202 Great
Resumes

ALSO BY JAY A. BLOCK AND MICHAEL BETRUS...

101 Best Resumes

101 More Best Resumes

101 Best Cover Letters

101 Best Resumes to Sell Yourself

101 Best Resumes for Grads

101 Best Tech Resumes

2500 Keywords to Get You Hired

202 Great Resumes

JAY A. BLOCK, CPRW

MICHAEL BETRUS, CPRW

McGraw-Hill

New York   Chicago   San Francisco
Lisbon   London   Madrid   Mexico City   Milan
New Delhi   San Juan   Seoul   Singapore
Sydney   Toronto

The McGraw·Hill Companies

4 5 6 7 8 9 0 QPD/QPD 0 9 8 7 6 5

ISBN 0-07-143316-3

McGraw-Hill books are available at special discounts to use as premiums and sales promotions, or for use in corporate training programs. For more information, please write to the Director of Special Sales, Professional Publishing, McGraw-Hill, Two Penn Plaza, New York, NY 10121-2298. Or contact your local bookstore.

This book is printed on acid-free paper.

Contents

Contributors

Ann Baehr, CPRW
Best Resumes
122 Sheridan Street
Brentwood, NY 11717
Resumesbest@earthlink.net

Jacqui D. Barrett, CPRW
Career Trend
11613 W. 113th Street
Overland Park, KS 66210
Careertmd@aol.com

Beverly Baskin, MA, NCC, CPRW
Baskin Business and Career Services
Woodbridge, Princeton, and Marlboro, NJ
800-300-4079

Alesia Benedict, CPRW
Career Objectives
Rochelle Park, NJ 07662
800-206-5353

Liz Benuscak, CPRW, IJCTC
Bi-Coastal Schoolhouse Road
New York, NY 10956
Bi-coastal@prodigy.net
www.bi-coastalresumes.com

Dr. Jerry Billis, IJCTC, CPRW
The Resume Center, Inc.
Theresumecenter@aol.com

Paula Brandt, CPRW
The Resume Lady and Associates
228 Donner Ave.
Monessen, PA 15062
Wewrite@resumelady.com

Tracey A. Bumpus, CPRW, JCTC
RezAMAZE.com
1807 Slaughter Lane #200
PMB366
Austin, TX 78748
Tbumpus@rezamaze.com
www.rezamaze.com

Diane Burns, CPRW, IJCTC, CCM
Career Marketing Techniques
5219 Thunder Hill Road
Columbia, MD 21045
Dianecprw@aol.com
www.polishedresumes.com

Camille Carboneau, CPRW, CEIP
CC Computer Services and Training
459 Gullane Circle
Idaho Falls, ID 83401
www.cccomputer.com
camille@cccomputer.com

Annemarie Cross, CPRW
Advanced Employment Concepts
www.aresumewriter.net
success@aresumewriter.net

Carla Culp, CPRW
Best Impression Resume Writing and Design
Edwardsville, IL
618-692-4090

Jean Cummings, MAT, CPRW, CEIP
A Resume for Today
123 Minot Road
Concord, MA 01742
www.aresumefortoday.com
careers@aresumefortoday.com

Barbie Dallman, CPRW
Happy Fingers Word Processing & Resume Services
Charleston, WV
304-345-4495

Darby Deihl, CPRW
D'Scribe Resumes
Irving, TX
972-556-1945

Deborah Wile Dib, CPRW
Advantage Resumes of New York
77 Buffalo Avenue
Medford, NY 11763

516-475-8513
gethired@advantageresumes.com

Anne-Maire Ditta
First Impression Career Services
58 Lincoln Ave.
Tuckahoe, NY 10707
Amditta@firstimpressioncareerservices.com

Marta Driesslein, CPRW
Cambridge Career Services
Knoxville, TN
423-539-9538

Michelle Dumas, CPRW, NCRW, CCM
Distinctive Documents
Somersworth, NH 03878
Resumes@distinctiveweb.com
www.distinctiveweb.com

Wendy Enelow, CPRW
Career Masters Institute
119 Old Stable Road
Lynchburg, VA
Wendyenelow@cminstitute.com

Dayna Feist, CPRW, CEIP
Gatehouse Business Service
265 Charlotte Street
Asheville, NC 28801
www.bestjobever.com
gatehouse@aol.com

Susan Higgins, CPRW
Q Resume Service
Plain City, OH
614-873-3123

Nancy Karvonen, CPRW
A Better Word and Resume
Willits, CA
707-459-4066

Louise Kursmark, CPRW
Best Impression
Cincinnati, OH
513-792-0030

Lorie Lebert, CPRW, JCTC
Resumes for Results, LLC
PO Box 267
Novi, MI 48376228
www.domyresume.com

Nick Marino, CPRW
Outcomererz@earthlink.net

Debra O'Reilly, CPRW, JCTC
ResumeWriter.com/A First Impression Resume Service
16 Terryville Ave.
Bristol, CT 06010
Debra@resumewriter.com
www.resumewriter.com

Tracey M. Parish
Career Plan, Inc.
PO Box 325
Kewanee, IL 61443
www.careerplan.org
resume@careerplan.org

Barb Poole, CPRW
Hire Image
Eink@astound.net

Jennifer Rydell
Simplify Your Life Resumes
6327-C SW Capitol Hwy
PMB 243
Portland, OR 97239
Simplify@spiritone.com

Walt Schuette, IJCTC, CPRW
The Village Wordsmith
931 S. Mission Road Suite B
Fallbrook, CA 92028
800-200-1884
wschuette@aol.com

Makini Siwatu, CPRW
Accent on Words
Belmont, CA
415-595-2514

Becky Stokes, CPRW
The Advantage
1330 Walnut Hollow Road
Lynchburg, VA 24503
800-922-5353
advresume@aol.com

John Suarez, CPRW
Executive Career Fitness
132 Kansas Ave.
Belleville, IL 62221
Jasuarez@aol.com

Vivian Van Lier
Vvanlier@aol.com

Susan Britton Whitcomb, NCRW, CPRW
Alpha Omega Career Services
757 Fast Hampton Way
Fresno, CA 93704
Susan@careerwriter.com
www.careerwriter.com

Tracey Laswell Williams, CPRW, JCTC
Careerwriters
5738 Olde Wadsworth Blvd.
Arvada, CO 80002
Tracey@careerwriters.com
www.careerwriters.com

Janice Worthington, CPRW
Worthington Career Services
6636 Belleshire Street
Columbus, OH 43229
Janice@worthingtonresumes.com
www.worthingtonresumes.com

List of Resumes by Industry/Job Title

202 Great
Resumes

1

Why This Book Is Unique . . .

Our business was booming in the 1990s. Companies were growing like crazy, hiring employees at every level. Unemployment was under 4%, and starting salaries were skyrocketing, especially in the technology sector. With all that hiring activity, there was a big need for services like ours to help people conduct an effective transition from one career choice to another.

The days of very low unemployment have passed, at least for now. The stock market has been crushed, and it may take another decade to reach the levels we saw in 2000. *Fortune* magazine even ran a cover story (June 2003) on white-collar layoffs. It's tough out there, and the competition for jobs is even tougher. That is why we are focusing this book on spinning your accomplishments to meet the needs of the hiring company.

Higher Unemployment + Contracting Workforce = MORE COMPETITION

This guide offers a new approach to resume writing and lists steps to take to ensure that your profile is reviewed by both decision makers and hiring managers. It is unique in the following ways:

How to research a company to uncover its needs. Nearly all resume books focus all their effort on developing a resume that illustrates the career background of the candidate. Great. The shortfall here is that too little time is spent understanding the needs of the target company, and then structuring your story (of which your resume is only a part) around that. Job searching today is analogous to sales: You *must* understand the needs of the hiring company (the buyer) in order to get hired (make the sale).

How-to section showing how to "*spin*" your resume to match the requirements of the target company. Danielle Sabian worked in various marketing and sales capacities for 12 years. She decided to test the employment waters and see if she could better her current position as a creative director for a Big Five advertising agency. She had one resume and circulated it to several other firms and companies that could use an experienced marketing or sales director or vice president. One resume! A true professional with terrific credentials for marketing consumer products had only one resume to use to market herself for a myriad of sales and marketing positions. Do you see the flaw? Danielle should have had several resumes, each with a factual but different emphasis. We developed six "boilerplate" resumes: one for agency marketing, one for in-house marketing, one for agency sales, one for sales management, one for agency VP positions, and one for client VP positions.

How to get in the door, network, and get yourself exposed to the hiring managers. Anyone in sales will tell you that the toughest part of sales is prospecting. Once you get in front of the decision maker, it's generally downhill from there—and fun. The toughest part of job searching is getting in front of the hiring manager. We will share some tactical actions you can take to help you get in front of the decision makers and influencers at the company you are targeting.

Create and articulate your value to the hiring managers and spin the right message, depending on whom in the target company you are meeting. Statements versus value statements. A resume focused on the candidate includes statements about the candidate. These statements may or may not be relevant to the hiring manager or the person reviewing the resume. A resume with statements that are tailored to match the accomplishments of the candidate with the needs of the target company provides *value*. Value statements will get you through the screening process and in front of the hiring manager.

Includes thousands of keywords and action verbs to help you write a resume. Resumes today frequently are sorted electronically, searched by keywords. Keywords are industry-specific or discipline specific terms that help define and distinguish your qualifications from those of other candidates. Examples of keywords can be found in Chapter 8.

How to overcome obstacles such as being laid off, taking a leave of absence, and being demoted. Are you feeling that you have a personal situation that might hinder your marketability? Were you laid off, did you take time off to be with your family, were you fired, are you underemployed? There are many things you can do to position yourself better. Chapter 9 details many of these challenges and shows how to overcome them.

Street-smart tips to help you job search, negotiate your salary, work through the Internet, interview, and much more. Our books have always included street-smart tips to get you hired. In fact, those tips are among the most popular elements of our past books. This book contains street-smart tips on interviewing, writing letters, writing resumes, using the Internet, working with recruiters, getting started, and networking.

THE HIRING COMPANY WANTS TO HIRE YOU

It is time-consuming and expensive to hire new employees. The quicker the search for a new candidate is ended, the happier everyone is. Your number one objective is to make the hiring decision easier for the company. Position yourself as the best candidate and things will fall into place for you and the company.

2

Creating a Solutions-Based Resume

Joe Pascual is a 36-year-old sales manager. He has worked in the telecommunications industry for his entire 14-year career. He began as a sales representative, moved to marketing, moved back to sales, became a general manager, and even started up new operations for one of the largest telecommunications companies in the world.

In 2003 Joe decided to look for a new position. He had rock-solid credentials and experience and plenty of references. He began circulating his resume and applied online and directly to a few companies that posted director-level opportunities.

After three months of doing this he had made no real progress. There was no follow-up, but in the worst telecommunications market in recent history, he felt fortunate to have his current position. He did not have high expectations.

One night he was scanning Monster.com and saw a terrific opportunity. It was a regional director of sales position for one of the few really stable telecommunications companies left. The job posting included the following job description:

> *This Regional Sales Director position will be responsible for launching and operating a profitable sales territory that satisfies [hiring company's] customer requirements & meets the territory's revenue objectives. You will manage five acquisition & retention focused sales branches selling local, long-distance, and Internet services to businesses. This position requires the candidate to have successful sales management experience, verifiable, and experience starting up new sales operations. This position will also be responsible for the selection, training and development of a professional sales staff.*

Joe posted his resume for the position. The name of the company was provided in the posting. He also began networking to try to find out whom he could meet at the hiring company. It was a great opportunity, and he needed to put his best foot forward. Following is the resume he posted for the position:

Joseph Pascual

1111 Roadway Road, Cincinnati, OH 45000
JP@appel.com Mobile: (513) 555-7707; Home: (513) 555-0133

SPRINT COMMUNICATIONS COMPANY, LTD.–Cincinnati, OH

April 1998-Present	**Regional Sales Director**

Manage sales teams in new markets by developing and executing marketing strategies and administering forecast and budget. Profile market demographics and analyze inbound traffic to identify viable collect markets for future launch. Collaborate with internal departments and external partners to execute implementation plans. Evaluate, select, and manage in-country agents and advertising agencies. Executed successful launches in multiple markets. In 1995, 1996, and 1998, averaged 113% of plan.

BELL SOUTH–Atlanta, GA

Oct 1992-April 1998	**Sales Manager**

Managed seven sales reps. Launched new data products for BellSouth in Atlanta area. Achieved over 100% of sales target through grassroots lead generation and prospecting.

EDUCATION	**Bachelor of Arts,** Finance, Northwestern University 1992

He never heard anything. After about five days and not wanting too much time to pass, he called and asked for help with his resume and cover letters.

After examining his resume and the advertisement, we saw no apparent connection between his experience as depicted on his resume and what the company was trying to hire. He sent his generic resume to the company and did not **customize** it for this opportunity. He saw a great opportunity and did not think to spend an extra 20 minutes tailoring the resume to meet the needs of the company.

Here are the changes we made to his resume:

1111 Roadway Road
Cincinnati, OH 45000

JOE PASCUAL
JP@appel.com

Mobile: (513) 555-7707
Home: (513) 555-0133

REGIONAL SALES DIRECTOR

Sales Management Executive with 14 Years of Experience in Telecommunications

Accomplished executive with 14 years of experience in sales and marketing management with Fortune 50 telecommunications provider. Successful track record in building sales teams from scratch and developing them into top national performers, consistently reaching President's Club status. Accomplished at managing multiple sales branches to sell integrated telecommunications services—local, long distance and data solutions. Sales results and stack ranking will all be validated.

AREAS OF EXPERTISE

- Account Planning
- Sales Management
- Network Engineering
  Competency

- Integrated Solutions Selling
- Sales Employee Development
- Multi-Branch Management
- Low Employee Churn
- New Business Development

- Contract Negotiation
- High Closing Rate
- Small Business Sales
- National Account Sales

PROFESSIONAL PROFILE

SPRINT COMMUNICATIONS COMPANY, LTD. (www.sprint.com)–Cincinnati, OH

Regional Sales Director (1998–Present)

Primary focus is to oversee and manage Midwest region for Sprint Business sales. Recruited and trained five sales managers to lead sales teams in local markets. Experienced zero turnover in sales managers and lowest turnover nationally in account executives. Also realized highest account executive participation in sales plan.

Areas of Accountability:

- Complete go-to-market responsibilities for Midwest region of Sprint broadband services, one DSL-based and two fixed-wireless (via MMDS technology), including hiring all staff and managing all marketing and public relations. Led market to 3rd highest customer penetration in 2001 out of 26 markets nationwide.

- Managed five direct B2B sales teams. Direct sales channel was most productive in this Sprint division, generating over 60% of regions sales. AEs averaged 83 sales/month each due to specific targeting and sales incentives developed, as well as very targeted marketing. Local marketing decisions included some print and radio placement, local events, direct mail, and some creative development. Created event channel, which resulted in generating almost 25% of market sales. In the absence of structured events, partnered with the likes of Home Depot, Wal-Mart and local malls. This was "out-of-the-box" distribution but extremely successful.

- Developed regional affinity program for selling to both major and national accounts as well as B2C sales to their employees. Secured many of the highest profile accounts in all markets.

- Created complete retail network in each market to distribute Sprint products, both national and local retailers, and created POP materials, local promotions, co-op and training programs. Secured local and two national retailers locally to sell Sprint products.

BellSouth (www.bellsouth.com)–Atlanta, GA

Sales Manager   (1992–1998)

Senior Sales Manager challenged to plan and orchestrate an aggressive market expansion for Atlanta market and launch the company's entry into data services throughout the U.S. Scope of responsibility includes recruiting sales representatives, strategic planning, contract negotiation, general business development, and client relationship management. Direct a team of seven.

Areas of Accountability:

❑ Led the successful market launch of new data product set in Georgia. Achieved President's Club award in 1994, 1995, and 1997.

❑ Built and managed key account relationships with major accounts and national accounts. Realized net gains over the interexchange data providers.

❑ Experienced lowest churn in direct sales group, losing no more than one AE per year. This was a key contributor to the President's Club wins. Also achieved highest AE participation in plan, with over 70% of the AEs reaching plan each year.

EDUCATION

Bachelor of Arts, Finance, Northwestern University; Honors Graduate—GPA 3.95. 1992

HONORS & ASSOCIATIONS

- President's Club, 1994, 1995, 1997, 1999, 2002
- Nationwide Leadership Award—Third Quarter 1999
- Nationwide Teamwork Award—June 2002
- USAF Exceptional Performance Award recipient 1989, 1990, 1991, and 1992
- Communicative Skills Award recipient, Emory Leadership School—1995

Joe did end up receiving a call when his second resume was sent because it directly mirrored the objectives of the hiring company. Customizing his resume to meet the needs of company got him through to the next step. This is the primary objective of a resume.

Chapter 5 will cover the basics of crafting an effective resume. This chapter is designed to get you thinking about factors motivating the hiring company and then draw a relationship between their needs and you, the solution to their problem (needs).

It's Really All About *THEM*

In order to develop a solutions-based resume, you need to uncover and understand the needs of the hiring company. What are its hot buttons, its key business drivers that keep its executives up at night? Identify those, and position yourself as a contributory solution to them, and you've really scored.

Research the Company

Researching a company or anything else today is much easier than it was even a decade ago. You can spend 90 minutes on the Internet and learn more than you could in a full day of research the old-fashioned way at the library.

Why Research?

The reason you want to research the company is to

- Understand how it stands financially (no finance background required for this).
- Identify its key partners, vendors (companies it buys from), and customers (companies it sells to). This is helpful when you are trying to network to get to key decision makers for referrals. Think of drawing out the six degrees of separation, the shortest connection between you and the company (preferably the hiring manager).
- Understand the company nomenclature and terminology so that you "speak their speak" when you finally meet.
- Discover areas where the business might need you to help it.

GREAT RESEARCH TOOLS

Here is a list of tools that can be accessed through the Internet to learn more about the target company:

- You must visit the company's Website, which in all probability it does have. Review its products and news releases first and the rest second. This should give you a good grounding of its business operations and approach.
  - **Annual report**. The annual report for a company provides the company's strategic direction, financial standing, and health.
- **Hoovers.com**. Even if you don't have a subscription, terrific information can be gathered by searching for information on the company.
- **Google.com**. This is one of the best search engines. When you get to the search screen, search the company name, the name of the hiring manager, and anything else relevant (such as industry data).
- Search in **Yahoo.com** (finance), **MSN.com** (finance), and **Quicken.com**.
- **Lexis-Nexis.com** is another terrific research tool.

RESEARCH

Now What?

Every time you research or learn something about the company, ask yourself, *So what*? You need to digest the information, interpret it at some level and determine how you fit into what you're reading to enable the improvement of the business.

Here are some sample *So what?* questions you can ask yourself as you conduct your research:

- Who are the company's major strategic partners, vendors, and customers?
  - Who do I know at these companies who can provide me with a referral, a contact name, or a reference to separate me from the pack?
- What are the company's major business units?
- What are the company's key business drivers, key challenges, and areas of pain?
- Who are its major competitors?

- What has happened recently that is of interest (new hires, reorganizations, product launches)?

You = Value

Now that you've researched the company properly, you can understand how you fit in the picture. In the following chapters we will discuss

- Creative getting-in-the-door tactics
- What is happening at the other end, at the company
- How to spin, or customize your message to meet the needs of the company and interviewer
- Crafting strong copy for the body of your resume
- Putting the whole resume together

WHY DO THIS AT ALL?

At home you probably get hit with a lot of direct marketing in form of junk mail, spam e-mail, and telemarketing calls. These contacts companies make with you are not specific; they're the same calls they make to everyone. How do you feel about that? Right. Now suppose a telemarketer called you and actually knew what your hot buttons were, understood your values, and was presenting something to make your life genuinely easier.

That's where we would like to get you. Understanding the target company allows you to do the following:

- Understand the company's business and communicate using their language. This will increase your credibility.
- Understand the ways the business needs help and position yourself as a value-adder by:
  - Helping them make (or save) money
  - Helping them increase profitability
  - Helping them increase the productivity of their assets

WHAT TO KNOW WHEN YOU CONTACT THE COMPANY

At a minimum, when you get a serious interview, strive to understand the following elements of that company:

- The company's major business units
- The company's recent changes in the organizational structure or otherwise
- Major business initiatives
- Major costs and expenses, areas of best revenue (read, most stable for some people), and profit margins
- Key challenges and areas of pain

HAVE CONFIDENCE

Why do this? So that you're the confident candidate with the resume that best fits the company's needs. So that you can communicate value to the company and so that you will secure that key interview and that desired position.

3

Getting in the Door

There are several primary sources of job leads:

- Networking
- Contacting companies directly
- Classified advertisements
- Executive recruiters and employment agencies
- Online services

Other sources include trade journals, job fairs, college placement offices, and state employment offices. One of the most difficult tasks in life is securing work and planning a career. A career is important to everyone, and so you must create a plan of action, utilizing more than one of the career design strategies at the same time.

NETWORKING

Without question, the most common way people find out about and obtain new positions is through networking. Networking is *people connecting*, and when you connect with people, you begin to assemble your network. Once your network is in place, you will continue to make new contacts and communicate with established members. People in your network will provide advice, information, and support in helping you achieve your career goals and aspirations.

Networking accounts for up to 70% of the new opportunities uncovered. So what is networking? Many people assume that they should call all the people they know personally and professionally and ask if they know of any companies that are hiring. A successful networker's approach is different.

A successful networker starts by listing as many names as possible on a sheet of paper. Those names can include family members, relatives, friends, coworkers and managers (past and present), other industry contacts, and anyone else you know. The next step is to formulate a networking presentation. Keep in mind that it need not address potential openings. In networking the aim is to call your contacts to ask for career or industry advice. The point is that you're positioning yourself not as a desperate job hunter but as a researcher. It is unrealistic to think that you will go far by asking people for advice like this:

> *Mark, thanks for taking some time to talk with me. My company is likely to lay people off next month and I was wondering if your company had any openings or if you know of any.*

This person hasn't told John what he does, has experience in, or wants to do. Mark is likely to respond with "No, but I'll keep you in mind should I hear of anything." What do you think the odds are that Mark will contact this person again?

A better approach is to ask for personal or industry advice and work on developing the networking web:

> *Mark, Paul Jonathan at CNA suggested I give you a call. He and I have worked together for some time, and he mentioned that you work in finance and that you are the controller of Allied Sensors. I work in cost accounting and feel you'd likely be able to offer some good career advice. I'd really appreciate some time. Could we get together for lunch sometime in the next week or so?*

You have now asked for advice, not for a job. People are much more willing to help someone who has made them feel good about themselves or who appears genuinely to appreciate their help. This strategy can be approached in many ways. You can ask for job search advice (including resume or cover letter advice), overall career advice (as shown above), industry advice, key contacts, information about various companies/people/industries, and other people they may know.

It is important that the person you network through like you. When someone gives you a reference, it is a reflection of that person. People will not put themselves at personal or professional risk if they aren't confident that you will be a good reflection on them. Finally, send each person you speak with a thank-you letter. That courtesy will be remembered and lead future contacts.

Six Degrees of Separation

In addition to traditional networking for opportunities, there is another very effective way to leverage networking in today's economy. Suppose you go to Monster.Com and uncover a great opportunity with Cisco Systems, Bristol-Myers Squibb, or a new company. Before blindly sending in your resume and a brief cover letter to that company (or recruiter), immediately ask around and try to find a reference you can leverage to get to them. If you follow the rules of "six degrees of separation," there is a good chance you can ask around and get a personal introduction to the hiring manager.

The idea behind the six degrees of separation is that you may be no more than two or three people, or degrees from networking to get connected with an employee at the company you are targeting. When you do, you have engineered a reference and network through the back door. Another terrific strategy to help you in this quest is to have your best references send in letters of recommendation to the hiring manager during the interview process. The determination you demonstrate by developing these references from your network will be perceived as the kind of determination you will demonstrate on the job. Companies desperately need good employees. Sell yourself as one of those employees and most companies will find a place for you.

A client of ours, Mark, was looking to find a position with Voicestream (now T-Mobile), a fairly new wireless telecommunications company. The company's Website had a posting for a position they wanted filled that was located in Atlanta. But how do you avoid being batched in the plethora of resumes these companies receive for each posting, especially in today's economy? Here is what we did: We worked with the candidate to see if he knew ANYONE at Voicestream. After a few days of asking around, it turned out that Mark's girlfriend's friend (in Chicago) used to work there. So we called her and got the name of her vice president.

Mark called the VP in Seattle, and he actually picked up the phone, in part because Mark called before hours when things were slow and waited until he answered the phone, not leaving a voicemail. Mark gave him a quick "elevator pitch" of his background and what his goals were, and the VP referred him to that region's VP. Mark then reached that VP and by then had a few names to drop, positioning himself as a referred candidate.

The new VP had Mark get in touch with a human resources recruiter in Kansas City, and a few weeks later Mark secured an interview and a position. That whole networking exercise took just two days but enabled Mark to scoop thousands of other candidates. You too should think of creative ways to network "internally."

CONTACTING COMPANIES DIRECTLY

Aren't there one or two companies you've always been interested in working for? Ideally, you may know someone who will introduce you to key contacts there or inform you of future openings. The best way to get introduced to a targeted company is to have a current employee personally introduce you or make an introductory phone call for you. You could make the introduction and reference the employee you know. We'll get into this later, but if you don't know anyone at a targeted company, a recruiter may be a good source of contact for you, even if it involves no job order for him or her.

You could send an unsolicited resume, but the likelihood of this working is low. Most large profile companies receive thousands of resumes a year, and few are acted on. Corporate recruiters Jackie Larson and Cheri Comstock, authors of *The New Rules of the Job Search Game*, don't take mass-mailed resumes very seriously. Part of the problem is that too many resumes are written as past job descriptions **and are not customized to a targeted position.**

Conrad Lee, a retained Boca Raton recruiter, believes "information is the most important thing in contacting companies directly. Don't call just one person in the company and feel that is sufficient. That person may have their own job insecurities or be on a performance improvement plan. You should contact five to ten people and only then can you say you contacted that company directly." New job search strategies all suggest targeting a select few smaller companies (under 750 employees, as larger companies are still downsizing) intensely rather than blanketing a thousand generically.

Contacting the head of your functional specialty in that company is a good start. Is it hard? Of course. You're facing rejection, probably feeling like you're bothering busy people, begging, maybe even feeling inferior. Would you feel inferior if you were calling hotels and ticket agencies for Super Bowl information? Of course not. What if someone can't help you? You just get back on the phone until you achieve your goal. These contacts should be approached the same way. You have a great product to sell—yourself. Position yourself as someone of value and as a product that can contribute to the target company.

The key is to position yourself for individual situations. This requires specialized letters, resumes, and strategies tailored for each situation.

One trick is to call the company you are targeting and try to get the name of the person in charge of the department where you would like to work. If you don't know, call the receptionist and ask her or him who that is and perhaps who a vendor or two might be (such as an accounting firm or ad agency) and then check the company Website for latest company news. Now you have something interesting to talk about when you reach the hiring manager.

Increase Your Odds: *GET IN*

There are two different things you need to try to do increase your odds in contacting companies directly. The first is to network your way internally to the decision maker. The second is to get an internal reference.

With small companies this can be difficult, but not with large Fortune 1000 companies. If you circulate and network effectively, you should be no more than two or three degrees from any major company employer, particularly if you're grounded in that industry.

Create a "family tree" of relationships you have with others and map out each one by industry. Start asking around for people who work for your targeted company or an affiliate (key customer, strategic partner, vendor) of that company. Keep looking. If you come up empty, go to a local restaurant for lunch or a happy-hour spot that is near their office. Be subtle and ask around. You will find someone. Strike up a neutral conversation and then offer to treat a person to lunch in return for some fact-finding information. If they like you, they will in almost all cases refer you internally. You've scored. An internal reference is worth more than any other kind of reference.

CLASSIFIED ADVERTISEMENTS

When you depend on classified advertisements to locate job openings, you limit yourself to only 7 to 10% or less of all available jobs, plus you are competing with thousands of job hunters who are reading the same ads. Keep in mind that the majority of these ads are for lower-wage positions. Do not disregard the classifieds, but don't limit your options by relying too heavily on them. Answering ads is more effective at lower levels than at higher ones. An entry-level position or administrative support position is more likely to be found by using this method than is a director's position. But it is easy to review advertisements. Check the local paper listings on Sunday, the paper of the largest metropolitan area near where you live, and even a few national papers such as the *Wall Street Journal* (or its advertisement summary, the *National Business Employment Weekly*) and the *New York Times*.

You may gain insight by looking at ads that don't necessarily match your background. You may see an ad that says, "Due to our expansion in the Northeast we are looking for. . . ." You have just learned of an expanding company that may need you. Review papers that have good display ads such as the *Los Angeles Times,* the *Chicago Tribune,* and other major Sunday editions.

Tactically, here is an interesting suggestion. Follow the thought process above and call them. Many classified ads list a fax number but no company name or main number. They encourage you to fax your resume but not to call them. Well, in most companies a fax number is a derivative extension of the main number. If the fax number is NXX-5479, there is a good chance that the main number is NXX-5000 or NXX-5400. With that you can call them and hunt for information, write them a more interesting and industry-specific letter, and position yourself ahead of the people who didn't use this method.

Then, when you write them, write about the company, not just "I am answering your ad." Package the resume and cover letter in a U.S. Priority Mail envelope so that it stands out, and you will be guaranteed to at least be reviewed, which when answering an ad is your first objective.

EXECUTIVE RECRUITERS AND EMPLOYMENT AGENCIES

Without some knowledge of the recruiting industry, choosing an appropriate recruiter can be as difficult as choosing an employee. There are over 6,000 recruiters of some kind in the United States. Some are large chains such as Robert Half Inc., and some are private recruiters that are more like consultants. Here is a brief overview on the recruiting industry as it relates to doing a job search and developing your resume.

Types of Recruiting Agencies

Executive recruiters fall into two major categories: contingency employment agencies and retained search firms. Traditionally, contingency agencies focus on the lower end of the hiring segment, from entry level through middle management. Retained search firms specialize in senior-level professionals and executives. The two types are different in the way they recruit and charge for their services too.

Retained Search Firms

Retained search firms are hired by a company for a period of time. They are paid as a consultant whether they fill a search or not. These firms are paid by the employers, like a contingency, but they act more like an employee of the company, as many consultants do. They are less receptive to a candidate approaching them than is a contingency recruiter. Still, this is a channel worth pursuing.

One reason they are retained and paid anyway is that they are searching for hard-to-find positions, which takes time and money. There is no guarantee they will find them, and so they need some working capital to carry them through. A retained recruiter may get about a third of the employee's first-year salary. The salary range of a position this recruiter might fill might vary from $100,000 to a senior-level executive earning millions.

Contingency Recruiting Agencies

Contingency agencies such as Management Recruiters charge a fee to the employer only when the candidate is hired. The contingency recruiter will generally perform some prescreening for the employer and then send a pool of candidates to the employer to screen and interview. Rates usually range from 20% to 30% of the employee's first year's salary. The salary level of a position a contingency firm may fill can range from $40,000 to $150,000.

Do's and Don't's

- Don't ever sign an exclusive with a recruiter.
- Don't pay a recruiter; that should come from the employer.
- Do focus on recruiters that specialize in your industry (health care, etc.), discipline (accounting, etc.), or geographic area.
- Do try to get a referral to a recruiter. This will help you find a good one, help you gain more credibility with the recruiter, and get the recruiter to become your advocate.
- Do make friends with some headhunters while you are employed so that they know you when you're hottest—employed and most marketable.

Online Services

Information technology is changing the way job seekers locate employment opportunities. Job hunters are now connecting with hiring authorities electronically. Thousands of astute individuals have already tapped into these powerful new technologies (databases, electronic bulletin boards on the Internet, and other online employment services) to help them achieve their career goals.

There are many books dedicated to this subject. Many independent Web pages are dedicated to such a cause. You can set up your own Web page, directing prospective employers to that page, or look at your targeted employer's page; they frequently have job postings listed. However, the best methods of contact are still personal, because frequently the best and higher-level positions are not posted. However, they are inexpensive to access, and you may identify a lead through e-mail contact with hiring managers or other job seekers.

On the Web, do several different searches for both job search keywords and the industry or discipline that is your specialty. Also, contact the local newspaper for additional online sources specific to your metropolitan area.

The top sites that house these opportunities include the following:

- Monster.com (www.monster.com)
- Headhunter.net (www.headhunter.net)
- Jobs.com (www.jobs.com)
- America's Job Bank (www.jobsearch.org)
- HotJobs (www.hotjobs.com)
- JobOptions (www.joboptions.com)
- Career mosaic (www.careermosaic.com)
- CareerBuilder (www.careerbuilder.com)

Though there are many great resources to help you in your online search, here are a few tips to keep in mind:

1. Have a good idea of what types of jobs you are seeking. That will make the search on these online sites more narrow in scope and more productive. Have geography and keywords prepared in advance. These two objectives should be part of developing your resume.

2. Have two resumes ready at hand: a "finished" Microsoft Word document to send as an attachment and a nonformatted text-only resume to copy and paste in an e-mail. The content should be the same, but the latter should be stripped of formatting that will not be preserved through the e-mail exchange.

3. Plan to post your resume at these sites as well as sending them directly to recruiters and employers.

4. Take the time to read and understand how the sites work before jumping in.

5. Print out copies of everything you see of interest on a site. It will help you for future reference. Also, catalog whom you send e-mails and resumes to so that you won't send redundant "applications."

6. Provide a personal e-mail address, not the one of your current employer. Check your e-mail daily, as an e-mail is a common first reply you will receive.

7. We will cover this in more detail in Chapter 6, but make sure your resume is very tight in your experience and what you want to do. The folks reading these resumes are doing so online and will not lend a lot of time to each one, so make it easy for them to get to your qualifications and objectives quickly and effortlessly.

4

What's Happening on the Other End?

Steven Pellar was interested in a position he saw posted on Monster.com: regional director of business operations with a national health-care firm. He read the advertisement and posted his resume. He never heard from the firm, and his application seemed to fall into the dark hole of cyberspace. Here's what happened to him:

When he posted his resume, it, along with many others, was sent electronically to an internal human resources recruiter. That recruiter reviewed a sampling of the resumes based on specific criteria posted, such as years of industry experience and years in a relevant discipline. Steven's resume made the first cut. The recruiter did not allow any resume that did not specifically match the desired qualifications. Within an organization, the hiring manager is the "customer" of the human resources recruiter.

The recruiter thought Steven was qualified enough to make the first cut. The recruiter then forwarded about ten resumes to the senior human resources manager for screening. This layer may not always be in place, but for a director-level position at a large company it is common.

The second human resources manager reviewed all ten resumes. Some really stood out: They had crisp summaries, and in less than one minute the recruiter could determine that the candidates were qualified and worth passing on. Since the next cut was to only include five candidates for the area vice president to review, the "sure things" were forwarded. Steven's resume was not a sure thing. Steven did not make the second cut.

Why? Two reasons. First, he did not customize his resume enough, matching it to the requirements of the position. Second, he did not make his qualifications and achievements readily understandable to the recruiter. A recruiter is not a line manager and functional manager. The recruiter's screening is usually based on connecting dots between the hiring manager's requirements and the resumes the recruiter reviews. In most cases resumes do get reviewed when you send them in the mail or post them electronically. What happens next is determined by how well you prepared your resume.

When you apply online or answer an advertisement, the first objective of the recruiter is to eliminate resumes from the stack and narrow the search for the hiring manager. When you see fields in the online application that give you the option to select "willing to relocate," "salary range," and "specific discipline" (marketing, sales, engineering), these are things that help recruiters eliminate you from the pool. Be cognizant of this. You may want to keep the selections specific if you fit the position very closely, or you may want to keep it general. You need to make that decision as you complete the application.

A NEW KIND OF ONLINE ASSESSMENT

One of our clients applied for a general manager position with a top three nonprofit organization. Once the application was complete with a resume posting, the next step was to take a 45-minute online personality assessment test.

The eliminator in this process was the personality review. Of course, there is no right or wrong answer to these things, and unless you know the hiring company's criteria and how your answers influence the assessment, you can't trick the system. Nor would you want to. Getting hired under false pretenses is a waste of your time and the company's money.

Employers more than ever are struggling to reduce their workforces to remain competitive in a shrinking global economic marketplace. One of the challenges they are facing is ensuring that they have the "right" people in the "right" positions to accomplish more with less. The U.S. government is doing the same thing, according to the outplacement firm Challenger, Gray, and Christmas, where a study revealed that the government sector is starting to pare its workforce.

High-impact management tools such as Six Sigma are being instituted by major corporations on an international scale to do more with less, to increase bottom-line profits through technology optimization (such as scanning your own purchases and checking yourself out at the grocery store without the help of cashiers), cost controls, and efficiency/quality control enhancements. What this means for job seekers is more competition for fewer and fewer top jobs.

Resumes, according to a growing number of Fortune 500 human resources professionals, can no longer be long-winded chronological, biographical obituaries that communicate little more than one's work history and educational experiences. They must be easy-to-read marketing profiles that sell and promote one's value. "Tell us what you can do for us, how you can contribute to our organization, and why you are the best man or woman for the job, and do it in less than 15 seconds," says Eartha Genece, CPCC, of the Newgen Results Group.

Today, with e-mail, voicemail, U.S. mail, and all other voices vying for attention in the course of the day, a job candidate has very little time to get his or her message across. Not unlike a 30-second television or radio commercial, a full-page magazine advertisement, or a headline on the front page of a newspaper, we have only a few seconds to capture the attention of the readers to get them to want to read on!

The following are seven mistakes made on resumes that employers claim hinder a job seeker's chances of securing an interview and eventually a job.

1. Lack of Organization

You must organize the resume and the information contained within it so that the reader is able to read the important information first. The important information is information that communicates your value—your ability to contribute in a meaningful way—in less than 15 seconds. A good question to ask when organizing your resume is, "What do I need to communicate to the reader that will ignite interest in me so that he or she will want to read the rest of the resume with interest and then invite me into the interview?" If you put education first and your education is at the same level as that of most other candidates competing for the same job, you are wasting that valuable 10 to 15 seconds communicating things that *don't* separate you from your competition. In elementary school, English teachers call this the "hook." You must organize your resume so that the first 10 to 15 seconds delivers the hook that creates interest in you and your qualifications so that the reader eagerly reads the rest of the resume with interest.

2. Information That Is Too General

What does "good communication skills" mean? Does it mean you can give a speech to 2,500 people, negotiate an arms deal, or write a best-selling book? What does "problem-solving skills" mean? What is a "people person"? My dog is a people person. As you can see from these examples, far too many job seekers are using the same common phrases, words, and concepts on resumes that look like those of most other job candidates and don't specify exactly how the concepts can benefit the prospective employer. If applicants used the same words and phrases on their resumes, which would be like watching a NASCAR race with 14 cars that looked exactly alike, you'd never know who was who! When writing your resume, instead of saying you have good communications skills, say that you have high-impact negotiating or presentation skills, solid public speaking abilities, or strong writing and editing skills. Instead of saying you are a problem solver, state that you can troubleshoot technical equipment, resolve human conflicts in the workplace, or resolve customer service issues professionally and effectively.

3. Lack of Achievements

A resume without achievements is like a report card without grades. It's not what you have done that is important but how well you have done it. If 10 secretaries are competing for the same job and they all provide previous job descriptions/responsibilities and nothing more, they will all say about the same things on their resumes and thus look alike. If 25 students in a class take math, English, science, history, and social studies, what differentiates them? Grades—results! Resumes are like report cards: What did you do, and how did you do it? Achievements come in two forms: qualitative and quantitative.

Quantitative achievements are specific achievements, for example, increased sales $1.2 million a year, improved customer service levels from 91.3% to 98.7%, enhanced market share from 18% to 23%, or increased profits $3.12 million a year or $1.03 per share. Qualitative achievements are nonmeasurable results but are accomplishments just the same: significantly increased sales, dramatically improved the level of customer service, decreased expenses while improving market share, or improved efficiency and productivity while lowering personnel turnover. Remember, a resume without achievements is like a report card without grades, and when you look like everyone else, you can't possible get noticed. When it comes to resumes, conformity is a recipe for disaster.

4. Resumes Not Written for Both Human and Technology Evaluations

Today many larger corporations are using computers with keyword software to read the plethora of resumes sent to them by job seekers. Most of the technology today has changed from past years when scanning devices could only read text files—without enhancement like **bold**, *italics*, underlining, and graphics. Most electronic resumes are sent as an e-mail attachment, and the integrity of the formatted resume can be retained because the improved software can read the document with the enhancements included. Note: Your resume must be compatible with Microsoft Word.

The goal is to write an effective resume that includes all the "relevant" industry keywords. Keywords are descriptive words, usually nouns, that are associated with specific disciplines or industries. Keywords (refer to *2,500 Keywords to Get You Hired*, McGraw-Hill, 2003) play an integral role in two areas of the resume screening process. One is the human element—the eyes only element—in which hiring and nonhiring managers are screening resumes for words and phrases that match their criteria. The second is the computer search, where software is developed to seek out keywords that also match the criteria of employers. When you are writing a resume, industry keywords need to be identified and used throughout the resume.

5. Resumes That Tell but Don't Sell

Resumes should not be long-winded biographies. Rather, they must communicate what you can do for the company and how you can improve its economics—its goals and objectives. You have never seen an advertisement for Coca Cola providing you with the complete history of Coca Cola. General Motors doesn't provide a year-by-year historical account of the company when selling automobiles. Employers don't want to know about your history. What they want to know is what your value is to them: how you can benefit them and how they can profit from you!

Your work experience, education, and other resume sections are relevant only to the extent that they provide *evidence* of how you can help the company. You are using your resume in what we call the "job market," and the job market is no different from the marketplace in general in that there is stiff competition. To attract the outstanding jobs, you must stand out on your resume and subsequently in the interview. Your job is to sell your value, not relate your historical biography. That's how to stand out and shout, "I'm the best candidate for the job!"

6. Resumes That Contain No Value-Added Messages

This mistake can often be the difference between victory and defeat. A value-added message shows how a candidate can add value to an organization in a way that is not specific to the hiring company. Companies want to know what you can do for them, how you can contribute to them. If a company is seeking a sales professional and the top three candidates all have about the same education, work experience, achievements, and credentials and are all well liked, what will tilt the scale in one candidate's favor? Often it's that "value-added" dimension that one of the candidates brings to the table. If one candidate speaks English, Spanish, and French fluently, that value-added dimension may be helpful in opening new markets that use those languages, and thus that person will be offered the job based on that. If a licensed esthetician is also an effective salesperson and can bring in new business as well as do facials and spa treatments, that added dimension would be instrumental in giving that person an advantage over other estheticians who do only treatment work. As you think about identifying the value you bring to your next job, think about what value-added aspects you bring to the job that would benefit the company or organization and differentiate you from the competition.

7. Resumes That Are Riddled with Typos and Grammatical Errors

Yes, this still occurs on a regular basis and remains a major irritant for those who read resumes. Spell Check won't catch a misused tense ("achieved" instead of "achieve"), won't catch a misused word ("in" instead of "if"), and won't catch a wrong date (1989 instead of 1998).

When you are finished writing your resume, select a handful of qualified people you know and trust to read and proofread it. One little typo on your resume read by the wrong person can be disastrous to landing the interview and winning the job. Have your resume proofed by competent people so that you don't put yourself out of contention for the top jobs.

5

Crafting the Resume

On the front page of the employment section of a late 2003 Sunday edition of one of the largest newspapers in the country, there was an article debating the pros and cons of using a resume. One commentary was that the resume is outdated and that in today's world of electronic-based communications it will go away. It went on to say that the resume has long evolved and that the days of using nice stock paper and matching envelopes has passed. At one point it even questioned whether hiring managers want to be bothered with reviewing resumes.

The article was partly correct. The traditional uses of a resume have evolved. Among all the clients we have advised over the last year, none have concerned themselves with paper stock. However, hiring managers and internal and external recruiters do need resumes. What they detest are poorly written resumes that make them work to understand the profile of the candidates.

Resumes are still a huge part of the job search process. The first step in any selection process is to review the resumes of candidates, even those with inside sponsorship. In this section we want to teach you that

- You need to create an effective and useful career summary for your resume.
- You need to document your accomplishments in the employment history sections and make them line up as closely as possible with the requirements of the company.

These two things are the most important uses of the resume and what many people pay hundreds of dollars to have a professional teach them.

RESUMES AND THE 80/20 RULE

Recently I was traveling from Tampa to Dallas. At the Tampa airport I was looking for a couple of magazines to read on the plane. The magazine rack was large and the selection of magazines was quite broad. I browsed the news periodicals (like *Time, Newsweek, US News*), the sports magazines, and some others. I bought two magazines after very casually perusing over 50 magazine covers.

Why did I buy those two magazines out of the whole lot? **Their covers and headlines**. In most cases, that is not unlike the initial resume screening process for candidates. You see, resumes are important because they can cause you to be deselected before you ever get to the plate. You need a good resume to keep your job search process open and alive with options.

A good resume is no guarantee of obtaining a great position, but a poor one may very well result in your not getting the interview.

Being computer-literate is an absolute requirement for any white-collar job today. To be considered a good prospect and good candidate, good presentation skills can be viewed as job-critical by hiring managers. Hiring managers view the resume and the cover letter as an indication of how well you may perform in the job. The resume is an indicator of a candidate's

- Organization skills
- Writing skills
- Presentation skills
- Ability to "net it out" effectively, meaning to communicate clearly in as few words as possible

Our objective in this section is to help you craft an information-rich, concise summary of qualifications and descriptive statements of your past accomplishments.

Up to 80% of your resume rests in the summary. If you were to poll hiring managers, human resources recruiters, and external recruiters and if they were honest, fewer than 10% would say they ever read every bullet a candidate writes to support the description of each of his or her jobs. If the summary section is weak or nonexistent, there is even less likelihood that the whole resume will be read.

YOUR RESUME IS YOUR MARKETING BROCHURE

When you see a marketing brochure advertisement, it has been carefully crafted with several things in mind: key messaging, copy positioning, colors, graphics, and so on. Positioning is a critical part of connecting the key message of the advertisement to the instinctive viewing center of the reader.

One more reason the summary is the most important single piece of information in your resume is because of where it rests—right in the visual center of the reader. Imagine an 8½ by 11 paper. This is where the visual center of a document is and where your summary should reside:

```

              Your Summary Resides Here—
              The Reading Center of the Page


```

On the next page is an example of a real resume used by a marketing manager with a Fortune 50 company whose earnings exceed $100,000 a year, a top earning percentile in the country. Note the areas of improvement for this resume.

Cathy Quigley

9911 42nd Street • Atlanta, Georgia 30003 • Home 404.555.5555 • PCS 404.555.5555

Sprint Telecommunications

April 2001-Present   **Mass Markets Organization (MMO) Off Shore Collect**
Marketing/Sales Manager
Implement collect service in new markets by developing and executing marketing strategies and administering forecast and budget. Profile country demographics and analyze inbound traffic to identify viable collect markets for future launch. Develop proposals and negotiate mutually beneficial agreements with foreign telecom carriers. Collaborate with internal departments and external partners to execute implementation plans. Evaluate, select, and manage in-country agents and advertising agencies. Executed successful launch of collect service in Egypt. Within one month, billable minute results exceeded forecast by 165%. Launched collect service in Pakistan and Vietnam; directly managed advertising agency and in-country Sprint representatives. Responsible for maintaining estimates, processing invoices and monthly accruals for General International team.

Oct 2000-April 2001   **National Consumer Organization (NCO) Integrated On-Demand Network (ION) Regional Marketing**
Regional Market Manager
Determined leads and expenditures required in achieving sales forecast. Developed and implemented media plans for each market. Developed and implemented marketing strategies for new and existing markets. Created sales incentive programs targeted at inbound and outbound telemarketing representatives. Achieved 100% of sales target through grassroots marketing and partnership acquisition. Analyzed in-market competitors; monitored and coached sales productivity.

Budget $6M, 60,000 sales

Jan 2000-Oct 2000   Long Distance International (LDI) Alternate Channel
Channel Sales/Marketing Manager
Developed and executed long-distance acquisition strategies for new sales channel. Recognized new revenue channels by establishing partnerships whose customer base consisted of international long-distance users. Managed end-to-end partnership implementation, ensuring program launched successfully and on targeted launch date.

Budget $12M, 90,000 Sales

Jan 1998-Jan 2000   Long Distance Division (LDD)/Consumer Service Group (CSG), Prepaid Card
Regional Sales Manager
Managed distribution, marketing, and sales efforts for the retail Prepaid Phonecard business within a specific region. Principal responsibilities include managing 10 independent brokers to sell and service Prepaid Card customers. Develop creative account specific promotions to enhance sales as well as new acquisition.

Budget $8M

1995-1996   **Deployment Analyst**
Developed and implemented training programs to support the objectives for Marketing, Sales, and Service of CSG Prepaid Card and FonPromotion groups. Developed and delivered internal and external customer training program. Staff: 25 (contract employees).

1993-1996   **Sr. Account Specialists**
Maintained direct relationships with high-profile and high-volume revenue Fax and Voice customers. Provided personalized service for each customer, including technical support, account status, and issue resolution. Focused on sales objectives.

1989-1991   **Pricing and Marketing Specialist**
Responsible for coordinating pricing policies for 20 international airline carriers. Implemented and tested new enhancements.

University of Missouri–Kansas City, Bachelor's Degree, Business Administration

THE SUMMARY

You can see the markups of places where this resume can be improved. For this individual, we are going to craft a new resume. Let's begin with the summary section. A summary section is needed because you need to provide a foundation of the candidate, an overview of what the candidate has accomplished and her key disciplines. The summary dictates whether the rest of the resume gets read.

Cathy Quigley

9911 42nd Street • Atlanta, Georgia 30003 • Home 404.555.5555 • PCS 404.555.5555

Career Summary

- 12 years in telecommunications industry, all with Sprint Communications Company, LTD.
- 4 years consumer sales experience
- 5 years traditional marketing experience, with an emphasis on channel distribution and promotion
- 3 years managing pricing for air travel vertical industry
- Subject matter expertise in consumer telecommunications applications, such as traditional long distance, prepaid calling, calling cards, CLEC bundled offers

---

This is a brief summary. It provides the reader with an information-rich snapshot of the accomplishments of this candidate. Each bullet does not necessarily have to define the number of years in each discipline. It's a great starting point. If you have experience starting up a new business, that could be a valuable summary bullet. If you successfully launched a new product or have some other unique or good skill, that could be a summary bullet.

The last bullet in this summary includes an acronym, CLEC. Is this proper? Within this industry, CLEC is not a unique acronym, and so it's acceptable. In fact, spelling out "Competitive Local Exchange Carrier" would send a message of being less a player. Use your judgment and always think of the **mindset of the reader**.

THE EMPLOYMENT SECTION

Value Statements		*Value Proposition*
□ Your Results		Result in actual value
□ Your Accomplishments	Written to meet the needs of the company	you will deliver to the
□ Your Skills		company

One key element to writing killer copy on your resume is to represent a value proposition to the targeted company.

On most resumes, the writers list their job responsibilities based on what they did in the past, not spun to what they intend to do in the future. Here are steps to take to turn passive copy into action-oriented, laser-targeted resume copy.

This section will focus on writing job descriptions and accomplishments that are relevant to the reader, the hiring manager.

The employment module normally begins with your most recent position and works backward (allocate the most space to the most recent positions and less space as you go back in time). If you have a sensible and strategic reason to deviate from this guideline and it enhances your document, go for it. Otherwise reference the following information for each employer:

1. Name of company or organization
2. City/town and state where you worked
3. Dates of employment (usually the year is enough; no need for month)
4. Titles or positions held

How far back do you have to go? That's entirely up to you. You do not have to go back more than 10 to 12 years unless you have a good reason to do so. For instance, if you want to get back into teaching, something you did 18 years ago but stopped so that you could raise your children, you'll want to go back 18 years. But the rule of thumb is 10 to 12 years. For the most part, what we did 15 years ago is of little consequence to an employer today.

Experience is not limited to paying jobs. Include volunteer work if it enhances your candidacy. Do not include salary, reasons for leaving, or supervisor's name unless you have a very specific reason for doing so. Salary history and requirements, if requested, should be addressed in the cover letter.

The listing of your job responsibilities should read like a condensed job description. Bring out only the highlights, not the obvious. Finally, use positive and energy-oriented words. The words you choose should reflect your energy level, motivation, charisma, education level, and professionalism. Emotion and action sell; use action and power words.

Briefly describe any special skills you used in carrying out past responsibilities. These skills might include computers that you operated, special equipment you used, and bilingual capabilities. Other examples of skills that you might have employed include problem solving, communications, organizational, and technical mastery. Review your daily tasks and you'll be surprise at the skills you use every day but take entirely for granted.

The major focus of the employment/experience section should be on your specific accomplishments, achievements, and contributions.

Employment (Other)

Quite possibly your employment history will go back 20 years or more. Focus the majority of your resume on the most recent 10 to 12 years and provide a brief synopsis of the rest. You are not obligated to account for every minute of your life, so use this section to summarize activities performed many years ago if it will round out your employment background.

Step 1: Focus on Accomplishments

Every descriptor should address and answer the question "So what?"

The first step to writing great copy for your resume is to itemize your accomplishments. In the spirit of writing with the reader in mind, this candidate should not use any descriptors that are not known to be clear to the reader. In the first bullet, the candidate writes about a "collect" service. This is not a widely understood term, and so it must be defined or removed. Here is an example of some accomplishments this candidate should have itemized for some of his positions:

Marketing/Sales Manager
- Developed and executed marketing programs designed to improve the consumer collect-calling service internationally.
- Executed successful launch of this collect calling service in Egypt. Within one month, billable minute results exceeded forecast by 165%. Launched collect-calling service in Pakistan and Vietnam; directly managed advertising agency and in-country Sprint representatives.
- Profiled international demographics and analyzed inbound traffic metrics to prioritize launch order of new international markets. This analysis resulted in Sprint launching the most lucrative markets first and exceeding market forecasts by 43% overall in 2001–2003.

Regional Market Manager
- Developed channel distribution plans for the launch of a new integrated telecommunications service targeted at consumers in Top 15 markets nationally.
- While developing media plans for new market launches, made contacts with local PR representatives and bought media locally, saving over 30% off traditional national rate card purchases.
- Created sales incentive programs targeted at inbound and outbound telemarketing representatives, which resulted in exceeding sales target in each market. Also develop training for telemarketing reps and troubleshooting call center processes.

You get the idea. You need to be clear and to the point and provide as much information as the reader needs to grasp what you've done, provide an indication of what you can do for them, and then stop.

THE EDUCATION SECTION

The education section, like any other section, should position your credentials in the best light without being misleading. List your highest degree first and work back. If you have attended six different colleges but have no degree, you might think that these efforts indicate that you are a lifelong learner. But this could also be interpreted as project incompletion and work against you. Think carefully, strategize, and do what's right for you.

Generally, the education section appears at the beginning of the resume if you have limited work experience. A recent high school, technical school, or college graduate will in most cases fall into this category. As your portfolio of experience and achievements gains momentum, the education section will drop toward the end of the resume as newly formed experiences, skills, and accomplishments begin to outweigh educational experience in the eyes of a prospective employer. Finally, if your educational credentials are seen as critical or are superior to those of competing candidates, you'll want to place this section early in the resume.

If you have a post–high school degree, do not list high school credentials on the resume. A job seeker with no post–high school degree should include high school graduation on the resume. Particular details you might want to address under the heading of education include

---

- ☐ Grade point average (GPA) if 3.0 or higher and only if a recent graduate
- ☐ Class ranking, again only if a recent graduate
- ☐ Honors and awards
- ☐ Scholarships
- ☐ Relevant coursework if directly related to your target profession (mostly for recent graduates)
- ☐ Special theses or dissertations
- ☐ Internships
- ☐ Research projects

This is a good place to talk about hiding information. There are some very imaginative methods of trying to hide weaknesses, and without exception they all fail. But that doesn't mean you should accentuate any flaws in brilliant colors for all to see. The best way to overcome a weakness is to identify a corresponding strength that more than makes up for that weakness. If you have an associate's degree in business when a bachelor's degree is required, what can you do? Pinpoint areas of experience where you've proved yourself, especially areas where practical experience and a proven track record stand out. Demonstrate high energy and enthusiasm and stress your commitment to give 200 percent. Also, enroll in a community school and begin earning your bachelor's degree and state this in your resume and/or cover letter.

You need to address your weakness honestly by demonstrating powerful strengths and assets. Even if you are successful initially in fooling a hiring authority, you can be sure that the interview will be quite uncomfortable. If questions are asked that you can't answer satisfactorily, you're in for an embarrassing, defensive, and unproductive meeting. You will come across as conniving and unethical.

MISCELLANEOUS SECTIONS

Military

If you served your country and received an honorable discharge, it is fine to mention this briefly in your resume. Unless your experience in the military is directly related to the profession you are pursuing (e.g., a U.S. Navy aircraft mechanic applying for a job as a mechanic with an airline), keep it very short, one to two lines at most. The more your military background supports your future career goals, the more emphasis you should give it. Underscore key skills and achievements.

Finally, and this is very important, translate military jargon into English. Many civilian employers were not in the military and can't relate to or understand the military vernacular. If you are not sure of the proper equivalent civilian terminology when translating military verbiage to business terminology, seek out assistance. After going through the painstaking effort of getting a hiring or personnel manager to read your resume, you want to be absolutely certain she or he can understand the messages you are sending.

Interests

Interests are inserted to add a human element to the resume; after all, companies hire people, not robots. This is a section that should be kept brief, tasteful, and provocative insofar as the interviewer can use this information as an "icebreaker" and to set the tone of the interview. It helps to build rapport.

Obviously you will want to use an interest section when your interests match job requirements, skills, or related activities that enhance your chances of getting an interview and a job offer. A country club manager may want to include tennis, golf, and swimming as hobbies. A computer teacher may want to list reading, attending motivational workshops, and surfing the Internet as hobbies. A salesperson may want to include competitive sports because many sales managers view strong competitive skills as a valuable asset in the highly competitive sales arena.

Provide one line (no more unless you have a compelling reason to do so) of information to show the reader your diversity of interests. You might try two or three athletic interests, two or three hobbies, and/or two or three cultural interests. This gives the prospective employer a good profile of who you are outside of work.

Community Service, Special Projects, and Volunteer Work

Many organizations place a high degree of importance on community service. They value fund-raising efforts, volunteering time to charities, and contributing to community improvement. In many cases it is good PR and enhances a company's image in the eyes of the public. Organizations that value these activities believe in the adage "what we get back is in direct proportion to what we give." If you feel that supporting community activities, the arts, and other causes will enhance your overall credentials, by all means include them on your resume.

Professional and Board Affiliations

Memberships and active participation in professional and trade associations demonstrate to a prospective employer that you (1) are a contributing member of your profession, (2) want to advance your own knowledge and improve your skills, and (3) are committed to the future of your vocation. Pertinent affiliations should appear in your resume.

If you sit on boards of directors, this indicates that you are well respected in your community and give of your time to other organizations, be they for-profit or nonprofit entities. These distinguishing credits should be included in your resume.

Awards, Honors, and Recognitions

No doubt these are critical to your resume because they represent your achievements in a powerful and convincing manner. It's one thing to boast about your accomplishments—and that's good. But if you flaunt accomplishments supported by specific awards and recognitions, that will often be the one thing that separates you from your competition.

You can illustrate your honors and recognitions

1. In the introduction section
2. Under professional experience
3. As a separate section

Technical Expertise/Computer Skills

Incorporating a section describing your specific technical and computer skills may be an effective way to introduce your skills to the reader quickly. In a high-tech, ever-changing business environment, employers are looking for people with specific skills and, even more important, people who have the ability to learn, adapt, and embrace new technologies.

In this section consider using short bullets so that the information is easily accessible. Information and data tend to get lost and confused when lumped together in long sentences and paragraphs.

Teaching Assignments

If you have conducted, facilitated, or taught courses, seminars, workshops, or classes, include this on your resume whether you were paid for it or not. Teaching, training, and educating are in-demand skills. They exhibit confidence, leadership, and the ability to communicate. If you have experience in this area, consider stating it on your resume.

Licenses, Accreditation, and Certifications

You may choose to include a section exclusively for listing licenses, accreditation, and certifications. Consider using bullets as an effective way to communicate your significant qualifications quickly and effectively.

Languages

We live and work in a global economy where fluency in multiple languages is an asset that is in great demand. Be sure to list your language skills at the beginning of the resume if you determine that these skills are critical to being considered for the position. Otherwise, note them clearly toward the end.

Personal

Personal data consist of information such as date of birth, marital status, Social Security number, height, weight, sex (if your name is not gender-specific), health, number of dependents, citizenship, travel and relocation preferences, and employment availability.

Employers, by law, cannot discriminate by age, race, religion, creed, sex, or color. For this reason, many job seekers leave personal information off the resume. Unless you have a specific reason to include it, it's probably a good idea to limit or eliminate most personal information. For example, if you are applying for a civil service position, a Social Security number may be appropriate to include on the resume. If you are applying for a position as a preschool teacher and have raised six children of your own, you may want to include that information.

Here's a good test for determining whether to include personal information on a resume: Ask yourself, "Will this information dramatically improve my chances for getting an interview?" If the answer is yes, include it. If the answer is no or I don't know, omit it.

TWO DIFFERENT RESUME TYPES

Chronological Format

The resume we redid earlier in this chapter is in the chronological format. The chronological format is considered by many employment professionals and hiring authorities the resume format of choice because it demonstrates continuous and upward career growth. It does this by emphasizing employment history. A chronological format lists the positions held in a progressive sequence, beginning with the most recent and working back. The one feature that distinguishes the chronological format from the others is that under each job listing you communicate your (1) responsibilities, (2) skills needed to do the job, and, most importantly, (3) specific achievements. The focus is on time, job continuity, growth and advancement, and accomplishments.

Advantages

- You are planning to stay in the same field/work area.
- You want to show off your promotions.
- The name of your last employer is highly prestigious.
- Most people prefer this format to the other formats listed here because it is easy to see whom you have worked for and what you did in each particular job.

Disadvantages

- Not necessarily a great format if you are planning to change career direction.
- You have frequently changed employers; this will highlight each one listed.
- Your work history has been inconsistent in recent years through unemployment, time taken off, job hopping, and so on.
- You do not have many achievements or your achievements are not consistent with what you are targeting. Of course, this is limiting with any format.

Functional Format

A functional format emphasizes skills, abilities, credentials, qualifications, or accomplishments at the beginning of the document but does not correlate those characteristics with any specific employer. Titles, dates of employment, and employment track record are deemphasized in order to highlight qualifications. The focus is squarely on what you did, not on when or where you did it.

The problem with the functional format is that some hiring managers don't like it. The consensus seems to be that this format is used by problem career designers: job hoppers, older workers, career changers, people with employment gaps or academic skill-level deficiencies, and those with limited experience. Some employment professionals feel that if you can't list your employment history in a chronological fashion, there must be a reason and that reason deserves close scrutiny.

Advantages

- You may emphasize abilities and achievements that have not been used in your most recent work.
- You are changing your career direction.
- You have had a large number of jobs and would prefer to describe the experience you have gained in total.
- Your work history has been patchy in recent years through unemployment, redundancy, self-employment, ill health, and so on.

- You want to highlight promotions and career growth. You could include this sort of information on the second page of a functional resume, but it would not be as prominent as it is on a chronological resume.

- Your most recent employer is highly prestigious, but its name will not be prominently displayed on the first page. You can get around this by putting the name in both the profile and the cover letter.

- Your job has only a limited number of functions.

- Because of its unusual layout, many hiring managers don't like this format and may generalize that it is used by people with employment gaps or problems.

An example of the functional format can be found on page 368.

Curriculum Vitae (CV)

A CV has different meanings in different places. In the United Kingdom, for example, the "CV" is an interchangeable term for "resume." In America, it is a type of resume, a subset of the genre. For this discussion, we'll use the American understanding of the CV.

A CV is a resume used mostly in professions and vocations in which a mere listing of credentials describes the value of the candidate. A doctor, for instance, would be a perfect candidate for a CV. A CV is void of anything but a listing of credentials such as medical schools, residencies performed, internships, fellowships, hospitals worked in, public speaking engagements, and publications. In other words, credentials do the talking.

An example of this type of curriculum vitae is found on pages 325–326.

A CV is also used as a more detailed biographical document of your background, accomplishments, and skills. CVs of this sort can run from three to eight pages. Think of your attention span. Even if you're interested in something, such as a good *Time* magazine article that runs for eight pages, it can strain your attention span. Now consider reading that much about someone else. Right—it can be too tedious to complete.

There are few instances where a document of this magnitude is required. If you can avoid it, do so.

How to Select the Correct Format

Consider using a chronological format if you have a solid work history and your future ties to your past. Contemplate using a combination format if you have few deficiencies in experience, education, or achievements. Consider a functional format if you are a student, are returning to the workforce after an extended absence, are changing careers, have worked many jobs in a short period of time, have had employment breaks, or have any other history that would make using a chronological or combination format problematic. Feel free to use a CV if your credentials speak for themselves and no further information is required of you until the interview.

6

An E-Guide to the Electronic Resume

We have been discussing how to develop a resume primarily by traditional means. Nearly everyone is used to writing up a resume in a word processing document, finding nice stationery, printing it out, and sending it out in the mail with a stamp.

The Internet has brought a new way of distributing resumes. Mail with a stamp is still useful, to be sure, but so are e-mail and Website postings. In fact, for those in Internet-related industries, e-mail and Website communications are so prevalent that you should consider those communications vehicles your first priority.

Two Golden Rules

1. Do not e-mail from your current employer.
2. Use a conservative or professional e-mail address. If your name is Sandy Layton, select an e-mail address such as *sandylayton@communications.com*. If you normally use something casual and fun such as *funnygal@communications.com*, drop it for your job search.

SCANNING?

A few years ago scanning seemed to be an emerging way to inventory resumes at the external recruiter and large company levels. But like beta video machines, it never really stuck. As soon as technology got easy to use for scanning, the

Internet exploded and Web-based data transfers and shared drive storage capabilities became the standard for resume inventory and management.

KEY DIFFERENCES BETWEEN AN E-RESUME AND A TRADITIONAL RESUME

First, let's assume there are two kinds of e-resumes. One is the resume as an e-mail attachment. The other is the resume as a text copy inserted into a Website's input field or pasted directly into an e-mail.

E-Resumes as Attachments

This is the easiest method with the fewest implications. You take the file of your resume that you created in a word-processing software program such as Microsoft Word and "attach" it to the e-mail. We will assume that you know how to do this.

We recommend that you attach your resume in e-mail/posting communications where possible. The hiring managers/recruiters will invariably print the e-mail with your resume on it. If you have a good version attached, that will be easier to read than will a text-only file that might be graphically displeasing or difficult to sort through. If you attach your e-mail, all the resume guidelines previously discussed still apply.

E-Resumes as Text Files—ASCII Format

Another way to offer your resume is as a text file. This means you are providing the bare content of your resume in text, without the graphical enhancements. This can mean that you no longer get to use tabs, bullets, certain spacing, boxes, shading, bold print, and the like. This can make the creation of the resume both easier and more difficult.

It can be easier to create a resume in text-only format because you are eliminating the graphical enhancements and formatting. You're simply writing in straight text. However, making an effective presentation without the ability to format actually makes this a more difficult task. This is very important! You need to make your resume appealing in light of the limitations just described.

ASCII (pronounced "Ask-ee"), is nonformatted, "universally compatible" text, the format of choice for large companies that scan or download resumes into keyword-searchable databases. You may even encounter an employer that specifically requests that a resume be in the ASCII format. If you ignore a company's request and try to go around the system by submitting an MS Word version of your resume or the URL for your Web resume, your qualifications may never be seen by your intended audience.

ASCII resumes' compatibility and total search/scan ability make them very desirable in "high-volume" arenas where speed and ease of processing are more important than aesthetics. Unfortunately, ASCII's lack of visual appeal can be a hindrance when image and design are important to a candidate. However—and this is critical—when employers request an ASCII resume, send them an ASCII resume and don't be concerned about its appearance.

E-resumes as Text Files—Writing Modifications

For the next few sections please refer back to Chapter 5. We will take each section that defined how to write up a resume and offer up tips on modifying that information for the text-only version.

THE HEADING

Keep the heading free of any bullets, changes in fonts, and underlines. Use commas instead. Your new text-only heading might look something like this:

```
Richard Twilley, 3628 Eastmore Street, San Francisco, CA 94123, 415-555-1257,
rtwilley@winklink.com
```

THE INTRODUCTION

Since this section is going to be reviewed online, you need to get to the point as concisely as possible. A good introduction is very important here. Try to boil your profile down to three or four bullets, preferably quantifiable ones, and make them as terse as possible. Whatever a reader's attention span is on paper, it is less when one is reading plain text on a monitor.

```
* 15 years experience in telecommunications
* Accomplished background in telecommunications engineering and product
  development
* Sales and product management background in Wide Area Network (WAN)
  design, ATM, Frame Relay, and Internet services
```

THE EMPLOYMENT SECTION

Keep this section free of bullets, changes in fonts, and underlines. Use commas instead. Your new text-only employment section might look something like this:

```
ABC CORPORATION, San Francisco, CA, 1996 to Present
Advanced Sales Support Manager/Field Product Manager
- Provided technical and product-related support for Sales Support divi-
sions on leading-edge technologies for approximately 200 engineering and
sales management employees.
- Led sales support for data services for highest performing region in ABC,
which in 2003 was 213% of plan
- Developed analyses of competitors' product offerings and evaluated cus-
tomer demand for new product feature offerings through market surveys. Pro-
vided recommendations to Marketing and Business Development on needed
enhancements to product portfolio.
```

THE EDUCATION SECTION

Keep this section free of any bullets, changes in fonts, and underlines. Use commas instead. Your new text-only education section might look something like this:

```
EDUCATION
COLLEGE OF WILLIAM AND MARY, Williamsburg, VA,
Bachelor of Science, May 1996
```

Here is an example of what a finished product might look like. This is a good example of how the completed resume would be formatted.

```
Richard Twilley, 3628 Eastmore Street, San Francisco, CA 94123, 415-555-
1257, kmorris@winklink.com

PROFESSIONAL PROFILE
- 15 years experience in telecommunications
- Accomplished background in telecommunications engineering and product
development
- Sales and product management background in Wide Area Network (WAN) design,
ATM, Frame Relay, and Internet services

ABC CORPORATION, San Francisco, CA, 1996 to Present
Advanced Sales Support Manager/Field Product Manager
- Provided technical and product-related support for Sales Support divi-
sions on leading-edge technologies for approximately 200 engineering and
sales management employees.
- Led sales support for data services for highest performing region in ABC,
which in 2003 was 213% of plan.
- Developed analyses of competitors' product offerings and evaluated cus-
tomer demand for new product feature offerings through market surveys. Pro-
vided recommendations to Marketing and Business Development on needed
enhancements to product portfolio.

EDUCATION
COLLEGE OF WILLIAM AND MARY, Williamsburg, VA,
Bachelor of Science, May 1996
```

Quick Text-Only Resume

You have a beautifully formatted resume, right? At this point you don't feel like rewriting the entire document or editing it all. That can take some time. Here is a quick MS Word tip for putting your formatted resume into a text-only document. You'll still want to edit it from here, but that won't take very long after you do this.

1. Pull up your resume and from the "Edit" menu and "Select All"
2. Then, go to the "Start" menu at the bottom and select "Programs," then "Accessories," then "Notepad"
3. Paste the copied text in the Notepad and you will have an unformatted resume.
4. Finally, save it. You can then e-mail the resume when you need to or copy and paste it in an online resume field that is commonly found on many companies' internal Website job postings or on Monster.com and the like.

Following are two more examples of e-resumes written in plain ASCII format, that is, stripped of all formatting. Note, these are not specific to students but are taken from our previous guides for professionals.

Robert Atkinson
4548 Sierra Lane
Jupiter, FL 33445
(561) 555-5934
robert.atkinson@aol.com

ACCOUNTING MANAGER

PROFILE:
Passed CPA exam in State of Florida
Well versed in all relevant computer software programs, including Peachtree, DacEasy, Lotus 1-2-3, AccountPro, Excel, and most other Windows-based applications

Experience in cost accounting in manufacturing environments and public auditing

Develop plan, conduct audits and variance analyses, process payroll and payroll tax reports and filings, and maintain/update accurate inventories.

KEY ACHIEVEMENTS:

- Instrumental in the negotiation and acquisition of $3 million home care and retail pharmacy stores; negotiated a $14 million contract for pharmaceuticals resulting in a savings of 1.5-3% on cost of goods for each retail store.

- Saved $87k in annual corporate management salaries through comprehensive management of the financial programs and credit administration of the group.

- Managed accounting department consisting of controller, billing auditor, and accounting staff.

EMPLOYMENT:

Wellington Regional Medical Center, West Palm Beach, FL
1994 - Present
Accounting Manager

- Managed accounting staff, reporting to CFO

- Design, implement, and manage all centralized accounting, management information systems, and internal control policies and procedures

- Manage accounting department consisting of A/P, A/R, cost management, and general ledger maintenance

- Prepare all Federal and State tax requirements, including corporate, partnership, payroll, and property tax returns.

Diversified Centers, Inc., Palm Beach, FL
1988 - 1994
Staff Accountant

- Staff accountant for real estate development firm

- Coordinate all financing and external reporting with financial institutions for the group

- Full general ledger management responsibility

- Managed accounts payable for two years

- Managed accounts receivable for 18 months

- Prepare and administer operating and cash budgets for each retail profit center.

EDUCATION: Florida Atlantic University, Boca Raton, FL
    Bachelor of Arts: Accounting, 1987

RESUME

Coury Rau
2724 Cameron Street
Washington, DC 20008
W (703) 555-1212, H (202) 555-1212
corey.rau@mail.argi.net

EXPERIENCE

A.T. Kearney - EDS Management Consulting Services
Washington, DC
Principal, 1996-present
Senior Manager, 1994-1996

Specialized in the development of business plans for emerging wireline and wireless telecommunications companies. Responsible for client relationship management and sales into preexisting client base. Responsible for managing large (up to 30 people) work teams. Provided advice to senior management on a broad variety of strategic and operational subjects, including:
-Business strategy and planning
-Financial modeling
-Competitive assessment
-Market segmentation
-Operations design and optimization
-Mergers and acquisitions
-Implementation assistance
-Churn management

Deloitte & Touche Management Consulting
Washington, DC
Manager, 1993-1994
Senior Consultant, 1991-1993

Primarily focused on developing market entry strategies for telecommunications clients. Developed very strong financial modeling skills. Responsible for managing smaller projects and developing client deliverables.

EDUCATION

B.S. in Physics, Montana State University, 1989
MBA in Finance, Carnegie Mellon University, 1991

PUBLICATIONS/SPEECHES

"An Ice Age Is Coming to the Wireless World: A Perspective on the Future of Mobile Telephony in the United States," 1995
Thought Leadership Series, EDS Management Consulting

"Analysis of the FCC's Order Regarding Ameritech's Application to Provide InterLA-TA Toll Services within the State of Michigan," A.T. Kearney White Paper, 1997

Presented at over two dozen industry conferences, workshops, and panels

Creating a PDF Resume

Have you ever seen a PDF file? They look great. Why? Because their format is set by the creator of the document (you) and can't be changed or edited. You'll see many corporate documents and forms in this format for that very reason. There are pluses and minuses to using a PDF format.

Pluses

- You set the formatting, and the reader sees it just as you intended. It won't be distorted from one recipient to the next. This is the primary advantage, a huge one.
- Demonstrates your extra resume creation effort and software savvy.
- PDF files can be created easily from MS Word and WordPerfect documents.
- PDF resumes cannot be altered or easily pasted into mailing list databases.
- PDF resumes do not contain viruses; recipients value that.

Minuses

- The text cannot be edited. It cannot be searched or scanned for keywords, which can limit its utility.
- Some recipients might not have Adobe Acrobat Reader software. However, it is free and can be downloaded at *www.adobe.com*.

To create a PDF file resume, you need the Adobe Acrobat program. It is not free, unlike the Reader software referenced above. However, once you have it, it's very easy to use. The key is to make sure it's reviewed comprehensively for layout and format. No typos! This is a good consideration if you have access to the Adobe software or don't mind buying it. However, solely for resume development, it is not necessary.

Web-Based Resume

Web resumes are based on HTML, the same protocol with which Web pages are created. They offer an array of creative options, from navigation within the resume to links to employers, products, distributors, and other areas at the click of a mouse.

Very Aesthetic

HTML formatting enables endless options with respect to layout, color, and overall design. HTML features can dramatically improve a resume's appearance and project an image of creativity, professionalism, and skill. With HTML you can create an endless amount of resume looks; they can be very edgy to very conservative. If you work in a high-tech or marketing-oriented field, this is definitely worth considering.

Very Compatible

HTML resumes are essentially Web pages. They can be viewed by anyone with Internet access. You don't run into compatibility issues with access to the links.

Go High and Wide

Like all Web documents, HTML resumes can be linked to other Web pages. The World Wide Web and the nature of linking one site to another are perfect for creating resumes, support documents and contacts, business associations, letters of recommendation, photos, and so forth. The Web enables you to better go "high and wide" in contacting and being contacted by more decision makers.

Developing Web Resumes

First, apply the same principles we discussed in Chapter 5 for developing a resume. Your options for linkages generally fall into two areas. First, you can provide navigation links to aid with the navigation of your resume. For example, take the following resume: Look at the boxed section at the upper left. If you were click on each of those links, the resume image would jump to that section.

Appearances

Try to use a light background and black (or dark) body text. Also, when designing it, consider what the resume will look like if printed or if there can be an option to select a PDF version for printing. Do not underline, save that for the hyperlinks.

Online resumes offer many advantages and are gaining in acceptance, as long as they do not depart too far from the general look of a traditional resume format. The example on the next page is produced by Image Marketers (*http://www.ImageMarketers.com*) and is interactive through the use of Infobytes, or additional pieces of background information that relate to sections on the resume (see the icon). This additional information can be very helpful in giving the story behind the resume and in introducing a personal touch. The resume is actually a Website with a unique URL that can be forwarded as a link rather than an e-mailed attachment. The "before-and-after" example shows how an Infobyte works when a reader moves their mouse over the icon on the screen. In addition, this resume can easily be responded to, forwarded, printed, and links can be added to give the reader a whole new dimension of information.

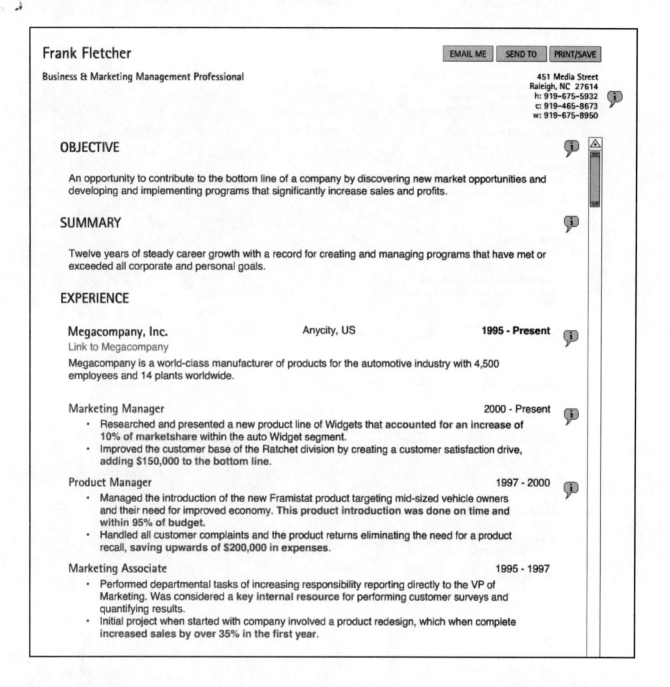

Frank Fletcher

EMAIL ME   SEND TO   PRINT/SAVE

Business & Marketing Management Professional

451 Media Street
Raleigh, NC 27614
h: 919-675-5932
c: 919-465-8673
w: 919-675-8950

OBJECTIVE

An opportunity to contribute to the bottom line of a company by discovering new market opportunities and developing and implementing programs that significantly increase sales and profits.

SUMMARY

Twelve years of steady career growth with a record for creating and managing programs that have met or exceeded all corporate and personal goals.

EXPERIENCE

Megacompany, Inc.   Anycity, US   **1995 - Present**
Link to Megacompany

Megacompany is a world-class manufacturer of products for the automotive industry with 4,500 employees and 14 plants worldwide.

Marketing Manager   2000 - Present
- Researched and presented a new product line of Widgets that accounted for **an increase of 10% of marketshare within the auto Widget segment.**
- Improved the customer base of the Ratchet division by creating a customer satisfaction drive, adding **$150,000 to the bottom line.**

Product Manager   1997 - 2000
- Managed the introduction of the new Framistat product targeting mid-sized vehicle owners and their need for improved economy. **This product introduction was done on time and within 95% of budget.**
- Handled all customer complaints and the product returns eliminating the need for a product recall, **saving upwards of $200,000 in expenses.**

Marketing Associate   1995 - 1997
- Performed departmental tasks of increasing responsibility reporting directly to the VP of Marketing. Was considered a **key internal resource** for performing customer surveys and quantifying results.
- Initial project when started with company involved a product redesign, which when complete increased sales by over 35% in the first year.

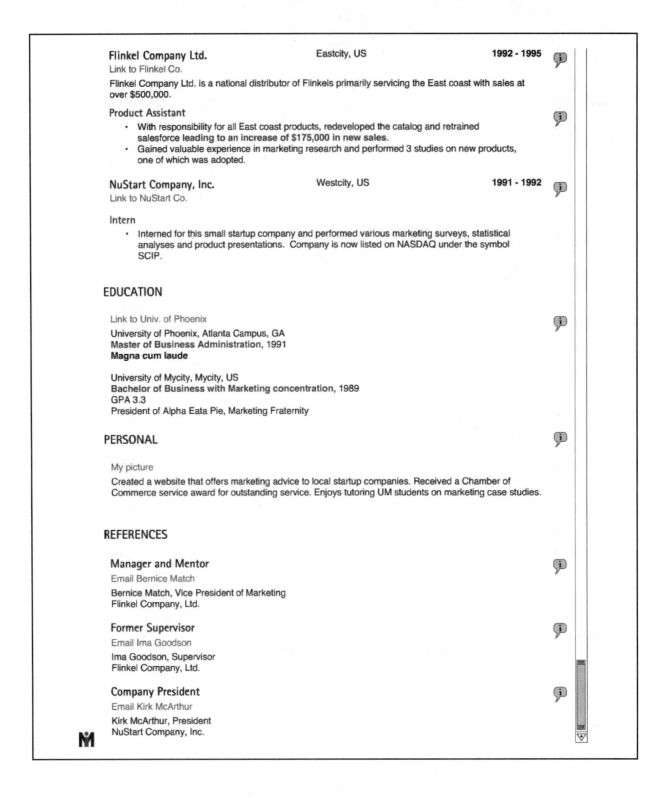

Flinkel Company Ltd.   Eastcity, US   **1992 - 1995**

Link to Flinkel Co.

Flinkel Company Ltd. is a national distributor of Flinkels primarily servicing the East coast with sales at over $500,000.

Product Assistant
- With responsibility for all East coast products, redeveloped the catalog and retrained salesforce leading to an increase of $175,000 in new sales.
- Gained valuable experience in marketing research and performed 3 studies on new products, one of which was adopted.

NuStart Company, Inc.   Westcity, US   **1991 - 1992**

Link to NuStart Co.

Intern
- Interned for this small startup company and performed various marketing surveys, statistical analyses and product presentations. Company is now listed on NASDAQ under the symbol SCIP.

EDUCATION

Link to Univ. of Phoenix

University of Phoenix, Atlanta Campus, GA
Master of Business Administration, 1991
Magna cum laude

University of Mycity, Mycity, US
Bachelor of Business with Marketing concentration, 1989
GPA 3.3
President of Alpha Eata Pie, Marketing Fraternity

PERSONAL

My picture

Created a website that offers marketing advice to local startup companies. Received a Chamber of Commerce service award for outstanding service. Enjoys tutoring UM students on marketing case studies.

REFERENCES

Manager and Mentor

Email Bernice Match

Bernice Match, Vice President of Marketing
Flinkel Company, Ltd.

Former Supervisor

Email Ima Goodson

Ima Goodson, Supervisor
Flinkel Company, Ltd.

Company President

Email Kirk McArthur

Kirk McArthur, President
NuStart Company, Inc.

Web Resume after an Infobyte of information is selected.

Frank Fletcher

EMAIL ME   SEND TO   PRINT/SAVE

451 Media Street
Raleigh, NC 27614
h: 919-675-5932
c: 919-465-8673
w: 919-675-8950

OBJECTIVE

An opportunity to contribute to the bottom line of a company by discovering new market opportunities and developing and implementing programs that significantly increase sales and profits.

- 12 years marketing experience in automotive industry.
- Top performance recognition for top sales performance in 1994, 1996, 1999, and 2001.
- Full sales/marketing go-to-market experience with new widgets. Marketing experience with various automotive products, including auto parts, SUVs, electric hybrids, and full-size trucks.
- Led 2001 product team to top-ranked performance in Megacompany division; met or exceeded plan from 2001 to 2003, and team had zero turnover. Proven marketing and product management leader, distinguished contributor as marketing organization leader.

SUMMARY

Twelve years of steady career growth with a record for creating and managing programs that have met or exceeded all corporate and personal goals.

EXPERIENCE

Megacompany, Inc.   Anycity, US   1995 - Present
Link to Megacompany

   Megacompany is a world-class manufacturer of products for the automotive industry with 4,500 employees and 14
   plants worldwide.

Marketing Manager   2000 - Present
- Researched and presented a new product line of Widgets that accounted for an increase of 10% of marketshare within the auto Widget segment.
- Improved the customer base of the Ratchet division by creating a customer satisfaction drive, adding $150,000 to the bottom line.

Product Manager   1997 - 2000
- Managed the introduction of the new Framistat product targeting mid-sized vehicle owners and their need for improved economy. This product introduction was done on time and within 95% of budget.
- Handled all customer complaints and the product returns eliminating the need for a product recall, saving upwards of $200,000 in expenses.

Marketing Associate   1995 - 1997
- Performed departmental tasks of increasing responsibility reporting directly to the VP of Marketing. Was considered a key internal resource for performing customer surveys and quantifying results.
- Initial project when started with company involved a product redesign, which when complete increased sales by over 35% in the first year.

Flinkel Company Ltd.   Eastcity, US   **1992 - 1995**

Link to Flinkel Co.

Flinkel Company Ltd. is a national distributor of Flinkels primarily servicing the East coast with sales at over $500,000.

Product Assistant

- With responsibility for all East coast products, redeveloped the catalog and retrained salesforce leading to an increase of $175,000 in new sales.
- Gained valuable experience in marketing research and performed 3 studies on new products, one of which was adopted.

NuStart Company, Inc.   Westcity, US   **1991 - 1992**

Link to NuStart Co.

Intern

- Interned for this small startup company and performed various marketing surveys, statistical analyses and product presentations. Company is now listed on NASDAQ under the symbol SCIP.

EDUCATION

Link to Univ. of Phoenix

University of Phoenix, Atlanta Campus, GA
Master of Business Administration, 1991
Magna cum laude

University of Mycity, Mycity, US
Bachelor of Business with Marketing concentration, 1989
GPA 3.3
President of Alpha Eata Pie, Marketing Fraternity

PERSONAL

My picture

Created a website that offers marketing advice to local startup companies. Received a Chamber of Commerce service award for outstanding service. Enjoys tutoring UM students on marketing case studies.

REFERENCES

Manager and Mentor

Email Bernice Match

Bernice Match, Vice President of Marketing
Flinkel Company, Ltd.

Former Supervisor

Email Ima Goodson

Ima Goodson, Supervisor
Flinkel Company, Ltd.

Company President

Email Kirk McArthur

Kirk McArthur, President
NuStart Company, Inc.

7
Happy Graduation: Uncovering Job Opportunities

For students and recent graduates there are several primary sources of job leads:

- On-campus recruiting
- Networking
- Career fairs
- Contacting companies directly
- Classified advertisements
- Executive recruiters and employment agencies

There are several unique elements to job searching when one is fresh from school compared with having several years of experience. There are differences in the tactical approaches to the job search, and we will provide some suggestions and guidelines to help you get a resume in front of the right people.

ON-CAMPUS RECRUITING

You will find that different companies recruit at different universities, trying to be geographically diverse, focusing on the top schools only, or focusing on the schools that have brought them the best recruiting success in the past.

Resumes from these targeted schools often are reviewed with a little more attention than are resumes sent through the mail or by fax. There are a few exceptions, however.

If the company you are targeting doesn't recruit at your school, you still have good options and may have to employ the tactics discussed later in this chapter. If your targeted company is visiting your campus to recruit, you should register with the school's career center to obtain an interview. When that is scheduled, do some preliminary research on the company. Most of those companies are large enough to have a detailed Website and be "in the news." Visit their sites so that you can see their direction and conduct media searches to learn more. Then drop this information into the interview where appropriate. You will learn more and make a stronger impression on the interviewer.

Suppose your targeted company is visiting your campus but you cannot secure an interview because of your major or grades. Don't give up; instead, try to employ some creative tactics.

- Have a favorite professor "sponsor" your effort and work with the campus career center or the recruiter to get you an interview.
- Make a special effort with the dean of your department and the director of the career center to convince them you are worthy and should not be overlooked. If your grades are poor, it may help to have some justification, such as working 20 or more hours a week. If you have a different major, point out that over two-thirds of all professionals work in fields that are different from their majors in college.
- Suppose the company is large, such as Verizon. Go to a Verizon store, network with the store manager, and see if someone internal can help you secure an interview.

There are many ways to get in the door, and you should not give up after the first push back. Also, if the company is recruiting, perhaps you can get an interview there even if you do not get one on campus. If you know that a company such as Verizon is recruiting, go directly to it and apply for a position.

If you have secured an interview on campus, do some research on the company so that you are prepared to discuss how you can fit in its organization. Your research should stimulate good questions to ask the recruiter. In addition, here are some sample questions to consider if you are interviewing with Verizon:

- What brought you to Verizon, and how does it differ there from other places?
- How would you rate the overall leadership and direction at Verizon, and how is morale overall?
- How would you describe the management culture at Verizon?
- What is one characteristic that demonstrates leadership skills in your organization?
- What do you feel is your biggest competitive threat in the next several years?
- How would you describe the culture of your company?
- Could you describe a typical day in the life of a [whatever discipline you're interviewing for] person?
- What are some of the challenges you face on a day-to-day basis?

- What is the average length of time entry-level recruits remain with Verizon?
- Did your company face significant layoffs in the most recent recession, and if so, how were those laid off selected?
- What types of continuing education programs do you offer your employees?
- What support mechanisms are currently in place that foster your company's innovative culture?

NETWORKING

The buzzword of job searching is *networking*—connecting with people. It's your best strategy today. Networking is people connecting, and when you connect with people, you begin to assemble your network. Once your network is in place, you will continue to make new contacts and communicate with established members. People in your network will provide advice, information, and support in helping you achieve your career goals and aspirations.

Networking accounts for up to 70% of the new opportunities uncovered. So what is networking? Many people assume that they should call all the people they know personally and professionally and ask if they know about any companies that are hiring. A successful networker's approach is different.

Leverage Alumni and Faculty

College grads and seniors should use the college's alumni as networking sources. Generally speaking, most people are willing to help you network if they can be persuaded by you to do something specific, or give you general advice. The trick is getting in the door to see those connected professionals. Here are some tips on networking with alumni.

- If you hear about an alumni doing a presentation at your college in your area of interest, go there and make sure to make contact with the presenter and ask for his or her card for future reference.
- Ask professors in your discipline if they know of any graduates who work in the area in which you are interested or for companies you are targeting. Here is another trick: Suppose you are interested in obtaining an accounting job with Ford Motor Company. Go to other professors, such as those in the engineering department or marketing department, who may be connected with alumni or managers at Ford. Large companies employ countless disciplines, and you need to leverage any "in" you can uncover.
- Find out which faculty members work in the consulting arena in the private sector and seek their advice and contacts.
- Focus on recent graduates and alumni. They were more recently in your shoes and may be better sources of tips and leads than are more established alumni.
- Go to alumni gatherings such as football games at sports bars. In Dallas, the Michigan State University alumni association has over 100 members, to put this in perspective. Alumni, especially from major universities, are *everywhere*. Visit them in the market in which you wish to live and/or work. Become friendly with the chapter president.

Make sure to treat alumni as respected networking sources and utilize the principles outlined later in this section. Don't send them your resume and don't ask them for a job. Be well organized and think through what you want to ask them so that they can give you very targeted advice. If you are not focused, they will not be able to help and may find the whole exercise frustrating.

CAREER FAIRS

Career fairs are an overlooked opportunity to uncover good career opportunities. In 1997, Grace Matherly, age 26, was looking for a marketing job in Dallas. She networked with some former colleagues, checked the classifieds, and contacted some executive recruiters. Still, she did not uncover the position that was the best fit. Then she heard about a career fair for engineers and technical managers. Though she was not looking for that type of position, she went to network.

There she met some recruiters from Sprint, and they informed her that Sprint had a big marketing presence in Dallas and that they were hiring. They put her in touch with Sprint, and within 60 days she secured exactly the position for which she was looking. She had uncovered an opportunity that had not been advertised and had no executive recruiter supporting it.

Even if the career fair is for a specialty different from your own, it still provides an excellent networking opportunity to uncover new leads. Generally, career fairs are advertised in local papers and held at hotels or convention centers, and from 5 to 15 companies may participate, even more in large fairs in major markets.

Career fairs can be crowded, with long lines of candidates waiting to interview. You can maximize your productive time with good preparation. Try to register electronically at the organizer's Website if possible; this eliminates standing in line at the entrance. Get there before the long lines form if you can. No matter what time you show up, go first to the companies your research has indicated will be the best match and then hit the rest. Take the time to visit as many companies as you can. Below are some tips to ensure that you get noticed:

- Develop your "elevator pitch." This is a two-minute overview of your background and the type of position for which you are looking. It should include professional and/or academic information, not personal information. However, when delivering it, you can interject some personal information to build rapport, demonstrate a high-energy personality, and distinguish yourself. Just don't overdo it.

- Bring at least one good copy of your resume for each company participating in the fair as well as a few extras in case you network in other areas.

- Research the employers that are attending. Learn more about each company, its product and services, and its current challenges. You can find terrific information on company websites and in media reviews. Some of these reviews can be garnered by going to the company's trading symbol on financial Websites and looking in the "news" sections. Also, type in the name of the company in a good search engine and click on what comes up.

- Bring a folder to carry resumes and a notepad for notes.

- Dress professionally.

- Prepare for the interviews. Review the tips for interviewing section in this book as well as our interviewing book *Great Questions, Great Answers* (McGraw-Hill, 2004).

- Prepare questions you want employers to answer.
- Go alone; if you go with friends or family, walk the fair by yourself.
- Be aware of time demands on employers. Do not monopolize an employer's time. Ask specific questions and offer to follow up after the fair as appropriate.
- Be direct. Introduce yourself. If you are job seeking, state the type of position in which you are interested. If you are gathering information, let employers know that you are interested only in materials and information.
- When greeting a recruiter, introduce yourself and look confident by initiating a handshake with a smile.
- Ask the company what the next step is and how to follow up.
- Get appropriate contact information and ask for a business card.
- After the career fair, send a thank-you card and reconfirm interest in the position and company. In the note, indicate exactly when you will follow up and then do so. Put the burden of follow-up on yourself because they may intend to follow up but be too busy and put it off or forget.

CONTACTING COMPANIES DIRECTLY

When you contact a company, you can do it directly or through a reference/networking source. A third-party endorsement lends credibility and will differentiate you from the other applicants. The networking section in this chapter is a good guideline for contacting companies directly. See also the discussion in Chapter 3.

CLASSIFIED ADVERTISING

See Chaper 3 for a discussion of classified advertisements as a source for job openings.

EXECUTIVE RECRUITERS AND EMPLOYMENT AGENCIES

Employment agencies and executive recruiters work for the hiring companies, not for you. There are thousands of employment agencies and executive recruiters nationwide. Employment agencies generally place candidates in positions with a salary range under $40,000, which may bode well for many recent graduates. Executive recruiters place candidates in positions ranging from temporary service at the administrative or executive level to permanent senior-level management. Recruiters can be a great source of hidden jobs even if they do not have a position suitable for you at a given time.

Recruiters and agencies will have a greater chance of locating a position for you if your professional discipline is of a technical or specific nature, such as accounting, engineering, or sales. See also Chapter 3.

STUDENT-SPECIFIC RESUME TIPS

Sample student resumes can be found on pages 362–372.

For functional resumes (the choice of most students), you should consider leading with your education and associated academic skills as the lead summary. The purpose of this introduction is to convey the scope of your experience and background and indicate to the reader your key strengths and areas of expertise. *The first section of the introduction must ignite initial interest and make the reader want to continue.*

Here is an example of a student's introductory section, focusing on educational experience:

SUMMARY OF QUALIFICATIONS

EDUCATION   **Master of Business Administration,** (expected 1999)
Central Michigan University, Midland, Michigan
GPA 3.0/4.0

Bachelor of Arts in Communications, 1996
Central Michigan University, Midland, Michigan
GPA 3.4/4.0

HONORS/AWARDS
- High School Valedictorian.
- Won citywide Essay Competition senior year in high school.
- Won "Best Essay" Contest out of 800 students at Armstrong State College.
- Invited to statewide Academic Recognition Ceremony at State Capitol.
- Awarded distinguished *Silver A* award from Armstrong State College.

SKILLS/STRENGTHS
- Strong understanding of financial markets and market development.
- Proficient with all Microsoft Windows-based programs.
- Extensive background with performing strategic analysis of corporations.
- Developed multiple presentations outlining strategic recommendations.
- Proven tact and diplomacy in handling interpersonal relationships.

The Education Section

The education section, like any other section, should position your credentials in the best light without being misleading. List your highest degree first and work back. If you have attended six different colleges but have no degree, you might think that these efforts indicate that you are a lifelong learner. But this could also be interpreted as *project incompletion* and work against you. Think carefully, strategize, and do what's right for you.

Generally, the education section appears at the beginning of the resume if you have limited work experience. A recent high school, technical school, or college graduate will in most cases fall into this category. As your portfolio of experience and achievements gains momentum, the education section will drop toward the end of the resume as newly formed experiences, skills, and accomplishments begin to outweigh educational experience in the eyes of a prospective employer. Finally, if your educational credentials are seen as critical or are superior to those of competing candidates, you'll want to introduce this section early in the resume.

If you have a post–high school degree, you need not list high school credentials on the resume. A job seeker with no post–high school degree should include high school graduation on the resume. Particular details you might want to address under the heading of education include the following:

Grade point average (GPA) if 3.0 or higher

Class ranking

Honors and awards

Scholarships

Intramural or varsity sports

Clubs and special classes

Relevant coursework if directly related to your target profession (mostly for recent graduates)

Special theses or dissertations

Internships

Research projects

Extracurricular activities (tutoring, volunteer work, student activities/politics, working on school newspaper)

Career-related jobs and activities while attending school

The following is an example of what the education section of a student's resume might look like. It is the same as that illustrated in the introduction section because these sections often are the same on student resumes that list little professional experience.

EDUCATION	**Master of Business Administration** (expected 1999) *Central Michigan University*, Midland, Michigan GPA 3.0/4.0 **Bachelor of Arts in Communications**, 1996 *Central Michigan University*, Midland, Michigan GPA 3.4/4.0
HONORS/AWARDS	♦ High School Valedictorian. ♦ Won citywide Essay Competition senior year in high school. ♦ Won "Best Essay" Contest out of 800 students at Armstrong State College. ♦ Invited to statewide Academic Recognition Ceremony at State Capitol. ♦ Awarded distinguished *Silver A* award from Armstrong State College.

The Employment Section

The employment section is a very important part of the resume for an experienced professional. However, for a student, the emphasis is more academic; a robust professional background is not expected. If you do have good work experience relevant to the position for which you are applying, list it here.

Experience is not limited to paying jobs. If applicable and advantageous, include volunteer work that enhances your candidacy. Do not include salary, reasons for leaving, or supervisor's name unless you have a very specific reason for doing so. Salary history and requirements, if requested, should be addressed in the cover letter.

When using a chronological or combination format, provide specific information for each employer you worked for and each job you performed. Include three pieces of information for each employer/job:

1. Basic accomplishments and industry- or company-specific information
2. Special skills required to discharge those responsibilities
3. General responsibilities

The listing of your job accomplishments and responsibilities should read like a condensed job description that shows how you made a difference. Bring out only the highlights, not the obvious. Finally, use positive and energy-oriented words. The words you choose should reflect your energy level, motivation, charisma, education level, and professionalism. Emotion and action sell; use action and power words.

Briefly describe any special skills you used in carrying out past responsibilities. These skills might include computers that you operated, special equipment you used, and bilingual capabilities. Other examples of skills that you might have employed include problem solving, communications, organizational, and technical mastery. Review your daily tasks and you'll be surprised at the skills you use every day but take for granted.

The major focus of the employment/experience section should be on your specific accomplishments, achievements, and contributions. What you did in terms of day-to-day functions has little impact. *What you accomplished through those functions determines your hireability.*

When using a functional format, simply list the information—company name, city/state, dates of employment, and titles—and leave it at that.

Here is an example of what this section might look like:

VOLUNTEER ACTIVITIES AND PREVIOUS WORK EXPERIENCE

Merrill Lynch, Lansing, Michigan
Intern (Summer 1997, 1998)
Performed financial analysis of prospective investment opportunities and worked directly with clients to support account manager. Helped develop new process flow that reduced temporary help expenses by over 22%.

SIGMA ALPHA MU FRATERNITY, Central Michigan University, MI
Kitchen Steward (Academic Season 1996, 1997, 1998)
Established kitchen procedures, many still in use, for newly chartered chapter of this fraternity. Responsible for food budget, purchasing food and supplies, interviewing and hiring kitchen personnel, supervising kitchen and dining room operations, and preparing food. Also held positions of Scholarship Chairman and Fundraising Chairman.

FINAL NOTES

Be Specific

Don't create a resume with a flowery introductory objective like the following:

My objective is to obtain a challenging position that will enable me to utilize my excellent communication skills and high motivation.

You may be laughing at this, but it would shock you how often this kind of fluffy, nondescriptive copy is offered on resumes. Actually, it shocks us how often that fluffy copy ends up in other resume guidance books.

Pack It Up Front

As with any resume, the introduction is 80% of the resume. Stack it with your best stuff. Leave the questionable or weaker material to the middle or end. Then think. Really think. Think about what the employer is looking for and find ways to interpret what you've done in the past that can lend itself to getting that job. This is remedial, but I remember when I was in high school and going for a promotion at a grocery store, from bag boy to produce clerk. I didn't get it. Why? Because another bag boy highlighted his experience working in his garden and preparing various vegetables for storage and consumption. Pretty creative for a 16-year-old.

8
Keywords and Action Verbs

Keywords are descriptive words, usually nouns, that are associated with specific disciplines or industries. Keywords are important because they are considered standardized for specific industries. For example, if you were an accountant, keywords would include cost accounting, budget analysis, auditing, tax, and so on. Keywords can be critical in the world of software management and job searching. Employers and recruiters may take your resume and cover letter (especially if sent electronically) and do a search for keywords/descriptors that match the profile they are seeking. Think of it as a prescreening process. For example, a finance director for Microsoft who is hiring a staff accountant might do a scan/search of resumes and cover letters for the words listed above, and if those words aren't in your materials, you could miss the first cut.

Keywords play an integral role in two areas of the resume screening process. One is the human element, where hiring and nonhiring managers are screening resumes for words and phrases that match the criteria they are using. The second is the computer search, where computers search the data on many different resumes to select those which match the words and phrases. That is how posted resumes on Websites such as Monster.com work.

PRESCREENING BY PERSONNEL

Keywords can be very important outside the computer search arena. In many cases, the initial scan of resumes is completed by either a human resources person or an assistant to the hiring manager. Even the most competent people doing this job can do a high-level job of resume scanning only if they are not intimately aware of the position or are not hiring for themselves. That is why it is important to keep a certain amount of "boilerplate" in your resume.

A client of ours named David Robinson comes to mind. He worked for Verizon Wireless and was curious about an advertisement he saw for a position with Ericcson. We updated his resume in the style that looks like that on pages 56–57 of our first book, *101 Best Resumes*. The key to that resume style was the use of the left column for a listing of accounts that becomes the core of the resume if you work in an account-driven environment such as sales. The hiring manager called David for an interview and told him: "We've had so many resumes that I told my assistant not to bring me any more unless they look like a perfect fit. The way you listed your accounts on the first page of the resume was a great way to show us who your contacts are." The initial screening was conducted by his assistant, who was only scanning resumes for key items (words, even things such as industry-specific terms, product names), and his resume effectively illustrated his sales accounts.

Don't make the readers work to learn what you're all about. Even in a low-unemployment environment, the competition for good jobs is too stiff.

THE ONLINE ENVIRONMENT

The Internet environment has created a new way of distributing resumes. As part of the boilerplate activities one does when beginning to market oneself to potential employers, using the Internet is now a standard resource tool. One of the first things many people do is post their resumes on Websites such as Monser.com and Headhunter.net. Corporate recruiters and independent recruiters review resumes posted on those sites. It works best when the search field is very narrow. If you were to do a keyword search of all the resumes posted on Monster.com for *telecommunications*, for example, the return would be in the thousands. However, if you narrowed the search to *MMDS narrowband spectrum management*, the return would be significantly lower. Thus, you need to whittle your skills keywords down as much as possible to help the right people find you through these keyword searches. Keywords make a traditional resume electronically retrievable in resume databases such as Monster.com and Headhunter.net.

After your resume is entered electronically into a resume database such as that on Monster.com, it is ready to be searched and ranked. A hiring manager/recruiter then decides which keywords best identify the skills needed in a candidate and, based on those keywords, has the system search the resume database. Typically, the reviewer will have several keywords that are required and others that are optional.

When the search engine recognizes a keyword in your resume, that is called a "hit." Your resume is ranked according to the number of keyword hits. Only resumes that have the required keywords are found. Among those, resumes that have more of the desired keywords rank higher and will be selected first to be read by a human reviewer. Other factors that can affect search rankings include proximity to other keywords and how close to the top of the page keyword hits occur. Therefore, in addition to placing keywords relevant to your field throughout your resume and cover letter, you should create an extra "keyword summary" near the top of the resume specifically for a resume search engine. Our resume guides provide many examples of how to do this in constructing the opening part of a resume.

Keywords and Action Verbs

A good summary of qualifications provides an opportunity to include listings of keywords that may not fit in the rest of the written part of the resume. The more keywords, the greater the likelihood of ranking high.

KEYWORDS

Below is a plain-formatted resume that is representative of something that might be pasted in the application area on Monster.com. Highlighted in gray are the keywords. Granted, this resume is an exaggerated version of the use of keywords. Still, it will give you a good perspective. Also, it's no secret that the more specialized the position, the greater the role keywords play. However, even if you're in sales or general management, key industry terms can be very helpful.

Dan Schmitz
1234 Hereford Highway
Kansas City, MO 12345
H: (913) 555-1111 W: (913) 555-1111; e-mail: danschmitz@technology.net

Keyword Summary

Systems Engineer. Client Server System Architect. Systems Analysis. Systems Integration. Network Administration. Database Administration. Systems Administration. Software Engineering. Troubleshooting Computing Systems. C++. Visual Basic. SQL. UNIX Shell Script. Windows. MS DOS. Windows NT. TCP/IP. OSI. Microsoft LAN Manager. Novell Netware. Project Management. Trade Studies. Consulting. BETA Tester. Technical Presentations. Sales Presentations. Instructor. BS Degree. Mathematics and Computer Science. UCLA. Air Force Institute of Technology. Computer Engineering.

Summary of Qualifications

Seven years of experience in designing, installing, and troubleshooting computing systems

Programming: C, C++, Visual BASIC, FORTRAN, Pascal, SQL, OSF/Motif, UNIX Shell Script (sh, ksh, csh), BASIC, Clipper, Algol 68, and 80X86 Assembler.

Operating Systems: UNIX (bsd & SVr3/r4), MS Windows, MS DOS, MS Windows NT, Solaris, HP-UX, Ultrix, AIX, VAX/VMS, and Macintosh System 7.

Networking: TCP/IP, OSI, Microsoft LAN Manager, Novell Netware, DDN, Internet, Ethernet, Token Ring, SNA, X.25, and LAN-WAN interconnection.

Applications: Microsoft Office, Microsoft Access, Microsoft Visual C++, Microsoft Project, Microsoft Publisher, Lotus 123, Lotus Freelance, System Architect, and others.

Professional Experience

Network Engineer

Netcom, Dallas, Texas 1996-Present

* Provide systems engineering, software engineering, technical consulting, and marketing services as a member of the Systems Integration Division of a software engineering consulting company.

* Designed and managed the development of an enterprise-level client/server automated auditing application for a major financial management company migrating from mainframe computers, db2, and FOCUS to a workgroup-oriented, client/server architecture involving Windows for Workgroups, Windows NT Advanced Server, Microsoft SQL Server, Oracle7, and UNIX.

* Designed an enterprise-level, high-performance, mission-critical, client/server database system incorporating symmetric multiprocessing computers (SMP), Oracle7's Parallel Server, Tuxedo's online transaction processing (OLTP) monitor, and redundant array of inexpensive disks (RAID) technology.

* Conducted extensive trade studies of a large number of vendors that offer leading-edge technologies; these studies identified proven (low-risk) implementations of SMP and RDBMS systems that met stringent performance and availability criteria.

Education

University of Kansas, BS Software Engineering and Computer Communications

GPA: 3.43

Specialized Training

Database Administration, Performance Tuning, and Benchmarking with Oracle7; Oracle Corporation.

Interactive UNIX System V r4 (POSIX) System Administration; ETC, Inc.

Effective Briefing Techniques and Technical Presentations; William French and Associates, Inc.

Transmission Control Protocol/Internet Protocol (TCP/IP); Technology Systems Institute.

LAN Interconnection Using Bridges, Routers, and Gateways; Information Systems Institute.

OSI X.400/X.500 Messaging and Directory Service Protocols; Communication Technologies, Inc.

For a more in-depth look into thousands of keywords for all professions, check out McGraw-Hill's *2500 Keywords to Get You Hired* by Jay Block and Michael Betrus.

9

Special Cases: Resume Challenges

BABY BOOMERS PASS MIDDLE AGE

Focus on Experience

There is little doubt that age bias exists in the marketplace, and there is no doubt, with the baby boomer population reaching 50, that the pool of professionals is growing. Many companies hire employees well into their fifties. In fact, my mother is over 70 and just got a job with the second largest U.S. cable television operator. Jobs can be obtained; it's just that doing it may be tougher than it used to be.

You have one plus on your side: experience. You need to focus on showing that you have a wealth of experience and seasoning while being as up to date on business practices and business technology as the young ones, and that you aren't materially more expensive.

All the "older" candidates I've worked with and interviewed have been willing to work for a competitive wage, not requiring a premium salary. Get that message out to the hiring managers when you can, preferably in the interview.

As with all other candidates, focus on accomplishments. There is a good chance you've solved a problem the new company is facing.

Presentation Tip

You might consider putting together a mini-business plan for your interview or even in the preinterview stage if you can figure out how to get it to a decision maker. This business plan might consist of about 10 slides (PowerPoint). Here is a breakdown of what this presentation might look like:

- The first couple of slides state the problem the company (or department) is facing.
- The next four slides might address how you would address the problem.
- The final three slides can tout your accomplishments (graphs are great) that line up perfectly with those stated needs.

This plan format was developed for a client of mine, and it resulted in his being positioned as the lead candidate for a $155,000 regional director position, distinguishing him from eight other final candidates.

Consider Not Focusing on Upward Mobility

When I was hiring a sales manager a few years ago, one candidate stood out. He was in his early fifties, the oldest member of the candidate pool from which I was selecting. I hired him for the following reasons:

- He had a lot of experience but was no more expensive than anyone else.
- He was well connected in the local market, which is equivalent to some of you having comparatively better industry connections.
- The biggest reason: He was not looking to become the CEO of the company. He wanted to do a great job, make good money, and stay in that role. That may contradict some job theories, but a major hiring problem is hiring someone who will not stay in the position long, get bored, or expect rapid career progression. I was convinced he would be a good hire. He was. He consistently achieved top 30% performance and was a very low maintenance employee.

The biggest challenge with hiring is achieving the lowest turnover possible. Turnover kills productivity more than almost any other internal management action does. Try explaining that you're very qualified and would be very happy excelling at this position but are not interested in becoming the CEO of the company.

Condense Your Resume

If your resume has 30 years and seven companies with which you were employed, consider cutting some down or out. You may need to list only the last 15 years or so. You might also consider a functional format resume.

The benefit of doing this is that it calls attention to your skills and accomplishments, not to your actual employers. You can summarize your skills as we've done on our sample resumes and then itemize your employers at the end, without placing the emphasis there. The difference lies in not listing several support bullets for each employer that can get tedious to read, especially given the short attention spans of resume readers.

Make Sure You're Hip on Today's Skills

You have to make sure you're **computer-literate** and **Internet-and e-mail-savvy**. If you're not, take a cheap class at a local college or adult learning center, or at a training center offered at some retailers, such as Comp USA. It's important to fight the perception that your skills and knowledge are not on the cutting edge. Stay up to date with technological trends and be sure to demonstrate your savvy.

Other Tips

- Networking is important for older workers because jobs at the senior levels are the least likely to be advertised.

- Try offering to put in nontraditional hours that younger workers with family obligations might not be able to work.

- Use networking as an opportunity to show what you can do. Get involved with professional associations by volunteering or consulting. Consider joining the board of a professional association in your discipline, industry, or geographic area (such as a county economic advisory board) and then demonstrate your skills to the membership. You could also seek a volunteer or consulting role that will enable you to build relationships with a larger group of people. As you become a valuable team member, your age will not be a prevailing descriptor. You will be thought of as Mike, the person who created a new process to cut costs and/or increase revenue, as opposed to Mike, the older guy looking for a new job.

- Whether you use a functional resume format or not, make sure to use a crisp summary of your skills and accomplishments (see page 31). This will help keep you and the hiring folks focused.

- Make sure your resume looks contemporary—nothing fancy. It has to be laser-printed and designed with a good word-processing program. Basically, make it look like it could fit in this book.

- Increase the number of targeted companies or employers.

- A woman went to work for Sprint in the early 1990s after putting in 20 years at and accepting early retirement from AT&T. AT&T was paying her lifetime health benefits, and so she was able to take a job without needing health care. That made her a little more marketable. It's ironic when you think about it: If you're retired and already have a pension and health benefits from your previous employer, consider working for salary only.

- Register with a temp agency so that you can generate some income, update your skills, and build your resume while waiting for the perfect job. Try to find an agency that specializes in older workers.

LAID OFF . . . AND SCARED

It's Not Your Fault

More people have been laid off from white-collar jobs in the early 2000s than at any other time. According to a June 2003 *Fortune* magazine article, white-collar workers now constitute over 17% of the unemployed, the highest proportion ever. Some industries, such as telecommunications, have been hit particularly hard.

In fact, the total number of jobs lost in 2001–2002 just from Sprint, AT&T, WorldCom (another story), Lucent Technologies, and Nortel Networks exceeds 100,000.

There Is An Upside !

Searching after a layoff is not considered the challenge it once was. Well, it may be to the person who is looking. But hiring managers do not usually consider a person who was laid off a higher-risk hire anymore.

First tip: Don't do it. You don't have to. It is not customary to specify why you left any job on a resume whether you were promoted or laid off.

Second tip: If you have job hopped, you might consider putting a short explanation in one of the supporting accomplishment bullets to address the employment shifts. An example might be a final support bullet that reads: *"Position eliminated because office relocated to Wisconsin and the only way to remain with the company was to relocate."*

Third tip: Your odds are much more favorable when you are job seeking in your established industry after being laid off than they are when you make this an opportunity to change careers.

Fourth tip: Focus on accomplishments. We've discussed in Chapters 2, 4, and 5 how to represent the true value you brought. The objective here is to demonstrate that you were a top player while there and that it was not for lack of performance that you were let go. Try to show management or professional career progression, which will position you as a top performer even though you are no longer there.

Fifth tip: Hold your head high. Even though you were laid off, so were a lot of other great employees. At one Fortune 50 telecommunications company, the company recruited its best and brightest to start a new division in the mid-1990s. Three years later they shut the division down in one giant cut, with virtually no regard for performance. This cut many of their best people. It happens, and these days hiring professionals know it. In fact, many hiring managers salivate about hiring because they know there is better talent on the street than ever before.

Job Hopping

If you are concerned you've job hopped throughout your career, try combining several jobs into one grouping. Here is an example.

- □ 1999-2002 Secretary/Receptionist: AD&F Law Firm, AirTouch Teletrac, Huff and Associates
- □ 2002-Present Bookkeeping: Dallas Security Systems, Southern Methodist University and North Dallas University

---

KIDS ARE GROWN: BACK TO WORK

If a mother is returning to the workforce after an extended absence during which she has raised three children, she can confidently showcase her transferable skills that were used as a "home" manager and also can be used as a "business" manager: complex scheduling, crisis management, purchasing, budgeting, inventory control, conflict resolution, and so on. A manager who was demoted to an assistant manager can reverse the order on the resume and list the manager's position first and the assistant manger's position second as long as this is done consistently with all the other jobs on the resume.

What we see frequently is the insecurity that many women returning to the workforce feel. Usually it is unnecessary. Taking a break on your own terms for a respectable reason will not diminish your credibility in the workforce, at least not to anyone you would like to work for.

Here are some tips for those returning to the workforce after a voluntary departure for maternity leave, medical leave, or a similar reason:

- Don't be ashamed of why you left. We're assuming you left on your own terms for a personal reason that any reasonable person would respect. This is not considered to be the same situation as that of someone who woke up one day and casually decided to quit his or her job.
- Volunteer in the interview and the cover letter that you have made arrangements to be able to meet the hourly/daily/weekly requirements of the job.
- Demonstrate that you are still up to date on current technologies, such as basic office software. Make an effort to do some research in your industry or discipline so that you really are up to date. Find ways to interject this in a cover letter or interview. This may be a big differentiator.
- Play on your reliable past employment record. This will lessen the impact of the leave of absence.
- As with all other candidates, focus on accomplishments. There is a good chance you've solved a problem the new company is facing.

THE "RESUME CHALLENGE" METHODOLOGY

The "Resume Challenge" Methodology is a method for attacking and overcoming challenges that might otherwise hinder a successful job search. The methodology is made up of four parts:

1. Identify your strengths, skills, abilities, and qualifications and be sure those assets are valuable to a prospective employer.
2. Determine what strategy you are going to use (the whole truth or the truth without offering the whole truth).
3. Identify the specific "challenges" you had to overcome and show how you developed tactical resolutions to overcome them.
4. Test the methodology with people you know who can provide an honest, professional, and objective opinion.

When you identify your strengths, skills, abilities, and qualifications, you are identifying your value. You will be hired based on (1) your ability to perform in a job as well as or better than anyone else and (2) your personality—whether they like you. If you have superior skills to perform in the job but aren't well liked, your odds of getting hired aren't as good. Once you have identified your value (step 1), you must select a strategy that will not jeopardize your ability to build rapport, confidence, and trust in the interview. Once you know your value (step 1) and have a good strategy (step 2), it's time to neutralize or eliminate the challenge.

Each resume challenge requires an in-depth strategic review of *problem versus solution*. **Each resume challenge requires that a strategic review be done from the perspective of the hiring entity.** Think about things from their perspective; position yourself so that you are conveying what is in it for them.

10

The Resume Workshop

Let's develop your resume from strategy to finished product. This personal resume workshop consists of six exercises and related worksheets you can follow step by step.

Each exercise includes an example you can use as a model for creating your own resume. Worksheets may be completed on your computer or typewriter or by using pencil and paper. *Don't* limit your responses to the spaces on the worksheets. Use extra space or paper if necessary so that your answers are comprehensive, detailed, and well thought out.

EXERCISE 1: LISTING YOUR CONTACT INFORMATION

Name: _____ Professional / Career Objective:_____

Address: _____ City/State/Zip _____

Daytime Phone: _____ Evening Phone: _____ Fax:_____

Cell Phone: _____ E-mail: _____ Other: _____

Name: Carol Pappas	Profession / Career Objective: Operations Manager	
Address: 123 Diamond Street	City/State/Zip Coral Springs, FL 33341	
Daytime Phone: (954) 555-1212	Evening Phone: (Same)	Fax: N/A
Cell Phone: (954) 555-3232	E-mail: cpappas@email.com	Other:

EXERCISE 2: CREATING YOUR PROFILE

As we have discussed, the most important part of your resume is the career profile, or summary. The summary is an at-a-glance description of who you are and what you have accomplished. We reviewed this in Chapter 6. Here is our example of a crisp career profile:

- ☐ 9 years experience in telecommunications industry, both wireless for consumer and businesses, and high-end voice and data products for businesses
- ☐ 6 years experience in sales and field management, 3 years in corporate marketing management
- ☐ Full go-to-market responsibility for two Sprint broadband markets
- ☐ Hands-on experience in leading direct, retail and inside sales teams at branch and regional levels in selling wireless telecommunications services to businesses and consumers
- ☐ Managed overall market plan development, marketing communications, B2B sales strategies and training development for Sprint ION.

It would not take more than 15 seconds to grasp what this person has accomplished in his or her career.

Worksheet: Create Your Career Profile

List about five different descriptors for your professional career. Here you are not promoting your accomplishments but just scripting a highlights section of your career.

1._____

2._____

3._____

4._____

5._____

EXERCISE 3: PRESENTING VALUE TO PROSPECTIVE EMPLOYERS

You typically will be hired based on your value to your prospective employer. As expressed on your resume, value is a combination of skills, abilities, and qualifications that enable you to meet job responsibilities—to meet or exceed organizational goals and objectives.

1. *Job responsibilities* are specific duties required of your position. They're tangible and set the level of your skills and qualifications that will be transferable to the position for which you are pursuing. Consider job responsibilities as table stakes, a general requirement just to be able to be considered.

2. *Accomplishments* represent the *results* you have attained in past positions that clearly show how you have been able to contribute in a positive way. They are the grades on the report card. A resume without accomplishments is like a report card without grades. There are a lot of professional baseball pitchers in the major leagues. All could put down pitching as a job responsibility, but only a select few could promote accomplishments such as "led the league in strikeouts," "lowest ERA in American League," or "led team in wins."

The objective is to incorporate the responsibility with a corresponding accomplishment.

SO WHAT?

Job searching has a lot in common with sales. When you sell, your product has attributes called features and benefits. What that really means is, **"so what?"** **So what** is how you evolve from writing about what you did to why it mattered. When you itemize what you did in past jobs, take the next step and ask yourself, **"so what? What did I do that made a difference to that business?"**

EXAMPLE

Responsibility **(without a "so what")**	*Accomplishment* **(with a "so what")**
Launched new product in market.	Launched new product in market and achieved third highest market penetration out of a total of 11.
Implement collection service in new markets by developing and executing marketing strategies and administering forecast and budget.	Created and implemented collect service that resulted in a 30% reduction in bad debt and reduction in customer churn from 8% to 5% in one year.
Developed and executed long-distance acquisition strategies for new sales channel.	Developed sales acquisition strategies resulting in sales performance that exceeded business case by 12%.

Examples: Carol Pappas's Accomplishments: Value Messages

1. *Launched new product in market and achieved third highest market penetration out of a total of 11.*
2. *Created and implemented collect service that resulted in a 30% reduction in bad debt and reduction in customer churn from 8% to 5% in one year.*

3. *Developed sales acquisition strategies resulting in sales performance that exceeded business case by 12%.*
4. *Recruited and developed only sales team in company to meet revenue objectives in 1999, 2000, and 2001.*
5. *Sold largest account in division, a Fortune 50 manufacturing company that secured revenue objective in 2001.*

Worksheet: Identify Your Value Messages and Employment History

After giving it careful thought, list four to six responsibilities and corresponding accomplishments from each employer that you might bring to a potential employer: Remember, your value messages should answer this all-important question: "Why should I hire you?

Employer 1: _____

1. _____
2. _____
3. _____
4. _____
5. _____
6. _____

Employer 2: _____

1. _____
2. _____
3. _____
4. _____
5. _____
6. _____

Employer 3: _____

1. _____
2. _____
3. _____
4. _____
5. _____
6. _____

EXERCISE 4: CREATING YOUR EMPLOYMENT HISTORY

Company/Organization Name   City and State   Dates of Employment

---

Your Title

Environment (Type of business or organization/annual sales/what they do.)

Example: Carol Pappas's Work History

GREAT SCOTT! Uniform Company, Boston, Massachusetts   1992 to Present
(A law enforcement uniform company specializing in private/corporate security organizations nationally)

General Sales and Operations Manager
Directed the successful start-up of a law enforcement uniform company specializing in private security and in-house security organizations. Created a new market segment – wholesale – not previously available to this target audience. Presently direct 11 employees, including warehouse manager, alterations manager, and office manager. Personally direct both sales and operations activities to ensure "we deliver what we sell and sell only what we can deliver."

Specific Accomplishments

- Started company in 1992 with $1,500 and $100 a week in sales to an industry leader with $1.6 million in sales by 1997
- Develop/manage company "brand label" (Great Scott!) to enhance market presence and maintain market dominance
- Private labeling efforts increased pant/shirt sales 47% and boosted gross profit margins 74%
- Spearheaded high-tech inventory JIT system – reduced inventory 18% while improving service
- Identified three solid acquisitions, performed due diligence, and negotiated successful purchase – adding $600,000 in sales
- Closed and managed four national accounts—IBM, Wackenhut Security, Pinkerton Security, and Raytheon Corp.
- Awarded "Distributor of the Year" by Made to Measure Magazine (Industry Trade Publication)
- Awarded "Quality Dealer" award by Made to Measure Magazine 7 consecutive years (Industry Trade Publication)
- Positioned company for successful sale – with one-year working contract

---

Allied International/Bromley's Security, Lynn, Massachusetts   1986 to 1992
(A security guard/alarm company serving accounts in Massachusetts)

Security Director
Recruited after graduating from UNH as a Management Trainee – working in a supervisory capacity to ensure security officers at client locations are performing as expected. Promoted, after three months, to Honeywell Manager - in charge of seven locations and 100 security offices throughout eastern Massachusetts for the lucrative Honeywell contract. Took over as Security Director in 1988 with full charge responsibility for 13,400 weekly billable hours or a $6.2 million operation consisting of 350 security officers servicing more than 60 accounts. Worked closely with VPs of sales and operations to ensure quality service and profitable performance. Purchased $85,000 a year in uniforms and equipment, oversaw alarm division personnel, and managed the operational integration of two major acquisitions.

__Specific Accomplishments__

* Managed unprecedented growth spurt from 6,000 weekly **hours to 13,000** hours in 18-month period
* Increased profit margin from 3.9% net profit to 7.4% - or $242,000 to more than $458,000
* **Negotiated lower process** and longer payment terms from vendors, saving more than $23,000/year
* Improved customer retention from 78% to 87.4% in highly volatile and competitive industry
* Reduce employee turnover from 357% to 89% in high-turnover industry
* Worked closely with management (Bromley's Security) to position company for sale to Allied International

EXERCISE 5: LISTING YOUR SUPPORTING INFORMATION

List your formal and informal education and other academic experience (seminars, workshops, self-taught courses, etc.). Begin with your highest degree or most recent training and work backward chronologically. If you have a college degree, you do not need to list high school. Include the names of the schools you attended, cities and states where they are located, years attended, curricula, and any special awards you received.

Example: Carol Pappas's Supporting Information

Formal Education: B.A. Business, University of New Hampshire, Durham, NH, 1986   (GPA: 3.1)
Continuing Education – Seminars – Workshops – Other
Dale Carnegie – Successful Selling, Tom Hopkins Sales Seminar; Anthony Robbins Sales Seminar; Johnston's Customer Service **Excellence, High**-Tech Inventory Management Systems, by Creative Software.
Professional Affiliations
American Association of Uniform Retailers (Cofounder); National Uniform Association America (NUAA); ASIS; (local Chambers)

Volunteer Work / Civic and Charitable Involvement / Community Service
Make a Wish Foundation; Special Olympics; Little League Coach; President/member of the Board - POA

_____

Formal Education _____

_____

_____

Licenses / Certifications _____

_____

_____

Continuing Education, Seminars, Workshops, Other _____

_____

_____

Other _____

Professional Affiliations _____

_____

Volunteer Work / Civic and Charitable Involvement / Community Service _____

_____

Special Awards and Recognitions _____

_____

_____

EXERCISE 6: THE FINISHED PRODUCT

Carol Pappas

123 Diamond Street • Coral Springs, FL 33341
(954) 555-1212 • Cell: (954) 555-3232 cpappas@email.com

Career Summary

- □ *Launched new product in market and achieved third highest market penetration out of a total of eleven.*
- □ *Created and implemented collect service that resulted in a 30% reduction in bad debt and reduction in customer churn from 8% to 5% in one year.*
- □ *Developed sales acquisition strategies resulting in sales performance that exceeded business case by 12%.*
- □ *Recruited and developed only sales team in company to meet revenue objectives in 1999, 2000, and 2001.*
- □ *Sold largest account in division, a Fortune 50 manufacturing company that secured revenue objective in 2001.*

Professional Experience

GREAT SCOTT! Uniform Company, Boston, Massachusetts   1992 to Present
(A law enforcement uniform company specializing in private/corporate security organizations nationally)
General Sales and Operations Manager

Directed the successful start-up of a law enforcement uniform company specializing in private security and in-house security organizations. Created a new market segment – wholesale – not previously available to this target audience. Presently direct 11 employees, including warehouse manager, alterations manager, and office manager. Personally direct both sales and operations activities to ensure "we deliver what we sell and sell only what we can deliver."

Specific Accomplishments

- Started company in 1992 with $1,500 and $100 a week in sales to an industry leader with $1.6 million in sales by 1997
- Develop/manage company "brand label" (Great Scott!) to enhance market presence and maintain market dominance
- Private labeling efforts increased pant/shirt sales 47% and boosted gross profit margins 74%
- Spearheaded high-tech inventory JIT system – reduced inventory 18% while improving service
- Identified three solid acquisitions, performed due diligence, and negotiated successful purchase – adding $600,000 in sales
- Closed and managed four national accounts – IBM, Wackenhut Security, Pinkerton Security, and Raytheon Corp.

Allied International/Bromley's Security, Lynn, Massachusetts   1986 to 1992
(A security guard/alarm company serving accounts in Massachusetts)

Security Director
Recruited after graduating from UNH as a Management Trainee – working in a supervisory capacity to ensure security officers at client locations are performing as expected. Promoted, after three months, to Honeywell Manager – in charge of seven locations and 100 security offices throughout eastern Massachusetts for the lucrative Honeywell contract. Took over as Security Director in 1988 with full charge responsibility for 13,400 weekly billable hours or a $6.2 million operation consisting of 350 security officers servicing more than 60 accounts.

Specific Accomplishments

- Managed unprecedented growth spurt from 6,000 weekly hours to more than 13,000 hours in 18-month period
- Increased profit margin from 3.9% net profit to 7.4% – or $242,000 to more than $458,000
- Negotiated significantly lower process and longer payment terms from vendors, saving more than $23,000/year
- Improved customer retention from 78% to 87.4% in highly volatile and competitive industry
- Reduce employee turnover from 357% to 89% in high-turnover industry
- Worked closely with management (Bromley's Security) to position company for sale to Allied International

Education

Bachelor of Arts degree: Business, University of New Hampshire, Durham, NH, 1986
(GPA: 3.1)

Continuing Education

Dale Carnegie – Successful Selling, Tom Hopkins Sales Seminar; Anthony Robbins Sales Seminar; Johnston's Customer service Excellence – the Weeklong Seminar; High-Tech Inventory Management Systems, by Creative Software.

11

Consultative Sales Approach and Cover Letters

In the last several chapters we've tried to show you the parallels between the job search process and marketing a product. Marketing principles revolve around the 4 P's: product, place, promotion, and price. Your self-marketing principles should revolve around the same principles. Thus, it makes sense to draw the parallels even further.

Marketers attempt to create and position a product to meet the needs of their target sales segment. You should position yourself in a manner that meets the needs of your targeted employers. Once marketing does its thing, it is up to sales to complete the process. This is the place: the distribution element of the marketing mix. Your sales element is in full force when you are in the interviewing stage, but even before that you need to set up the stage for a strong sell.

In some industries, the nature of sales is transactional, meaning that the sales department is selling a commodity type of product, simply taking and filling orders. A company that provides long-distance telephone service to businesses is a good example. It is selling a simple product that has many alternate vendors, and the product may have few differentiators other than price. The salesperson doesn't have to sell a concept and doesn't stress the relationship between customer needs and the product beyond the ability to make calls for less.

However, what if the salesperson worked for IBM's consultative branch, touting *Real Solutions*? Then the salesperson would sell an integrated solution that might include long-distance along with managed network services, Internet access, data transport products, and WAN service. To make the sale, the salesperson would have to understand the needs of the customer.

Enter consultative sales. Consultative sales calls for you to understand the needs of the customer (or your prospective employer) and sell the customer on the idea that you have a product to meet those needs. To rise above the pack in the job search process, you need to demonstrate to the prospective employer that you clearly understand its needs and you can fill the gap the gap in its organization to meet those needs.

Here are a few examples of things to look for in an organization. These are things you should understand and research before beginning the process of writing the cover letter and sending your resume so that you can address those items in your communications, just as in sales and marketing.

- Existing products
- New products
- Geographic presence
- Climate of the industry
- Competitive products and companies
- Emerging trends in the industry and within the organization
- Profile of the current staff
- Profile of the desired staff skill set
- The company's key business or market drivers

There are many others, but you get the point. You need to try hard to learn about these things. Then you can better position yourself as someone who can help the company achieve its goals rather than someone who needs a job. The research should take place before you send the cover letter and resume so that you can customize them to meet the needs you uncovered.

You can learn about these things in several ways. Chapter 2 explored this in more depth. When you have uncovered that information, you can use it in two ways. In your resume you should position, spin, or highlight your accomplishments to make them consistent with the company's overall goals. Your cover letter is the vehicle to address what you have learned and how you can help them meet their goals.

THE FORMULA

Here is the basic formula for a consultative cover letter:

Part 1. This first section of the letter should be about *them*. Based on research you've completed, this is an area where you state the needs of the company or hiring manager. The purpose is to demonstrate your understanding of their situation and business. If nothing else, it shows the reader you know something about his or her situation and needs.

Part 2. This is the bridge. Draw the connection between what the business's needs are and how its people resources address them. You can see multiple examples of this on the following pages.

Part 3. This is where you begin with information about you. You've now stated the company's needs and how people will meet those needs. Now you need to connect yourself to the solution. Write just a couple statements about how your skills and accomplishments will solve the company's problems and meet its needs.

Take a look at the following letters and look for the ways each letter opens with a level set of where the company is and where it is going. Then look for the way the writers are connecting the company's needs with their skills. If you can master this concept, you will be very successful not just in your job search but in your overall career.

Melissa Sumner

9981 Southern Boulevard • West Palm Beach, Florida 33409 • (561) 555-5719

March 29, 1999

Ms. Theresa Mascagni
Vice President Technical Operations
4800 Oakland Park Boulevard
Fort Lauderdale, FL 33341

Dear Ms. Mascagni:

After completing much research on the wireless communications industry over the last few months, it has become apparent that NextWave holds a unique position in the market. NextWave has secured multiple C-Block licenses across the country and when built out will have a national presence comparable to AT&T and Sprint.

In order to meet your aggressive growth goals of launching this market by next fall, you will certainly need a strong RF team that has experience in the CDMA platform. Specifically, you will need a team that has experience optimizing the Lucent and Nortel base stations.

As a consultant, I led RF teams from network design to launch with both PrimeCo and Sprint PCS in the Chicago and Dallas MTAs, both of which were on a Lucent platform. I can provide excellent references from both. I think NextWave is a cutting-edge operation, one in which ingenuity, creativity and drive can make a material impression. I want to be a part of your team.

My experience is in perfect line with your needs right now and what you will need after launch. I will give you a call next week to set up some time for us to talk further.

Sincerely,

Melissa Sumner

Glenna Hazen

2357 Golf Drive Lane
Coppell, TX 75220
(817) 555-5974

June 9, 1999

Mr. Grant D. Powers, CEO
Golden Bear International
Golden Bear Plaza
11712 U.S. Highway 1
North Palm Beach, FL 33412

Dear Mr. Powers:

Your Controller, Mr. Gerald Haverhill, told me over golf a few weeks ago that you are looking for an MIS director. He told me some very interesting things about GB, and I was impressed, not only with the growth and profitability but in the similarities between GB and Diversified Centers, my current employer. GB has added 23 new training centers in the U.S., as well as overseen the design of all Jack Nicklaus courses. With that much widespread activity, MIS needs must surely be exploding.

With that much national activity, you must need each site to be networked with your home office for both voice and data transport, as well as establish a WAN to improve real time connectivity. As well, the design aspect of the business must eat up a lot of bandwidth in data transport, so it would surely help if you could share information more quickly and efficiently, while maintaining your privacy "firewall."

My current operation is quite similar. I have built a very efficient network for our many regional locations to communicate. Diversified Centers builds and manages strip mall shopping centers for Tom Thumb grocery stores. Our network enables each regional office to stay in touch via e-mail and shared drives through our WAN, as well as utilize the Sprint ION network for real-time communications of high bandwidth development plans, similar to your use of golf course designs.

It appears that my accomplishments with Diversified Centers is in line with your MIS needs at GB. I will give you a call next week to set up a meeting to talk further.

Looking forward to meeting you,

Glenna Hazen

PS - Gerald told me you are quite close with Mr. Nicklaus. Please congratulate him on his fine Masters showing!

CAROLYN KELLENBURGER

5534 College Parkway, Cape Coral, FL 33410 (941) 555-9753

March 15, 1997

Ms. Kimberly Houston
Paramount Pictures
4800 Hollywood Boulevard
Santa Monica, CA, 90211

Dear Ms. Houston:

Jim Talley at Touchstone recently informed me that you are overseeing costumes and makeup for the new film *The Nutty Professor*. Jim shared with me some of the effects that you are planning to use to transform the lead character between the thin professor and the very overweight professor. In order to pull this off, you will undoubtedly need artists skilled in this field.

Experience with plastics, makeup, special wraps, and the various maskings takes a great deal of skill to apply in a way that is transparent to the viewer. I know; I was the lead artist for several movies and clips, including Michael Jackson's *Thriller* video, *Halloween H₂0* and several *Tales from the Crypt* episodes.

My experience is very consistent with what you will need for your upcoming film. Please review my attached resume for the specifics of my film credits. You will see that I would be a good fit for helping you with all of the makeup and related preparations for the demanding transformation scenes. I will call you next Tuesday and set up a time to stop by the studio to meet you.

Sincerely,

Carolyn Kellenburger

MISTI DEORNELLAS

45227 Michigan Avenue, Chicago, IL 24197 (312) 555-3125

March 9, 1999

Ms. Maria Lane, Executive Vice President
Hyde and Smithson Public Relations, Inc.
1800 Scenic Way
Mountain View, VT 19877

Dear Ms. Lane:

Over the last few months I've noticed your firm moving into consulting with several healthcare firms. After speaking with Tom Aimee, I am aware that you are bidding on the upcoming opening of two new Columbia hospitals. You will no doubt need significant healthcare industry expertise to drive this account. Healthcare can really get complicated when trying to balance aggressive marketing and sales techniques along with a more public entity image.

The two new locations in Portsmouth and Springfield will be delicate openings given the amount of bad press Columbia has received in the last year or two. Columbia has been in trouble with both the IRS and the FBI for tampering with federal aid and overbilling to Medicare. They will undoubtably need good advice on how to position their openings to get off on the right foot.

I have been working in marketing and public relations for 9 years, most recently with Humana in Florida. We successfully opened 11 new hospitals over the last six years, and even experienced a storm when we opened the one in Orlando. That one opened in the midst of a major city-wide controversy regarding the for-profit nature of Humana versus the for-the good-of-the-people persona hospitals have maintained. Under my direction Humana successfully overcame that encounter, and now that hospital is one of the most successful in the region.

My skills are very much in line with the needs of both your firm and your clients:

*   15 years in public relations
*   15 years in the healthcare industry
*   Expertise in new launches and crisis management
*   Key contacts within the industry

Please expect my telephone call in the next week so that we might be able to set a time to meet and discuss employment possibilities that would serve our mutual interests.

Sincerely,

Misti DeOrnellas

Walt Johnson
2357 Indiana Lane • Indianapolis, Indiana 49877 • (317) 555-5687

September 8, 1998

Ms. Christy Garcia
Director Sales and Marketing, AT&T Data Services
3333 Westwood One
Indianapolis, IN, 49557

Dear Ms. Garcia:

I have been researching AT&T and their play in the integrated services offerings for some time. I was intrigued to read about the upcoming INC announcement that is currently scheduled for this fall. INC is reportedly going to converge data and voice transport products into a single, more cost-effective transport that can support virtually unlimited bandwidth demands.

In order to pull this off, you will surely need to have strong relationships in place with the CLECs or ILECs in given markets. For in the short run that is the only way you can provide the local access "last mile."

I have a lot of experience working with Bell Atlantic/Nynex and Bell South in xDSL. xDSL will surely be your plan for last mile access when it is built out, and you will need skilled network data engineers to optimize and design that integration.

Please take a look at my resume, which reflects the broad experience I have developed in data transport and xDSL technology. I will call you next week for an appointment when we can review this further.

Sincerely,

Walt Johnson

CHARLENE W. PARKER
668 West Hannover Boulevard
Chicago, IL 60623
Phone: (718) 555-2486
E-mail: Fivestar10@Main.net

July 9, 1999

Mrs. Grace Billings, Customer Service Manager
United Parcel Service
1000 State Street
Chicago, IL 60602

Dear Mrs. Billings:

Congratulations on the recent contract between the pilot's union and management. The strike of 1997 was surely devastating, not only to UPS, but the nation as a whole who depend on and trust UPS. The agreement signed last week ensures that the good name of, and extraordinary service provided by, UPS will not be tarnished.

I read in the Business section of the Chicago Times, over a month ago, that UPS was expanding its call center operations in the Chicago area and that a "benchmarking" effort was going to be made to bring the center back in-house after many years of contracting the service. Now that the talk of a strike has been put to bed, I am sure you will be focusing attention again on this project. I believe I can help!

I work as a Call Center Manager for Sears Roebuck and Company here in Chicago. They too once contracted out their call center/customer service operations and made the decision to bring it in-house six years ago. I was one of nine team leaders responsible for the strategic planning and implementation of the conversion from contracted to in-house call center operations for Sears. I was part of this team from the very beginning to now - where over a six-year period we have improved our customer service rating from 93.7% to 99.2% while saving the company approximately $1.2 million. I have implemented a tactical plan to further enhance the rating to 99.7%, and now I am seeking new challenges.

Some of my career highlights include the following, which actually tie in closely with the emerging needs at UPS:
- Personnel management and team building; directing a team to consistently exceed organizational expectations
- Systems and operational benchmarking; developing systems of operations that can be replicated in other operations
- A highly competitive but jovial manager who inspires success and while demanding results
- Strong finance/budget management skills; bottom-line oriented

I am sure that you see connection between my five areas of strength above and the criteria by which UPS evaluates potential managers. I know your time is extremely valuable, and so is mine. Therefore, I would enjoy speaking with you for a few moments over the telephone to determine if an in-person meeting might be beneficial to us both. Please expect my call next Monday afternoon. If this is not a good time to chat for a few minutes, we can arrange another time that is mutually convenient.

Thank you for your time and consideration.

Sincerely,

Charlene W. Parker

Leigh Milford
21 Lighthouse Way, Nubble Light, ME 02779 (707) 555-9375 Jblawrence21@aol.com

May 30, 1999

Mr. Paul Graves, Executive Vice President
Horrace Small Manufacturing
120 Opreyland Commercial Park
Nashville, TN 46732

Dear Paul:

Bob Harris let the cat out of the bag! I think it is the best long-term interests of our industry that Horrace Small Manufacturing enter the retail segment of the law enforcement uniform industry and compete with the other manufacturers who have begun to travel this road. There is no doubt, you will assume a leadership role in the retail operations as you have in the manufacturing arena. And I believe I can contribute to this success.

I have enjoyed working with you and your company over the past nine years as a vendor and retail client. We have certainly shared some great success stories together. When I first began Professional Image Uniform Company in 1990, few people gave me a chance to succeed, but Horrace Small (Bob Harris in particular), the giant of the uniform industry, saw my potential and accepted me as a retail customer. Today, nine years later, Professional Image Uniform Company is one of the largest uniform companies in the nation. We even bought out Simons Uniforms, a company that tried to thwart our success. I am proud of what we accomplished and feel no regrets about selling the company to FSS, Inc., because I am now seeking new and more exciting challenges.

Might that challenge be to spearhead your national retail operations?

Bob mentioned that you are presently looking for a retail manager to direct operations at your flagship location. I would be interested in meeting with you to discuss this exciting opportunity. I have one more week to finish up things with FSS, and then I am available to meet with in Nashville. I will call you tomorrow to discuss this fax.

There are six areas of accomplishment that truly do connect closely with the needs of Horrace:

1) An industry-recognized track record for successful retail start-up management - conception to implementation
2) Multiple retail operations management
3) Creative sales, marketing, and promotions tactics to accelerate growth
4) Inventory management expertise to ensure 5-star customer service with minimal inventory levels
5) Competitive positioning - understanding competitive influences and developing tactical strategies to be #1
6) Organizational/personnel leadership; hiring "attitudes" and inspiring peak performance

Paul, thanks for taking the time to review this note. I'd really love to get together for a few minutes soon to talk a little more. There is no doubt in my mind that we'd make a great team in pursuit of your retail growth objectives.

Sincerely yours,

Leigh Milford

2121 East 75th Street
Fort Lauderdale, FL 33304
(954) 555-5945

March 21, 1999

Mr. Howard Finelaw, President
Valet Services of South Florida
9205 Dixie Highway, Suite 200-B
Pompano Beach, FL 33360

Dear Mr. Finelaw:

Our paths have met on at least two occasions, and I was truly impressed each time. Please allow me to explain. I attended the Executive Women's Association gala event three weeks ago at the Cypress Creek Marriott, where more than 400 people attended. When I drove my car to the valet, I was awe-struck by the professionalism of the attendants, the uniforms, and the courtesies extended, not only to me, but to everyone. I mean to say that the valet service was so exceptional, it was the talk of the evening!

When I asked to speak to the hotel manager to rave about the valet service, he told me that it had nothing to do with the Marriott. I found out that your company is responsible for this level of service. Last Saturday night my wife and I went to the Kravis Center to see Phantom of the Opera. Needless to say, half of South Florida was there - and so were you! Again, I could not believe the level of service provided - simply exceptional.

So our paths have met on two occasions over the past 4-5 five weeks - and I'd like to propose a 3rd. I am a highly successful sales professional, and I will represent only companies with top-rated products and services. I would like to propose a meeting to discuss how I can best help your company grow and prosper even beyond the success you have had to this point.

After completing some research online, I discovered your Website. I noticed that your company has plans to expand into Broward County as well as Martin. I know I can use my plethora of corporate contacts to help you build your company. And if you decide you want to go regional, state, or national, I have the experience and verifiable track record to assist in this area as well.

And here's the best part - I enjoy being compensated for results, and I guarantee results. I do not require a high base salary compensation plan, but actually prefer an attractive commission program. I am a six-figure earner and am compensated only when I bring in the business. My past sales experience has been focused on hospitality-oriented business, so I have key contacts with companies that can use professional valet services. In fact, I have spent the last three evenings studying the valet business and have familiarized myself with the competition, past and future trends, and growth/profit potential. Based on my preliminary findings, you are in a niche market with almost unlimited potential.

I have enclosed a detailed resume of my qualifications and will contact you early next week to discuss possible scenarios for future employment with your company.

Thanks for taking the time to read this letter. I do hope we can meet in the next week or so.

Sincerely,

Cynthia E. Goodman

HELEN R. HENDERSON
21 Village Street
San Francisco, CA 99465
(302) 555-6102

February 22, 1999

Ms. Alice Greene
Center Plaza Hallmark
201 Broadway, Center Plaza
San Francisco, CA 99427

Dear Ms. Greene:

Bonnie Taylor provided me with your name and suggested I contact you regarding summer employment this season. Apparently, Bonnie has worked for you for the past three summers but will be in Europe this year and thought I might work in her place.

I understand you are looking for people who have experience in retail environments, are customer service oriented, are loyal and dependable, have working knowledge of point-of-sales computer technologies, and are drug free. In retail environments like this it can be so difficult to find good people. The retail stores I have worked with at school have really struggled to get good, bright and courteous people on staff.

I am in my third year at UCLA, majoring in Business Administration. As well, I have five years of retail experience (The Body Shop, Wolfe Camera, and The Gap) and am very familiar with POS computer systems.

I will be off for the summer as of May 29th. However, I will be home for Spring Break (April 7-15) and would like to stop by and introduce myself to you. We can both be sure that Bonnie would not have introduced us to each other if she didn't feel I could fill her shoes in a way that measures up to your high standards.

I will call you next week to see if we can arrange an interview during my Spring Break. Thanks in advance for your consideration.

Sincerely,

Helen R. Henderson

TONI MASTERS
3232 West Collings Avenue, Windsor Heights, IA 50311 (508) 555-9526

March 2, 1999

Mrs. Shirley Snife, Chairperson
Windsor Heights Girls Softball League
99 Town Center Road, Dept. A-6
Windsor Heights, IA 50398

Dear Shirley:

It is no secret that Windsor Heights has developed a woman's softball program that is the talk of the state. I read in the local newspaper a week ago that there are more than 160 women participating in the league and that the emphasis on skills training is so intense that Windsor Heights has won the State All-Star Championships in each of the past two years. It is a credit to you and your staff that you have met an important need in our community - namely providing our children with the resources and opportunity to compete in an area that they love to compete in.

I also read in that same article that you are looking for volunteers to coach these girls - that there are four or five openings for coaching and assistant coaching positions. I have a fifteen-year-old daughter who has played the last two years in the league. Having been an active parent, I think I have a good idea as to what you are looking for in a coach. I offer you the following:

1) More than 11 years coaching experience as an Assistant Athletic Director at the high school level
2) Able to grasp and teach the fundamentals of the game
3) Ability to inspire players in a positive way, to give 100% and achieve peak-performance levels
4) Teaching emphasis on sportsmanship
5) To work with parents, league staff, and others involved in making this program a success

I know that there are limited head coaching positions available, and I would very much entertain the opportunity to assist a head coach in hopes of demonstrating my abilities for a future coaching position.

I will be attending the Board Meeting scheduled for the 24th of this month, and I hope to meet with you before the meeting to properly introduce myself to you. If you would like to speak/meet with me prior to the meeting, I will make myself available at your convenience.

I look forward to another great season and hope to become a participating member of your coaching staff.

Sincerely,

Toni Masters

12

Resumes by Profession

ERIC D. SCHMIDT, CPA

1685 Crestview Drive
Lake Oswego, Oregon 97035
(503) 534-2265
eschmidt@yahoo.com

Senior Financial Analyst

Professional Summary

Diligent Senior Financial Analyst with 7+ years' experience in financial analysis, planning, and budgeting. Demonstrated expertise in and dedication to innovating process improvements that positively affect company profitability. Saved one employer well over $35K in process improvements alone. Post-baccalaureate accounting certificate, CPA, strong PC skills. Self-starter, creative problem solver, top performer.

Areas of Ability

- Financial Analysis and Management Reporting
- Interdepartmental Coordination and Collaboration
- Short- and Long-Range Budgeting
- Capital Expenditure Analysis
- Financial Modeling

- Process Design and Development
- Profitability and Credit Analysis Reports
- General Accounting Procedures
- Staff Supervision and Training
- Financial Forecasting

Professional Experience

POPPYBOX GARDENS, Portland, Oregon   2002–2004
Accounting Manager (Senior Financial Analyst)

Built accounting department for fast-paced start-up company, a division of the #1 company in the U.S. for sales of container nursery stock, with $70 million in annual sales. Designed and documented processes and procedures and hired support personnel. Supervised and trained accounting staff on general accounting procedures, spreadsheet models, and technical best practices. Provided senior-level financial support in forecasting of cash requirements, capital expenditures, and labor costs, integrating input from sales director and operations managers/controllers.

Developed financial models, including long-term forecasts for accounts payable payments, labor cost forecasts, capital expenditure forecasts, key measurement ratios and graphs, and monthly financial statement models using standard GAAP format. Completed financial reporting and consolidation of four subsidiary companies. Actively interpreted and reviewed financial results with/made recommendations to senior leaders. Researched and corrected variances and omissions.

- Reduced labor costs by average of $500 per month by cutting two days off monthly close schedule.
- Saved company approximately $22K in additional labor costs by completing increased department tasks without adding headcount. Facilitated savings through improved communication, giving staff opportunity to take on more responsibility and improve skills.
- Saved countless hours of clerical staff time spent filing and making copies by developing process and procedures to convert existing paper filing system to electronic filing process.
- Commended by CFO for developing model for long-term forecast of accounts payable payments to determine cash requirements and timing of bank borrowing.
- Earned 10% increase in pay for 2003 as result of cost-saving achievements and value to company.

(Continued)

ERIC D. SCHMIDT, CPA

MAGINNIS & CAREY LLP CERTIFIED PUBLIC ACCOUNTANTS, Portland, Oregon 1999–2002
Staff Accountant

Compiled and reviewed financial statements for small, local public accounting firm to acquire relevant public accounting experience. Prepared corporate, partnership, and individual tax returns. Developed projections of income and cash flow statements. Carried out other projects typical of certified public accounting firm, including monthly close process for clients, correspondence with taxing authorities, client memos, and special projects.

GARDENBURGER, Portland, Oregon 1996–1999
Financial Analyst

Provided senior-level financial support in areas of strategic planning and forecasting for national corporation with $2 billion in annual sales. Prepared forecast schedules for payroll reserve requirements and recommended rates to reserve manager. Prepared various monthly accounts receivable reports and graphs for senior management/operations and additional ad hoc analysis reports as needed. Reviewed income statement and balance sheet accounts and researched and corrected variances. Created A/R management reports in Oracle and automated using Cognos Impromptu report writer software program.

- Reduced labor costs $500 per month on average by cutting two days off total report time for monthly accounts receivable reports. Worked with senior management and operations, analyzed issues, and developed automated system using Oracle.
- Increased efficiency of reconciliation process by working with IT department to develop custom program in Oracle to track and reconcile prepaid accounts. Successfully migrated from existing legacy program to newly created Oracle version.
- Acted as member of Y2K Oracle implementation team responsible for successful migration from legacy GL system.

Education/Certification

Two-Year Post-Baccalaureate Accounting Certificate, University of Oregon, Eugene, Oregon, 1996

Bachelor of Science in Business, University of Portland, Portland, Oregon, 1994

Certified Public Accounting Certificate, State of Oregon

Recent Professional Development Coursework:

Controllership: Leading Skills for Corporate Performance, American Institute of CPAs (AICPA), 2004
Organizational Skills for Time and Stress Management, Click2Learn, 2003
Management Basics: Thriving as a New Manager, Click2Learn, 2003
New CPA Ethics, AICPA, 2002
Compilation and Review Engagements, AICPA, 2002
S-Corporations, AICPA, 2001
Advanced Managerial Accounting, University of Portland, 2000
Advanced Microsoft Excel, Portland Community College, 2000
Cognos Impromptu Workshop, Gardenburger, 1999
Oracle General Ledger Financials, Gardenburger, 1999
Corporate Finance, University of Portland, 1998

Computer Skills

Strong PC skills, including Microsoft Windows, MS Word, MS PowerPoint, MS Excel, Oracle, and Cognos Impromptu.

Professional Affiliations

American Institute of Certified Public Accountants and Institute of Management Accountants

Drew Atkinson
4548 Sierra Lane
Jupiter, FL 33445
(561) 555-5934
drew.atkinson@aol.com

ACCOUNTING MANAGER

PROFILE:
Passed CPA exam in State of Florida
Well versed in all relevant computer software programs,
including Peachtree, DacEasy, Lotus 1-2-3, AccountPro, Excel and
most other Windows-based applications

Experience in cost accounting in manufacturing environments and
public auditing

Develop plan, conduct audits and variance analyses, process
payroll and payroll tax reports and filings, and maintain/update
accurate inventories.

KEY ACHIEVEMENTS:

- Instrumental in the negotiation and acquisition of $3 million
home care and retail pharmacy stores; negotiated a $14 million
contract for pharmaceuticals resulting in a savings of 1.5-3% on
cost of goods for each retail store.

- Saved $87k in annual corporate management salaries through
comprehensive management of the financial programs and credit
administration of the group.

- Managed accounting department consisting of controller,
billing auditor, and accounting staff.

EMPLOYMENT:

Wellington Regional Medical Center, West Palm Beach, FL
1994 - Present
Accounting Manager
- Managed accounting staff, reporting to CFO

- Design, implement, and manage all centralized accounting,
management information systems, and internal control policies
and procedures

- Manage accounting department consisting of A/P, A/R, cost
management and general ledger maintenance

- Prepare all Federal and State tax requirements, including
corporate, partnership, payroll, and property tax returns.

Diversified Centers, Inc., Palm Beach, FL
1988 - 1994
Staff Accountant

- Staff accountant for real estate development firm

- Coordinate all financing and external reporting with financial
institutions for the group.

- Full general ledger management responsibility

- Managed accounts payable for two years

- Managed accounts receivable for 18 months

- Prepare and administer operating and cash budgets for each
retail profit center.

EDUCATION: Florida Atlantic University, Boca Raton, FL
                  Bachelor of Arts: Accounting, 1987

Dax Dawsonn

917-555-0000
SAG

Height: 6'1"
Weight: 180 Lbs.
Hair: Brown
Eyes: Brown

Accents
New York,
New Hampshire,
New Orleans, Southern,
Midwestern, Irish,
English, French
Pirate

Vocals
Folk, Rock, Jazz, Soul,

Instruments
Saxophone, Trumpet

Dance
Irish Jig, Step, Tap

Circus Skills
Clown

Movement
Stage Combat,
Swordsmanship
Physical Comedy

*Dawsonn wraps
himself around
Stanley's psyche in
an emotionally
charged presentation.
He is the bad boy
that your mother
warned you about.*

*Seth Samuals
The Villager*

*Dax Dawsonn is eery
and comical as Ben.*

*Michael Feingold
Village Voice*

THEATER
NEW YORK STATE

Henry IV	Hal	Lincoln Center, Vivian Beaumont Theater
The Dumb Waiter	Ben	La Mama, Etc.
Betrayal	Waiter	Roundabout Theatre
Silence	Bates	Repertory Theatre of Lincoln Center
Macbeth	MacDuff	Elm Shakespeare Company
King Lear	France	Shakespeare & Company
Streetcar Named Desire	Stanley	Gallery Players
Angels in America	Prior	Gallery Players
Chicago	Amos	Heights Players
Arsenic and Old Lace	Raymond	Heights Players
Sweet Sunday, Sour Monday	Jake	East Side Players

REGIONAL

Limonade Tous Les Jours	Andrew	Zachary Scott Theater Center, Austin, Texas
Side Man	Al	Generic Theater, Norfolk, Va.
Catch Me If You Can	Frank	Kansas City Players, Kansas City, Ks.

FILM & TELEVISION

Law & Order: Sundown	Court Officer	NBC
Sex and The City: Girls Night Out	Guy at Bar	HBO Productions
Oz: Sonata de Oz	Street Junkie	HBO Productions

COMMERCIALS

Beck's Beer	Mountain Climber	M & R Productions
Manhattan Shirts	Military Man	Mac Donald & Associates Productions

TRAINING

Brooklyn College	BFA	Judylee Vivier, Polina Klimovitskaya, Charles McNulty, Rose Burnett Bonczek
HB Studios	Acting Technique	Trudy Steibl, Edith Meeks, Michael Beckett
	Scene Study	Bill Hickey
	Voice	Bill Hickey
	Acting	Elizabeth Hodes
Shakespeare & Company	Voice	Rocco Sisto, Michael Hammond, Edga Landa
	Movement / Fight	Molly Murray
	Clown	Brent Blair, Normi Noel
Light Hearted Comedy Company	Comedy Camp	Jim Jarvis
	Viewpoints/Grotowski	Jill Samuals

LEAH BROOKS

195 North Union Boulevard • Colorado Springs, CO 80909 • (719) 632-9074 (A/H)

RECEPTIONIST / ADMINISTRATIVE SUPPORT SPECIALIST

Professional Representation ♦ Outstanding Communicator ♦ Customer Service Excellence

Commercial Construction / Financial & Investment / Health & Medical Field

QUALIFICATIONS PROFILE

Highly motivated, solutions-focused professional with extensive experience and an impressive record of achievements within all facets of reception, administrative and customer service management across diverse industries. Combine sound time- and resource-management skills to implement strategic administrative and operational initiatives to enhance productivity, quality, client service and overall bottom line performance.

➢ Exceptional interpersonal and communication skills with proficiency to promote confidence and build and maintain strategic business/client relationships, while interfacing positively with people of diverse backgrounds.

➢ Ability to manage multiple tasks without compromise of quality or productivity.

➢ Sound organizational skills achieving results that surpass company goals and objectives.

CORE COMPETENCIES

- Client Relationship Management
- Switchboard/Telephone Answering
- Process & Productivity Improvement
- Functions Planning & Management
- Vendor & Supplier Negotiations
- Correspondence/Report Authoring
- Diary Management & Scheduling
- Executive & Administrative Support

PROFESSIONAL EXPERIENCE

ADCO CONSTRUCTIONS   2001–Present

Receptionist /Administrative Support

Professional representation as first point of contact for this high-profile commercial construction company, implementing initiatives to ensure the smooth functioning of a busy reception area and efficient operation of an extremely demanding switchboard. Type and distribute highly confidential documentation, correspondence and relevant reports, including site-meeting minutes. Oversee and coordinate incoming/outgoing correspondence upholding internal mail protocols and meeting deadlines. Monitor and procure inventory, office stationery, and kitchen consumables.

Diverse administrative and clerical procedures; prepare subcontractor agreements, cover letters and associated photocopying/dissection into relevant procedures; order and maintain stock of Adco procedural manuals for site foreman, including site instruction, site diary, request for information; and multiple photocopying as required. Organize mailouts and special notices; compile and prepare priority invoices utilizing sophisticated database; author accompanying letter.

♦ Played key administrative role in successful completion of multi-million-dollar construction projects.

♦ Placated irate and concerned customers, infusing diplomacy and tact, ensuring clients' needs were responded to appropriately and professionally.

♦ Exceeded all corporate standards for productivity, administrative and reception management.

Continued…

LEAH BROOKS

PERPETUAL   1995–2001

Receptionist/Telephonist

Distinguished track record within all facets of receptionist/telephonist procedures when interfacing with clients to meet/greet and respond to their needs, while optimizing Perpetual's overall corporate image through professionalism and outstanding customer service. Diary management and appointment scheduling for Financial Consultants; directed client introductions for Senior Consultants involving research and reporting of client's relevant data; and collaborated with Client Relationship Managers and Senior Financial Consultants.

Supported Executive Personal Assistant with word processing, inward/out mail, reconciliation of accounts, and preparation of invoices. Coordinated conference rooms and car bookings; maintained tearooms; monitored and procured supplies; and ensured reception area was well presented at all times.

- ◆ Spearheaded development and implementation of benchmarking customer liaison techniques, which secured ongoing accolades from senior executives and clients.
- ◆ Empowered relief staff through training, supervision and support in company procedures.
- ◆ Skilled operation of a 20-line Meridian 2000 switchboard, implementing outstanding communication skills/telephone techniques; requested to record corporate business message on answering machine and mobiles across the entire company.

HOSPITAL MANAGEMENT ASSOCIATION   1990–1994

Corporate/Customer Service Officer (1993–1994)

Steady promotion demonstrating expertise and professionalism through increasingly responsible positions, becoming fully accountable for the research, planning and implementation of innovative product marketing and promotional initiatives to a diverse corporate client base. Responded to technical enquiries; supported and advised companies providing Payroll Deduction Schemes to H.M.A. clientele on a global level; provided on-site support to businesses; and assisted with general telephone enquiries.

- ◆ Enhanced company's corporate image through continual professional representation of H.M.A., while maintaining key alliances with a diverse client base of business customers.
- ◆ Provided strategic customer relationship management techniques to maintain client satisfaction, retention and ongoing business.

Front Desk Receptionist (1990–1993)

Maintained highest level of professionalism when greeting and assisting clients; handled internal/external telephone enquiries, and coordinated internal/external deliveries. Prepared correspondence and reports; maintained H.M.A.'s library, including distribution of daily papers, periodicals and associated literature.

EDUCATION & PROFESSIONAL DEVELOPMENT

PERPETUAL IN-HOUSE TRAINING
Professional Letter Construction / Concise Writing ◆ First Impression
Customer Service ◆ Telephone Techniques ◆ Time Management

BS Degree – Business Administration – ST. LOUIS UNIVERSITY

TECHNOLOGIES

MS Word ◆ MS Excel ◆ MS Outlook

KATHY HUDDLESTON

2412 SE 24th Avenue
Portland, OR 97214

(503) 234-8919   kathy_h@verizon.net

Administrative/Executive Assistant

SUMMARY OF QUALIFICATIONS

Hardworking, thorough administrative professional with 5+ years of experience successfully managing administrative offices/processes. Adept at troubleshooting and resolving issues. Background includes experience creating databases and maintaining networks. Proficient in MS Office products, including Word, Excel, Access, and Outlook. Positive, adaptable, and motivated.

Areas of expertise include:

Efficiency: Handled the work of 3.5 people after rest of department was merged to another office.

Organization: Designed infallible tickler file that ensured high organization and attention to detail.

Computer Literacy: Maintained networks, designed presentations, created databases. One database increased office efficiency by days.

Supervision: Supervised up to 21 staff members at a time. Mediated employee disputes. Received excellent performance ratings for writing constructive employee reviews.

Research/Analytical Skills: Researched and analyzed complex data for presentation to high-level audience.

PROFESSIONAL EXPERIENCE

Portland Classical Chinese Garden, Portland, OR   2001–2004
Administrative Assistant/Computer Application Specialist

Researched and analyzed MS database system and data to facilitate development of Web-based database. Created database for association directory. Redesigned charts and reports. Performed any computer tasks as needed: spreadsheets, letters, templates, graphics, greeting cards, invitations, event programs, and databases. Maintained four-station network, including virus protection and performance.

- Instrumental in development of MS Access database to process benefits for staff of 150.
- Installed, tested, and evaluated 1.5 years of data in two-month period.
- Assembled data and created charts presented at national association meetings.

Northwest Regional Educational Laboratory, Portland, OR   2000–2001
Office Manager and Executive Assistant to the President

Supervised two customer service and two front office staff members. Hired two accounts receivable staff members. Purchased all office supplies, computer hardware, and software warehouse equipment. Wrote president's correspondence, both domestic and foreign. Made all travel arrangements. Worked with attorneys conducting research and verification for patent filings and patent infringement cases. Settled personnel conflicts.

- Oversaw construction and equipping of new office/warehouse building. Move was completed without disruption to product sales or distribution.
- Saved company both time and money by changing phone system and provider.
- Found suitable CFO candidates for president's review.

(Continued)

KATHY HUDDLESTON   Page Two

PROFESSIONAL EXPERIENCE, CONTINUED

U.S. Bank, Portland, OR   1997–2000
Employee Benefit Trust Specialist

Made lump sum benefit and withholding payments to retirement plan recipients. Prepared and balanced out-of-state withholding taxes. Met all state and federal standard accounting requirements. Reconciled tax issues with various states and retirees. Resolved all tax problems, recalculated tax amounts, and reissued 1099's where necessary. Solved client problems and answered questions.

- Made recipient state withholding tax payments, which required knowledge of 39 different tax regulations.
- Stepped up and replaced 2.5 employees when rest of department merged to out-of-state location.
- Met all deadlines, maintaining high level of accuracy for one of Oregon's largest banking institutions.

Wells Fargo Bank, Portland, OR   1994–1997
Trust Operations Specialist

Utilized technical ability to work with bank databases to generate reports, enter transactions, verify assets, and balance asset positions. Read and analyzed large volumes of time-critical and complex investment material. Wrote client investment alert summaries.

- Standardized investment alert bulletin to minimize risk of loss. Made it user-friendly for banking and national investment managers who represented retirement funds and wealthy private clients.
- Dealt with transactions in the thousands of shares and millions of dollars.
- Reduced time to calculate and balance shares and costs from days to hours by designing and implementing Excel database.
- Handpicked to go to California to oversee department transfer and monitor merger of accounts.

EDUCATION AND PROFESSIONAL DEVELOPMENT

B.A. in English, University of Oregon, Eugene, Oregon

Related Professional Development Coursework:

Computer Classes in Word I and II, Excel I and II, PowerPoint, Access, and Integrated Computer Projects, Portland Community College, 2002–2004

COMPUTER SKILLS

MS Windows; MS Office, including Word, Excel, Access, PowerPoint, Publisher, and Outlook; McAfee and Norton Anti-Virus Software; Netscape, Visual Basic, and proprietary software applications.

AFFILIATIONS

Volunteer: StRUT (Students Recycling Used Technology)
Evaluate, repair, and refurbish donated computers, which are then given to public school system.

Member: WITI (Women in Technology)

. . .

CAROL POVEROMO

9843 South Parkland Drive
Dallas, Texas 76545
(214) 555-9875
cp@aol.com

EXECUTIVE SECRETARY / ADMINISTRATIVE MANAGER

Ten years' experience planning and directing executive-level administrative affairs and support to Chairmen, Boards of Directors and Executive Management. Combines strong planning, organizational and communication skills with the ability to independently plan and direct high-level business affairs. Trusted advisor, liaison and assistant. Proficient with leading PC applications, including word processing and presentation programs. Qualifications include:

Executive & Board Relations
Executive Office Management
Staff Training & Development
Confidential Correspondence & Data
Special Events & Project Management
Crisis Communications

PROFESSIONAL EXPERIENCE

Executive Secretary -- GLOBAL TECHNOLOGY, INC. (GTI) -- 1991 to Present

Recruited to administration/office management position and promoted to Executive Secretary in 1992 as the personal assistant to the Chairman of the Board and CEO of this diversified research venture. Executive Liaison between Chairman/CEO and Executive Management Committee, Business Departments and employees to plan, schedule and facilitate industry and intercompany business functions. Manage confidential correspondence, meetings, travel and schedule for the Chairman/CEO. Coordinate quarterly shareholders meetings, manage liaison affairs and facilitate print production of shareholder communications. Led team of 40 and managed $1.5 million budget.

- Recruited 50+ personnel responsible for all office management functions for the Chairman/CEO, Senior Vice President and CFO and CTO.
- Played key role in the successful completion of a multi-million-dollar construction project to support the company's rapid growth and expansion. Negotiated contracts for the purchase of equipment and supplies.
- Exceeded all corporate standards for productivity, efficiency and operating management.

Executive Secretary / Stenographer -- UNITED STATES AIR FORCE -- 1982 to 1990

Fast-track promotion through several increasingly responsible administrative management positions throughout the U.S. and abroad. Advanced based on consistent success in effectively managing high-profile, sensitive military affairs for commanding generals and other top military officers. Received numerous commendations and awards for outstanding performance. Significant projects and achievements:

- Managed confidential correspondence, schedule and meetings for Judge Advocate. Independently researched, and responded to requests for legal documentation for a team of 10 attorneys managing 100+ cases per week.
- Planned and directed security, logistics and administrative affairs for visiting foreign dignitaries, congressional leaders and military officials.
- Selected from a competitive group of candidates for exclusive joint military Leadership Development Course.

EDUCATION & PROFESSIONAL TRAINING:

- Graduate of 200+ hour intensive U.S. Air Force executive administrative and secretarial training program.
- Attended seminars while continuing with higher education sponsored by universities and professional associations.

JOHN HARRISON

777 Winding Road
Brentwood, New York 11717
(631) 555-6777
killersale@artofpersuasion.net

APPROACH • NEEDS • PRESENTATION • OVERCOME • CLOSE • SERVICE

ADVERTISING DIRECTOR

Accomplished advertising professional with a dynamic career leading a major media production company to success. Known for strengthening the organization to compete in competitive markets both directly and through leadership of others. Record for delivering innovative marketing concepts and strategies that work. Effectively manage the sales cycle process from client consultation to closing. Core strengths encompass:

– **Key Account Development**   – **Media Relations**   – **Sales Analysis & Reporting**
– **Solutions Selling & Marketing** – **Public Speaking**   – **Project Management**
– **Team Building & Leadership**   – **Advanced Presentations**   – **Contract Negotiations**

PROFESSIONAL EXPERIENCE

Senior Advertising Manager   1985 – 2004
CABLE MEDIA PRODUCTIONS, INC., New York, New York
— *Animal World, Global Travel, Health Line*

- Spearheaded key account development programs that targeted, penetrated, and launched business growth throughout Northeast, Southeast, and Midwest regions.

- Overachieved projected sales volumes for 1999 by 74% with revenues in excess of $16 million.

- Established senior-level contact with 43 advertising agencies throughout New York City and Boston.

- Effectively negotiated and sold 30-second units of commercial advertising space to client agencies with major accounts that included Coors, AT&T, Lucent Technologies, Clorox, and Avon.

- Positioned Discovery Communications as a viable advertising avenue to target viewer audiences inclusive of preschool to elementary aged children and adults in the 25-54 age category.

- Orchestrated the promotion of in-banner advertising and hotlinks.

- Secured Cable Media Production's first million-dollar advertising sale with AT&T.

- Single-handedly negotiated and closed network's first online deal with Independent Films in 1998.

- Pioneered the organization's cross-channel promotion programs, heightening American Production's visibility with additional coverage in U.S. News and World Report magazine.

- Captured the interest of clients and professional audiences of up to 300, with powerful, invigorating presentations illustrating the benefits and value-added solutions of cable network advertising.

- Created innovative account retention programs to protect key clients from competition.

- Pioneered the development of sales and marketing strategies and advertising plans.

- Chaired weekly competitive meeting to discuss season networks, market segments, and departmental issues with senior management, account executives, account planners and sales assistants through open discussions and persuasive presentations.

— Continued —

JOHN HARRISON

Page 2

PROFESSIONAL EXPERIENCE
Cable Media Production, continued

- Launched the business growth and development of this fledgling network cable start-up company.
- Developed convergence marketing proposals tailored to $500,000 budgets, mapping multifunctional advertising packages that incorporated the Discovery Channel's magazine, Website, and network.
- Spearheaded the development and execution of Internet-based hotlinks advertising.
- Collaborated with the International Education Society on the introduction of an online chat room to encourage post-viewing discussions among students.
- Technically astute and aware of our full product set, including software solutions.
- Allocated airtime programming that strategically assigned segmented advertising blocks on a regional level.

EDUCATION

Bachelor of Business Administration
PACE UNIVERSITY, Pleasantville, New York

SALES AWARDS

Recognized at 25 Top National Sales Organizations, Media and Marketing Magazine, 2002
Excellence in Salesmanship based on Meyer's Survey, 1997 – 2001

PARTICIPATORY MEMBERSHIPS

Vice President, American Management Association, 1995 – present
Heart Walk Captain, American Heart Association, 1995 –1998
Committee Member, Community Mainstreaming Program, 1995 –1996
Committee Member and Fundraiser, National Committee For Aids Research (NCFAR), 1994 –1995

PROFESSIONAL DEVELOPMENT

Extensive presentations and skill development workshops / Communispond / Speakeasy

ROBIN YARBOUROUGH
567 Alamo Avenue, San Antonio, Texas 78228
Residence: 555 555-1234 • Office: 555 555-2345 • email@email.com

ATTORNEY AT LAW

EXPERIENCE

LAW OFFICE OF GEOFFREY CISNEROS, San Antonio, Texas
Attorney-at-Law, 1993 to present
Solo practitioner with a diversified caseload of real estate transactions and litigation; business transactions and litigation; corporate and partnership matters; estate planning; probate, bankruptcy; mortgage foreclosures.

GEOFFREY CISNEROS, A Professional Corporation, San Antonio, Texas
President/Owner, 1991 to 1993
Real estate transactions and litigation; business transactions and litigation; corporate and partnership matters; estate planning; bankruptcy; mortgage foreclosures; homeowner associations.

GLADYS P. KNIGHT & ASSOCIATES, San Antonio, Texas
Associate Attorney, 1988 to 1991
Real estate transactions and litigation; business transactions and litigation; corporate and partnership matters; estate planning; bankruptcy; equine law; homeowner associations.

BLANCA, BLANCO, BLACK & WHITE, San Antonio, Texas
Associate Attorney, 1985 to 1988
Real estate transactions and litigation; business transactions and litigation; corporate and partnership matters; estate planning; bankruptcy; equine law; homeowner associations.

BLOCK & BLOOM, San Antonio, Texas
Associate Attorney, 1981 to 1985
Real estate transactions and litigation; business transactions and litigation; corporate and partnership matters; estate planning; bankruptcy; personal injury.

EDUCATION

TEXAS WESTERN SCHOOL OF LAW, San Antonio, Texas
Juris Doctor, 1978
• Phi Delta Phi International Law Fraternity

UNIVERSITY OF TEXAS, Austin, Texas
Bachelor of Arts in Political Science

PAST AND PRESENT AFFILIATIONS

Member, State Bar of Texas
Member, American Bar Association
Member, Bexar County Bar Association
Member, San Antonio County Bar Association

ADMISSIONS

Texas State Courts
Bexar County Courts

Federal Courts:
Southern District of Texas
Central District of Texas
District of Texas

Judge Pro Tempore:
Alamo Municipal Court

Arbitrator:
San Antonio Municipal Court

Appropriate personal and professional references are available.

DANIELLE S. VAN LIER

555 Murietta Avenue   (818) 555-9196
Valley Glen, California 91405   danielle@vanlierlaw.com

ATTORNEY AT LAW

Proven ability to work independently as well as collaboratively; learns quickly and enjoys challenges. Strengths in research and analysis with an ability to recognize and understand diverse viewpoints. Served on law review at top tier law school. Excellent client relations, writing, and oral presentation skills. Possesses a positive work ethic with strengths working with cross-cultural populations. Experience in emerging technologies, including multimedia, Internet, e-commerce and Website development.

Bar Admissions: State Bar of California; Ninth Circuit Court of Appeals, Central District of California

PROFESSIONAL EXPERIENCE

Counsel
SCREEN ACTORS GUILD, Los Angeles, CA May 2000 to Present
Promoted from initial position as Residuals Claims Business Representative, 2001
$ Conduct due diligence and determine most effective dispute resolution strategies.
$ Interpret and apply SAG agreements, security agreements, distribution and licensing agreements as well as applicable Copyright Law.
$ Review, negotiate, advise and redraft contracts in conjunction with Information Technology department.
$ Pursue arbitration remedies for disputed claims from initial referral through award enforcement.
$ Consult on Internet and Intellectual Property issues including matters related to SAG website.
$ Educate coworkers, producers, distributors, performers and attorneys on provisions of SAG agreements and policies, relevant legal standards and other related issues.

Freelance/Contract Legal   1999 to Present
$ Production counsel and associate producer for feature film shot on location in Los Angeles.
$ Performed research for Internet company on legal issues including business immigration, online banking, encryption, digital signatures, electronic funds transfers and electronic commerce. Drafted and reviewed contracts, evaluated Website for compliance.
$ Assisted filmmaker with issues related to financing of two films, including potential foreign coproductions.
$ Prepared comprehensive business plan and provided legal consultation for nonprofit wildlife organization.
$ Assisted pair of screenwriters in negotiating screenplay option agreement.
$ Additional topics include new media, Internet, trademark infringement, and corporate issues.

Litigation Associate
FEINBERG & WALLER, Encino, CA 1998 to 1999
$ Participated in all aspects of litigation for civil litigation firm with diverse caseload.
$ Areas of practice included trademark licensing disputes, malicious prosecution, fraud, insurance litigation, wrongful termination, unlawful detainer and family law.
$ Law and Motion appearances before trial courts throughout California.
$ Prevailed by motion for summary judgment in bankruptcy adversary proceeding.

Legislative Fellow (Jan.– Aug.) 1997
UNITED STATES HOUSE OF REPRESENTATIVES, Washington, D.C.
Representative Howard L. Berman, 26th Congressional District, California
$ Performed research, drafted memoranda, and provided assistance on diverse subjects, including intellectual property and judicial issues. Monitored pending legislation. Drafted official and constituent correspondence.
$ Interfaced with various legislative offices and foreign embassies.
$ Designed and implemented Representative Berman s official Internet Website.

(Continued)

DANIELLE S. VAN LIER   PAGE TWO

ADDITIONAL EXPERIENCE

Founder ForLawyersOnline.com 1999 to Present
$ Conceived, developed and launched Internet legal resource site. Performed in-depth research and developed content. Explored and discussed partnership and affiliation opportunities.

Legal & Business Affairs Associate (Mar–Aug.) 1998
JULIA BUG ENTERTAINMENT, Beverly Hills, CA

U.S. House of Representatives Intern August 1997
U.S. CONGRESS/KOREAN NATIONAL ASSEMBLY EXCHANGE; Seoul, South Korea
$ One of eight students nominated by Members of U.S. House of Representatives to participate in jointly sponsored government exchange. Met with representatives of U.S. and Korean political and nongovernmental organizations, members of the Korean National Assembly and U.S. Congressional representatives.

EDUCATION

Juris Doctor, WASHINGTON UNIVERSITY SCHOOL OF LAW, St. Louis, MO; December 1997
*Completed 80% of course work toward **Master of Arts in East Asian Studies***

Honors and Activities
- *Washington University Journal of Urban and Contemporary Law*, Associate Editor
$ *Jessup International Moot Court*
$ Negotiation Competition; Finalist
$ Phi Alpha Delta (Justice); Student Bar Association (Social Committee Chairperson); East Asian Law Society (Co-Founder/Vice President); Sports and Entertainment Law Society (Vice President)

Publications
- *"Boy, You Possessed My Body and Soul; Now I'll Possess Your Woman": A Post Modern Noh Play*, Occasional Papers in East Asian Studies, Spring 1998

Bachelor of Arts in Japanese; UNIVERSITY OF CALIFORNIA, Santa Barbara, CA; Spring 1994
$ Charter member Toastmasters International, U.C.S.B. Student Chapter
$ "Youth in Action" cultural exchange program in Netherlands and Spain; Summer 1991

Japan Studies Program, TOKYO INTERNATIONAL UNIVERSITY, Kawagoe, Japan; Fall 1993

CONTINUING EDUCATION / PRESENTATIONS *Full list available upon request.*

$ Extensive continuing education in areas including Intellectual Property, Entertainment Law, Cyber Law (*details available upon request*)
$ 2001 Los Angeles County Bar Association Entertainment Industry Labor & Employment Law Conference Planning Committee: Comoderated and organized panel on runaway production featuring Congressman Howard L. Berman, Jean Prewitt (AFMA), Karen Constine (CA Film Commission) and Cody Cluff (EIDC)

FOREIGN LANGUAGES—Japanese (conversational)

COMPUTER SKILLS—*Highly computer-literate, including all major operating systems*

$ Applications include Microsoft Office Suite, WordPerfect Suite, and legal research applications.
$ Web page design. Familiarity with relevant Macromedia, Microsoft, and Adobe programs.
$ Above-average familiarity with Internet use, including legal, political, and social research and issues.

ERIKA GARDNER
erikagardner@email.com

6655 Oak Tree Lane   Residence (818) 555-1111
Tarzana, California 91356   Mobile (818) 555-1112

ATTORNEY
Expertise in Litigation, Appeals & Business Development
Product Liability • Contracts • Workers Compensation • Labor Law • Personal Injury • Construction • Unions

Trial Attorney with ten years experience managing all aspects of trials, administrative hearings, depositions, motions and appeals. Excellent qualifications in the independent planning, management and representation of clients. Skilled negotiator. Excels in developing relationships and generating new business.

Admitted to Practice in California and Hawaii

ILLUSTRATIVE EXPERIENCE

- Generated product liability case that resulted in $6.1 million award.
- Won highest jury award for firm.
- Argued before three-judge panel, obtaining $1.2 million verdict.
- Prevailed at appellate level—and recovered substantial verdict—in precedent-setting case.
- Successfully defended state employee in high-profile case.
- Prevailed in numerous personal injury, product liability and construction law case appeals.
- Cultivated relationships with numerous labor unions and community organizations, generating substantial business.

PROFESSIONAL EXPERIENCE

Attorney • 2001 to Present
ABBOT & BARRETT, Beverly Hills, CA
Joined 20-attorney firm to develop new business in addition to litigating personal injury cases.
- Generated approximately 60 cases within two years, resulting in average annual revenues of $500,000 to $1 million.
- Brought in case that resulted in $6.1 million—largest in firm's history.
- Cultivated relationships, and captured contracts with several construction industry unions.

Attorney • 1993 to 2001
COLLINS, DUBROW & GARDNER, Century City, CA
Coestablished successful practice as Trial Attorney, achieving outstanding record of success in litigation and appeals. Managed day-to-day marketing, administrative and financial affairs with full P&L and budget accountability. Directed staff of attorneys, paralegals and administrative assistants. Conducted jury trials, arbitrations, administrative hearings and depositions pertaining to all aspects of personal injury law.
- Developed niche personal injury clientele, specializing in on-the-job accidents and labor law.
- Cultivated and managed relationships with various union clients; interfaced on daily basis with insurance companies.
- Negotiated profitable sale of practice, upon dissolution of partnership, to large personal injury law firm.

(Continued)

110

Erika Gardner • PAGE TWO

EDUCATION

SOUTHWEST SCHOOL OF LAW, Los Angeles, CA 1992
Juris Doctor

Honors/Activities

Received numerous moot court awards
Awarded Dean's Fellowship.

UNIVERSITY OF HAWAII, Honolulu, HI 1988
B.S. in Political Science

Professional Development / Continuing Education

Medical Trial Skills College—American Trial Lawyers Association (26 hours)
Essentials of Civil Litigation—American Trial Lawyers Association (36 hours)
Advocate Status Attained—Trial Advocacy College

LICENSES

Admitted to Practice Law in California and Hawaii

PROFESSIONAL AFFILIATIONS

Member—Los Angeles County Bar Association
Member—American Trial Lawyers Association
Member—Hawaii Bar Association

ADDITIONAL INFORMATION

Computer Skills

Computer-literate on PC and Macintosh
Applications include Windows, Microsoft Word, WordPerfect

Community Activities

Volunteer—SPCA, APLA, Humane Society
Board Member—Tarzana Community Homeowners Association

BRAD T. BOWMAN

555 Lakeshore Drive ◄ Atlanta, Georgia
Home: 404-377-5555 ◄ Cell: 404-555-5551
bbowman@email.net

SENIOR AUTOMOTIVE INDUSTRY EXECUTIVE

Inspiring World-Class Leadership Teams That Drive Growth- and Profit-Focused Operations

Accomplished Executive with a 23-year career in the automotive dealership industry. Combines expert qualifications in sales, marketing, business development and customer relationship management with equally strong operating unit and P&L management qualifications. Extensive experience in leading start-up companies from scratch to profitability, recruiting and leading high-performing management teams. Proven ability to exploit technology to enhance revenue base, cut costs and bridge communication gaps. Strong vision and proven skill at achieving ambitious goals. Aspires to excellence in every endeavor.

◄ Financial Statements / Profit & Loss (P&L) and Balance Sheets / Return on Investment (ROI)
◄ Customer Satisfaction (C.S.I.) / Manufacturer Relationships / Communications
◄ Operating Infrastructure / Multisite Operations / Departmental Processes / Service Design
◄ Strategic Sales Processes / New Business Development / Advertising & Marketing
◄ Market Expansion / Start-Up Operations / Operational Relocation
◄ Employee Management / Team Building / Retention / Motivator / Mentor / Coach

LEADERSHIP / BUSINESS DEVELOPMENT ACHIEVEMENTS

Deliver strong operating and financial gains within highly competitive markets. Track record of recruiting exceptional start-up management teams to ensure strong profitability for the investors.

◄ **Met the challenge of launching multiple start-up operations**, originating productive and revenue-driving management teams over relatively short periods of time.
  - **Built Acura / Hyundai / Suzuki dealerships** from the ground up. At Acura, catapulted **sales from zero to 100 cars / month** across a 90-day time frame. At Hyundai, **boasted 150 car sales / month** after only 90 days in operation. (Genuine Chevrolet)
  - **Drove net profits from $300,000 to $1.3 million during first year, capturing total sales of $72 million** for start-up auto operation. (Brown's Auto Mall of Atlanta)
  - **Recruited profit-producing management team for start-up dealership.** Same management team is still entirely in place. (Brown's Auto Mall of Atlanta)

◄ **Outdistanced colleagues** in nationwide performance (sales, customer service and operations).
  - **Named Genuine Leader** (Top 150 of 4,900 U.S. Chevy Dealers), 2000. (Genuine Chevrolet)
  - **Won Precision Team Award** (Top 25 U.S. Acura Dealers), 1989. (Genuine Chevrolet)
  - **Earned the Highest Levels of Customer Satisfaction** (C.S.I.) among 31 marketwide Chevy dealers. (Genuine Chevrolet)
  - **Vaulted Group Sales from zero to 950 cars / month.** (Genuine Chevrolet)

◄ **Drove sales, profits and cost-containment efforts** that mirrored strengths in P&L management.
  - **Earned 100% of objective,** month over month, 2002 to present. (Genuine Chevrolet)
  - **Vaulted sales approximately 40%** after innovating / implementing a volume-based sales incentive program spurring a focus on monthly sales, 2003. (Genuine Chevrolet)
  - **Captured double-digit profit improvements** after establishing a commercial department that introduced business-to-business sales. (Genuine Chevrolet)
  - **Cut $190,000 / year in spending** (by eliminating two management positions) and increased sales volume and effectiveness after installing new technology. (Genuine Chevrolet)

(Continued)

PROFESSIONAL EXPERIENCE

GENUINE CHEVROLET, INC., Atlanta, Georgia   1986 to Present
(Awarded the 2002 Mark of Excellence Award by General Motors. Genuine Chevrolet started in 1935 and currently houses over 400 new Chevrolet cars, trucks and custom vans). [www.genuinecars.com]

Vice President / Executive Manager (Chevrolet Dealership), 1997 to Present
Vice President (Chevrolet / Honda / Acura and Two Hyundai Dealerships), 1995 to Present
General Manager, 1986 to 1995

Full P&L responsibility across a $75 million, 72,000 sq. ft. dealership operation with 145 employees (office, body shop, parts, service and sales departments). Direct Genuine's operational strategies and oversee the day-to-day employee, sales, service and customer relationship management initiatives. Scope of diverse accountability includes managing five dealerships (including a total of 34 managers), analyzing monthly P&L (via financial statements and balance sheets), leading, motivating and building employee teams, and developing meaningful relationships with manufacturers and their financing divisions.

Notable Contributions:
- ◀ Recognized by Chevrolet: **Top 150 of 4,900 dealers,** nationwide (Genuine Leader designation). Recognized by Acura: **Top 25 dealers,** nationwide (Care Award).
- ◀ **Spearheaded three start-up operations** during tenure (Acura, Hyundai and Suzuki), performing all the start-up operation / staffing functions, accomplishing full-scale operation / consistent revenue streams.
- ◀ **Employed a commercial department** composed of outsides sales professionals selling the product business to business and improving **net profit 18% per month**.
- ◀ **Deployed ADP technology** that **curbed expenses nearly $190,000 / year,** increased sales volume / effectiveness and created a real-time communication channel among managers.
- ◀ **Pinpointed and derailed** an employee's deceptive practices, **saving $525,000 / year.**
- ◀ **Incentivized sales team** via an inventive pay plan, spurring double-digit sales growth.
- ◀ **Maintained consistently positive performance record** in regard to Chevrolet's financial objectives.
- ◀ **Earned an exceptionally high employee retention rate** with an average employee staying 10+ years.

BROWN'S AUTO MALL, Atlanta, Georgia   1984 to 1986
Vice President / General Manager

Notable Contributions:
- ◀ **Tapped to assemble a management team for start-up operations** involving three franchises (Honda, Mazda and Nissan) and two large used car lots.
- ◀ **Successfully created an effective, cohesive management team** / operation that drove $2.5 million in first-year revenues.

EARLY CAREER EXPERIENCE: Under the mentorship of Dan Svenson of Svenson Ford, climbed the ladder, working in every department of the Ford dealership, 1980 to 1984

PROFESSIONAL DEVELOPMENT

Bachelor of Science in Business Administration
Oglethorpe University, Atlanta, Georgia

Member, Board of Directors
Chevrolet Marketing Group, Atlanta, Georgia
- ◀ BOD is charged with investing $5.2 million marketing budget.
- ◀ Increased sales 20% in the marketplace to date.

CHRISTOPHER HERRING

7759 Ace Drive • Baltimore, Maryland 21203
(410) 555-1212/e-mail@email.com
SS#: 000-00-0000/Veteran Status: N/A/U.S. Citizen

Department of Transportation—Federal Aviation Administration
Applying For: Civil Aviation Security Investigative Officer
Investigative Specialist—Maintenance Expert
GD-111-222-33/4

Licenses/Credentials

Top Secret Security Clearance
Private Pilot's License
Level 4 Investigative Grade

U.S. Army Maintenance Certification—L12
Advanced Navigational Training
Aviation Regulations 76, 88, FR6, and RR52

Education

GEORGE WASHINGTON UNIVERSITY, Washington, D.C.
Bachelor of Technical Science: Aviation Management, 2000
Aviation Planning
Aviation Technology
Aviation Disaster Investigation I, II, III

Aviation Safety and Security
Aviation Crisis Management
Aviation for Future Generations

Internship: Dulles Airport—Security Officer/Investigator, Small Aircraft
- Inspections
- Evidence Gathering
- General Security

Computer Skills: SourceBook, AviatePro, NavSystems 6.0, Simmod, Office, and Internet

Professional Experience

AVIATION CONSULTANTS INTERNATIONAL, Baltimore, Maryland   1995 to Current
Aviation Investigator/Assistant to Lead Investigator

- Hired on a part-time basis while attending school to assist and support Lead Investigator in aviation and aviation-related accidents/incidents. Utilized extensive technical and mechanical experience to fit the pieces of the aviation puzzle back together, including crashes, near misses, callbacks, and airline mechanical records and reports. Most assignments are requested by the FAA through Aviation Consultants International.

- Advanced to Aviation Investigator upon completion of BTS degree in Aviation Management in 2000. In the past eight months, successfully investigated six private-aircraft crashes, nationwide, and developed three comprehensive reports for FAA regarding maintenance records of two major airlines for an eight-month period.

- Trainer of new recruits hired on as Assistants to Lead Investigators. Developed comprehensive orientation program that significantly reduced overall "break in time."

Affiliations/Activities

American Pilots Association
National Aviation Association of America

National Association of Aviation Investigators
Aviation Mechanics Association

References Furnished upon Request

114

13—BALLET DANCER

Audrey Soffitt

2045 West 45th Street, #306 ■ New York, NY 10019 ■ (212) 555-2362 ■ asoffittdance@email.email

"Dance is the hidden language of the soul." - Martha Graham

PROFILE

Professional dancer committed to dancing and working consistently to participate in the highest level of the art form, while bridging the gap between classical ballet and contemporary dance. Maintain a sense of empowerment and responsibility for my physical and energetic presence and promote respect for self through my dance.

STATISTICS: ■ 5'7" ■ 125 pounds ■ Brown Hair ■ Brown Eyes

TECHNIQUES: ■ Ballet ■ Modern ■ Jazz ■ Tap ■ Street ■ Salsa ■ Tango ■ Rumba ■ Funk ■ Swing ■ Hip-Hop

SPECIAL SKILLS: ■ Floor Gymnastics (cartwheels, round-off, split, back bends, head stand, hand stand, forward roll, backward roll) ■ Yoga ■ Pilates ■ Martial Arts ■ Singing (13 years formal training as a 1st soprano).

PRINCIPAL DANCE PERFORMANCE EXPERIENCE

TOURS

EDGE PERFORMING ARTS CENTER: *Swan Lake & Millennium* – Tokyo, Japan	2002 – 2003
JOE ALTER DANCE GROUP: *Esmeralda* – Hannover, Germany, and Geneva, Switzerland	2001
PERKSDANCEMUSICTHEATER: *Mass & Festival of Art*s – New Orleans, LA	2000
JOEL MARQUETTE BALLET THEATER: *Giselle* — Minneapolis, MN, and Chicago, IL 2000	2000
MARK MORRIS DANCE GROUP: *The Hard Nut* – Berkley, CA	1999
ACTIVE CULTURES DANCE GROUP *Tri-City Tour* - Taiwan	1999
JULLIARD DANCE ENSEMBLE: *Paul Taylor's Esplanade* – Amsterdam, Holland	1998
LINCOLN CENTER INSTITUTE: *Cross Cultural Tours* – New York City [Schools]	1997

NEW YORK CITY

LIMON DANCE INSTITUTE: *Second Hurricane, Nutcracker* and *Paquita*	2002 – 2003
THE METROPOLITAN OPERA BALLET: *War and Peace* and *Don Quixote*	2003
PILOBOLUS DANCE THEATER: *Slippery Hearts*	2002
HUNTINGTON BALLET THEATER: *Nutcracker*	2001 – 2002

EDUCATION & TRAINING

BROADWAY DANCE CENTER/ALVIN AILEY ADC/DANCESPACE – New York, NY	2000 – 2001

Ballet: Jack Hertzog ■ Modern: Bill Hastings ■ Jazz: Ray Leeper

SAN FRANCISCO DANCE CENTER, ODC – San Francisco, CA	1999

Ballet: Summer Rhatigan ■ Modern: Veronica Combs (Horton) and Kathleen Hemmesdorf

THE JULLIARD SCHOOL – New York, NY	1997 – 1999

Bachelor of Fine Arts in Dance Performance (1999)

JOFFREY BALLET SCHOOL AMERICAN BALLET CENTER – New York, NY	1995 – 1997

Ballet Technique

PROFESSIONAL HONORS

- The Julliard School Grant toward Active Cultures Dance Group company tour
- Princess Grace Award Foundation Award in modern dance
- Broadway Dance Center Outstanding Performance in Dance award
- National Society of Arts and Letters competition award
- National Choreographer Conference scholarship award

MICHAEL S. FROMM

555 NE Shore Drive
Portland, OR 55555

(503) 555-2303

fromm@hotmail.com

Financial Services Customer Service Representative

SUMMARY OF QUALIFICATIONS

Hardworking Financial Services Customer Service Representative with 10+ years' experience providing patient, compassionate customer service. Strong knowledge of Adjustable Rate Mortgage Indexes, Principal and Interest type loans, and the escrow process with regard to insurance, taxes, and escrow analysis. Won multiple awards for providing outstanding customer service. Strong ability to both get along with coworkers and work independently. Diligent, organized, and thorough. Additional expertise in handling the following:

- New Customer Calls
- Year End 1098 Tax Information
- Rate Change Information
- Requests for Copies of Documents

- Account Balance and Payment Verification
- Payment of Taxes and Insurance
- Missing Payments
- Vendor Contact

HIGHLIGHTS OF ACHIEVEMENTS

- **Consistently provide service to 250 to 300 customers per day,** way above department average of 200 customers per day.

- **Known as the one who can be relied on** to solve customer service issues, leaving both customers and bank management satisfied with solutions provided.

- **Act as resource to coworkers** on bank policies and procedures after completing thorough study of procedure manual outside of work hours.

PROFESSIONAL EXPERIENCE

KENNEDY FINANCIAL SERVICES GROUP, Hillsboro, OR   2002–Present
Customer Service Representative

Earned "employee of the month" customer service award on numerous occasions. Respond to incoming calls and qualified written requests. Handle customer inquiries pertaining to mortgages and consumer loans. Respond to customer inquiries and needs, providing quality customer service.

U.S. BANK OF OREGON, Portland, OR   1996–2002
Customer Service Representative, Commercial Markets (2001–2002)

Represented and supported all Oregon Commercial Markets at Oregon Emergency Operations Center for Y2K event management. Monitored system through Y2K. Tested each system for functionality to make sure it transferred over from 1999 to 2000. Utilized understanding of all aspects of normal business operations, contingency planning and operations, as well as critical system requirements and dependencies of each individual commercial market.

Customer Service Representative, Teleservicing Center (1996–2001)

Provided general account servicing and problem resolution to banking clients. Received and responded to clients via telephone regarding bank products and services. Researched and maintained accounts. Prepared debits/credits for service charges and/or reversals. Substituted for production officers in absence as needed.

(Continued)

PROFESSIONAL EXPERIENCE, CONTINUED

WELLS FARGO BANK, Portland, OR   1993–1996
Customer Service Representative, Consumer Loan Servicing

Received Chairman's Award for providing outstanding customer service. Responded to customer and branch inquiries by telephone and in writing. Performed online or manual adjustments and file maintenance to customer accounts. Responded to credit information requests. Provided oral and written payoff information. Researched accounts and reports. Received and disbursed funds. Maintained ledgers, accounts, and records in accordance with regulations and policies.

EDUCATION

A.S. in Business Administration/Accounting, Mt. Hood Community College, Portland, OR

Recent Professional Development Coursework:

Top Customer Service Skills for Top Customer Service Representatives, SkillPath Seminars, 2004
Communicating Successfully with Difficult People, Portland Community College, 2003
Microsoft Word I and II, Portland Community College, 2003
Microsoft Excel I and II, Portland Community College, 2002

COMPUTER SKILLS

Word, Excel, PowerPoint, Access, and various proprietary software applications.

PROFESSIONAL AFFILIATIONS

Professional Member, International Customer Service Association

■ ■ ■

BRIDGET D. BROWNING

15 Grove Street ❐ Patchogue, New York 11772 ❐ (516) 555-8203′ ❐ bb117@aol.com

❐ PROFILE

Professional abilities in general bookkeeping. Excellent analytical skills; develop operative systems to reduce expenses and protect revenue. A versatile team player who can work effectively and independently in challenging environments. Proficient on Lotus, Great Plains accounting software, and Officewriter programs.

❐ ACHIEVEMENTS AND QUALIFICATIONS

❐ **Designed original program to correct inefficient hotel reservation system;** reduced expenditures by clarification of authorizations and billing.

❐ **Partnered with CEO to develop detailed medical coverage cost analysis schedule.**

❐ **Authored clearly understandable manuals** on accounting office systems and procedures.

❐ **Developed financial tracking system** to maximize dollars spent on temporary help.

❐ **Created innovative procedures** that dramatically increased data entry productivity.

❐ PROFESSIONAL DEVELOPMENT

Arrow Electronics, Yaphank, NY
Accounts Payable Manager 1989 to present

Oversee accounts payable department of electronics production facility ($115M sales).

❐ Coordinate and implement all aspects of general bookkeeping. Reconcile bank statements and accounts. Utilize chart of accounts to code vouchers and enter accounts payable invoices. Prepare cash disbursements, apply cash receipts, research bills, check batches and day reports for accuracy. Generate computerized end of month reports. Utilize trial balance for various schedules.

❐ **Develop and execute numerous special projects.** Determine budgets, establish hotel accounts, travel arrangements and itineraries for conventions, etc. Maintain individual files and process payroll of each freelancer and temp used on jobs. Compile monthly special reports; prepare American Express schedule. Act as backup for vacation coverage in department.

Video Today Magazine, New York, NY
Accounts Payable Manager 1987 to 1989
General accounting with concentrated focus on vendor and customer relations.

❐ Addressed and resolved client problems and concerns. Performed customer credit verifications. Entered and prepared cash disbursements, invoices, and cash receipts. Assembled and tested voucher packages and coded account distribution. Monitored aging report, tracked collection of past due accounts, reviewed expense reports.

❐ EDUCATION AND TRAINING

Hofstra University, Uniondale, NY Courses toward B.A. in Liberal Arts.

Company training: Journal entries, adjustments and accompanying schedules. Client billing systems (actualizations, etc.).

118

Alexis Zolac ▣ Television and Video Production

▣ Professional Profile

Produce daily interview segments airing on Bloomberg Terminals, Bloomberg News and BIT (Bloomberg Information Television) worldwide. Handle live, two-way satellite and remote preproduction, production, postproduction, and editing.

Setup and tape live news programming and studio, satellite and remote television interviews with business leaders, heads of state, celebrities and newsmakers.

Professionally committed, focused, responsible, and cool in chaos. Utilize an effective combination of technical abilities, creativity, and good humor to produce excellent interviews and programming in normal or unforeseen situations.

▣ Technical Equipment and Abilities

Switchers	☐ Abekas A34, PDG 418 Videotek
Cameras	☐ Sony BetaCam, Hitachi studio camera
Remote Controls	☐ Fujinon, Radamec advanced robotic cameras
Audio	☐ Mackie 32x8 Audio Console
Routers	☐ BTS Digital CP-300, SYC-3200 Sigma, Codec
Editing	☐ AVID / Video cube, Abekas A34, RM-450, PVE-500
Computers	☐ Audio Video Capture Computer (AVC), PC, Mac

☐ Pre- and postproduction and basic editing for live and remote newscasts.
☐ Live production transmission utilizing multimedia computer.
☐ Dubbing and duplication of tapes and tape format changes.
☐ On-air switches and master control duties. Live daily newscast teleprompting.
☐ Remote and studio control cameras. Live and taped.

▣ Employment and Education

Bloomberg, LP, New York, NY   1996 to present
Video Forum Technician and Segment Director

WLNY, Melville, NY   1994 to 1996
Studio Technician and Editor for live daily news show

Bachelor of Fine Arts in Broadcasting   1994
New York Institute of Technology, NY

610 Broadway, Amityville, NY 11701   ☐   516-555-5555   ☐   alexz@aol.com

PAUL SMITH
Home: (718) 555-5566 / Cell: (718) 555-8899

Residence
555 East 3rd Street
Brooklyn, NY 55555

Mailing Address
P.O. Box 555
Brooklyn, NY 11220

FACILITIES MAINTENANCE DIRECTOR / DIRECTOR OF BUILDING OPERATIONS
Multiple Unit Dwellings / City Housing / Commercial

Proactive building systems expert with 27 years' experience. Successfully manages costs and scheduling of capital improvement projects. Encourages maximum productivity from maintenance teams. Delivers highest standards of routine building maintenance. Effectively communicates with all levels of management, staff and residents. Strengths include:

Strategic Planning & Management • Purchasing • Budgeting • Cost Control • Team Leadership and Development
Plumbing • Electrical Repair • Welding • Roofing • Heating and Fire Safety Systems • Grounds Maintenance

---

EMPLOYMENT

COALITION FOR THE HOMELESS, New York, NY   2001 – Present
Director of Building Operations
Selected to direct routine maintenance, cleaning, mechanical operations and repairs of three brownstone units housing 38 families on the Upper West Side. Supervise superintendent and maintenance / porter teams in providing painting, vacuuming, carpet shampooing, dusting, mopping, buffing and other cleaning tasks. Oversee all plumbing, electrical and door lock repairs.

- Converted standard lighting fixtures to fluorescent lighting with a 12% reduction in lighting costs.
- Restructured staff scheduling, increasing delivery of vacant apartment from one to three units daily.
- Identified faulty boilers and oversaw subsequent replacement with Lockivar boiler system.
- Initiated painting of boiler room, clearly marking area with boiler operation directions, delivering consistent heating.
- Directed two-month elevator renovation project while maintaining safe passageways for residents and staff.

NEW YORK CITY HOUSING AUTHORITY, New York, NY   1980 – 2001
Superintendent

Red Hook Houses, Brooklyn, NY (1998 – 2000)
Brooklyn's largest development with 2,873+ units, including senior citizen housing /recreation center, outside recreation and seating areas.

Queensbridge Houses, Queens New York, NY (1990 – 1998)
The largest development in New York City with 3,100 apartments

Administered maintenance and mechanical operations of city owned housing developments. Supervised maintenance, caretaker and heating plant technicians. Ensured resident safety and cleanliness of all inside/outside common areas. Conducted daily premises and grounds checks. Documented general condition of apartment entrance doors, cabinets, countertops, ceilings, beams, columns, electrical and plumbing fixtures. Maintained and repaired basic plumbing fixtures. Spot-checked fuel oil deliveries for compliance with inspection requirements. Coordinated qualitative maintenance inspections with NYCHA representatives.

- Oversaw $1.5 million lobby entrance renovation for five residential buildings. Completed renovations within record time of three months.
- Alerted management to asbestos hazards, which prompted prompt removal. Oversaw removal project from inception to early completion within 90 days.
- Reviewed and revised plans for installation of boiler upgrade. Replaced two malfunctioning boilers posing heat and hot water interruptions. This upgrade reduced tenant complaints by 100%.
- Instituted spot checks with 100% of work orders completed on time and within budget.
- Coordinated with contractors in grounds upgrade, which included replacement of cracked mason sidewalks and hazardous playground equipment.
- Reversed violations issued by Keyspan Energy (Brooklyn Union Gas) three days earlier than time allotted.
- Organized tenant / management meetings with strengthened tenant relations.

Page 1 of 2

PAUL SMITH

NEW YORK CITY HOUSING AUTHORITY continued…

Armstrong Houses, New York, NY
Assistant Superintendent (1983 – 1990)

Supported building superintendent in grounds and premise maintenance for this 1500+-unit development. Contracted carpenters, tile installers, painters and plaster repair crews. Reviewed and approved fuel oil consumption readings. Oversaw boiler room equipment maintenance and upkeep.

- Dramatically reduced maintenance backlog from over 1000 to 30 repair orders within three months.
- Boosted boiler efficiency to 80% of allotted fuel.
- Reduced time to prepare units for new occupancy from 12 to 10 days.

Pomonok Houses, Flushing, NY
Maintenance Worker (1980 – 1983)
Performed general building repairs in this 1200-unit complex. Maintained elevators in reliable working condition. Conducted electrical, plumbing, appliance and door lock repairs.

Heating Plant Technician (1975 – 1980)
Charged with providing adequate heat and hot water to tenants.

LICENSES / CERTIFICATES

THE CITY OF NEW YORK ENVIRONMENTAL PROTECTION ADMINISTRATION,
DEPARTMENT OF AIR RESOURCES, New York, NY
Certificate: Operation of Residual Fuel Oil Burners and Incinerators

NEW YORK CITY HOUSING AUTHORITY, New York, NY
Certificate: Fundamentals of Heating Plant Operation (Housing Firemen)

BRONX COMMUNITY COLLEGE, Bronx, NY
Certificate: Vehicle Emission Program

NEW YORK STATE DRIVERS LICENSE
Class E

EDUCATION

BROOKLYN COLLEGE, Brooklyn, NY
Major: Liberal Arts

MEMBERSHIP

Teamsters Union Local 237, New York, NY

STACEY KROSS

312 Belleview • Palm Beach Gardens, Florida 33410
Day: (561) 555-1212 • Evening: (561) 555-5454
email@email.com

BUSINESS DEVELOPMENT/RELATIONSHIP MANAGEMENT
Seven Years' Experience in Diversified Environments—Pharmaceuticals/Automotive
"Top producer in all positions held"

- **Senior-level presentation and closing skills**
- **Start-up and turnaround management experience**
- **New-product rollout-management expertise**
- **Team/organizational leadership**

A highly competitive, tenacious, and results-oriented professional combining polished interpersonal and rapport-building skills to significantly enhance growth, profits, and return on investment.

Core Strengths

Total account-relationship management (long-term)	Strategic market domination and leadership
Tactical alliance/partnership development	Negotiating complex contracts/special terms
Product, service, and sales training—all levels	Brand development and management
Customer-service and retention management	Time management

Professional Experience

PharmCo, Inc., Central/South Florida 2000 to Current
Institutional Account Specialist
Full accountability in developing mutually productive business relationships with key influencers and decision makers to gain formulary access for new products. Responsible for maintaining stringent sales quotas for designated priority accounts. Work with sales management in investing resources with priority customers to optimize sales and return on investment.

"100% of accounts added new product on formulary"

- Promoted to highest performance category—only 19 professionals out of 298 in the United States.
- Achieved 105% of quota with successful launch of Zyvox.
- Attained 110% increase in sales of Fragmin over 1999 sales in the Miami market.
- Promoted after four months—as a result of top performance.

Pfizer Pharmaceuticals, Miami, Florida 1995 to 2000
Institutional Healthcare Representative (1999–2000)
Directed sales and account-management activities targeting institutional accounts. Mentored and trained institutional healthcare representatives, initiated and led institutional sales projects, and demonstrated and provided key information to increase sales.

"Ignited Sales from $556,000 to $2.1 million"

- Trained and mentored 25+ new pharmaceutical representatives—elevating district to #1 ranking status.
- Consistently ranked in top 5% of institutional representatives—exceeding quotas in all product areas.
- Achieved formulary acceptance (all products) at Jackson Memorial, Miami FL, and Mt. Sinai Medical Center.a
- Created sales rep. resource book that was adopted by Pfizer USP Training and Curriculum Department.
- Contributing team member in developing a cost-analysis program for specialized treatment program.

Page 1

Stacey Kross
Page 2

Professional Experience

Pfizer Pharmaceuticals
(Continued)

Professional Healthcare Representative (1995–1999)
Managed physician and hospital accounts in the private sector. Developed efficient call cycle, managed district projects, implemented and assessed sales-action plans, and managed formulary approvals.

"Increased sales from $600,000 to $3.1 million"

- Initiated new sales tactics to achieve maximum productivity and profit.
- Achieved 222% of quota—for all products sold.
- Successfully and professionally exceeded all established sales objectives.
    - Awarded: Circle of Excellence
    - Awarded: Topper Club
    - Named: Rookie of the Year

Ford Motor Company, Dallas, Texas   1/94 to 4/96
Market Area Manager
Sales and marketing liaison between Ford Motor Company and 17 Ford/Mercury dealerships—wholesaling 16 vehicle lines. Traveled among the 17 locations providing consultative advice and support on key areas, including inventory management, advertising and marketing, pricing, and profit building.

"Ranked #1 in sales for both car and truck offerings"

- Ranked #1 in sales—managed $250 million in annual sales (17 dealerships)—wholesale sales.
- Earned *#1 Select Manager Award* honors for achieving highest percentage of quota.
- Coordinated and facilitated high-energy motivational programs to achieve top levels of individual/team performance.
- Promoted four times in recognition of sales and marketing achievements.

Education/Professional Development

Florida State University, Tallahassee, Florida
Bachelor of Science: Marketing Major; Management Minor, 1993
GPA: 3.75/Summa Cum Laude

Selected Professional Development
Target Account Selling, Targeted Selection, Conflict Resolution, Speed Reading, Public Speaking

License
220 Insurance License (General Lines)

Computer Skills
Windows, Word, WordPerfect, Excel, PowerPoint, and Internet Applications

Activities

Running, Physical Fitness, Skiing, Interior Decorating, Reading/Personal Development, and Community Service

References and Professional Portfolio Furnished upon Request

Bonnie Herbert

5699 Glen Trail • Austin, Texas 78127 • 512.555.5555 • bh@austin.rr.com

CALL CENTER MANAGER • CUSTOMER SERVICE MANAGER

Highly experienced Call Center Manager with over 20 years' experience in Customer Service Program Development, Call Center Management, and Quality Improvement. Excellent success in managing and improving large call centers. Resourceful problem solver with proven record of achievement in operational turnaround of lagging ventures, successful shaping of new programs, and improvement of productivity in established departments. Positive individual able to build and motivate telemarketing and sales teams to self-improvement. Highly ethical professional, able to improve revenues without sacrificing values.

Highlights of Performance

Instituted program improvements that resulted in "Call Center of the Year Award" by Telemarketing Magazine for the Harte Hanks Response Management - Austin Call Center in 1998

Managed Telemarketing Department to achievement of 3.86 out of 4.0 rating on Price-Waterhouse telemarketing audit, affecting an increase of .76 points.

Reduced TSR agent turnover rate of 77% to 14%

Increased productivity by 90% through implementation of improved technology

Boosted sales by 25% for Q1 1998 through establishment of sales goals and quotas

Elevated appointment hold rate from 25% to better than 90% through electronic transfer of appointment data

Areas of Expertise

Program Improvement

> Established performance measurement metrics and internal/external processes standards for Call Center to achieve COPC-2000 Certification
> Formulated improved screening and hiring processes for telemarketing agents to improve productivity and quality of service
> Set communications procedures to improve interdepartmental communications and build common goals among geographically separated branch offices
> Developed Disaster Recovery Plan that set a global standard for Response Management
> Masterminded Career Advancement Program that significantly impacted agent turnover rate and improved depth of training of employees
> Spearheaded formation of Performance Initiative Team for improvement of service and performance award selections
> Created Quality Control procedures and set benchmarks for quality goals achievement

Technology

> Developed standardized, online account tracking application that allowed secure documentation tracking, quality measurements, and autogenerated reports resulting in reduced processing/billing errors .
> Designed "pop up" technology for quality control of appointment confirmation using proprietary Unix-based software
> Migrated operating environments from Unix to NT based platforms
> Improved overall technology environment through workstation upgrades and integration of cutting-edge support peripherals for information sharing
> Trained Tech Support Agents on SAP, PeopleSoft, MediLife, Dialogic, and other applications for various high-tech accounts

(Continued)

Professional Experience

PC.com
INFORMATION TECHNOLOGY MANAGER   1999-2003

SecuritySystems.com
QUALITY CONTROL SYSTEMS MANAGER   1999

Harte Hanks
QUALITY IMPROVEMENT COORDINATOR   1996-1997
TELEMARKETING MANAGER OF TRAINING   1995-1996
TELEMARKETING PRODUCT TECH SUPPORT REPRESENTATIVE   1994

1973-1994
Career history in Sales, Business Development, and Entrepreneurial endeavors developing multi-million-dollar
revenue-generating ventures and growing successful Sales/Marketing divisions
Details happily provided in an interview situation

Technical Skills

Windows NT Server	UnixWare	MS Access
Novell NetWare	HP-UX	MS Office Suite 95/97
Ethernet	Solaris	Executone ACD
Token Ring	Visual Basic	ACT!
LAN Manager	Visual FoxPro	GoldMine
LAN Server	AlphaFour	Netscape
NetDirector of Unix	Lotus Notes	Communicator
System Management	Lotus 123	Internet Explorer
Server	FoxBASE	NFS
Enterprise/Solver	FoxPRO	

Protocols and Processes:

SMTP	IPX/SPX	PPP
IMAP	TCP/IP	DNS
IP	Telnet	ZIP
SNMP	TFTP	FTP
IPSec	POP3	

Military Service

United States Navy • Honorable Discharge • 1971

Education

Associates Bachelor of Arts – Business and Marketing
Richland College • Dallas, Texas

JANICE BASKIN, M.A.

6 Alberta Drive, Marlboro, New Jersey 07746
(908) 555-4860 - home
email@email.com

STRENGTHS AND ABILITIES

- Career and Mental Health Counseling
- Organizational Consulting
- Empowerment Counseling
- Training and Development

PROFESSIONAL ACCOMPLISHMENTS

Individual Counseling and Organizational Consulting

- Serve as Executive Director of Baskin Business and Career Services, a private practice specializing in career and mental health counseling, as well as issues facing employees in the workplace.

- Conduct nationwide three-day outplacement seminars and one-on-one executive coaching sessions for Fortune 500 corporations.

- Currently negotiating "Lunchtime Career Seminar" series for 1996 with NOVA Corp., Princeton, New Jersey.

- Served as Keynote Speaker and workshop leader, Professional Association of Resume Writers Convention, 1991 and 1992. Chosen Keynote Speaker for the New Jersey Home Economists in Business, 1994-1995 Conference.

- Enlisted as guest speaker on New Jersey Talk Radio, WCTC, "The Liz Maida Show," and WRFM, "About Money."

Seminars/Training

- Presented "Multimodal Therapy, the Cutting Edge of Psychotherapy Today," with Dr. Alice Whipple, New Jersey Mental Health Conference, Rider University, October 1995.

- Recommended by the New Grange Community Center for Adults with Learning Disabilities, Princeton, New Jersey. Developed a program entitled, "Making the Correct Vocational Choice," 1994 conference. Presented workshop to members of the Monmouth County Board of Social Services, 1994.

- Contracted as a workshop leader for Brookdale Community College Community Services Division. Assist with career workshops, business seminars, and women's conferences.

- Listed with the NJEA's Speaker's Bureau. Conducted a full-day seminar entitled "Career Education in the Public Schools" for the Sayreville Public School System.

- Lead half-day seminars for Rutgers University Student Services, Monmouth County Library Headquarters, and Monmouth County Vocational School Districts.

Presentations and Publications

Contributing Author, *Key Careers* by Robert Noe. Contributing Author - *Targeted Cover Letters* by Mark Ince. Contributing Author - *Executive Job Search Strategies* by Robert Hines. Contributing Author, **Using WordPerfect** in Your Job Search by David Nobel

(Continued)

JANICE BASKIN, M.A. **Page 2**

EXPERIENCE

EXECUTIVE DIRECTOR
1984-Present
Baskin Business and Career Services
Offices in Woodbridge, Princeton, and Marlboro, New Jersey

Additional Counseling Experience:

Beverly Baskin, M.A. - Private Counseling Practice
Dr. Alice Whipple, Licensed Psychologist, Princeton, New Jersey
Jewish Family Services, Edison, New Jersey

WORKSHOP LEADER, Community Services Division
Brookdale Community College, Freehold, New Jersey   1984-Present

ADULT EDUCATION TEACHER
Freehold Township Public Schools, Freehold, New Jersey   1981-1984

BUSINESS EDUCATION TEACHER, Facilitator of Co-Op Program
Jamesburg High School, Jamesburg, New Jersey   1971-1981

EDUCATION

MA in Counseling Services, Rider University, Lawrenceville, New Jersey
Graduate Studies, Career and Vocational Counseling, Rutgers University
Selected by the New Jersey Employment Counselors Association as recipient of a Counseling Student
Grant to further my education
Bachelor of Science in Education, City University of New York, Baruch College

American Counseling Association and
New Jersey Counseling Association and Affiliates
National Career Development Association
National Association of Employment Counselors
Member, Career Planning and Adult Development Network
Member, National Association of Job Search Training
Middle Atlantic Career Counseling Association
American Psychological Association, Student Member

CARTOONIST
SPORTS / HUMOR

JERRY P. KRAUSS
1824 5th Avenue
New York, NY 10021
(212) 555-8263
email@email.com

PROFILE:

More than 15 years of successful experience as a freelance cartoonist specializing in the field of sports and humor. Have appeared regularly in the following publications:

*	*Golf Digest*	1987 - Present
*	*Golfer's World*	1990 - Present
*	*Sports Illustrated*	1990 - 1994
*	*Sporting News*	1989 - 1993

Recent Work:

- Six-year contract with *British Golfing Journal*, 1990 - Present
- Seven-year contract with Walt Disney Publications, 1989 - 1996
- Eight-year contract with PGA of America (Promotions Dept.), 1989-1996
- Eight entries with the *New Yorker Magazine*, 1989 - 1995
- Three entries in NBA All-Star Program, 1989, 1992, 1993

Education:

B.A.: Animation Science; University of Vermont, Burlington, VT
With Honors, 1986

Awards:

ACA National Honorable Mention (1988-1996)
NACA National Recognition (1991-1996)
IACA International Recognition (1987 - 1996)

References and Professional Portfolio Furnished
upon Request

RONALD C. GARRISON
55555 Springbranch Drive ▪ Austin, TX 55555
gar@earthlink.net ▪ 512-555-8714

SENIOR EXECUTIVE MANAGEMENT
CEO / PRESIDENT / COO

Over 25 Years' Profit-Building Experience in Competitive Aerospace Markets
Strategic Planning / Turnaround / Start-up Operations

Key Top-Level Contacts throughout Industry and Government

Consummate, visionary Senior Executive with aggressive record of increasing sales, achieving market leadership, and restructuring operations. Demonstrated domestic and international experience in complex and demanding roles leading start-up and growth organizations. Results-oriented, decisive leader with proven success in new market identification, strategic thinking, and problem solving. Cultivated command presence and strong repertoire of cross-functional corporate knowledge and skills.

CORE EXECUTIVE COMPETENCIES

- Business Development
- P&L Management
- Operations Management
- Sales & Marketing
- Strategic Business Planning
- R&D Management

- Relationship Building
- Strategic Alliances
- Government Contracting
- Large-Scale Negotiation
- Global Product Development
- Niche Market Identification

EXECUTIVE EXPERIENCE

Northlink, Inc., Austin, TX   1999–Present
President / CEO
Recruited to turn around Global Positioning System (GPS) "S" Corporation engaged in design, manufacture, and distribution of electronic equipment for core products and related applications. Direct P&L responsibility for $10M in annual revenues.

- Negotiating sale for $18M to largest customer. Buyer senior management forecasts $1.5M profit in first quarter following sale.
- Spearheaded vision, strategy, and execution of $1.5M niche marketing campaign, targeting agriculture, aviation, geographic information systems, and animal tracking.
- Increased sales from $3M to $7M plus, more than doubling revenue base with 20% plus net profits in first 18 months.
- Sustained profitability and financed high-level growth with earnings achieved from targeting best-in-class engineering and customer service to high-margin, niche markets.

StarLock, Inc., Tempe, AZ   1995–1999
CEO / COO
Recruited by John Walton (Wal-Mart) to build start-up for introduction of world's first successful aerial GPS Parallel Tracking and Guidance System. Directed all phases of start-up with bottom-line P&L responsibility for $100M in capital.

(Continued)

129

Ronald C. Garrison

Executive Experience (Continued)

- Achieved $200M plus gross sales, 100% investor return, 60% plus market share, and 1688 systems deployed over 3.5 years, overcoming strong competition to become market leader.
- Orchestrated exclusive $450M, five-year agreement to sell cost-effective, satellite-based trademarked positioning signal to agricultural interests.
- Established "new" industry estimated at $100M annually by forging integration of differential GPS (DGPS) and major growth market of "precision farming."
- Built grassroots relationships with early industry leaders, such as AgriCad, Ag Leader, Applications Mapping, Soil Teq, Deere, Case IH, and USDA on technology benefits and preferred status.
- Led implementation of cost-effective, breakthrough, value-added technology for precise positioning industry

Bede Jet Corporation, St. Louis, MO   1993–1995
Executive Vice President / COO / Director
Led program for world's first general aviation, supersonic aircraft that attained international recognition, including Aviation Week cover story. Directed international sales and marketing with full accountability for staffing and strategic directives. Established strong worldwide marketing relationships.

- Booked 55 orders estimated at $30-40M while still in developmental stage.
- Positioned aircraft for $25M international sales and candidate for Department of Defense multibillion-dollar, 10-year Joint Primary Aircraft Training System (JPATS).
- Won $11M contract to license airframe for military drone use.

AirFoil Technologies, Inc., San Diego, CA   1991–1993
President / CEO / Director
Founded research and development company to develop high-tech airfoil for gas turbine, airframe, and hydrodynamic applications. Built operations from ground up, including planning, successful patent application, project management, wind tunnel testing, technical reporting, industrial liaison, and financial reporting. Organized board of directors around selected Fortune 500 leaders and world-class consultants, including Time magazine's engineer of the century, and a Nobel Prize winner in Physics.

- Raised $15M from Private Placement Memorandum and $5M from IPO Prospectus, leading due diligence presentations to financial community.
- Negotiated Non-Disclosures with Allison, Grumman, Solar Turbine, among others.
- Structured teaming agreement with SAIC, UCSD, Aerovironment, Cal Tech, Stanford, Georgia Tech Research Institute.
- Patented Venturi Enhanced Airfoil and positioned technology for advanced systems analysis, prototype development, and licensing.

United States Navy, Worldwide Assignments   1970–1990
Naval Officer/Aviator (Commander)
Documented career as leading Naval Officer, pioneering manager, and groundbreaking aviator. Served in highest positions of authority and responsibility, including White House Aide, Congressional Liaison, Air Wing Commander, and Blue Angels Commanding Officer. Authored and managed operational-budgetary plans involving assets over one-half billion dollars. Directed Foreign Military Sales mission to Norway.

Education

Bachelor of Arts in Economics, University of Missouri, Kansas City, MO

EVA RAMIREZ avaramirez@abx.com

_____ 111 SW 81st Street ♦ Pullman, Washington 99163 ♦ Home: 509.555.1193 ♦ Cellular: 509.555.1165

CHIEF FINANCIAL OFFICER ♦ DIRECTOR OF FINANCE
Proven Expertise in Commanding Health-Care Fiscal Environments

Accomplished financial executive with over 14 years' experience. Progressively responsible and diversified experience in accounting, budgeting, and strategic planning. Valuable combination of financial acumen integrated with highly developed interpersonal skills. Exceptional overall business perspective, demonstrated ability to exceed goals, and a proven history of providing valuable financial advice. Solid project management skills with effective combination of directing multiple priorities and generating innovative strategies to meet and exceed performance objectives.

Key role in streamlining efficiency: astute at recognizing areas needing improvement, with the vision to develop and implement necessary changes. Known for team-based management style, value-based leadership skills, and vision-based organizational design. Articulate communicator at all organizational levels. Demonstrates ability to exceed goals through relationship building and team leadership. Skilled supervisor, trainer, leader, and motivator. Proficient in Microsoft Office, Lotus Notes, and healthcare platforms Meditech and HBOC.

AREAS OF EXPERTISE

- Contract Negotiations
- Annual Financial Audits
- Insurance Coverage Evaluation
- Collective Bargaining Agreements
- Financial Institution Communications
- Multi-Million-Dollar Financial Planning
- Capital/Operating Budget Development

- Project Management
- Payroll Administration
- Medicare/Medicaid Systems
- Federal Guideline Compliance
- General Ledger Administration
- Employee Compensation Plans
- Statistical Information Accumulation

CAREER PROGRESSION

St. Mary's Memorial Hospital – Tacoma, Washington
A forty-two-bed acute care hospital with 65 staff physicians, 225 employees, and annual revenues of more than $25 million; combined with medical office building and satellite building for therapy, foundation, and billing services. Located on the campus of Washington State University accredited by the Joint Commission on Accreditation of Healthcare Organizations. **(www.stmarys.org)**

Chief Financial Officer (1995 – Present)
Orchestrate and administer all facets of financial agendas, including budget/forecast development, cost report preparation, financial audits, and tax preparation; liaise with department staff, physicians, and board members to accumulate financial data used to identify trends and perform historical analysis. Participate in third-party payor contract negotiations and internal audits to ensure proper service according to negotiated parameters. Ultimately responsible for profit and loss administration, progressive departmental efficiency, adequate insurance coverage on hospital assets, and overall fiscal stability. Embrace GAAP rules and progressive educational course attendance to ensure required accounting consistency.

Representative Achievements:

- **Steered hospital to favorable financial status, opening door for funding of $20 million replacement hospital** by aggressively maintaining low debt service ratio, promoting and passing $8.2 million community tax bond, and assisting in the planning phase to secure $4 million hospital foundation contribution; balance realized through cash reserves, hospital debt funding, and private partnerships.

- **Intensively maintained comprehensive log of Medicare claims resulting in receipt of $200,000 underpayment** from Financial Intermediary; original request was made from Intermediary **to seek** a refund but did not get approval and was reversed by internal accounting records.

- **Successfully developed Employee Incentive Plan to promote performance improvements hospital-wide.** Plan entailed reformatting organization pay structure from **budget**-based to **goal**-based which proved positive, thus was approved for second year **implementation. Participated in collective bargaining agreements discussions with WSNA (Nursing Union) and SEIU (LPN Union).**

(Continued)

- **Clearly visible in evaluation and selection of information system resulting in 1997 platform movement to Meditech;** motion involved shared arrangement realizing approximately **$1 million** in capital costs with ongoing cost savings in the hundreds of thousands.

- **Implemented rolling CD portfolio to provide maximized rate of return despite limited investment avenues.**

- **Heavily involved in Healthcare Financial Management Associations (HFMA) Annual National Institute;** received 34 hours of CPE training, including Creating a Planning Culture, Integrating Financials & Strategic Goals, Bottom Line Impact, HIPAA Privacy, Rural Hospital Regulatory Issues, Proven Cost Management, and How to Hire the Right Person, etc.

- **Consistently maintains progressive knowledge of changes in healthcare financing and disperses information appropriately;** currently training with **GE Medical Solutions** on **Six Sigma and Change Acceleration Process & Work-Out™** processes involving intense six-month training on statistical analysis. Previously completed six-month training regimen on investment and financial management with **Money®** intended to help with personal finances and financial management/training for others.

- **Established formidable relations with bank and County Treasurer officials** to secure line of credit with no service fees or annual fees proving beneficial in securing short-term cash needs.

- **Shared service with Director of Quality Services as Corporate Compliance Officer (CCO) to** implement a corporate compliance plan and training schedule to new employees; participated in development of legal and ethical issue clarifications.

- **Progressive determination to implement functional changes in accounting procedure has moved accounts receivable days (gross) from a high in 1997 of 104 days to a low of 49 days.**

Director of Patient Financial Information Services /Interim CFO/Chief Accountant (1988 – 1995)
Charged with full accountability for directing all aspects of account receivables, admissions, and comprehensive oversight of fiscal services. Established department goals, objectives, and priorities, with direct involvement in various projects; monitored project progress and results while defining staff and resource limitations. Participated in committees or task forces as requested or required. Responsible for associate hiring, scheduling, and support providing insight relative to billing, cashiering, admitting, and customer service issues; acted as substitute during employee absences. Communicated appropriately with patients, coworkers, physician offices, and members of ancillary departments to perform essential job functions.

Presided over meetings with management and line staff to facilitate consistency of personnel policies; utilized staff meetings, customer comments, and employee input to research and identify internal and external departmental process and system components enabling solutions to department-wide objectives. Maintained Patient Financial Information Services policies and procedures manual, staying up to date with current state and federal regulations. Oversaw medical records and transcriptions and scrutinized charity care applications ensuring guideline adherence.

Representative Achievements:

- **Assessed department policies and procedures and implemented required changes** to ensure accurate billing, prompt reimbursements, and proper patient handling according to PMH corporate customer standards. Successfully set systems in place resulting in significant decrease of Accounts Receivables days.

- **As required attended progressive educational conferences and seminars** as well as possess appropriate reading material necessary to acquire and maintain competency in admissions compliance/management and Medicare and Medicaid regulations and compliance.

EDUCATIONAL PROFILE

UNIVERSITY OF PHOENIX – Phoenix, Arizona
Candidate MBA

WASHINGTON STATE UNIVERSITY – Pullman, Washington
Bachelor of Arts – Business Administration (Accounting)

College of Ministry Training – Pullman, Washington
Bachelor of Arts – Biblical Studies

JANKO M. HUBERNESH

138 Commonwealth Avenue
Boston, MA 01960
email@email.com

(617) 555-0878

EXECUTIVE CHEF

Specializing in Italian, French & Continental Fine-Dining Cuisine

Dynamic, Results-Oriented & Team-Spirited

OVERVIEW	Over fifteen years of professional cooking and kitchen management experience. Exemplify leadership qualities and professionalism, backed by a consistent, verifiable record of achievement. Consistently maintains 5★/5★ and Michelin 2★ rated restaurant establishments including the Hubernesh Imperial (Boston, MA), the Hubernesh Imperial (Vienna, Austria), Boulderfrach International (Transkai, South Africa), and Klosterbrau (Seefeld, Austria)

AREAS OF EXPERTISE	Master Chef designation Executive/Sous-Chef experience with million-dollar, upscale establishments Trained by Paul Bocuse, Gaston Lenotre, Roger Verge, M. Matt and R. Gerer Training & development specialist; teaching instructor Successful catering experience (1,200+ people) Maximizing kitchen productivity and staff performance

---

PROFESSIONAL EXPERIENCE	The Hubernesh Imperial, Boston, MA 5★/5★ **GM / EXECUTIVE SOUS-CHEF** 1993 - Present Executive Sous-Chef for restaurant serving Italian, French, and Continental cuisine, producing $2.4 million in revenues. Hire, train, and direct six cooks/chefs. Plan menu, assure quality control, and minimize waste. The Hubernesh Imperial, Vienna, Austria 4★/4★ **GM / EXECUTIVE CHEF** 1987 - 1993 Supervised 28 cooks/chefs, managed back house operations, and performed purchasing function for this $7 million upscale establishment specializing in Italian and French cuisine. Les Chef de France, Epcot Center, Orlando, FL 5★/5★ **CHEF - FOOD PRODUCTION FACILITY** 1989 - 1990 Managed 15 people and oversaw production of high-volume establishment, for this $16 million upscale restaurant specializing in French cuisine.

(Continued)

24—CHEF (CONT.)

Janko M. Hubernesh
Page Two
Resume

EXPERIENCE
(Continued)

<u>Hotel Klosterbrau</u>, Seefeld, Austria   5★/5★ Michelin 2★
EXECUTIVE SOUS-CHEF   1987 - 1989

Supervised 35 cooks/chefs, for this internationally renowned hotel boasting two award-winning restaurants ($7 million in food volume/year). One of just two restaurants in Austria with a Michelin 2★ rating.

<u>SUN International</u>, Transkai, South Africa   5★/5★ Michelin 2★
SOUS-CHEF   1986 - 1987

Oversaw 48 people for Chico's Restaurant, one of the hotel's 14 restaurants producing a total of $50 million/year in food revenue.

<u>Hotel Palaise</u>, Vienna, Austria   5★/5★ Michelin 2★
CHEF   1985 - 1986

A landmark hotel with a 400-year history, considered one of the top upscale hotels in Europe. Served Traditional and Continental cuisine. Annual F&B revenues of $20 million.

EDUCATION &
QUALIFICATIONS

<u>W.I.F.I.</u>, Innsbrook, Austria
Graduate: CERTIFIED MASTER CHEF

Silver Medalist:	International Cooking Olympics, Germany, 1983
Guest Chef:	Cuisine de Chefs, Paulos Cafe Restaurant
	Les Chef de France Epcot Center, Orlando, FL
Instructor:	Culinary Arts to Aspiring Sous/Executive Chefs
Guest Appearance:	Sunny 104.3 FM Radio - *Kevin's Kitchen*

- References & Supporting Documentation Furnished upon Request -

BROOKE STEVENS

555 West 15th Street
New York, NY 10011
347-555-4456

PRIVATE CHEF with 10 years experience available for live in, live out and travel. Pleasant accommodating style with culinary talents in Asian Fusion, World Beat, Mediterranean, vegetarian, and gourmet raw cuisines. Offers creative menu planning from both clients' and personal recipes for individual dining through large soirées. Maintains well-organized pantries with a quick orientation to new environments. Flexible work ethic with acceptance of last-minute changes, unexpected guests, special diets, and schedule changes.

Special Talents

★ Accumulated extensive shopping portfolio with the finest provisions and specialty products to orchestrate sumptuous meals. Portfolio includes organic produce, imported fish from clean waters, and freshly pressed oils in addition to kitchen outfitters and mail order catalogues.

★ Artisan Baker experienced in producing high-quality breads such as sourdough, pane, panini and focaccia.

★ Experienced in food set-ups, including five-course meals, buffet and family-style, plated, grill cooking, travel lunches and picnics.

Culinary Experience

CONFIDENTIAL CLIENT, New York, Arizona, Aspen, Massachusetts   **2000 – Present**
Selected to manage three kitchens and prepare up to 10 meals per week for this social leader. Select fresh seasonings from client's gardens, including herbs, vegetables, and fruits. Coordinate with butler in planning small intimate dinner parties through large social gatherings. Direct kitchen maintenance to ensure safe, clean and efficient workspace. Maintains well-stocked pantries.

- Interpreted recipe selections from both personal files and notable chefs such as Daniel Boulud and Charlie Trotter, incorporating lighter, healthier products while maintaining a flavorful essence.
- Thoroughly reequipped kitchens, removing all toxic cookware and expired condiments.

CONFIDENTIAL CLIENT, Connecticut, Beverly Hills, New York   **1997 – 2000**
Oversaw four kitchens totally outfitted with commercial-grade equipment in the homes of this stage actor/singer. Frequently executed culinary selections for small, casual dinner parties as well as occasional luncheons, poolside barbeques and picnics. Packed small lunches and supervised cleaning staff.

- Facilitated client's successful transition to a whole foods diet, introducing both personally created recipes and those of Alice Waters, Ric Orlando and Lucas Rockwood.

CANYON RANCH, Lenox, Mass.   **1993 – 1997**
Collaborated with head chef in creating scrumptious and nutritionally satisfying cuisine, light meals and artisan breads at this world-class health resort's 126-room property in the Berkshires. Led cooking demonstrations with an emphasis on converting high-fat/high-calorie meals to health supportive alternatives.

Culinary Training

KURA HULANDA EXPERIENCE, HOSPITALITY AND CULINARY
INSTITUTE, Curacao, Netherlands Antilles

Basic, Intermediate and Advanced Culinary
Certificates

LUCAS ROCKWOOD
Caravan of Dreams, New York, NY

Group Classes: Live Food Preparation

NORMAN HARRIS

555 Columbus Avenue
Tuckahoe, NY 55555

Norman@online.com
914-555-1111

AWARD-WINNING CHEF WITH 10 YEARS EXPERIENCE
HIGHLY MOTIVATED AND COMMITTED TO CULINARY EXCELLENCE

CAREER HISTORY

HILTON HOTELS CORPORATION   1993 – Present
Shaped a path in culinary arts with this world-renowned hotel chain. Assignments include:

Banquet Chef
Promoted to direct banquet operations for the newly opened Millennium Hilton with eight banquet rooms. Design and plan banquet menu inspired by New York City's diverse ethnic populations. Collaborated with Executive chef in developing selections for Church & Dey Restaurant menu.

- Influenced design and setup of banquet kitchen with maximized efficiency of food preparation and delivery of service, resulting in minimal changes during first quarter operations.

Chef De'Parti (1999 – 2003)
Direct staff of 18 cooks responsible for producing provisions for corporate groups and private parties in six banquet rooms at McLean Tyson's Corner, McLean, Virginia. Plan and produce up to seven meals daily from buffet breakfasts to elaborate theme dinners, including the Lacrosse World Championships dinner and Women of Vision awards gala. Prepare tasting menus for committee approvals and kitchen executions.

- Invited to prepare appetizers and entrée for grand opening celebration of Alexandria Mark Executive Meeting Center.
- Named employee of the year in 2000, 2003.

Kitchen Supervisor (1998 – 1999)
Oversaw kitchen operations for this restaurant, upgrading breakfast selections and daily lunch specials to meet customers' requests. Ensured guest satisfaction by consistently creating outstanding meals and food preparation.. Trained new personnel on operations and procedures in accordance with Hilton Hotels Corporation.

- Restructured Penfield's menu, earning San Pellegrino Outstanding Restaurant Award
- Reorganized kitchen and utilized spare foods reducing operation costs by 15%.

Saucier / Roundsman (1993 – 1998)
Directed the daily production of soups and sauces for banquets and all hotel outlets

CAREER HIGHLIGHTS

JAMES BEARD FOUNDATION, New York, NY
Prepared annual board dinner for members.

AWARDS / HONORS

JAMES BEARD FOUNDATION, New York, NY
2002 – American Express Best Chef, New York City
2000 – Coca Cola Americas Classics
1998 – San Pellegrino Outstanding Restaurant Award

MEMBERSHIPS / ALLIANCES

AMERICAN CULINARY FEDERATION St. Augustine, Florida

EDUCATION

THE FRENCH CULINARY INSTITUTE OF AMERICA, New York, NY

PATRICIA NASLUND

12123 Bay Point Drive • Delray Beach, Florida 33444 • (561) 555-1222
email@email.com / http://portfolio.dooubleman.com (web resume)

CHIEF MARKETING OFFICER
Director of Marketing / Business Development
15+ Years of Real-World, Hands-On Sales & Marketing Leadership

Capitalize on Emerging Marketing Opportunities / Solid Organizational Leadership Skills
Long- & Short-Term Goal Setting & Strategic Marketing
Extraordinary Technical Aptitude

Robust business expansion experience allows this highly creative professional to generate compelling sales/marketing strategies to ignite revenue, enhance market share and improve bottom line performance.

Core Professional Strengths

Market analysis/marketing plan development
Building/maintaining key strategic alliances
Employee training, development, and supervision
Creative passion leading to extraordinary results

Lead generation – new business development
Senior level project and brand management
Executive level presentation/closing skills
Web marketing and e-solutions

Technical Proficiencies

WebMaster	Broadcast Producer	Online Media Expert	Print Graphics Artist
ColdFusion MX	FinalCut PRO	FLIX	Photoshop
Flash MX	Media100	MediaCleaner	Illustrator
Dreamweaver MX	AfterEffects	Real Producer Pro	QuarkXPress
Fireworks MX	Boris RED		Freehand

Professional Experience

webHORSE Digital Media, Delray Beach, Florida   2001 to Present
Chief Marketing Office / Director of New Business Development
Designed, produced and executed "start-up" marketing plan resulting in dramatic growth for this new media creative services firm, including webhorse.org. Project managed all targeted account/creative services, resulting in reduced costs, increased efficiencies, higher client spending and increased customer satisfaction. Some managed accounts include:

Central American Produce
Positioned the second largest importer of melons in the US to gain market share in the face of stiff competition and a fierce marketplace. Developed creative strategy/approach and managed production of channel sales and marketing campaign during 2002. Company surpassed more than $80 million in annual revenue. Leading deliverable was centralamericanproduce.com, a dynamic business-to-business website that enhances communications with growers and with buyers, leading to increased sales and all-around higher satisfaction. Additional elements included:

* Corporate and various brand logos
* Sales kit with CD-ROM insert
* Public relations elements
* Corporate brochures
* Nationally distributed magazine ads
* Product sales collateral materials

J.C. DeNiro & Associates
Facilitated successful launch of New York City and Vero Beach offices for this prominent luxury residential realtor and enhanced their public image in South Florida, resulting in a significant increase in listings and sales.

- Produced jcdeniro.com, a data-driven website, including an administrative client control panel, utilizing FLASH, ColdFusion and mySQL.
- Created and introduced new corporate logo.
- Developed a print advertising campaign, and streamlined their internal advertising process.

Galactic Communications
Information Architecture, Design, Implementation and Marketing of TelephoneServiceForLess.com. This e-commerce website and data-driven agent/reseller marketing tool has generated extensive online orders, driven agent acquisition with increase retention, and more for this multilevel marketer of local/long distance telephone services.

(Continued)

Professional Experience (Continued)

News Bureau Television Production & Media Services, Boca Raton, Florida   1996 to 2001
Director of Marketing and Business Development
Grew in-flight television business to more than $2 million in annual sales in under three years.

- "Bootstrapped" operation through personal first year sales of more than $600,000, winning the support of major accounts, including SONY, Microsoft, IBM, Olympus, Ricoh and KRAFT.
- Designed, wrote and executed all print, video and Internet marketing materials.
- Managed relationships with all media vendors, including Delta Air Lines, American Airlines, United Airlines, USAir, British Airways and many others.
- Built and coached sales and sales support staff, resulting in more cohesiveness and increasing sales.
- Developed and maintained a worldwide network of television production professionals.
- Personally produced more than 100 news shorts and feature segments.

Worldwide Target Demographic Television, Deerfield Beach, Florida   1991 to 1996
Director of New Business Development   (1993 - 1996)
Conceived, launched and personally sold magazine-style television programs, generating millions of dollars of revenue.

- Launched InFlight Division with introduction of Delta Air Lines' *Business and Technology Review*. Capitalizing on this exciting new market resulted in first year sales of more than one million dollars.
- *Healthy Living with Dr. Joyce Brothers…* an instant success with the aging of America and America's heightened health consciousness. Program ran for over two years on national cable television.
- Developed, produced and sold award-winning technology program, *Sights & Sounds…* Strategic partnership with Hachette Filipacchi for four-year cost supported run on CNBC and The Discovery Channel.
- Influenced initial advertising support and contributed significantly to the team development effort, resulting in the successful launch of *Modern Cuisine with Robin Leach.*
- Launched and garnered industry and media support for Multimedia Today, the first ever technology-based transactional television program through alliances with IBM, Redgate NewMedia, Tiger Electronics and others.
- Built, trained, coached and managed sales staff and exceeded personal and team sales projections each quarter.

Director: Advertising and Public Relations   (1991 - 1993)
Developed all sales and marketing materials of start-up operation, generating tremendous awareness and market penetration.

- Designed and executed a multitude of sales and marketing pieces, including national print advertising campaigns, press releases, brochures and promotional videos, leading to the ultimate success of the start-up operation.
- Generated profit and increased awareness producing a 4500 sq. ft. trade show presence by coordinating shared participation of more than 20 clients.
- Successfully bartered $1 million in advertising in fewer than six months in a zero-dollar budget environment.
- Facilitated program and content development, as well as advertiser participation through research.

Education

MOREHEAD STATE UNIVERSITY
Bachelor of Arts: Journalism, 1986

UNIVERSITY OF KENTUCKY
Post-Graduate Work: Communication / Persuasion Research, 1985-86

Additional Information, Documentation, and References furnished upon request

Claire James
1168 Jason Way
Los Angeles, California 90223
Home: (213) 555-2121 / Cell: (213) 5556565
Email: email@email.com

INDUSTRY LEADER - TECHNOLOGY EXECUTIVE / CONSULTANT
CIO / CTO / INFORMATION TECHNOLOGIST

Orchestrating Explosive Growth in Volatile and Down DOT-COM Markets

Expanding & Reengineering Organizations / Start-Up Management Expert
Organizational / IS Leadership of Public and Private Enterprises

---

High-profile career spanning 25 years spearheading the development, commercialization and implementation of emerging technologies across key industry sectors, including Internet, healthcare and high-tech environments.

CORE PROFESSIONAL STRENGTHS

Strategic Visioning / Planning	Management / IT Team Development
Corporate / Business Development	Product Development / Enhancement
System Integration / IT Infrastructure	Project Management / Leadership
Building Strategic Alliances and Partnerships	New Technology Development / Transfer

PROFESSIONAL EXPERIENCE

COURT-LAND, INC., Boca Raton, Florida   1998 to Current
Chief Technology Officer
- Spearheaded team to develop an Internet Healthcare plan that became the basis for Cybear's vision.
- Core management team member that took this developmental stage Internet Company public.
- Designed and implemented Court-Land's HIPAA ready National ISP network and Network Operations Center (NOC).
- Drafted initial specifications and developed "Dr. Cybear Internet Portal."
- Integrated strategic business partner's applications into the product.

CYBERMATRIX CORP., West Palm Beach, Florida   1995 to 1998
Chief Information Officer
- Directed IT strategic planning and implementations in preparing PhyMatrix for its IP.
- Built a national network to support corporate Medical Practice Management, Managed Care and Data Warehousing systems.
- Worked with the top management to identify, evaluate, and integrate organizations into PhyMatrix's core business systems.

PALM BEACH COUNTY HEALTH CARE DISTRICT, West Palm Beach, Florida   1991 to 1995
Chief Technology Officer
- Reengineered the internal infrastructure and implemented a new managed care system.
- Developed team to plan countywide managed healthcare network.
- Managed internal and consulting resources during this effort; project was on time and under budget.

DIGITAL OFFICE SYSTEMS INTERNATIONAL, West Palm Beach, Florida   1986 to 1990
Chief Technology Officer
- Developed the first Cable TV (CATV) Facilities Resource Management System for integration into the advance Geographic Information System (GIS) and Cable TV Engineering software.
- Headed the development team responsible for the D-tain House Arrest System. Developed all facets of the system: hardware, systems software, imbedded microprocessor software, unit fabrication and manufacturing. Product deployed nationally in 1987.
- Founded and managed DOSI operations and development teams.

EDUCATION & TRAINING

Bachelor of Science: Analytical Chemistry	University of Florida	1985
Associate Faculty Member	College of Engineering	1990-Current

Comprehensive Resume, Specific Achievements & References Furnished upon Request

LYNDA JACKSON

402 Rally Drive • Belleville, Illinois 62221 • (618) 555-8342
• email@email.com

SUMMARY OF QUALIFICATIONS

Six years experience as the Head Coach of highly competitive basketball, volleyball, and softball teams for a quality NAIA womenís intercollegiate athletic program in the American Midwest Conference (formerly the Show-Me Collegiate Conference). A successful track record for graduating student-athletes (97%), managing athletic programs, recruiting, and developing talent at the high school, junior varsity, and varsity levels. Actively involved in faculty, athletic, and student affairs committees. Proven athletic administration skills include:

Budgeting	Travel Planning	Public Relations
Staffing/Scheduling	Academic Standards	Recreational Programs

- Graduated 60 Academic All Conference volleyball and softball players in the last five years. Coached volleyball teams that qualified for postseason play each year and softball teams that have finished no less than fourth in the conference, including a regional championship and a 4th place national finish.
- Member of the American Volleyball Coaches Association, National Softball Coaches Association, and National Association of Intercollegiate Athletics.
- Served as the Director of Public Relations for the St. Louis Steamers Soccer Club from 1985-1987. Accustomed to developing a strong rapport with local media contacts.
- Hold an M.A. Degree in Speech Communication from Southern Illinois University at Edwardsville and a B.A. Degree in Communication from St. Louis University. Earned Academic All Conference honors in basketball as an undergraduate. Taught various Physical Education (activities and theory) and Communication courses over the last six years, including Public Speaking, Interpersonal Skills, Small Groups, and Persuasion.

COACHING HIGHLIGHTS/COMMITTEE WORK

Head Volleyball/Softball Coach, McKauliffe College, Livingston, Illinois   1989-Present

- 1995: American Midwest Rating Committee, Volleyball
- 1995: 4th Place, NAIA National Softball Championship, the highest national tournament finish for any athletic team at McKauliffe College
- 1995: NSCA Exposure Camp Director
- 1995: NAIA Executive Committee, Softball
- 1995: NAIA Midwest Region Champions, Softball
- 1995: NAIA Midwest Region Coach of the Year, Softball
- 1994: NSCA Exposure Camp Staff
- 1993: NAIA District #20 Chair, Softball
- 1992: Show-Me Collegiate Conference Champions, Volleyball
- 1992: Show-Me Collegiate Conference Coach of the Year, Volleyball

	1990	1991	1992	1993	1994	1995	Totals
SOFTBALL							
Won/Loss	29-14	19-9	21-10	22-8	28-18	41-16	160-75 (68%)
NAIA All Americans	1	n/a	n/a	n/a	n/a	2	3
All Conference	2	3	3	4	5	5	22
Academic All Conference	1	1	5	7	8	9	31
VOLLEYBALL							
Won/Loss	18-10	24-20	18-11	25-13	28-13	16-21	129-88 (60%)
NAIA All Americans	n/a	n/a	1	1	2	2	6
All Conference	2	2	3	4	3	3	17
Academic All Conference	2	2	5	6	7	7	29

ROBERTA LYONS

320 Brandies Street • Springfield, Illinois, 62232 • (618) 555-1212 • email@email.com

ATHLETIC COACH
Basketball

9 Years Successful Experience in High-Visibility Athletic Programs

"Improving Skills—Improving Character—Improving Basketball Programs"

Discipline/Reward/Growth

A positive-thinking, results-oriented, and team-spirited athletic coach with a sound, verifiable record of success in building winning programs and developing values-based students into contributing citizens in their communities.

CORE STRENGTHS

Athletic conditioning and fitness expert
Strategic planning—sound basketball fundamentals
Program marketing and promotions—on/off campus

Nutritional certification
Staff development
Concentration on grades and sport

EMPLOYMENT

Springfield County School System, Springfield, Illinois   1992 to Current
Girls Head Basketball Coach/Math Teacher—McKenner High School

Coaching Highlights:
2001   American Midwest Regional Finals—Top 12 in State
2000   American Midwest Regional Finals—Top 10 in State
1999   NCCA—Runner-up
1998   Northwest Conference Champions
1997   Northwest Conference Champions
1996   Runner–up Northwest Conference Champions

Coaching Record:

	WINS	LOSSES	PERCENTAGE	COMMENT
2001	15	3	83%	First in conference
2000	14	4	77%	Second in conference
1999	16	2	88%	First in conference
1998	12	6	66%	Third in conference
1997	13	5	72%	Third in conference
1996	13	5	72%	Third in conference
1995	9	9	50%	Sixth in conference
1994	10	8	55%	Fifth in conference
1993	9	9	50%	Sixth in conference
1992	6	12	33%	Last in conference

EDUCATION & TRAINING

Providence College
Rhode Island

Master in Athletic Coaching   1991
Bachelor of Science: Sports Science: Providence College   1988 (Dual)
Bachelor of Arts: Education: Mathematics and Statistics   1988 (Dual)

AFFILIATIONS

National Coaches Federation—Member/Former Board Member, Springfield County Chapter
American Heart Association—Board Member—Springfield County Chapter

References upon Request

JANET RACE

1610 Donovan Hill Road
Upperville, Virginia 20184
Phone/Fax: (540) 555-1212
email@email.com

SENIOR-LEVEL COMMUNICATIONS EXECUTIVE
20 Years' High Visibility in Washington, D.C.
Best-Selling Author/Crisis Management Expert

Government, Media, Communications, and Public-Relations Specialist
Top-Level Speech Writer/Resource and Economic-Development Management

---

A **well-connected, achievement-driven Public Relations/Communications Executive** with outstanding qualifications in all phases of corporate/governmental communications, with particular emphasis on strategic crisis management. Spearheaded the public-relations efforts for national and international crises, including:

- Tylenol Crisis
- Three-Mile Island Crisis
- Teamsters/Government Takeover

HIGHLIGHTS OF EXPERIENCE

- Association-management executive for trade associations
- Spokesperson for International Union representing more than two million members and affiliate members
- Director of Public Relations and Congressional Liaison for the American Revolution Bicentennial Administration
- Presidential Appointment, Vice Chairman, National Parks Advisory Board, 1991 to 1995
- Appointed Vice Chairman, Presidential Inaugural Committees, 1969, 1981, and 1989
- Nominee, National Mediation Board, 1995
- Featured guest on *Nightline*, *The Today Show*, *Dateline*, and all network news, including CNN
- Speechwriter (White House and three U.S. Senators); best-selling author of *Devil's Pact: Inside the Teamsters*

PROFESSIONAL EXPERIENCE

SOUTHEAST THOROUGHBRED ASSOCIATION, Warrenton, Virginia   1992 to Current
Executive Director

Developed programs to enhance breeding of native thoroughbred industry while promoting racing in Virginia. Created and implemented high-impact programs and interfaced closely with industry leaders, breeders, government officials, and the legislature to meet association goals and mandates. Oversaw budget processes, administered state breeders' fund, directed educational seminars, spearheaded fundraising activities, and serviced association members.

- Increased membership 12% a year, adding $124,000 a year to new business efforts
- Reduced attrition rate by 8%—from 12% down to 4%, through improved member-service management
- Increased profit center revenue by 32% between 1999 and 2001 by successful target-marketing efforts
- Significantly improved bottom-line results by an average of 11% per year

INTERNATIONAL BROTHERHOOD OF TEAMSTERS, Washington, D.C.   1978 to 1992
Director of Communications/Executive Assistant to the President

Served as international spokesperson, fully responsible for all communications and media-relations efforts for the two million-member union and its affiliates. Managed a staff of 20 in producing all publications, educational and policy material, and other pertinent collateral information for the membership.

- Served as Executive Assistant to the President, and Director of Government Relations
- Served as Senior Assistant and White House Liaison for international union activities

(Page one of two)

142

Janet Race
Page two

PROFESSIONAL EXPERIENCE (Continued)

NATIONAL CAUSE, Washington, D.C.   1976 to 1978
Assistant Director/Vice President

Established efforts to promote U.S. international policies, commerce, and trade to enhance targeted causes with government, industry, and business leaders. Wrote speeches and directed press/communications efforts.

- Directed policy development and communications on domestic and international policy for national think-tank organization founded by Senators George Murphy, John Stennis, and others, including the late John Wayne

AMERICAN BICENTENNIAL ADMINISTRATION, Washington, D.C.   1971 to 1976
Director of Public Relations/Congressional Liaison

Contributing leadership role in developing and implementing all aspects of communications and public relations, including promotional planning, for the National Bicentennial Celebration. Liaison with Congressional members relative to administration and federal development and planning for national observance.

- Chief of the News Bureau, responsible for all press relations, publications and media development, marketing, and high-level speech writing

HILL AND HILL PUBLIC RELATIONS, INC., Washington, D.C.   1967 to 1971
Vice President/Account Executive

Directed government-liaison activities and public-relations campaigns for several major accounts, including Ernest & Ernest, American Airlines, The Wine Institute, Gillette, Owens Illinois, Miles Laboratories, Procter & Gamble, Continental Can, Zenith Radio Corp., and the New York Times.

- Developed crisis-management strategies for the Tylenol Crisis and the Three-Mile Island Crisis

EDUCATION

Bachelor of Arts: Communications, Journalism	George Washington University	1966
Associate's Degree: Political Science	Dartmouth College	1962
International Law and Foreign-Relations Studies	Georgetown/Catholic University	1966–67

AFFILIATIONS

Virginia Society of Association Executives   Public Relations Society of America
National Press Club   Who's Who in American Politics

REFERENCES

Senator John W. Warner (603) 555-1212   Congressman Tom Davis (603) 555-1213
Lawrence J. Brady (603) 555-1212   Richard Quinn (603) 555-1232

Fitz Abercrombie

98033 North Addison ▪ email@email.com ▪ Chicago, Illinois 60000 ▪ (212) 276-2293

COMPUTER TRAINING & TECHNICAL SUPPORT PROFESSIONAL

Sales Automation Marketing Network Support

Results-driven training and support specialist with proven record of achievement in computer training and technical support. Produced measurable results in sales force automation through training and support of sales reps in multiple divisions. Outstanding project management, technical, networking, training, and presentation skills. Extensive PC software experience:

▪ WordPerfect	▪ DOS	▪ Procomm
▪ Lotus 123	▪ Norton Utilities	▪ Laplink Pro
▪ Microsoft Excel	▪ cc:Mail	▪ Paradox
▪ Lotus Freelance	▪ Windows 95	▪ Microsoft Access

PROFESSIONAL EXPERIENCE

Technical Administrator   1994-Present
SHELTON HOMES, INC., Chicago, IL

Manage, support, troubleshoot, and maintain sales automation system for 2 major divisions of large homebuilding corporation. Provide onsite training and telephone support for multiple sales offices for general PC projects. Produce computerized/multimedia presentation materials for employee meetings and other functions. Involved in development, testing, and training of new software programs distributed throughout the region to additional users.

- Solely responsible for installation, training, and sales support of WinSell program, a Windows-based sales/prospecting program for the homebuilding industry, resulting in 37% increase in sales rep efficiency.
- Instrumental in diagnosing major system problem and implementing solution in regional office affecting 25+ users. Kept repair costs under budget and completed job in 50% of projected time.

Information Resource Specialist / Network Administrator   1991-1994
ALUMINUM RECYCLING ASSOCIATION OF NORTH AMERICA, Chicago, IL

Managed and maintained online electronic bulletin board system for 2500+ users. Supervised holding library and database, information acquisition program, and publication ordering system. Developed procedures and other in-house documents.

- Learned Novell Network system independently; promoted to system administrator and liaison to outside vendor support after 1 year.
- Trained and supported 40 employees during network upgrade and installation of WordPerfect.

Membership Coordinator / Trainer   1989-1991
AMERICAN ASSOCIATION FOR MENTAL RESEARCH, Washington, D.C.

Managed database of 8000 members for 16 divisions. Identified and solved problems related to annual meeting registration and management of general session meeting.

- Served as backup to computer manager and liaison to vendor support.
- Provided training and support to member associations during conversion to proprietary software system.

Fitz Abercrombie   Page Two

RELATED EXPERIENCE

Operations Assistant   1988-1989
MAJOR DOMO ENTERPRISES, INC., Washington, D.C.

> Supervised preshow activities and preexhibitor fact books and information sheets. Supervised convention hall personnel and onsite registration.

General Manager   1986-1988
JAMES RADISSON PROPERTIES, Washington, D.C.
Supervised hotel employees; managed accounts for hotels, condominiums, and private customers. Extensive computer operation and accounting.

Public Relations Intern   1986
CINCINNATI BLUE BIRDS HOCKEY CLUB, Cincinnati, OH

> Served as marketing liaison with local media, developed marketing strategies, compiled market analysis information, prepared statistical analysis of team performance for media distribution.

EDUCATION

Bachelor of Science Business Administration   1986
ILLINOIS STATE UNIVERSITY, Normal, IL
Financed 100% of educational expenses.

Additional Training:

- How to Teach People to Use Computers" (3 days), SoftBank Institute, Washington, D.C. 1995
- Understanding the Internet," National Seminars Group, Bethesda, MD 1995
- Computer Training & Support Conference," SoftBank Institute, Orlando, FL 1995
- Advanced PC Troubleshooting, Essential Seminars," Tysons Corner, VA 1994

References furnished upon request

JACKI D. SMITH

3045 Information Highway, Villa #B-6, Cyberston, Montana 23456
(750) 555-2345 • E-mail: jackismi@aol.com

PROFILE
- **Expertise in Information Systems Development.** Over 15 years' direct experience in the analysis - design - development - quality assurance - testing - and implementation of large-scale information systems for both private and government clients. Proficient in software, applications, and database development. Successful in aligning IS strategy and architecture with corporate mission. **Professional Trainer. Willing to travel, relocate, or accept contractual assignments.**

- systems analysis, integration, lifecycle	- client-server technology
- Wide Area & Local Area Networks	- multivendor environment
- strategic IS planning	- telecommunications integration
- configuration management	- technology security
- business disaster recovery	- cost reduction through technology
- operations and process reengineering	- Continuous Improvement
- Deming Management Method	- ISO-9000
- Statistical Process Control (SPC)	- MRP II utilization
- Total Quality Management (TQM)	- APICS-certified
- Just-in-Time (JIT)	- distributed processing
- technical training (all levels)	- university-level curricula design

SELECTED ACHIEVEMENTS

TWENTY-FIRST CENTURY TECHNOLOGIES, LTD.

PROJECT LEADERSHIP
- **Directed the strategic and tactical growth and development of a Wide Area Network** (WAN) consisting of over 125 nodes and incorporating DOS and UNIX-based systems. Mobilized special task force to determine feasibility and technical requirements for this project.
- **Participated in strategic network planning and special studies** to enhance network utility. Optimized network availability and performance of all network resources.
- **Defined and developed software standards and documentation.**

PROGRAM IMPLEMENTATION
- **Trained line and senior management** on use of microcomputers and installed software (introductory, advanced, and recurring classes). **Served as key technical adviser** to CEO and his direct reports regarding Information Technology issues.
- **Spearheaded and comanaged the search and implementation of a fourth-generation MRP II package.**
- Served in several critical **leadership roles:** (Chair) Emerging Technologies Steering Committee - (Co-Chair) Reengineering Strategies Committee - (Member) Project Team Mobilization.

PROCESS REENGINEERING
- **Modernized the company's Information Systems department** to meet current and future data processing, transmission, and communication requirements.
- **Significantly improved Department's ability to manage the network.** Standardized software and hardware applications which decreased user training and equipment acquisition costs.

ALLIANCE DATA & TELECOMMUNICATIONS SERVICES CORPORATION

COST REDUCTION
- **Saved company $1 million annually by automating the production planning process.** Designed/directed an Ethernet-based LAN (Local Area Network) system to use MRP II technology (all company plants and product lines).
- **Wrote software that forward and backward-scheduled shop floor operations** and introduced a Just-in-Time use of raw materials.
- **Restructured inventory management procedures** using a time-phasing approach which decreased storage costs and resulted in **$345,000 annual savings.**
- **Conducted company-wide systems training** on use of MRP II software - microcomputers - micro-to-mini communications - word processing - spreadsheet and database managers - development software.

JACKI D. SMITH   PAGE TWO

SELECTED ACHIEVEMENTS (continued)

UNITED STATES NAVY

PROJECT MANAGEMENT & COORDINATION
- **Provided end-user training and documentation of computer and security systems.** Designed and instructed in use of Wide Area Network. **Received several commendations for improvements to command-wide training management systems.**
- Streamlined mission planning and reporting processes through use of automation. Certified computer systems for the processing of classified information.
- **Authored numerous Naval training manuals and developed procedures** for aircrew qualifications, testing / scoring, performance measurement, and certification. Served as Flight Examiner and Instructor Pilot on naval ship the U.S.S. Connecticut.
- **Technically prepared 175-member crew** for qualifications in General Damage Control and Fire-fighting. **Designed curriculum and performance measurement tests.**

WORK HISTORY

- TWENTY-FIRST CENTURY TECHNOLOGIES, LTD., Quality, Montana (HIGH-TECH DIVISION OF FORTUNE 1000 TECHNOSTAT & AN IS0-9000-CERTIFIED ORGANIZATION) **Information Systems Manager** (10/87-present)

- ALLIANCE DATA & TELECOMMUNICATIONS CORP., Secret City, Montana **Manager, Innovation & Technologies Department** (8/84-8/87)

- UNITED STATES NAVY (prior to 1984)
  - **Lieutenant Commander: Honorably Discharged**
  - Training Director: Naval Conference Center
  - Recipient: Meritorious Service Medal (2)

EDUCATION
- **Master of Science - Systems Management** Montana State College of Technology, Secret City, Montana
- **Bachelor of Science - Computer Science** Montana State College of Technology, Secret City, Montana
- American Production & Inventory Management Certification: **Certified in Production & Inventory Management (CPIM)**
- Numerous continuing education workshops: detailed list upon request.

COMPUTERS & SYSTEMS PROFICIENCY

OPERATING SYSTEMS
- NOVELL Netware 2, 3 - IBM AIX 3.2, 3.4 (UNIX) - OS/2 version 3 - WINDOWS 2.0, 3.0, 3.1 - PCDOS & MSDOS versions 3.0 through 6.22.

PROGRAMMING LANGUAGES
- PROGRESS - "C" - BASIC - dbase III, IV - PL/1 - COBOL (ANSI & pre-ANSI) -FORTRAN (ANSI & pre-ANSI) - IBM Assembly.

APPLICATIONS
- Word processors: WordPerfect - Microsoft Word / Works - PCWrite.
- Spreadsheets: Excel - QuattroPro - Lotus 123.
- Database Managers: PROGRESS - Access - PCFILE - dBase II, III, IV.

COMMUNICATIONS
- Hyper Access - IPX and TCP/IP protocols - Procomm and Procomm Plus - Internet and other online services.

THOMAS GREEN

Permanent Address
153 Blue Bird Drive
North Fort Myers, FL 33321
(813) 555-8822
(407) 555-0011 (Fax)

Local Address
266 Fallen Oak
Miami, FL 933781
(407) 555-6633 (Home)
email@email.com

CONSTRUCTION MANAGER / SUPERINTENDENT

OVERVIEW: Over 25 years' experience in Construction, 16 years as Construction Manager/Superintendent. A successful record of working on small/large projects ($5 million to $153 million). A **qualified and competent professional** recognized for completing projects *on time and under budget.* Extensive **national/international experience.** A troubleshooter able to turn around troubled projects to meet challenging goals and objectives.

PROJECT EXPERIENCE:
- Water Treatment Facilities
- Subway Systems
- Large Concrete Placement
- Embassy Renovations/New Construction
- Piping
- Culverts
- Excavation
- Power Plants

Have worked on Defense Contracts governed by the U.S. Army Corps of Engineers, Alexandria, Egypt (1989-90) and Almaty, Kazakhstan (1994 - Present).

PROFILE:
* Well organized; able to effectively manage **multiple projects** simultaneously.
* A solid record of **working well with people** at all levels including government officials, laborers & expats and clients' representatives.
* A proven and *verifiable* record for **profit attainment.** Recognized for containing costs, meeting stringent schedules, and earning profits.

EXPERIENCE:

4/92 - Present
Bill Harbert International, Birmingham, AL (*Project Site - Almaty, Kazakhstan*)
QUALITY CONTROL MANAGER - Hired and selected to take over as Quality Control Manager in charge of the construction and renovation of the new U.S. Embassy in Kazakhstan ($62 million project). Reestablished good working rapport between the contractor and the U.S. Army Corps of Engineers. During this 8-month assignment, inspected all phases of construction, directed all preparatory meetings and assured that all products used met original specifications. Project was successfully completed in December 1994.

3/82 - 4/92
L.A. Water Treatment Corp., City of Industries, CA (*Project Site - Egypt*)
SITE MANAGER - Hired to complete a troubled project (Potable Water Treatment Facility - Provincial Cities Development Project, $22 million project). Finished the project in 5 months and supervised **Plant Start-up. Disinfected & Sterilized 25 kilometers of pipe.**

10/84 - 10/86
Howard, Harbert, Jones, J.V., Greensboro, NC (*Project Site - Egypt*)
AREA SUPERVISOR / CIVIL FOREMAN - Upgraded sewer & pump stations. In addition, worked on the construction of a $125 million fresh water treatment facility. Poured over 8,000 meters of concrete and completed the project on time and under budget. Used an innovative approach to solve a pouring problem by designing and fabricating a *"Tapered Wall-Tie"* to pour concrete against dead-head concrete.

EDUCATION:
Educational Institute of Pittsburgh, Pittsburgh, Pennsylvania
A.A. Degree: Architectural & Mechanical Design (1965-66)

MILITARY:
United States Marine Corps
Honorable Discharge - Rank of Sergeant; Marine Corps. Silent Drill Team. Top Secret Clearance for *White House Details* and Presidential Guard at Camp David.

- References Furnished upon Request -

Maria Schinn

907 Main Street
Rochelle Park, NJ 07662
(201) 555-5555 ▪ email@email.com

**WEB CONTENT
DEVELOPER
. . .
ONLINE
WRITER**

**New Media
Writing & Editing**

**Web Site Content
Development**

**Project Planning
& Management**

**Research &
Journalistic Writing**

**Production
Coordination**

**Digital Copyright
Issues**

**HTML Coding
& Visual Design**

Overview

Professional writer offering 7+ years' experience coupling expertise in leading-edge technologies with powerful online content development skills.

Blend in-depth understanding of e-commerce issues with powerful writing skills to create compelling, original content that reflects e-business missions and strategies.

Demonstrated talent for transforming abstract ideas into high-quality written communications. Concise writing style proven effective in capturing and holding Web browsers' attention.

Strong team player with consistent record of contribution in collaborative efforts with interface designers, HTML editors, marketing specialists, and strategists.

Detail-focused and organized; proven time management and multitasking skills in coordinating the completion of complex research and writing assignments.

Professional Experience

Senior Content Developer – Omnipoint.com, New York, NY   **1997 – Present**

Meet daily production deadlines, planning and developing online content designed to build community for this dot.com company. Confer with management to brainstorm and crystallize content ideas. Define specifications, scope, and resources, and coordinate a team of associate writers. Write, edit, and disseminate Web content and articles targeting a high-tech audience.

Selected Achievements:

Developed creative, timely, and relevant content that was instrumental in generating 76% expansion in readership and a 30% increase in average time spent at the site.

Wrote intriguing introductions to site channels that increased click-throughs 45% and fostered a sense of community by doubling reader participation in online discussions.

Conceptualized and wrote hundreds of well-received articles, including 2 national award-winning pieces that produced widespread publicity and a 15% increase in site traffic.

Journalist/Editor – New Media Communications, Rutherford, NJ   **1993 – 1997**

Authored 200+ journalistic and editorial articles focusing exclusively on technological advancements and societal impacts. Served as top feature writer and assisted with editing the weekly publication distributed to government and social service agencies.

Education

B.A., Communications and Journalism – Magna Cum Laude
Fairleigh Dickinson University, Rutherford, NJ – 1993

Trained and experienced with most Windows-based applications, including MS Office Suite (Word, Excel, Access, PowerPoint), WordPerfect, and Lotus Notes. Skilled in Web page development with MS FrontPage and Macromedia Dreamweaver.

LOIS LANE

1504 Ocean Reef, Jupiter, FL 33477

Telephone (407) 555-8978
email@email.com

Experience and education have provided excellent working knowledge in the following key areas:

Sales & Marketing	**New Business Development**
Market Analysis	**Seminars & Presentations**
Sales Forecasting	**Program Development**
Account Development	**Budget Planning**

Highly regarded for consistently achieving *superior sales results* through leadership, planning and effective implementation. Management style is to lead by action, assess the situation, and create consensus through effective communications.

Senior Groups & Meetings Manager

PALM BEACH COUNTY CONVENTION & VISITOR'S BUREAU, West Palm Beach, FL 1994 - Present
Joined the bureau, serving 37 Gold Coast communities (1 million population), to cover the association, incentive, and corporate markets in the Midwest, West Coast and Canada. Named Senior Sales Manager after three months of goal-exceeding performance. Presently direct the Mid-Atlantic region.

- In late spring, 1995, monthly goals for confirmed bookings were at 325%, and 80% for the calendar year.
- Arrange sales missions to major cities and familiarization trips for association leaders and corporate travel planners.
- Increased sales leads 46% for 1994/95 by executing a high-volume direct mail campaign aimed at targeted prospects.

Director of Convention Sales

FRESNO CITY & COUNTY CONVENTION & VISITOR'S BUREAU Fresno, CA 1984 - 1994
Played a key role developing aggressive short-term strategic marketing plans that recaptured Fresno's top ranking as a convention site during economic doldrums. Joined the Bureau as Membership Director. Named Senior Convention Sales Manager in 1988 and promoted to Director in 1990 for a Bureau serving a half-million population in Central California.

- Led the convention sales department in the reversal of a three-year downturn. Fresno moved from fourth place as a state, regional, and district convention site in 1989 to third in 1990 & 91, and second in 1992.
- Starting in 1989-90, which saw a $36.6 million decrease from the previous year, began producing consistent revenue increases, totaling more than $91 million, over four consecutive years.
- Increased sales leads to 207 in 1992-93 from 60 in 1989-90, with a corresponding 25% growth in actual bookings.
- Advanced average convention attendance by 50% and increased revenues to $38 million from $10 million.
- Launched a national athletic marketing program, resulting in 10 events and $7 million in future business.
- Successfully orchestrated several sales blitzes, one of which led to $3 million in future business.
- Earned the *Outstanding Achievement Award* in 1991 from the Western Association of Convention & Visitors Bureaus and *Business Associate of the Year Award* in 1993 from the American Business Women's Association.
- Presented talk, <u>*Getting More Business with Less Money and Fewer Staff Members*</u>, at the 1992 Annual Convention of the Western Association of Convention & Visitors Bureaus.

A.S. Degree Program - Business Administration

Fresno City College, California, 1984

Mark F. Denning

3592 Glenhurst Drive ▪ St. Louis Park, MN 55416 ▪ (952) 555-7821 ▪ markfdenning@email.email

SENIOR OPERATIONS, SALES, FINANCE & BUSINESS DEVELOPMENT EXECUTIVE
20+ Years' Management Experience Leading Medical Supply Distribution & Manufacturing ...
Seek COO opportunity to maximize business performance

Energetic, passionate and forward-thinking executive offering expansive, cross-functional, "multihat" qualifications and operations leadership expertise to build corporate value for diverse organizations. Experienced in start-ups, turnarounds, joint ventures, restructurings and mergers. Empowering, fair and high-expectation leadership style. Tenacious, with a strong belief that destiny is related to the faith and effort poured into life. Set high standards but can flexibly "roll with the punches" in the 21st century workplace. Management style focuses on matrix teamwork and clearly articulated mission and values for buy-in of all levels.

Value Offered

Strategic Visions & Mission Planning	Selling & Sales Management
Revenue Growth / Brand Identity & Market Positioning	Integration/Change Management/Culture Shift
Market Expansion & Growth	Team Building & Staff Leadership
Asset Productivity & Profit Margin Growth	Customer Care
Structure Simplification and Standardization	Efficiency & Technology Systems
Bargaining & Negotiations (Union, Buyer, Vendor, Government)	Articulate Communication & Relationship Building

Career Highlights

MEDSOURCE INDUSTRIES, INC. – Minneapolis, MN   2002 – present
Consolidated affiliate/$400 million joint venture of MedSource Industries, Inc. ($8 billion global manufacturer of medical devices, sterilants and water purification products), with Adamson Technologies and Zanic Resources, medical supply distribution and aftermarket sectors.

SENIOR VICE PRESIDENT: INTERNATIONAL
- Recruited as a senior executive change agent to manage pivotal integration of new joint venture partners. Maintain direct P&L responsibility for 39 global distribution branches (340 teammates) generating $225 million in revenues annually.
- As company officer, participate in long-range planning, business objectives, policies and procedures, human resource issues, operating budgets, capital expenditures, safety and partnership issues.
  Key Contributions:
  - ➤ Directed the international expansion, developing core technologies in hollow fiber membrane devices, chemical sterilants, dialysis solutions and electronics for kidney dialysis, open-heart surgery, endoscopy and pure water preparation.
  - ➤ Led the execution of an integration plan for the newly created joint venture partnership, completed within 30 days (exceeding 90-day challenge). Simultaneously exceeded year-end revenue and EBIT targets.
    - · Convinced top 50 customers to buy from the new company and its new service model.
    - · Reduced excess labor and delivery vehicles; consolidated redundant customer service centers from 40 to 6. Combined inventory and consolidated information systems to provide immediate and seamless service.
  - ➤ Planned, structured, orchestrated, negotiated and closed the sale of company's instrument division. Reduced overhead costs by more than $.5 million, while winning customer support throughout the transition.

ADAMSON TECHNOLOGIES, INC. – Minneapolis, MN   1993 – 2002
$800 million medical supply technologies and aftermarket distributor of customized dialysis, cardiosurgery, medical device reprocessing, biotechnology and filtration/separation products.
EXECUTIVE VICE PRESIDENT, SALES & SERVICE (1998 – 2000)
- Oversaw P&L, balance sheet and strategic planning for company, generating revenues of $190 million annually through 400 shops/service centers and 700 mobile service trucks in 40 states (1,200 teammates).
  Key Contributions:
  - ➤ Reorganized the reporting structure to local markets and led the implementation of "Market Power" to drive local brand identity and eliminate unnecessary management. Reduced annual overhead costs by $2.6 million.
  - ➤ Spearheaded and led an e-based sales management process and training for a national sales team of 80, successfully shifting sales and support to the company's focus on the local market.
  - ➤ Achieved the rollout of new point-of-sale software in 240 production shops within 9 months.

Mark F. Denning / Page 2 of 2 / Career Highlights (Adamson) continued

VICE PRESIDENT, PARK CORPORATION (1997 – 1998)
Adamson's distribution business, merchandising medical products to the healthcare industry.
- Recruited to drive and lead business growth through strategic and tactical direction.
- Maintained P&L/fiscal and strategic responsibility for company generating annual revenues of $175 million through 76 branches and 450 teammates in 35 states.
  Key Contributions:
  ➢ Served on the team that grew the company threefold, through prudent use of capital, in a business dominated by two OE manufacturing competitors with a combined market share over 40%.
    · Centralized all back office functions, including purchasing and inventory; minimized costs and capital employed.
    · Mentored key talent and empowered them to run the wheels of the business, securing managed, profitable growth and succession.
  ➢ Restructured purchasing patterns to optimize best pricing, while negotiating supply contracts of $60+ million/year.
  ➢ Established national sales training and account profitability programs, enabling the management team to make sound business decisions, customer by customer.

MANAGER / GENERAL MANAGER, PARK CORPORATION (1993 – 1997)
- Managed the single largest distribution branch and promoted to manage the facilities within the business unit's Northern Region, including the market and investment analysis and start-up of 6 new distribution facilities.
  Key Contributions:
  ➢ Led team that defined, selected and rolled out/installed centralized inventory management and point-of-sales software to 60+ distribution centers nationwide. Negotiated discounted pricing and training costs. This resulted in the most efficient use of capital, personnel productivity, and profit margins while creating the support structure for future growth.
  ➢ Accessed the reality of the interdependent business' financial economics and resource allocation. Initiated action to analyze two businesses separately.

SCANLON, INC. – Minneapolis, MN   1992 – 1993
   CONSULTANT / GENERAL MANAGER
- Retained to restructure the business for eventual sale to a primary competitor.

FARMINGTON MEDICAL SUPPLY – Farmington, MN   1986 – 1991
$4.3 million distributor of wheelchairs, lifts and seating systems for all applications throughout the Midwest.
   VICE PRESIDENT / OWNER
- Directed all sales activities. Oversaw family-owned company's transition.
  ➢ Secured partners and outside capital to recharge investment/reorganization. Business stabilized and thrives today.

EARLY CAREER INCLUDES PROGRESSIVELY RESPONSIBLE POSITIONS IN 5 YEARS:
   SENIOR MERCHANT: AGRICON - Minneapolis, MN (1983 – 1986)
- Traded foodstuffs worldwide with Intercorp Trading Company.
   REGISTERED REPRESENTATIVE: MORGAN STANLEY – Minneapolis, MN (1982 – 1983)
- Sold securities as a licensed agent by the SEC, NYSE and NASD, with Series 7 and 63 credentials.
   MANAGER, CITIBANK, N.A. – AbuDhabi, United Arab Emirates (1981 – 1982)
- Challenged to expand Citibank's commercial presence in this province without formally establishing a branch, to avoid confrontation of the Saudi Government mandate. Served on a 3-person team that defined the target market, prospected business with commercial entities, identified with that target, and helped manage banking activities with those businesses.
  ➢ Grew business from a $20 million Loan Production Office to $120 million (asset) business unit lending short-term and long-term. Business operated as self-funding (deposits) entity; issued Letters of Credit, Letters of Guarantee, and Forward Foreign Exchange Contracts. Business generated $1 million in EBIT within one year (1981 – 1982).

Education

E.M.B.A. and B.A. in Finance & Economics, Magna Cum Laude: COLUMBIA UNIVERSITY – New York, NY (1981)

▪ Varsity Hockey ▪ ISEC

PROFESSIONAL DEVELOPMENT
Strategic Management, Wharton School (1997)
Minnesota Executive Program, University of Minnesota (1996)
MENA CAD (Accelerated Program), Citibank, Glyfada, Greece (1982)

ROBERT MURRAY

880 King Street • New York, New York 10004
Office Number: (212) 555-6392 • Cell Number: (917) 555-8664
Fax number: 212-555-0468 • email@email.net

President and Chief Operating Officer

Seasoned professional, known for creative solutions and delivering bottom line results
A consistent record of delivering superior results over 20 years
Diversified background in communications and healthcare

Exceptional experience guiding and managing all business challenges encountered by fast-paced, aggressive, growth-oriented companies. Team spirited, hands-on management style with strong analytical and strategic planning expertise. Recognized for strategic, cutting-edge management decision skills with a consistent record of building and managing successful teams, enhancing growth, and increasing shareholder value.

Core Professional Strengths

Build and manage national sales/service organizations
Develop key strategic alliance and significant relationships
Corporate finance/expense management – P&L management
Negotiation complex agreements – government contracting

Develop winning sales strategies for global accounts
Creative, high-impact marketing/sales expertise
Real estate acquisitions and contract administration
Start-up, turnaround and growth leadership

Professional Experience

GGC ADVISORS, LLC., New York, NY   2003 to Current
Managing Partner
GGC Advisors, LLC, provides a comprehensive suite of Telecommunications and IT consulting services across all market segments. Consulting services include three primary practice areas: 1) Telecommunications infrastructure, inventory and assessment management solutions, carrier pricing and contract renegotiations support. 2) IT consulting and implementation specializing in IP Telephony/Unified Messaging solutions in all markets focusing on increasing user productivity, lowering operational costs, and improving our client's return on investment (ROI). 3) Outsource sales and marketing support to new and emerging telecommunications equipment and service providers with primary focus on providing sales support into the top 100 enterprise clients in the New York tri-state area

RICHARDS NETWORKS, Denver, CO   2002
Chief Operating Officer
COO of a high-speed wireless Internet technology purchased out of Chapter 11. Responsible for the recovery and reactivation of nationwide wireless assets.

- Hired team and successfully implemented the turnup of two markets for commercial services.
- Successful recovered intellectual assets required to turn up Micro-cell data network across 20 markets.
- Reduced operating expense required to turn up recovered markets by 40%. Significantly altering the cash flow required and the time in each market to be cash-flow-positive.
- Create unique "win-win" with municipalities who held the real estate leases on the wireless network assets through a "barter for services" exchange.

KRAMER COMMUNICATIONS, INC., New York, NY and Herndon, VA   1996 to 2002
COO, Kramer Sales and Service Organization (2001 to 2002)
Responsible for national sales and service organization including selling Kramer's portfolio of products and management of the existing customer base. P/L responsibility including credit, collections and capital expenditure recommendations

- Responsible for 240 representatives nationwide; consistently exceeded all net-new revenue objectives.
- Supported and grew $260 million+ in existing annual revenue across all size markets .
- Developed successful marketing techniques/themes - awarded for excellence by the marketing industry.

1

ROBERT MURRAY

Professional Experience

KRAMER (Continued)

- Effectively managed national customer service organization: lauded for superior customer support.
- Implemented 13 Federal Government service contracts - exceeded all SLAs
- Designed complex customer solutions that paired enterprise and legacy systems with innovative technical solutions to enhance the entire business process including e-business objectives.

President and Chief Operating Officer, Kramer Large Account Solutions (1999 to 2001)
Developed/managed Winstar's National Account Program, including Fortune 1000, government agencies, and carrier and enhanced service providers. Managed 350 sales, service, marketing, complex solutions, finance and legal support representatives.

- Supported over $650 million in annual revenue. Completed sales to over 100 national accounts, including 10 master service agreements. Executed over $500 million in enhanced service contracts.
- Awarded 13 Federal Government contracts valued at over $2.7 billion.

President and Chief Operating Officer, Kramer Wireless (1996 to 1999)
Led the design, implementation, construction and operations management of the first national fixed wireless telecommunications network in the top 20 U.S. markets. Provided innovative product and design solutions for local, long-distance, data and network services. Recognized by industry for best-in-breed technical solution and design. Managed 400 full-time employees nationwide.

- Employed effective cost management methodologies for budget of over $250 million.
- Directed engineering, construction, operations, systems, logistics and wholesale sales and services.
- Managed RE acquisition team, leasing over 1,200 building rights and roof top leases in under one year.
- Directed the design, construction and operational management of the first national amp; local telecommunication network utilizing 38ghz fixed wireless technology for their first 10 US markets.

DBT SERVICES, New York, NY   1991 to 1996
Senior Vice President Account Management
Managed and grew DBT's entire national account base. Responsible for over 200 account management and claims processing service representatives nationwide.

- Supported $1.8 billion in annual revenue across all markets.
- Bid and won over $1 billion in contracted revenues.

SPRINT TELECOMMUNICATIONS, New York, NY   1986 to 1991
Senior Director National Accounts Northeast Region
Implemented Sprint's first major account program. Responsible for 150 sales and service representatives nationwide. Supported over $200 million in annual revenue.

- Managed account teams that sold over $500 million in multiyear master service agreements, including Time Warner, Bristol Myers Squibb, North American Phillips, CBS, ABC, Estee Lauder and 18 additional contracts.
- Developed the first on-site accredited MBA program for telecommunications professionals at Fordham University.

Employment Prior to 1986

Northeast Regional Director	CARTER'S BUSINESS SYSTEMS, New York, NY	1981 to 1986
National Account Manager	SPRINT TELECOMMUNICATIONS, New York, NY	1980 to 1981

Education & Affiliations

Bachelors of Science; Education   PENN STATE UNIVERSITY
    All-American, Football

Board Member: Dungeon's Integrated Systems (Fortune 200)

References and Supporting Documentation Furnished upon Request

2

154

RITA BIRCH, J.D.

1111 Little Road
Cincinnati, OH 45237

RitaBirch@pool.com

Mobile: (513) 555-7707
Home: (513) 555-0133

CORPORATE COUNSEL / COMPLIANCE / MANAGEMENT

Integrating & Protecting the Needs of Business in Domestic & International Environments

Accomplished executive with 17 years' progressively responsible and diversified leadership experience in competitive professional environments. Successful track record in building international, national, state, and local alliances. Talented leader and motivator with highly effective interpersonal skills and a global outlook. Extensive legal experience with reputation for negotiating win-win scenarios. Articulate communicator with proven ability to leverage relations with state, federal, and international officials. Highly motivated, enthusiastic, and committed to professional excellence.

AREAS OF EXPERTISE

- Mediation/Negotiations
- Litigation Management
- International Business
- Proposal Development
- Budgeting & Cost Reduction

- Contract Drafting/Review
- Compliance/Regulatory Reporting
- Large-Scale Project Management
- Marketing/Advertising Regulation
- Public Relations Management

- Dispute Resolutions
- Federal/State Legislation
- Risk Management
- SEC Rules & Regulations
- New Business Development

CAREER PROGRESSION

WORTHINGTON GLOBAL HOLDINGS, INC. (www.worthingtonglobal.com) – Cincinnati, OH
[International arm of Worthington Life & Health, a $115 billion insurance/financial services organization and Fortune 200 company employing over 35,000 with a market presence in 37 countries.]

Country Integrator (05/2000 – Present)
Promoted and challenged to develop, direct, and prioritize international business initiatives and utilize resources to meet existing needs. Primary focus is to oversee and manage international projects, particularly the development, installation, and coordination of a universal operating model. Identify, define, and articulate to the home office the process and product needs of local countries and resolve various defined business requirements.

Prepare/implement project charters and administrative portion of country work plans. Identify/coordinate resources to achieve business objectives in local operating companies. Analyze issues of international law and coordinate resolution and compliance activities. Keep current on trends and issues impacting corporate business and strategies both stateside and abroad. Report directly to Administrative Officer, Global Holdings.

Areas of Accountability:

- Review various legal agreements and international legislation; prepare presentations from a legal prospective for use in business initiatives.
- Communicate universal model functionality, priorities, and versioning process to staff in international locations. Utilize global perspective to convey relevant corporate activities, priorities, and decisions.
- Establish and maintain business relations with international staff, particularly host country leadership.
- In Greenfield situations, research products/services from local target markets, select operating sites, and help set up resident infrastructure. Procure equipment/supplies, resolve connectivity issues, conduct lease negotiations, obtain insurance, and assist in recruitment/hiring of in-country staff.
- Lead and coordinate administrative and IT teams to successfully integrate new business abroad. Oversee and direct procedures, controls, testing, and training initiatives for operating business locations.

WORTHINGTON FINANCIAL (www.worthingtonlife.com) – Cincinnati, OH
[$96.5 billion holding company for Worthington Insurance Services, and its major operating subsidiary, Worthington Life Insurance Company.

Attorney, Project Development & Dispute Resolution (05/1999 – 05/2000)

Areas of responsibility were diverse and included providing legal counsel to project staff on numerous project development, dispute resolution, and training issues. Liaisoned with outside counsel to resolve legal issues and questions of law. Recruited, trained, supervised, and mentored staff attorneys and product experts. Conducted and managed oral hearings before legal counsel representatives to advocate claims resolution and relief determinations. Prepared written reports and summaries regarding claims valuations, suggested relief, and final dispositions.

Representative Contributions:

- Instrumental in resolution of major class-action lawsuit. Coordinated project management, litigation management follow-up and dispute resolution activities; trained, supervised, and administrated staff performance and astutely leveraged project team to successful settlement.

- Designed, developed, and implemented scoring guidelines/adjustment criteria, evidence analysis/review guidelines, a comprehensive scoring matrix, and other legal assessment instruments to streamline claims review and valuation processes and to establish relief for an anticipated 18,000 class-action lawsuit claims.

- Formulated, drafted, and structured a comprehensive appeals package for the purpose of contesting dispute resolution determinations.

Senior Compliance Analyst (01/1997 – 05/1999)

Scope of responsibilities included monitoring legal and regulatory developments, performing quality assurance and risk management activities, and researching/analyzing state and federal regulations in order to meet procedural and substantive annuity guidelines. Negotiated and facilitated the approval of various annuity products and associated sales materials with state regulatory agencies. Coordinated and drafted individual/group annuity contracts and related forms. Assisted in the development of products for new business and led projects for various business and state filing initiatives.

PROFESSIONAL PROFILE

EDUCATION & TRAINING

Juris Doctorate, Capital University College of Law, Columbus OH; 1997. Top 3% of Legal Research and Writing class. Admitted to practice law in Ohio and Federal District Court for the Southern District Court of Ohio.

Bachelor of Arts, Human Resources Administration, Saint Leo College, Saint Leo, FL; Honors Graduate — GPA 3.95. 1992

Legal Principles Claim Specialist (LPCS), American Educational Institute, Inc., Basking Ridge, New Jersey; Professional designation. 1999

HONORS & ASSOCIATIONS

- Selected for Nationwide Leadership Development Program 2000
- Nationwide Leadership Award – Project Buckeye; Third Quarter 1999
- Nationwide Teamwork Award – Project Buckeye; June 1999
- USAF Exceptional Performance Award recipient 1989, 1990, 1991, and 1992
- Communicative Skills Award recipient, Air Force Leadership School – 1987
- Awarded top-secret security clearance with the U.S. Government
- Member; American, Ohio State, and Columbus Bar Associations

DOLORES RAMIREZ, J.D.

578 Alma Rio
Cincinnati, OH 45237

Email: dramirez@data.com

Home/Office: (513) 555-0254
Cellular: (513) 555-3604

Summary

Versatile corporate legal professional with diverse experience as in-house counsel to Fortune 500 corporations and general counsel to government, commercial businesses, and nonprofit organizations. Known for creativity, resourcefulness, innovation, and timely completion of major projects. Highly skilled negotiator with a reputation for consistently achieving win-win scenarios. Private practice experience includes corporate transactional, administrative, civil and criminal litigation, trial and appellate practice and public sector law.

Competencies

- Corporate Transactional support

- Investment Management Agreements

- Intellectual Property Agreements

- Complex contract creation and negotiation

- Due Diligence and Executive Summaries of the same

- Memoranda of Understanding

- Joint Venture Agreements

- Nondisclosure Agreements

- Confidentiality Agreements

- Vendor and Supplier contracts

- Outsourcing contract negotiations

- Administrative and Regulatory order review

- Uniform Commercial Code (UCC) Articles 2, 2A, 3, 4, 4A, 5, 8 and 9

- Code of Federal Regulations (CFR)

- Federal Energy Regulatory Commission (F.E.R.C.) rulings and bulletins

- Securities and Exchange Commission (SEC) rulings and bulletins pertaining to public utilities

- Residential, commercial and Community Development planning policy

- Nonprofit corporation formation, acquisition of tax-exempt status, governance and policy

- Civil and Commercial Litigation, trial and appellate practice

- Bankruptcy (Chapters 7, 11 and 13)

- Recruiting, hiring and training

- Community Development Block Grant (CDBG) packages

- Criminal Defense

- Breach of contract and collection cases

- Wills, Trusts, and Estates

- Personal Injury Defense

- Civil Rights cases

Practice

Pan American Electric Power & Utilities – Cincinnati, OH
Nation's eighth largest electric utility with 38 power plants serving 4.9 million in 11 states, Australia, Brazil, China, Mexico, the Philippines, and the UK. Employs 26,376 and yields $13.6 billion.

Senior Counsel, Corporate Development (11/2000 – Present)

Provided general corporate transactional support, advice, and counsel to unregulated wholesale and retail marketing departments. Created/negotiated contracts, nondisclosure agreements, and other documents related to sale of power to industrial, commercial, and residential users. Reviewed/negotiated all vendor/supplier contracts, joint ventures, and management agreements. Key member of team performing due diligence for construction/purchase of cogeneration plants.

Led teams that negotiated numerous multiyear transactions valued up to $400 million. Negotiated outsourcing contracts for Mutual Energy Service Company's (a division of American Electric Power) billing/statement printing, lock-box agreement, third-party bill payment/collection agreement, and other service center contracts. Secured and directly managed assistance from outside counsel for projects undertaken by the unregulated retail marketing and business development units.

Reported to Senior Vice Presidents of Wholesale Marketing and Retail Residential Marketing departments, providing all requisite legal support (contract negotiation/drafting/review, creation of nondisclosure agreements, negotiation/review of

(Continued)

intellectual property agreements, administrative/regulatory order review). Researched and kept unregulated marketing units informed of legal ramifications of bulletins and rulings from the F.E.R.C, the SEC, in the CFR and the UCC.

Contributions:

- Crafted and negotiated multiyear master investment management agreements with ten separate national and international investment management firms for placement of AEP's $2+ billion ERISA Pension Trust Fund into Index and Fixed-Income Investment portfolios.

- Created and negotiated a multiyear, seven-figure bill and invoice master agreement to print and distribute 3+ million monthly utility bills, statements, and marketing materials.

- Negotiated and successfully resolved securities fraud matter that named AEP as a defendant.

- Crafted and negotiated multiyear, $5 million call center master agreement (with the telemarketing division of a Fortune 500 communications conglomerate) that allowed customers to receive accurate and timely answers to questions regarding utility bills and statements.

- Designed, structured, and negotiated a multiyear, $5+ million agreement involving U.S. Bureau of Fish and Wildlife to reforest 10,000 acres with hardwood trees that, over the next 70 years, will reduce atmospheric emissions of carbon dioxide and greenhouse gases.

- Served as in-house counsel for negotiations to construct a $400 million cogeneration facility for a Fortune 500 international chemical company.

CITY/COUNTY OF PHILADELPHIA – Philadelphia, PA
Nation's fifth-largest municipal corporation, providing governmental services to 3.5 million people in the tristate region of Eastern Pennsylvania, Southern New Jersey and Delaware.

Divisional Deputy City Solicitor (02/1990 – 08/2000)
Served as General Counsel to Director of Office of Housing and Community Development (OHCD). Provided legal review, analysis, and oversight to the Director, who was tasked to allocate $70 million in federal community development block grant monies leveraged to fund $250+ million of infrastructure rebuilding/replacement, low to moderate housing, and community development projects.

Supervised Deputy City Solicitor, Assistant City Solicitor, a paralegal, and two support personnel in reviewing, amending, and certifying proposed funding contracts of up to $50 million. Served as legal adviser to City's Trade Representative, advising project managers regarding compliance with Housing and Urban Development (HUD) regulations on expenditures of $200+ million in Federal funds for commercial and industrial development.

Reviewed, coordinated, and amended all CDBG proposed commercial and industrial project funding. Also advised the Director of Public Affairs on the text of publications, brochures, flyers, and other printed materials sent out by OHCD. Served as the in-house counsel to the Vacant Property Review Committee, tasked with selling/donating liened/abandoned property, and advising the Committee on the legality of such conveyances.

Contributions:

- Saved City $9 million in funding by mediating and resolving three-year-old dispute with HUD, which prevented a threatened cutoff or retroactive denial of previously spent monies for a $47 million commercial development. Dispute centered on whether the project qualified as a Community Redevelopment Project under Federal guidelines.

- Played instrumental role in moving toward resolution of a $3 million intercity agency dispute between school district and various agencies. Negotiated with Mayor's Office, Revenue Commissioner, City's Redevelopment Authority, City of Philadelphia School District and the City Solicitor's Tax Division.

Professional Profile

Academic: **Duquesne University School of Law, Pittsburgh, PA**
Doctor of Jurisprudence

University of Detroit, Detroit, MI
Bachelor of Business Administration/Finance
Honors: ***Blue Key Honor Society***
Dean's Award for Exceptional Performance

Admissions: **U.S. Supreme Court; U.S. Court of Appeals, Third Circuit; U.S. District Court for the Eastern District of Pennsylvania; U.S. District Court for the Western District of Pennsylvania**
Supreme Court and all subordinate Courts of the Commonwealth of Pennsylvania
Supreme Court of Ohio, *Corporate Status until August, 2003*

THERESA DERBY

1827-B America's Cup Blvd.
Newport, RI 02840
(401) 555-3001
email@email.com

CUSTOMER SERVICE PROFESSIONAL

PROFILE:
- More than 7 years' successful experience in Customer Service & Support with recognized strengths in account maintenance, problem-solving & trouble-shooting, sales staff support, and planning/implementing proactive procedures and systems to alleviate problems in the first place.
- Possess solid computer skills. Excellent working knowledge using both IBM and Mac systems; Lotus 1-2-3, Excel, WordPerfect, MS Word, CT DataTrac.
- Ability to train, motivate, and supervise Customer Service employees. A team player, acknowledged as *"Total Quality Customer Service Professional."*
- Develop plan, conduct audits and variance analyses, process payroll and payroll tax reports and filings, and maintain/update accurate inventories.

Synopsis of Achievements

Increased customer retention by 19%, from 72% to 91%
Reactivated 9 key accounts ($253K/year), utilizing persuasion/mediation skills
Proactive planning led to notable increase in morale in all departments
Created customer satisfaction survey, drastically reducing potential problems

EMPLOYMENT:
1990 - Present

Cellular One,   Newport, RI
Customer Service Representative
Work with 28 sales professionals covering 2 states (Rhode Island and Connecticut), responsible for over 3,800 individual and corporate accounts.

- Support sales reps in opening new accounts and upgrading existing service
- Quickly and effectively solve customer challenges
- Maintain quality control/satisfaction records, constantly seeking new ways to improve customer service

1985 - 1990

Daniel Southerland, Public Speaker,   Newport, RI
Client Support
Worked with nationally acclaimed trainer and public speaker in booking programs. Work entailed heavy cold canvassing, working with speakers bureaus, and following up on referrals.

- Instrumental in igniting revenues from $58K in 1985 to $686K in 1990
- Received *Red Ribbon Award* from National Speakers Bureau for fine work
- Helped position Southerland to land VP position with Pilzer Seminar Group

EDUCATION:
Southern New England Junior College, Providence, RI
Associate of Arts: Communications & Public Relations, 1985

REFERENCES:
Furnished upon request.

Denise Corriander

73 Dearborn Avenue, Chicago, IL 60613   (773) 555-6543   emailaddress@emailaddress.com

Career Summary & Focus

Data Mining Specialist – Developing Solutions for Online Relationship Marketing

Specialist in developing customer affinity through the design, implementation, and management of data mining solutions for relationship marketing applications. Full lifecycle experience on enterprise-scale data warehousing/mining projects. Strong team leader and results-focused manager. Capabilities include:

Data Warehousing, Mining & Reporting	Mass Marketing Communication Tools
Data Analysis & Knowledge Discovery	Systems Design & Development
CRM Technologies & Tools	Web-Enabled Decision Support Applications

Technical Qualifications

Extensive experience in design and construction of data warehousing and processing systems.
Oracle Certified Professional - DBA; extensive Oracle PL/SQL qualifications.
In-depth understanding of OLAP, data mining, and ad-hoc query tools.
Experienced in UNIX/Perl scripting; C and C++ software development abilities.
Highly proficient with most popular reporting tools – Actuate, Crystal Reports, and Cognos.
Advanced skills with data analysis applications – SAS and SPSS.
Deep understanding of CRM tools - E.piphany, Broadbase, and Siebel eConfigurator.
Knowledgeable in strategies for linking data to Web content management platforms.

Professional Experience

Manager of Data Mining, Guardian.com – Chicago, IL, 1997 – Present

Assessed, procured, and implemented the vendors, tools, and technologies that enabled and facilitated data warehousing, mining, and analysis for this startup dot.com.
Designed and provide ongoing management of the systems allowing one-on-one relationship marketing within an e-commerce space.
Evangelized the role of knowledge sharing within the organization; credited with successful promotion of intimate relationships with consumers.
Initiated real-time processing and presentation of data on the Internet; linked to Web content management platforms to create instantaneous, personalized product offerings.

Data Warehouse Engineer, Norcross, Inc. – New York, NY, 1995 – 1997

Analyzed and specified requirements for scalable databases, data mining, and reporting.
Designed, constructed, maintained, and modified Oracle/UNIX databases to meet needs.
Researched and evaluated emerging data warehouse techniques and tools; recommended cost-effective solutions for data mining and reporting.

Education & Training

M.S., Computer Science
New York Institute of Technology (1995)

B.S., Electrical Engineering
Boston University (1993)

Associations & Memberships

Association of Database Developers,
Member (1995 – Present)

Customer Relationship Management Association, Member (1995 – Present)

43—DATA WAREHOUSE MANAGER

deborah lorenz .... data warehouse manager

101 W. 10th Avenue, Denver, CO 80201...e-mail@e-mailaddress.com...303.555.1010

core competencies...

- Data Warehouse Manager offering 10 years of experience and in-depth knowledge of the functional and data needs of e-businesses.

- Data warehouse development experience incorporates skills in programming, analysis, architecture, and project management. Expertise in high-level and detailed system design, requirements gathering, logical and physical data modeling, development, and implementation. Expert knowledge of data modeling in ERP and other major application areas.

- Well-versed in Oracle (Oracle Express, Oracle Reporter, Oracle Financial), Oracle tools, and Erwin products. Data migration experience using Informatica, C++, Java, Corba, multi-dimensional database, JavaScript, Oracle Web server, and Java. Exceptional use of CASE tools as part of an overall development effort.

- Extensive knowledge of DBMS: Oracle RDBMS, SQL, PL/SQL, STAR Schema Modeling. Experienced in UNIX operating system, Microsoft PC operating systems including NT, desktop productivity software, and client/server system architecture.

- Proven ability to assemble and mobilize project teams, building consensus among multidisciplinary technical and functional teams in the rapid development and implementation of data warehousing solutions. Recognized by managers and colleagues as a strong, positive leader and a sharp strategic thinker.

experience...

amazon.com, Denver, CO
Data Warehouse Manager, 1995-Present

- Drive the strategic vision and realization in the evolution from centralized data warehouse to distributed data marts. Report to divisional IT management with accountability for global processes. Manage a budget of $5.6 million.

- Provide guidance to software development teams on the use and purpose of data warehouses. Direct a team of seven data warehouse developers/analysts in the daily operations of the corporate data warehouse. Oversee all aspects of the warehouses, including data sourcing, data migration, data quality, data warehouse design, and implementation.

- Scope, plan, and prioritize multiple project deliverables, based on data warehousing dependencies and changing business needs. Develop project plans, identify and fill project resource needs, and manage projects to on-time, on-budget completion.

- Influence toolset and business needs assessment. Lead the selection of third-party software; manage vendor relationships. Successfully manage multiple projects in the design and implementation of warehouse functionality and interfaces.

Colorado Department of Revenue, Denver, CO
Data Warehouse Architect, 1990-1996

- Translated an enterprise data model, created dimension and fact tables to support budgeting, financial planning, analysis and data ware systems, in collaboration with the DBA and Data Steward.

- Determined database/data mart business requirements. Created the logical and physical database/data mart design for Relational and OLAP Data Warehouse environment.

education...

Master of Science, Data Warehouse Management, University of Denver, Denver, CO

Bachelor of Science, Computer Information Systems, University of Colorado, Boulder, CO

DIANA PACE, DDS, MSPH _____

864 East 19th Street • Fort Lee, New Jersey 07024
(201) 555-8638
email@email.com

PERSONAL PROFILE

By nature a powerful, analytical, scientifically disciplined professional seeking an opportunity to utilize demonstrated strengths in the public health sector. Superior technical knowledge, doctor/patient relationship, methodical analysis and research in a biomedical environment.

EDUCATION

DOCTOR OF DENTAL SCIENCE (DDS), December 1980
School of Dentistry, Federal University Espirito Santo
Vitoria Espirito Santo, Brazil

MASTER IN REMOVABLE PROSTHODONTICS, 1985
Thesis: Semi Rigid Prosthodontic Unilateral
Dental Conference in Guarapary, E.S. Brazil

MASTER IN SCIENCE IN PUBLIC HEALTH, 1992
University of Alabama at Birmingham, Birmingham, Alabama
Thesis: "Prevention of Caries in Pit and Fissure"
International Dental Public Health

Resident in General Dentistry, 1981 - 1982
Botafogo Polyclinic, Rio de Janeiro, Brazil

Dental Sculpture, 1981
School of Dentistry Federal University of Rio De Janeiro, Brazil

Dental Nutrition 1100, Six Hour Credit, 1992
Institute for Natural Resources, Miami Florida

CAREER PATH

THE METROPOLITAN ARES OF ESPIRITO SANTO'S CAPITAL, Vitoria, E.S. Brazil   1984 - 2003
Dentist
Worked as a dentist in a general practice. Spent three years training in prosthodontics. Quickly increased number of patients with a very high retention and loyalty level.

SAO JOSE RURAL HOSPITAL, Colatina, E.S., Brazil   1985 - 1986
Case Manager
Screened and referred patients to appropriate clinics. Followed up on case studies of the prevalent dental and medical communicable illnesses of patients seen and treated at the hospital. Processed patient information, and maintained active records to assist the appropriate clinic on the research data bank.

SAO JOSE RURAL HOSPITAL, Colatina, E.S., Brazil   1985 - 1986
Part-Time Health Educator
Provided technical assistance and training to patients in the areas of dental and physical health. Conducted lectures on matters such as hygiene, vaccination, nutrition, and the importance of breast feeding.

UNIVERSITY OF ESPIRITO SANTO, Vitoria, E.S., Brazil   1979 - 1980
Student Instructor
Supervised and assisted dental students with diagnostic, treatment plan, laboratory work, and orientation during their work with patients. Graded each student.

44—DENTIST (CONT.)

DIANA PACE • (201) 555-8638 • email@email.com

(CAREER PATH CONTINUED...)

UNIVERSITY FEDERAL, E.S., Brazil　　　　　　　　　　1979 - 1980
<u>Part-Time Assistant Professional/Instructor</u>
Taught dental procedure techniques. Assisted with diagnostic and evaluation treatment plan during treatments and laboratory assignments. Graded each student.

CERTIFICATIONS

CERTIFICATE IN INTERNATIONAL EPIDEMIOLOGY OF AIDS, 1993
University of Miami School of Medicine, National Institute
of Health, Forgaty International, Miami, Florida

ADDITIONAL TRAINING

Worked as Pediatric Dentist, Education, Public Health

Director of Laboratory Safety for Nutrition Laboratories,
Department of Epidemiology and Public Health

INTERNSHIP/CLINIC

Department of Public Health, Internship 325 Hours
Florida State Department of Public Health, Miami Florida

Visiting Research Associate in Dental Public Health
University of Alabama at Birmingham, Birmingham, Alabama

PROFESSIONAL AFFILIATIONS

American Dental Association　　　　　　　Brazilian Dental Association
Espirito Santo Dental Association　　　　Rio de Janeiro Dental Association
Paulista Dental Association　　　　　　　American Dental Association
Federal Dental International　　　　　　　West Dade Dental Society
American Academy of Cosmetic Dentistry　　Hispanic Dental Association
American Association of Public Health Dentistry

PUBLICATIONS

Researched and Wrote <u>Biomaterial on Microleage in Gallium</u>, Presented March 11-15, 1992
Meeting AADR in Boston, Massachusetts

Presented a Panel <u>Removal Prosthodontic with Free Unilateral</u>
6th Dental Meeting of Espirito Santo, April 18-21, 1986

LANGUAGES

Portuguese, English, Spanish; read and comprehend Italian

BRETT MICHAELS

555 Sherman Avenue   Brentwood, New York 11111   (631) 555-3211   BrettMichaels@grocery.net

Position of Interest: **Regional Director of Procurement**

Progressive career combines well-rounded experience in the broadline distribution of fresh produce, grocery, and frozen product categories, leading to current role as Director of Foodservice Sales.
➤ Expertise in retail management and wholesale distribution across foodservice and the airline catering industry.
➤ HACCP-trained with a certifiable knowledge of food storage and handling guidelines on the distributor side.
➤ Record for delivering sustainable revenue and profit gains within competitive regional markets.

Vendor Relations	Logistics & Transportation	Strategic Sales Planning
Product Acquisition	Competitive Bidding	Performance Measurement
Account Management	Contract Negotiation	Team Building and Leadership
New Business Development	Proposal Development	Management Reporting

PROFESSIONAL EXPERIENCE

Long Island Produce, Inc., Brentwood, New York, 1995 – Present
DIRECTOR, CORPORATE FOODSERVICE SALES
ACCOUNT MANAGER, LONG ISLAND AIRLINES
Total sales volume $75 million

Report directly to CEO and COO, in charge of regional sales operations for this major northeast produce distributor, and one of Long Island's first to receive HACCP certification.

- Positioned organization to compete as a leading distributor for the Long Island market with the introduction of contract sales and purchasing agreements.

- Drive a customer-focused sales organization through leadership and field supervision of CSR teams and route operators servicing foodservice vendors across travel, hospitality, and healthcare sectors.

Significant Contributions

➤ Led the account acquisition of a second casual dining chain with eight Long Island locations, realizing an increase in annual sales of $½ million (2002).

➤ Secured a $6 million contract with Long Island Airlines (LIA), assuming concurrent role as Account Manager for more than two years. Surpassed LIA's service expectations through hands-on leadership of Airline Account Managers assigned to nine LAG, JFK, and EWR airport-based locations (1998-2003).
- Achieved a 97% fill rate, and below 2% rejection rate, based on a weekly distribution of 6,500 cases.
- Enforced strict adherence to regulatory food handling and storage guidelines through implementation of a HACCP plan at Long Island Best, customer/employee education, and records management procedures.
- Coordinated annual audits with American Sanitary Institute.
- Currently provide backup support for LIA during periods of product availability and quality deficiency.

➤ Grew existing national casual dining chain account by 120% with the expansion of local distribution operations to regional level, reaching annual sales volumes of $1.1 million from $½ million (1997).
- Achieved six consecutive renewals from 1996 to 2003; favorably on track for January 2004.
- Negotiated purchasing agreements with growers, allowing for stabilized costs, consistent quality, and projected pricing on key menu items year-round.
- Maintain continuous interaction with internal/external contacts to monitor customer preferences and ensure order fulfillment of hard-to-find gourmet, specialty, and culturally specific food products.

(Continued)

BRETT MICHAELS

Page Two

Professional Experience
Continued

LI Partner Produce Co., Inc., Brentwood, New York, 1983 – 1995
OPERATIONS MANAGER
Total sales volume over $10 million

Served as second in charge to the Owner and CEO of this well-established foodservice distributor following a long-standing tenure in front-end and back-end positions of increased responsibility.

- Held full accountability for Sales, Procurement, and Transportation operations of fresh produce, groceries, and frozen products, including seafood, juice, and dietary supplements, across local and regional markets.

- Supervised fifteen employees across Warehousing, Route Management, and Accounting departments.

- Provided drivers with hands-on leadership and field training in areas of direct sales strategies, customer relations, and general business management.

- Planned, budgeted, and scheduled labor and equipment requirements to support the logistical management of broadline distribution operations.

Significant Contributions

➤ Steered company in the direction of broadline distribution, driving new business growth to $1.7 million in annual sales, expanding frozen food category with the introduction of grocery and frozen dietary supplements to accommodate a changing customer base.

➤ Merged business with LI Partner Produce, a nationally leading Long Island-based retail distributor (1995).

➤ Secured chain account with National Casual Dinning, serving as leading distributor for ten locations throughout the Long Island market with increased annual sales of $½ million.

➤ Negotiated and won a competitive contract bid servicing 35 nursing homes and four medical centers, successfully penetrating the healthcare sector and expanding distribution with annual gains of $2.5 million.

EDUCATION

State University of New York at Stony Brook
Bachelor of Arts, Communications, 1993

COMPUTER SKILLS

Windows 98 / UNIX; MS Word, Excel, Power Point, Publisher; Internet research

CAROLYN MARTIN

5987 Wadleigh Falls Road ▪ Boston, MA 02114
Phone: (617) 555-4536 ▪ Fax: (617) 555-3214 ▪ E-mail: emailaddress@emailaddress.com

DISTANCE TRAINER ▪ INSTRUCTIONAL DESIGNER ▪ CURRICULUM DEVELOPER
Computer, Internet, Video, & Telecommunications Technologies

Technically sophisticated professional well qualified by 10+ years' experience for creating and facilitating high-quality, high-impact internal/external educational solutions using innovative technologies. Rare depth and breadth of experience with distance learning tools and proven abilities in applying advanced technologies to enhance adult learning. Skilled in collaborating with subject matter experts to enhance course content and ensure technical accuracy. Extraordinary written and verbal communication skills. M.Ed., Educational Technology.

AREAS OF EXPERTISE

Computer- & Video-Based Training (CBT/VBT)	Instructional Systems Design (ISD) Methods
Web-Based Training Creation	Adult Education Needs & Theories
Online Course Development & Facilitation	Multimedia Authoring & Visual Design Concepts
Instuctor-Led & Self-Paced Training Delivery	Training Program Evaluation & Quality Standards
Curriculum & Course Materials Development	Project & Program Management

EXPERIENCE HIGHLIGHTS

DISTANCE EDUCATOR / ON-LINE COURSE DESIGNER   DXE Internet Training, Inc., New York, NY 1996   Present

Joined this cutting-edge Internet and Web-based training firm during the start-up phase. Manage and training projects from conception through delivery. Develop and design custom technology-based course content, lesson plans, and training materials for diverse customers, including major corporations, small e-business ventures, and government agencies. Teach and facilitate both technical and nontechnical courses using a variety of distance training delivery methods.

Key Achievements:

Combined expertise in instructional design methodologies, adult learning theories, and advanced technologies to create more than 30 online courses. Conferred with clients to assess needs and developed distance educational strategies and solutions successful for both internal and external training purposes.

Applied multimedia authoring and Web design tools such as MS FrontPage, PowerPoint, Dreamweaver, and NetObjects Fusion to create dynamic training and workshop materials proven through analysis of evaluation data to increase student learning and retention 24%.

Generated 16 new corporate training accounts valued at more than $1.2 million through referral and add-on business. Built solid client relationships and a reputation for ability to quickly create courses that consistently surpass quality and effectiveness objectives.

Led Web-based training on diverse subjects and utilizing both instructor-led and self-paced delivery methods. Interacted with students in realtime during scheduled online meetings. Facilitated self-paced study through e-mail correspondence and coordination of Web activities.

Achieved consistent 99% instructor effectiveness ratings through surveys of students' and educational sponsors' satisfaction. Overachieved goals for students' completion of self-paced study courses, with 92% of students finishing all coursework and examinations.

Introduced the use of Internet telephony as a cost-effective alternative to traditional long-distance student/instructor conference calls. Improved student communication and interaction by implementing and managing Web discussion forums and instructor moderated e-mail distribution lists.

(Continued)

CAROLYN MARTIN Page 2

DISTANCE TRAINER/CURRICULUM DEVELOPER – School of Lifelong Learning, San Diego, CA   1991 – 1996

Developed and taught coursework on a vast range of subjects for this accredited correspondence school specializing in home-study certification for adult students located nationwide. Researched and consulted with experts on topics spanning a wide range of industries and professions. Created and implemented curricula and lesson plans, authored course content, and designed training and evaluation materials.

Key Achievements:

Conceptualized and produced critically acclaimed multimedia computer- and video-based training modules that built student interest and are credited with increasing revenues 18%

Initiated the use of Web-based technologies that enhanced student/instructor communication while capitalizing on cutting-edge technologies to outpace the competition and establish the school as a pioneer in this area.

Exploited learning opportunities on the Internet by revising coursework to include Web-based activities; dramatically improved students' self-reports of learning and retention at a minimal cost to the school.

Provided guidance to students in completing self-paced training courses; counseled and instructed students needing special assistance and evaluated performance at the completion of each unit. Ranked consistently as the distance trainer generating the highest student satisfaction rate.

SALES TRAINING COORDINATOR, RMS Technology, San Diego, CA   1989 - 1991

Rejuvenated the sales training department of this premier telecommunications equipment manufacturer. Reengineered educational methodologies and processes, instituted department goals, and established training certification programs. Created a new training methodology that refocused emphasis to build consultative and solution sales competence.

Key Achievements:

Transformed the sales process by empowering the sales force with the knowledge and tools to assess customers' business needs and meet requirements through product solutions. Drove a 112% increase in sales.

Encouraged expansion into emerging telecommunications markets worldwide by creating special monthly workshops that introduced and familiarized the sales team with various industry segments.

Designed and developed a precedent-setting multimedia sales training module that taught the sales force both basic and advanced selling skills. Launched and delivered the module at a national sales conference.

Formulated and deployed an innovative customer training program on a new telecommunications switch. Successfully transferred technical knowledge and played a primary role in establishing top market positioning.

EDUCATION & TRAINING

M.Ed., EDUCATIONAL TECHNOLOGY, cum laude –1995
University of California, San Diego

B.S., BUSINESS ADMINISTRATION, MINOR IN COMPUTER SCIENCE – 1989
University of New Hampshire, Durham

Extensive training and experience with PC applications; advanced user of MS Office Suite (Word, PowerPoint, Excel, Access, Outlook), MS Internet Explorer, and Netscape Communicator. Skilled with multimedia authoring tools such as FrameMaker, Authorware, Director, and Dreamweaver, and Web design tools including HTML, MS FrontPage, NetObjects Fusion, and Lotus Domino Designer.

Member, Distance Education and Training Council

DOUGLAS DRAKEFORD

119 Old Stable Road
Lynchburg, Virginia 24503
(804) 555-4600
email@email.com

DISTRIBUTION OPERATIONS / WAREHOUSING / TRANSPORTATION EXECUTIVE
Building Profitable, Efficient & Quality-Driven National Logistics Operations

Well-qualified executive with 21+ years' experience in the strategic planning, development, staffing, budgeting, and management of large-scale distribution operations. Expertise includes:

- Multi-Site Operations Management
- Transportation Planning/Operations
- Carrier Selection/Negotiations
- Equipment Acquisition/Asset Management
- Human Resource Affairs/Labor Relations
- EDI/Supplier Partnerships

- Materials Planning/Management
- Capital Project Management
- Facility Design/Specification
- Budgeting/Financial Affairs
- JIT/Quick Response Inventory
- OSHA/DOT Regulatory Affairs

Managed up to 22 distribution sites supplying 130 sites nationwide with an inventory valued at $140+ million and a 140-vehicle fleet. Captured multi-million-dollar cost savings through efficiency, productivity, quality, and safety improvements.

PROFESSIONAL EXPERIENCE:

Senior Partner   1992 to Present
PENSKE TRUCKING, Lynchburg, Virginia

Recruited by executive team of this full-service transportation management firm to provide strategic and tactical leadership for an aggressive business growth and diversification program. Company specializes in the design and delivery of customized logistics operations to reduce costs of product acquisition, transportation, and warehousing for client companies.

Manage client projects from initial consultation, through a comprehensive service improvement, cost reduction and analysis program for design, development, and oversight of logistics operations. Evaluate existing logistics operations and integrate within newly-established programs. Analyze efficiencies of existing warehousing, fleet, and traffic management processes to determine alternative paths of supply management. Provide on-site training to company personnel and personally negotiate carrier price and service contracts.

- Won nine major traffic management contracts which generated over $1 million in revenues.

- Spearheaded three major logistics projects with full responsibility for design of turnkey warehousing, distribution, fleet, and logistics operations.

Vice President of Distribution   1978 to 1991
THE HOME CENTERS, INC., Lynchburg, Virginia

Senior Operating Executive responsible for the strategic planning, development, and management of a regional distribution program servicing 167 home centers in 10 states throughout the Eastern U.S. Total revenue volume exceeded $650 million. Total SKUs of approximately 20,000 items.

Scope of responsibility included five distribution centers, a 100-tractor private fleet, 400 personnel, a $31 million inventory and the entire domestic/import traffic management program. Managed a $17 million annual operating budget, administered all DOT and OSHA regulatory compliance programs, and introduced a complete safety, health, quality, and productivity improvement plan. Directed distribution, operations, purchasing and vendor management programs.

Conducted ongoing operational analyses to maximize operational efficiencies through redesign of warehousing facilities and realignment of regional distribution network. Analyzed cost factors to determine the need for facility expansion, closure and/or relocation. Negotiated contracts with common carriers to reduce transportation costs and administered union contract agreements for all employees.

DOUGLAS DRAKEFORD   *Page Two*

THE HOME CENTERS, INC. *(Continued):*

- Created an innovative cross-docking program in cooperation with major suppliers that reduced annual product acquisition costs by more than $15 million.

- Introduced a proactive program for inventory control that reduced shrinkage from $1.4 million to only $250,000 within two years.

- Consulted with professional firm to design and implement leading-edge computer technology for the optimal replenishment method for each SKU category.

- Implemented JIT and quick-response inventory and stock replenishment programs that resolved previous problems with merchandise distribution and provided adequate on-hand inventory at all 165 retail locations.

Assistant Vice President of Corporate Distribution   1970 to 1977
BLOOMINGDALES, Lynchburg, Virginia

Promoted from Director of Distribution to Assistant Vice President within one year of hire with responsibility for 22 distribution centers (3 million square feet), 1100 employees, 140-vehicle fleet, $140 million inventory, and $23 million annual operating budget. Directed stock replenishment and merchandise distribution (87,000 hard and soft goods) to 130 stores in nine states. Total revenues exceeded $1 billion.

- Launched a series of aggressive cost reduction initiatives that saved over $9 million in annual expenses. Realized savings through redesign of existing warehousing and transportation programs, negotiation of discounted purchasing and service agreements, realignment of staff requirements, and improved operating policies and procedures.
- Initiated and secured ICC approval for a wholly owned subsidiary contract carrier. Reduced annual costs to the corporation by $2.5 million through savings in payroll and equipment costs concurrent with a significant decrease in union exposure.
- Restructured the entire distribution network, consolidated operations, and eliminated four distribution centers for a net annual savings of more than $6.5 million.
- Negotiated favorable collective bargaining agreements with three Teamsters local unions and the International Ladies Garment Workers Union.

Traffic Manager / Customer Relations Manager   1966 to 1969
RCA-WHIRLPOOL DISTRIBUTOR, Lynchburg, Virginia

Supervised inbound traffic, public warehousing, customer delivery operations, dealer/customer relations, and warranty/nonwarranty repair programs. Facilitated significant improvements in the productivity, efficiency, and quality of operations.

EDUCATION: **Bachelor of Science / Business / Summa Cum Laude,** Lynchburg College   1994
                   Bachelor of Arts / Psychology, Liberty University   1966

Highlights of Continuing Professional Education:

- Traffic Management, Liberty University
- General Transportation Management, Liberty University
- Computer Applications in Distribution, American Management Association
- Warehouse Layout, American Management Association
- Materials Handling Management, International Materials Management Society

PROFESSIONAL AFFILIATIONS: American Management Association
                                     Council of Logistics Management
                                     International Materials Handling Society
                                     Warehouse Education & Research Council
                                     Private Carrier Council
                                     American Trucking Association
                                     Virginia Motor Truck Association

48—ELECTRICAL ENGINEER

SHANNON YATES

15857 60th Street North
Austin, Texas 78620
(512) 555-1212
email@email.com

ENTRY-LEVEL / INTERNSHIP
Electrical Engineering

Utilizing Outstanding Technical & Problem-Solving Skills
Currently Enrolled in Electrical Engineering Curriculum

A highly dynamic, team-spirited, and results-oriented individual seeking *entry-level or intern position in the area of power sources and systems as an electrical engineer trainee* while attending Austin Community College. Highly dependable with a strong desire to learn, contribute, and make a difference.

AREAS OF STRENGTH

Technical problems solving and troubleshooting	Logical reasoning and deduction
Maintenance and repair (grounds and equipment)	Purchasing and inventory control
Statistical analysis; factual recall and evaluation	Staff training and development
Communication and rapport-building skills	Organization and time management
Project planning and coordination	Customer service and quality control

■ Computer Skills: Microsoft Office 2000 (Word, Excel, Access) and Internet Research & Applications

EDUCATION

PALM BEACH COMMUNITY COLLEGE, Lake Worth, Florida
Bachelor of Science: Electrical Engineering, In Progress (EGD: Winter, 2002)

Selected Coursework:

Calculus	Chemistry I and II	Environmental Conservation
Trigonometry	Biology	Microcomputer Applications

HIGHLIGHTS OF PROFESSIONAL EXPERIENCE

- More than six years of working in electrical engineering (helping father in his engineering business)
- Utilizing solid technical and maintenance skills, ensuring proper maintenance and care of equipment
- Assisted in the automation/computerization of Stellar Equine Center – installed retail and inventory software
- Selected as lead project engineer for college project – junior year

CHRONOLOGY OF PROFESSIONAL EXPERIENCE (While Attending School)

Southgate Electrical Engineering Group, Austin, Texas **Electrical Engineering Apprentice (part-time and summers)**	1996 to Current
Stellar Equine Center, Austin, Texas **Sales Representative – Horse Trainer (Summers)**	1990 to Current

References and Supporting Documentation Furnished upon Request

SEAN H. RYAN

2578 South Haverhill Road
Rumney, New Hampshire 06222

Email: email@email.com
Telephone: (603) 555-1212

CERTIFIED ELECTRICIAN
12 Years' Professional Experience—Residential, Commercial, & Industrial

Loyal, Dependable & Trustworthy/Outstanding Technical Skills
Customer-Service Specialist/Excellent Training and Supervision Skills

---

A highly qualified, dedicated, technically skilled Electrician recognized as a team player seeking to contribute to and grow with a progressive and innovative company/organization.

AREAS OF STRENGTH

Basic electronics	Interior/exterior lighting	OSHA safety and regulatory compliance
Energy management	Diagnose/troubleshoot problems	Employee supervision
Project management	Communication skills	Customer service/quality control

EDUCATION/TRAINING/CERTIFICATIONS

CERTIFICATIONS:

Red Badge Certification	Thermolag Certification	Fire Watch Certification
"Hazmat" Certification	Respiratory Protection Certification	CPR and First Aid Certification

FORMAL TRAINING:

J.A.T. C., West Palm Beach, Florida
Journeyman Wireman, 1995 (5-Year Joint-Apprenticeship Curriculum, 8,000 on-the-job hours)

❏ Approved for work in nuclear facilities.

PROFESSIONAL EXPERIENCE

RUSSELL-THOMAS, Plymouth, New Hampshire **Master Electrician**	1995 to Current
FISK ELECTRIC, Medley, New Hampshire **Electrician**	1993 to 1995
NPS ENERGY SERVICES, Harrisburg, Pennsylvania **Foreman/Electrician (Seabrook Nuclear Power Plant)** **(Temporary Assignment—Requested by NHDE)**	1997 to 1998

❏ Recipient of numerous safety awards for safe workmanship.
❏ Worked as "Job Steward," acting as a liaison between employees and contractor.
❏ Performed the electrical work in an $11 million "smart house" in Plymouth.
❏ Worked in the Control Room and in the Containment Building at the Seabrook Nuclear Power Plant.
❏ Installed security and data systems for Barnett Banks throughout Northridge County.
❏ Worked on the fire alarms, power, and security systems at Manchester International Airport.
❏ Installed Emergency Generating System and Fire Suppression System at Logan Airport.
❏ Foreman for the Lighting Protection Project at the Southern Bell Central Office.
❏ Performed maintenance on more than a dozen Southern Bell buildings/locations.
❏ Installed and set up the Halon System at a large Concord Correctional Facility.
❏ Directed five separate Barnett Bank projects in Northridge and Becker Counties

References and Supporting Documentation Furnished upon Request

LORNE D. GINSBURG

335 Waterside Drive
Evansville, Indiana 47734
(812) 555-1212 / email@email.com

ELECTRONIC ENGINEERING / TECHNICAL PROFESSIONAL
Contributing to Growth & Profitability via Technical Project/Product Leadership

Product Delivery / Customer Relations / Quality Assurance
Complex Problem-Solving / Organizational Leadership

A dynamic, team-spirited, and bottom-line-oriented Electronic Engineer / Technician offering outstanding qualifications in equipment/product development to include **prototyping, testing and debugging, layout and documentation, production coordination, final testing/documentation, and delivery to end user (installation, training, and follow-up).**

CORE STRENGTHS

Analytical and technical aptitude	Team leadership and staff development
Assimilating and communicating complex information	Computer skills, including programming
Presentation and public speaking skills	Cooperative interdepartmental interface
Total quality management and customer service	Automated testing experience

PROFESSIONAL EXPERIENCE

TECH SERVICES, Indianapolis, Indiana
Electronic Engineering Technology Services
1994 to Current

Consistent and ongoing technical work assignments for three key client companies

MOTOROLA, Indianapolis, Indiana
(1999 to Current)
Testing Engineer / technician
Constructed automated test stations, including robotics for the development of personal communication devices. Utilize Hewlett Packard Test and Measuring equipment as well as Rhodes and Swartz and proprietary interfaces. Construct prototypes and design simple circuits and mechanical subassemblies to ensure proper interface with personal communication devices.

- Significantly reduced mechanical construction time by introducing templates and predrilled and tapped rails and plates.
- Decreased wiring time by using harness technicians.
- Successfully performed much of the work without formal documentation.

GEO FOCUS, Springfield, Indiana
(1995 to 1999)
Electronic Engineer / Technical Consultant
Responsible for building prototypes, testing, and coordinating with manufacturing for development of prototypes, ordering parts, field installation, testing, and service/repair to component level. Developed documentation, as-built drawings, and bills of materials. Designed simple mechanical and electronic subassemblies.

- Involved in the installation of Train Tracking System (GPS) on tri rail trains and platforms.
- Installed computer network at the Tri Rail Customer Relations Center, including wireless radio networking.
- Reduced downtime by reprogramming boards in the field.
- Dramatically reduced service calls by redesigning computer-networking connections.

(Continued)

PROFESSIONAL EXPERIENCE

IMAGE GRAPHICS INC., Holden, Indiana
(1994 to 1995)
Customer Service Technician
Responsible for troubleshooting and maintenance of E.B.R. (Electronic Beam Recorder) micrographics, and image setter used in micropublishing. Worked with Unix system – both hardware and software. Coordinated customer service efforts at customer site – troubleshooting both digital and analog systems.

- Successfully troubleshot equipment and systems, causing no down time to the client.
- Effectively trained customer personnel in EBR operations.

PROFESSIONAL EXPERIENCE (Other)

QUANTA CHROME CORP., Westin, Indiana   1992 to 1994
Electronics Technician
- Built and calibrated scientific equipment – repair to component level (digital and analog).

ENGINEERED COMPUTER SYSTEMS, Torrance, California   1991 to 1992
Systems Consultant
- Designed, installed, and trained on electronic publishing systems (including software applications).

AMP BUSINESS SYSTEMS, LTD., Dartmouth, Nova Scotia   1987 to 1991
Systems Consultant
- Designed, installed, and trained on 3M Optical Disk and Micrographic Systems.

BELL & HOWELL, Toronto, Canada   1985 to 1987
Assistant Regional Manager
- Hired, trained, and directed staff for presentations made in academic environments throughout eastern Canada to recruit students for Bell & Howell's DeVry Institute of Technology.

ACADEMIC / TRAINING HIGHLIGHTS

DeVRY INSTITUTE OF TECHNOLOGY, Toronto, Canada
Bachelor of Science: Electronics Technology, 1984

ROYAL CANADIAN NAVY, Halifax, Canada
Radar and Electronics Technician, 1980-84

References and Supporting Documentation Furnished upon Request

51—ELEMENTARY SCHOOL TEACHER

VIVIAN ALESSI

50 Ferne Lane
Seattle, Washington 98366
(941) 555-1212/email@email.com

ELEMENTARY SCHOOL TEACHER
Enhancing Academic Experience for All Children

A highly motivated, intuitive, and results-focused individual with 18+ years of successful
experience in diversified environments—the past eight years as an educator

A team player with solid leadership skills able to generate new ideas, analyze and resolve
challenges, and advance organizational goals and objectives

Creative, detail-oriented, and highly dependable; work effectively in stress/high pressure
situations; flexible and adaptable to ever-changing environments

Fluent in English and Spanish

Strengths

Communication skills (presentation/writing skills)
Interpersonal and "people" skills
Organization, administration, and time management
Start-up operations supervision and coordination

Coaching, teaching, and training
Multiple/complex project management
Problem solving and conflict resolution
Curriculum development/enhancement

Education

UNIVERSITY OF ILLINOIS, Urbana-Champaign, Illinois
Bachelor of Science: Psychology, 1983
- Specialization: Developmental Child Care Program
- CDA Equivalency through Seattle Community College, Early Childhood Educators Network

Professional Experience

BEGINNINGS PRESCHOOL, Seattle, Washington   1993 to Current
Teacher

- Plan and implement daily classroom activities for preschool education program. Assist children in academic and personal/social growth development—to include interpersonal, organizational, and conflict-resolution skills. Organize and prepare materials for daily activities; maintain clean, well-organized learning environment; and direct the children to appropriate activities throughout the day.

- Perform written evaluations three times a year and work as a team member in developing/enhancing academic curriculum. Create weekly lesson plans, train new teachers/staff in classroom procedures and curriculum development, and provide quality support to both the children and their parents/families.

- Played a team leadership role in the creation of a new library, including classification of books and category determination. Ensured all logistical efforts were in place for meeting Grand Opening deadline.

- Member—Teacher Parent Advisory Council, 1995 to Current

Professional Experience, Other (1983 to 1993)

Retail Experience/Customer Service
Teaching—Preschool and Public School

Byrons/Toys-R-Us, Seattle, Washington
Seattle School System, Seattle, Washington

References and Supporting Documentation Furnished upon Request

174

Brendan Ross

1234 Green Street NW • Washington, DC 20008
555.555.5555 • cell: 123.456.7890
br@yahoo.com

Objective

Telecommunications Engineer with in depth knowledge of **GSM communications** and software systems. Seeking full-time position with global telecommunications entity. Eager to bring extensive product and technology knowledge to benefit emerging wireless communications industry.

Technical Knowledge

GSM	Solaris
SS7 Networks	SQL
ETSI standards	Unix
ITU-T Standards	Axe Platforms
ISUP	TDMA
Intelligent Networks	FDMA
Assembler	Common Channel Signaling

Professional Experience

IRISH SATELLITE GROUP – IS, INC.

GSM SATELLITE SUPPORT ENGINEER

Falls Church, Virginia • 1999-present

Team Leader of consulting group serving Hughes Network Systems engaged in deployment of large satellite/wireless access network in the Middle East. Working directly with HNS engineers, advised on product specifications of Global System for Mobile Communications (GSM) node interfaces. Provided expertise on network operations and implementations for 200,000-subscriber switch in the United Arab Emirates that will extend coverage to Africa, the Middle East, Asia and Eastern Europe. Delivered and tested all software on the switch in anticipation of a go-live in 2001. Performed acceptance testing and documented findings/results. Performed internal planning and carried out process definition and implementation.

- **Consistently met all deadlines and performance benchmarks through dedicated work over an extended period**
- **Fostered positive, productive relationships with customer engineers and involved entities through singular effort in communication and cooperation**
- **Singled out for promotion to Verification Manager for Fairfax location**

(Continued)

INTELLIGENT NETWORKS GLOBAL CUSTOMIZATION COORDINATOR

Dublin, Ireland • z

Teamed on development of complete customization process from scratch, initiating existence of Global Customization department for Irish Satellite. Authored documentation and procedures for implementation of a customization process for all IS mobile IN services. Dedicated extensive man-hours over a 4-month period to establish functional entity and participated in several IN service customization prestudies.

SUPPLY AND SUPPORT TEAM LEADER • IRISH SATELLITE PREPAID LITE SOLUTION

Dublin, Ireland • 1998-1999

Led team of up to 3 engineers in supply and support of Irish Satellite prepaid lite solutions. Planned and executed functional system testing of product at customer sites. Assisted Marketing Department through provision of numbers series, tariff structures, and other data for strategic positioning against competing service providers. Trained local companies and colleagues on implementation, features, and functionality as part of technology transfer. Traveled extensively to customer sites in Turkey, Macao, Uganda, Azerbaijan, Serbia, and Zanzibar to provide troubleshooting and implementation of simple and efficient solutions.

- **Successfully implemented product for customers in six different global markets. Carried out an implementation in Serbia, working largely alone under wartime conditions. Completed implementation in location with less than adequate infrastructure and local support. Met all implementation deadlines and benchmarks.**

ISUP CERTIFICATION TEAM LEADER

Tel Aviv, Israel • 1997-1998

Lead team involved in Integrated Services Digital Network User Part (ISUP) testing and certification of system software for Public Telephone and Telegraph (PTT – Israeli publicly owned telco). Troubleshot software and wrote corrections in Assembler. Coordinated and documented software testing.

- **Played key role in contract award for Irish Satellite to supply network hardware and software for Israel's first GSM system. Beat competitors Siemens and Nortel Networks to certification finish line despite need to adjust platform to interface with Israeli protocols.**

ENGINEER IN TRAINING

Dublin, Ireland • 1996-1998

EDUCATION AND TRAINING

Bachelor of Science – Electronic Engineering
University College – Galway, Ireland
Graduated with Honors - 1996

Irish Satellite Engineering Training – 1996-1998

Walter A. Harris

123 Timberland Drive • Klamath Falls, Oregon 97600
(503) 555-2121
email@email.com

OBJECTIVE   Vice President for Programs with the Wildlife Habitat Enhancement Council.

PROFILE

- Over 25 years experience in ecosystem biodiversity and habitat management.
- Excellent communication, organizational, and time-management skills.
- Belief in straightforward and honest approach for soliciting cooperation.
- Motivated to *do the job well.*
- Fluent in Spanish and French.

EDUCATION

Bachelor of Science - Magna Cum Laude, Wildlife Management and Biology
Humboldt State University, Arcata, CA

RELEVANT EXPERIENCE AND ACCOMPLISHMENTS

ECOSYSTEM AND HABITAT MANAGEMENT

- Designed and introduced plant, fish, and wildlife species surveys, assessment, habitat protection, restoration, and monitoring programs to 3 districts.
- First biologist hired by Law Enforcement Division, US Fish & Wildlife Service, to enforce International Endangered Species Treaty Act.
- Developed and perfected Spotted Owl Survey techniques and identified habitat parameters in National Forest.

ENVIRONMENTAL PLANNING AND DESIGN

- As interdisciplinary team member, participated in development of Master Management Plans of Mt. Baker-Snoqualmie National Forest, Crystal Mountain Ski Resort, and 880-square-mile White River watershed.
- Evaluated and designed projects and plans.

MANAGEMENT

- Supervised 12 people directly and 82 indirectly.
- Promoted team building and collaboration to accomplish all multidisciplined tasks.

EMPLOYMENT HISTORY

Headquarters, US Department of Agriculture, Forest Service, Washington, DC

1991-present   **Resource Director**
Managed all natural resources and disciplines including cultural, recreation, plants, hydrology, soils, fish, wildlife, ecosystems, special uses, and volunteer programs.

1984-1991   **District Biologist**
Developed, implemented, and managed all plant, fish, and wildlife species and habitat programs for 3 National Forest districts.

1975-1984   **Timber Sale Administrator**
Ensured contract compliance of private timber companies' logging and timber sale activity, including erosion control, stream and wetland protection, threatened and endangered species habitat protection, road design and construction, and forest reclamation.

AFFILIATIONS/MEMBERSHIPS

President, Fallbrook Land Conservancy
Member, Habitat Restoration Working Group, The Wildlife Society

DOM KINSKI

3121 Village Crossing • West Palm Beach, Florida 33409 • (561) 555-9638 • email@email.com

---

ENVIRONMENTAL ENGINEER/CONSULTANT
3 Years' National and International Experience Working with Fortune 500 Companies/Clientele
Master's Degree in Environmental Engineering

A dynamic,team-spirited,and bottom-line-oriented Project/Environmental Engineer offering outstanding qualifications in all areas of Environmental Engineering —with emphasis on working on multi-million-dollar projects for key international clientele,as well as smaller national projects.

Environmental Management System/Water & Air Management/Waste Management
Environmental Impact Assessment/Environmental Annual Report/Cleanup and Remediation
Environmental Audit/Project Management/Power-Plant Water & Sewer Management

CORE STRENGTHS

Regulatory compliance   Project cost analysis
Contract negotiation/administration   Field-performance supervision
Budget and expense management   Multiple-project management
Complex problem solving/troubleshooting   Policy/procedure development

Computer Skills: Windows, MS Office (Word, Excel, PowerPoint, Outlook), Visio, and Internet applications

PROFESSIONAL EXPERIENCE

DELOITTE & TOUCHE LTD, Budapest/Miami   1992 to Current
Environmental Engineer/Consultant
Project Manager/Team Member in directing environmental engineering projects. Work in a team environment on diversified projects, interfacing closely with clients to ensure quality work and that all project/budgetary objectives are met.

- Prepared environmental report for multi-billion-dollar,international corporation for the purchase of a $50+million-dollar power plant.Provided comprehensive evaluation,including environmental-risk analysis and cost analysis.
- Managed the improvement of one of the largest Hungarian wine company 's water and sewage system and worked with environmental authority to accomplish stringent goals.
- Worked for local government —assessed the cleanup of polluted property (oil and gas),and analyzed cleanup strategy. Determined cost to complete work and oversaw the completion of the project.
- Project leader for Phase 1 Environmental Audit for Macedonian Government —a large-scale lead battery firm.
- Successfully directed a Phase 1 Environmental Audit for Punch Hungary LTD —a plastics-materials manufacturer serving the computer industry.
- Performed environmental risk analyses for European Union PHARE Programs for financing viable investment projects,with specific concentration on determining "environmental benefits " of the projects..

BUDAPEST POWER PLANT LTD, Budapest   1989 to 1992
Environmental Engineer
Prepared company 's first annual environmental report; contributed to remediation procedures and the improvement of the water-management system.

- Set up company's comprehensive environmental procedures program and improved company's image.
- Managed remediation project and helped complete project to come in under budget.
- Improved the safety and quality of the water system—addressing/resolving acid and oil contaminates.

ACADEMIC HIGHLIGHTS

Master's of Science in Environmental Engineering, 1989   University of Veszprem, Hungary
Course Certification (Environmental Industry and Ecology), Summer, 1996   University of Stockholm, Sweden

- Fluent in English, German, and Hungarian

MARK BARROW

3111 Crows Nest Circle
Ashville, NC 87163
(912) 555-1212

ESTIMATOR—for General Contractor
17 Years' Successful Experience—Field, Office, Project-Management Estimating
Hard-Bid & Negotiated Work

"A Competitive Estimator Who Knows How to Make You Money"
- J. Kline, Former Employer

SUPPORTING STRENGTHS

- ❑ Estimating costs in relation to manpower, equipment, and materials; preparing bid packages/proposals.
- ❑ Clarifying and interpreting bids; writing/developing scope of work and construction-related specifications.
- ❑ Supervising commercial, municipal, and residential construction projects—estimating/project management through completion.
- ❑ Assessing needs, and hiring, training, and scheduling men, contractors, and equipment, to ensure maximum efficiency.
- ❑ Monitoring work progress to ensure quality work.
- ❑ Ensuring compliance with blueprints and specifications; change order management.
- ❑ Developing and maintaining good customer relations.

PROFESSIONAL EXPERIENCE

CLARK CONSTRUCTION SERVICE, INC., Ashville, North Carolina   1992 to Current
Lead Estimator
- ❑ Responsible for estimating total job costs on commercial projects ranging in price from $400,000 to $4 million.
- ❑ Prepared project estimates through contract negotiation and supervised construction operations and personnel—start-up through completion/acceptance. Worked on government/municipal bids/projects.
- ❑ Initiated key contact, drew up bid specifications for $3.2 million school-renovation project, and was awarded the contract.
- ❑ Successfully estimated and awarded contract to refurbish Ashville City Hall—a $2.6 million project.
- ❑ Turned around a troubled project—six weeks behind and over budget. Came in on time and met all financial/quality goals.

INTERNATIONAL HOSPITALITY SERVICES, Greenville, North Carolina   1988 to 1992
Purchasing Agent, Estimator & Superintendent
- ❑ Initially employed as superintendent, responsible for providing on-site supervision in all phases of construction. Subsequently promoted to estimator—preparing estimates for hotel construction projects. Elevated to purchasing agent, responsible for negotiating contracts with subcontractors and purchasing materials for commercial projects.

MULCATHY, INC., Ashville, North Carolina   1986 to 1988
Carpenter
- ❑ Employed by company providing carpentry-subcontractor services on various government and institutional projects, such as schools, museums, and government-works buildings.
- ❑ Performed carpentry duties for the installation of acoustical tile ceilings, freezer panels, and freezers on various commercial construction projects.

Prior employment included eight years in various positions in the Construction Industry.

TRAINING/AFFILIATIONS

Harding Vocational and Technical School—Successfully Completed Two-Year Program   1975–77
Carpentry Apprenticeship, Ashville, North Carolina   1978
Member, American Society of Architects & Estimators
Computer Skills:
      - Timberline Estimating/Business software
      - Word, Excel, and Internet applications

Letters of References Furnished upon Request

BRENDA LEHY

555 West Baseline Road
Tempe, Arizona 55555

Home: 480-555-5555 Cell: 480-555-5551
E-mail: behy@mail.net

EXECUTIVE / PERSONAL ASSISTANT
"Committed to Making the Boss Look Brilliant"

Progressive, 11-year professional career managing cross-functional business affairs for diverse service organizations. Currently challenged with executing day-to-day administrative and relationship management initiatives for the Vice President of Business Marketing at a Fortune 500 organization. Flexible in an urgently paced environment. Expertise in building rapport; possess a special ability to mirror others, cultivating a trust situation. Dynamic telephone presence/etiquette with a knack for meaningful yet efficient telephone exchanges.

- Cross-Functional Executive Support
- Vendor & Customer Communications
- Special Events & Meetings Management
- Productivity & Performance Management
- Reporting, Recordkeeping & Documentation
- Senior Staff Relations & Communications
- Project Planning & Management
- Problem Solving & Decision Making
- Staff Training, Development & Mentoring
- Confidential Correspondence & Data

EXPERIENCE & ACHIEVEMENTS

MAJOR TELECOMMUNICATIONS COMPANY, Phoenix, Arizona

Executive Assistant to Vice President   2000 to Present

Transitioned through a series of increasingly responsible administrative positions supporting senior executives and their direct reports. Currently work in cooperation with the Vice President of Business Marketing and other senior management to plan and direct high-level administrative affairs in support of Major Telecommunications' strategic goals. Lead, mentor and coach two executive assistants.

Professional / Proactive Support

- As gatekeeper, constantly manage telephone communications (about 60% of the time), fielding and prioritizing calls from or initiating calls to customers, vendors and high-level executives, both internal and external. Average day involves 120+ telephonic communications.
- Coordinate calendars for 6 executives (vice president plus 5 directors), accommodating an average of 45 meeting makers, scheduling meeting priorities and adapting to continual scheduling nuances.
  - ✓ Designed and implemented an e-mail procedure that streamlined division's meeting management efforts, impacting approximately 130 meeting makers.
- Organize international travel schedules, interfacing with internal/external travel agencies to arrange ground/air transportation and hotel accommodations while adhering to strict budgets.
- Systematize executive's itinerary/travel folder to relieve travel stress.
- Aid in employee new-hire process from interview through hire, arranging series of interviews across a multiplicity of executive calendars, circulating resumes and completing HR application matrix.
- Support the purchase requisition purchase order process to ensure vendor/partner payment of invoices.

Meeting Management / Presentations

- Instituted and lead a weekly executive assistants group meeting as a forum to cross-reference and identify/resolve conflicts to executive calendars, and exchange solutions/promote mutual support on overflow projects. Serve as group representative and spokesperson during executive staff meetings.
- Spearhead weekly vice president staff meetings and monthly business unit team meetings, including meeting space reservations, catering arrangements and attendee scheduling.
- Develop digital presentations, establishing content and building, modifying and distributing slides.

EXPERIENCE & ACHIEVEMENTS, continued …

MAJOR TELECOMMUNICATIONS COMPANY, Phoenix, Arizona, continued …

Executive Assistant to Vice President 1999 to Present

Meeting Management / Presentations

- Assemble 13 executives' presentations across functional areas.
- Capture and disseminate meeting minutes, accumulating and then dispersing action items.

Special Events Management

- Key contributor in the orchestration of three major Major Telecommunications events: 1) Thrice-annual Advisory Council focusing on 15 key customers; 2) User's Conference, a larger-scale event hosting 800 customers; and 3) Key Dealer Event. Highlights of involvement include:
  - ✓ Communicate with C-level Major Telecommunications executives, their support staff and Major Telecommunications business clients, solidifying meeting dates and recruiting meeting presenters.
  - ✓ Attend regular meetings with the hotel management, performing site inspections, establishing the master account, creating a reception theme and scheduling meeting space, catering and overnight accommodations for customers.
  - ✓ Arrange Major Telecommunications executives' and customers' air/ground transportation and then closely monitor individual attendees' travel details. Intimately follow their airport check-in, seat assignment and arrival, and perform problem solving when even the slightest detail becomes askew.
  - ✓ Closely manage all other logistical and customer relationship management details.
- Spur team-building through research and planning of employee events. Coordinate site checks, setup, ground transportation, event contracts, agenda, giveaways and catering with various resources.
- Tapped for building's Chair of Community Relations Team interfacing with nonprofit organizations areawide and expanding relationships among Major Telecommunications associates.
  - ✓ Spearhead the Phoenix Zoo's Boathouse Project, organizing up to 60 volunteers.
  - ✓ Co-Chair the Trolley Run that involves 600 to 700 participants.
  - ✓ Member of a Steering Committee whose mission is to impart the "hope of a good Christmas holiday" for the individuals at Hope House.
  - ✓ Won the **2002 Spirit Award**, bestowed by Major Telecommunications President and COO.

CMG & ASSOCIATES, Tempe, Arizona
Client Services Manager 1998 to 2000

BART A. HANSEN, DDS, MS, Phoenix, Arizona
Staff Assistant 1995 to 1998

MAJOR OIL CORPORATION, Phoenix, Arizona
Executive Administrator to the President 1992 to 1995

PROFESSIONAL DEVELOPMENT

MAJOR TELECOMMUNICATION'S UNIVERSITY OF EXCELLENCE, Phoenix, Arizona
- How to Be Effective in Leadership
- Achieving the Competitive Edge with Customer Service
- Managing Organizational Change
- Building Blocks for Business Writing

COLLEGE OF THE DESERT, Palm Desert, California / Business Coursework

Computers: MS Office: Word, Excel, PowerPoint, Access, Outlook, Publisher, Photo Editor, Quicken.

JOHN TOMPSON

119 Old Stable Road
Lynchburg, Virginia 24503
(804) 555-4600
email@email.com

CORPORATE FINANCE / ACCOUNTING / ADMINISTRATION / MIS

Sixteen-year professional career directing domestic and international corporate finance for challenging and complex operations. Expert negotiation and transaction management qualifications. Skilled decision maker, problem solver and team leader. Fluent in French and Scandinavian languages. Conversational German.

- Merger & Acquisition Management
- Corporate Divestiture & Realignment
- Strategic Planning & Development
- SEC Regulatory Affairs & Documentation
- Securities & Investment Banking
- Public Relations & Investor Relations

- Financial Consolidation & Reporting
- Asset & Liability Management
- General Accounting Operations
- Operations & Financial Analysis
- Pension & Benefits Administration
- Domestic & International Tax

PROFESSIONAL EXPERIENCE:

Present   Since resigning my position with Williams Company, I have completed several contract/consulting engagements:

- Investor Group — Completed due diligence review for acquisition of start-up medical supply manufacturer.

- Software Company — Advised CEO and operating management in the preparation and presentation of capital investment solicitations to the venture capital community.

- Construction & Development Company — Prepared annual financial statement, operating and capital budgets, and forecasts.

WILLIAMS COMPANY, INC., Lynchburg, Virginia   1981 to 2004

Fast-track promotion throughout 23-year career with this $5.5 billion, 50,000-employee, diversified manufacturer. Promoted through a series of increasingly responsible senior accounting and supervisory positions to final promotions as:

Assistant Controller, Smithfield, Inc., spin-off of Williams Company (1993 to 1994)
Director of Financial Consolidations & Reporting, Williams Company, Inc. (1987 to 1993)

As Director, held full responsibility for directing all accounting operations and monitoring financial performance of each operating division. Defined MIS information requirements to meet operating needs and established corporate-wide accounting policies, procedures, and reporting packages. Led a professional staff of 16 (11 of whom were CPAs with Big 6 experience) with dotted line responsibility for 70+ Division and Group Controllers.

Directed accounting operations for international and domestic taxes, long-term contracts, foreign currencies and derivatives, pensions and retiree medical benefits. Prepared shareholder, SEC, and internal Board of Directors and Management reports and semiannual consolidated plans. Monitored financial performance of divisions, including receivables and inventory management, capital expenditures, R&D expenditures, and general administrative costs. Managed systems implementation and integration of MIS for all operating divisions.

(Continued)

JOHN TOMPSON - Page Two

WILLIAMS COMPANY, INC. *(Continued)*:

In 1992, selected to lead the management team responsible for orchestrating the spin-off of Williams commercial growth businesses to form Smithfield, Inc. Continued to manage ongoing responsibilities throughout 18-month project. Worked with SEC personnel, investment banking advisers, corporate securities counsel, legal transactions firm, and CFO. Directed strategic financial analysis, asset/liability allocation, and preparation of Form 10 SEC registration statement for new company shares.

Following transition to Smithfield, given full management responsibility for three corporate departments — Business Operations Analysis & Planning, Financial Consolidations & Reporting, and General Accounting. Coordinated with Tax Director on international tax planning and related legal structuring. Directed a staff of 10 headquarters personnel and a worldwide team of Division Controllers.

Career Highlights & Achievements:

- Directed the strategic analysis of Williams which resulted in spin-off of Smithfield.

- Established the entire accounting and financial infrastructure for new corporation. Developed policies and procedures for budgeting, financial analysis, financial reporting, tax accounting, and pension accounting. Coordinated with Treasury Department for international cash management.

- Directed complex financial analysis and integration of all accounting and financial operations for 19 acquisitions worldwide ($500,000 to $258 million). Integrated two acquisitions concurrent with company spin-off.

- Orchestrated accounting and financial affairs for the disposition of over 70 operating divisions of Williams during the company's realignment of its core portfolio. Consulted with Williams U.K. operations to resolve operational and financial issues related to the disposition of international business units.

- Developed economic analysis of impact on stock price of share buyback versus acquisition investment with the company's price/earnings ratio as measure.

- Served as the sole company representative on behalf of Smithfield in discussions and negotiations with the SEC on challenged issues regarding company formation and financial information.

- Successfully represented Williams in an arbitration of a disputed sales contract. Presented and interpreted financial and contractual documentation for the court and recovered $20.6 million of disputed $21 million for the corporation.

WATSON & WATSON, PLC, Forest, Virginia   1979 to 1981

Staff Accountant promoted to **In-Charge Accountant** promoted to **Senior Accountant** within 18 months. Heavy SEC experience (including 10-K and S-1 filings). Industry experience included oil and gas, manufacturing, and food distribution.

EDUCATION:

Bachelor of Science, Business Administration / Accounting Option, Summa Cum Laude Graduate, 1978
NEW MEXICO STATE UNIVERSITY *(passed CPA examination in 1978)*

PAUL J. MORGAN

555 North Gateway Lane • Edison, NJ 11111 • 856 555-7414 (AH)

ACCOUNTANT / FINANCIAL CONTROLLER

Start-up, Turnaround & High-Growth Organizations

Importers & Wholesalers / Manufacturing & Production

QUALIFICATIONS PROFILE

Solution-focused, multifaceted Senior Finance Executive demonstrating expertise building top-performing organizations consistently exceeding revenue and profit objectives within challenging, competitive and volatile markets. Outstanding accomplishments in business start-up, turnaround, and financial/operational management across diverse industries, reinvigorating organizational infrastructure, inventory, technologies, processes and financial measurement systems. Delivered strong and sustainable revenue/income gains with equal expertise in capturing cost reductions through process redesign and performance management.

Core Competencies:

- Forecasting, Reporting & Analysis
- Strategic Planning, Execution & Management
- Software/Hardware Analysis & Enhancement
- Staff Management & Performance Building

- Revenue, Profit & Market Share Growth
- Budgeting & Cash Flow Optimization
- Banking/Finance Liaison/Negotiation
- Corporate Finance & Asset Management

PROFESSIONAL EXPERIENCE

AGR SYSTEMS, Edison, NJ   1999 – Present
Multi-million-dollar importer/manufacturer, supplying raw materials to niche market of small/medium-size manufacturers within the surface coatings, ink & plastic batch manufacturing industry.

Financial Controller

Challenged to turnaround company with limited growth potential due to mature product lines and existing markets through strategic evaluation, development and execution of operational-enhancing solutions and initiatives that captured dramatic improvement across inventory management, financial reporting, cash flow and bottom-line profitability, transforming substantial losses into healthy returns.

- Championed **turnaround from $275,000 losses to $89,000 profitability** in only 12 months, with results currently on target for $150,000 profit for 2002-2003.

- Spearheaded change of finance facility to reflect business needs/cycle, **saving thousands of dollars in interest charges** through negotiation with bankers and utilization of Trade Finance Bills rather than overdraft. **Improved cash flow** allowing company to place $100,000 on term deposit, thus avoiding use of overdraft facility during last 12 months.

- **Enhanced stock management efficiency** through identification of significant levels of obsolete stock and subsequent initiation of major stock write-downs/disposals in June 2001 and **improved stock turns of 1.2 to 3.5** in less than two years.

- **Increased product margins** where possible in a price-driven marketplace and with majority of company products having low margin rates.

- **Transformed poorly managed, inaccurate financial accounts** with sporadic analysis and reporting **into highly efficient operation,** producing full management accounts within five days of month end, including KPI summary and budget variance analysis.

- **Streamlined financial accuracy and reporting** through conversion of manual GL into Attaché software and integrated debtors, creditors, stock, purchasing and payroll.

Continued...

PAUL J. MORGAN

DIAMOND LABEL INTERNATIONAL, Edison, NJ   1990 – 1998
Leading women's clothing manufacturer with annual revenues topping $42M.
Financial Controller
Identified, formulated and implemented problem-solving strategies, while uniting management's disparate viewpoints by convincing and encouraging change to management solutions to prevent ongoing dismal ROS of less than 2% on annual revenues of $42M. Created sound financial base in order to accelerate growth of company revenue and profitability; monitored company progress through strategic, accurate and timely financial reporting.

- Transitioned **group from severe negative cash flow position to healthy positive cash flow** within 12 months with $1.4M in funds, expanding to $2.7M during following two years, and in excess of $3M.
- Introduced cash forecasting model that phased in local/overseas purchasing with relevant payment terms, which facilitated negotiation with bankers for a short-term increase in finance facility from $600K to $2.6M (later being reduced to $1.1M).
- Ceased previous neglect of long-term cash forecasting by management to the point of near insolvency.
- **Secured strong cash flow**, which enabled group to establish new warehousing/logistics company and a new Hong Kong Branch office with operating capital funded by Diamond Label.
- Instrumental in improving results through focusing Directors' awareness on margin rather than sales as the key factor for profitability and retention of cash within the business.
- **Optimized ROS of 1.3% to nearly 7%** within 12 months and a **further increase to 8.5%** within 6 months, with industry average at that time around 4%.
- Successfully implemented, tested and achieved full operational functionality of all financial modules of new JBA computer system within specified time frame.
- **Finalized long overdue accounts with accounts from October 1989 and onward** not yet produced in February 1990. By end March 1990, all accounts including February were completed with a management summary presented to Directors.

EDUCATION & PROFESSIONAL DEVELOPMENT

MBA – Finance & International Business • Washington State University
BS (Finance) • University of Michigan

PROFESSIONAL ASSOCIATIONS

American Institute of Certified Public Accountants
National Association of Public Accountants

WILLIAM J. HUNTER

879 West Weeping Lane • Atlanta, GA 30374 • wjhunter@hotmail.com
(770) 555-2589 (Cell) • (770) 555-7857 (A/H)

SENIOR CORPORATE FINANCE EXECUTIVE

CEO-Finance & Administration/Financial Controller & Administrator/Group Accountant

Start-up Enterprises, Turnaround & Revitalizations, High-Growth & High-Profit Organizations

National & International business expansion and leadership scope

QUALIFICATIONS PROFILE

Hands-on, solutions-focused Senior Finance Executive with a career demonstrating visionary leadership, expertise and outstanding performance in business start-up and financial/operational management of multisite, nationally and internationally based operations. Proactive change agent, combining implementation of strategic operational initiatives with solid direction of cross-discipline departments to enhance bottom-line financial performance and company growth. Expertise verified within:

- Strategic Planning & Execution
- Multisite Operations Management
- Team Performance Optimization
- Forecasting, Reporting & Analysis

- Revenue, Profit & Market Share Growth
- Budgeting & Cash Flow Optimization
- Investor Presentations & Consultations
- Corporate Finance & Asset Management

PROFESSIONAL EXPERIENCE

MINING LIMITED, HOUSTON, TEXAS   1983 to Present

Internationally listed, U.S.-based oil and gas exploration and production company with joint venture explorations and gold mine production enterprises in U.S., South America and Australia.

CEO – Finance & Administration (1997 to Present)

Distinguished financial and business management performance securing rapid promotion through a series of increasingly responsible accounting, financial control and treasury positions, implementing core business and operational strategies to deliver strong investment and market share gains. Oversee preparation and filing of all U.S. statutory filings; prepare and submit accounting and monthly board reports for Australian gold production facility.

Strategic negotiation and management of revolving credit facilities and treasury funds. Perform presentations to represent company at investor conferences throughout U.S.; serve as main point of contact as Investor Relations adviser, answering public and investor-related queries. Facilitate coordination, preparation and submission of U.S. budget and three-year plans to Board of Directors. Director of U.S. subsidiary companies.

- Raised $220 million from U.S. institutions in 1995 U.S. listing and subdebt offering in 1997, through prospectus preparation and presentations at U.S. based road shows.
- Pioneered international business expansion establishing Houston, Texas operations in 1992, and successfully relocating corporate offices to Houston in 1993.
- Recommended numerous performance optimization initiatives to corporate C.E.O.; pioneered implementation of gold commodity hedging program.
- Championed development and execution of management and joint venture accounts for copper and gold exploration activities in South America.

Previous roles included Operations Manager, Financial Controller and Group Accountant demonstrating diversified accounting/financial expertise executing strategies that delivered sustainable revenue gains.

Continued...

WILLIAM J. HUNTER

CHAMPION OIL LIMITED, HOUSTON, TEXAS   1981 to 1983

Oil, gas and natural resource exploration, development and production company; managing partner of 17 joint ventures and operator of Surant gas field/LPG extraction plant.

Financial Controller / Joint Partnership Administrator

Diverse financial accountabilities with job scope involving preparation of monthly/year-end financial statements; invoicing and distribution of gas, crude and LPG revenue; budget preparation; and control of capital expenditure. Directed and oversaw renewal of joint venture and corporate insurance policies. Served as liaison, interfacing between technical and field operations staff. Reported directly to Manager of Finance and Accounting.

- Tripled performance output while effectively orchestrating downsizing of department staff from five to three.
- Spearheaded preparation and negotiation of joint operating agreements and accounting procedures for new joint ventures.
- Created strategic portfolio of financial models, indices and analyses to monitor and evaluate performance of production programs.
- Revitalized company by laying foundations to drive revenue and profitability growth and achievement of operating and financial objectives.

BHP REFINERY, HOUSTON, TEXAS   1980 to 1981

Multinational petroleum company with divisions consisting of refineries and coal exploration.

Accountant

Performed broad financial functions; budget preparation, and analysis of monthly sales, rebates and gross margins.

- Led computerization of entire business organization, including accounting, finance, billing, capital assets, customer management and human resources.

EDUCATION

Bachelor of Economics: Accounting, Texas University, Houston, Texas

PROFESSIONAL MEMBERSHIPS

Associate Member; National Association of Public Accountants

YU-CHEN (ALAN) FAN

555 Foxhollow Lane, Southampton, NY 55555 ▪ HP: 631-555-3431 ▪ CP: 917-555-4702 ▪ alanfan@m.com

---

SENIOR FINANCIAL PROJECT MANAGER

13 YEARS DIVERSE INTERNATIONAL FINANCIAL PROJECT MANAGEMENT EXPERIENCE

Well-Versed in Global Business Market Specializing in East-West Cultures

Certified Project Management Professional, PMI

Strategic Cost & Financial Management.Global Government & Public Relations

Fluent English & Mandarin Communication & Presentation Skills

---

Firsthand experience positioning global Fortune 500 companies for long-term growth and profitability. Demonstrated track record of consistently combining financial leadership with sound business practices to ensure bottom-line revenues and better, cheaper, faster business for total customer satisfaction. Reputation as self-directed professional with excellent problem-solving, communication, analytical, and management skills. Proficient in proprietary financial control software, including Oracle Financial Tools, TRAC, CRMS, Extra, and Remedy, among others.

CORE COMPETENCIES

- Strategic Business/Financial Models
- Project Financial Control Systems
- Hedging & Risk Analysis
- Resource Planning/Scheduling
- SWOT Analysis

- Financial Operations Management
- Cash Flow Forecasting/Management
- Pricing & Invoicing Management
- Rational Unified Process Estimation
- Project Profitability Modeling

- High-Level Contract Negotiation
- Capital Budget management
- Foreign Currency & Tax Regulation
- Risk/Business Valuation Models
- World Bank Procedures

PROFESSIONAL EXPERIENCE

American International Group (AIG), Inc., Fort New York, NY — 2001–Present
PROGRAM FINANCE MANAGER
Oversee program financial operations for largest US underwriter of commercial and industrial insurance and leading international insurance and financial services organization, with operations in 130 countries and $67.5B in annual revenues. Control hedging, risk analysis, operational budgeting, resource planning, invoicing, pricing, ordering, and scheduling.

- Led SWOT analysis of $530M international VCP (venture capital partnerships) transformation program that added to 2002 9.9% record increase of $2.19B international financial services operating income. Coordinated and directed project managers and budget authorities across all operations to develop business cases, funding structures, and budget matrices to ensure program objectives achieved on time and on budget.

- Designed and implemented comprehensive project financial controls to reverse previous years' losses, thus adding to foreign general net premiums for 2002 record of $6.01B.

- Designed complex resource and expense tracking systems to analyze over $5B in corporate program budgets against respective accruals and to generate corrective action recommendations to senior management with evaluation summary and variance analysis reports.

- Diagnosed risks of projects exceeding $5M for bid/no-bid decision-making process by building project rational unified process (RUP) estimation, creating risk and business valuation models, conducting *ad hoc* operation analysis, and collaborating with senior management.

General Dynamics Advanced Information Systems (GDAIS), Tinton Falls, NJ — 1997–2001
SENIOR BUSINESS ANALYST
Provide primary detailed analysis of $95M in annual program budgetary concerns and financial performance for integrated information-based systems and services of fourth largest US defense contractor. Evaluated new business proposals, interpreted financial data, forecasted corporate cash flow, and developed business models jointly with sales and marketing teams. Principal adviser to senior management.

- Pitched and developed $130M overseas operation business structure, based on in-depth analysis of local tax system, foreign currency regulation, and patent issues, ensuring accounting, billing, and contracting structures correlated with planned business models.

(Continued)

60—FINANCIAL PROJECT MANAGER (CONT.)

YU-CHEN (ALAN) FAN

PROFESSIONAL EXPERIENCE CONTINUED...

- Increased invoice turnover rate 150% and monthly cash flow 8% by creating consolidated tracking system to monitor real-time material/equipment traffic, billing, and payment status. New system procedures accepted by all stakeholders.
- Captured $55M in miscalculated profit by identifying and correcting errors to revise revenue projection and cost estimation, using performance-to-date analysis.
- Designed state-of-the-art financial project management performance and progress tracking system.

Duke Energy International (DEI), Inc., Houston, TX   1996–1997
INTERNATIONAL FINANCE ANALYST
Analyzed energy market trend in China for premier international energy trading company of $16.1B annually. Appraised financial activities, including capital budgeting, banking, hedging, risk analysis, and cash flow forecasting. Examined inquiries orders, pricing, and marginal profitability.

- Led $255M cost-efficient establishment of presence in Hong Kong and Beijing, China, by improving international communication and negotiating fair and reasonable tax payments.
- Decreased average contract management costs $22M annually by constructing more efficient strategies and project profitability projection with innovative financial models and tools for calculating project payback period, net present value (NPV), and modified internal rate of return (MIRR).

China Petroleum Material and Equipment Co., Beijing, China   1992–1995
BUSINESS MANAGER
Managed purchase group responsible for negotiation and implementation of capital equipment purchase contracts. Large projects included Sichuan Basin Gas Pipeline Rehabilitation ($420M) and Xingjiang Junger Basin Oil Reservoir exploration ($98M).

- Developed, justified, and managed $1.3B annual capital equipment purchasing budget.
- Won $66M contract as lead negotiator to close ceramic tile joint venture deal between Beichen Group and Italian manufacturer.
- Formulated and implemented new procurement procedure according to World Bank purchase guidelines. Introduced competition mechanism into solicitation process that ensured equal playing field for project negotiation.
- Established Houston, Texas, residence for company, serving first term as Houston Office Representative (1992).

China National Petroleum Corp. (formerly Ministry of Petroleum Industry), Beijing, China   1990–1991
WORLD BANK LOAN PROJECT COORDINATOR
Coordinated bid documents preparation, solicitation analysis, bid material review, and suppliers short-list selection. Assisted project financial appraisal, risks analysis, and post auditing.

- Supervised implementation of $900M World Bank loan for oil and gas projects, working closely with World Bank Task Managers and project stakeholders.
- Bridged gaps between World Bank, governmental regulators, and key stakeholders for $8.3M energy study project through thorough preparation of bid evaluation report to National Projects Evaluation Committee for approval.

EDUCATION & PROFESSIONAL DEVELOPMENT

MBA, Finance, University of Saint Thomas, Houston TX, 1995

BA, English Changsha Railway University (Honors), Changsha China, 1989

Professional Certificate in Business Analysis, George Washington University, Washington DC, 2001
International Business Training, Beijing Science and Technology Advanced Study Institute, Beijing China, 1991
World Bank and Foreign Loan Projects Operation Training, Beijing Education College, Beijing China, 1990

PROFESSIONAL AFFILIATIONS

Financial Management Association International (FMA)
International Project Finance Association (IPFA)
Project Management Institute (PMI)

189

SEAN O'DONNELL

1234 Myrtle Lane, Temecula, California 92591 (909) 555-1212

CAREER PROFILE

An experienced **Firefighter** whose professional responsibilities expanded his primary specialty into areas of operational management, staff training, administration and finance, motivational leadership, and decision making. Competent and knowledgeable in all phases of fire fighting with specific expertise in managerial activities. Qualified by:

- A proven record of success with progressively increasing responsibilities based upon experience, knowledge, and superior work performance.
- An innate ability to easily interface between both management and staff as well as with individuals of diverse backgrounds and cultures.
- Excellent communication, motivational, and time-management skills and abilities.
- Organizational and analytical skills, decisiveness in crisis situations, and adeptness in managing multiple tasks simultaneously.
- Hands-on experience in developing and training cohesive, dedicated, and loyal staffs.

PROFESSIONAL EXPERIENCE

NORTH COUNTY FIRE PROTECTION DISTRICT, Fallbrook, California - October 1992 to present

Fire Captain (Acting) responsible for supervising and coordinating day-to-day activities of assigned firefighters engaged in protecting lives and property. Functional authority includes: supervision of personnel; operations and maintenance of fire equipment, apparatus, and station facilities; response to alarms received and initial assumption of fire control activities; planning, supervising, and conducting training, fire prevention, and maintenance programs; station administration relative to personnel, emergency responses, inspections, station facilities, etc., by coordinating and supervising fire company policies, regulations, and procedures; enforcing and implementing department policies, regulations, and procedures; conducting prefire planning surveys and developing fire ground methodologies; and conducting preliminary fire company investigations to establish cause and point of origin.

NORTH COUNTY FIRE PROTECTION DISTRICT, Fallbrook, California - October 1986 to October 1992

Engineer responsible for controlling and extinguishing fires, protecting life and property, and maintaining assigned equipment under emergency and routine conditions. Additional responsibilities included performing assigned duties in preventive maintenance and repair of assigned equipment, apparatus, buildings, equipment, and facilities. Collateral duties involved providing instruction to Fire Fighting Team personnel.

NORTH COUNTY FIRE PROTECTION DISTRICT, Fallbrook, California - April 1983 to October 1986

Firefighter/Reserve Firefighter responsible for controlling and extinguishing fires, protecting life, environment, and property, responding to medical emergencies, and maintaining fire fighting equipment.

ACCOMPLISHMENTS

- Secretary and Crew Representative, Fallbrook Firefighters Association.
- Recipient, 5- and 10-year Dedicated Service Awards, North County Fire Protection District.
- Recipient, Crew Representative Service Award, Fallbrook Firefighters Association.
- Developed, implemented, and monitored Apartment and Street Map Books.
- Voluntarily installed new engine equipment and Communications Center upgrade machinery.
- Assisted in construction of Station #4 Apparatus Building and remodel of Headquarters Station.
- Conducted periodic inspections of emergency apparatus identifying numerous, potentially costly problems and initiating corrective actions to eliminate repair time and reduce expenditures.
- Enhanced the overall safety of firefighters and the general public.

RELEVANT COMPETENCIES

•Budget Preparation	• Strategic Planning	• Staff Training
•Hazardous Materials	• Communications	• Staff Development
•Station Management	• Motivation & Leadership	• Codes Compliance

---

(Continued on next page)

61—FIREFIGHTER (CONT.)

EDUCATION AND PROFESSIONAL TRAINING

Crafton Hills Community College, Yucaipa, California - 10 Credits
- Undergraduate Studies - Major Emphasis: Fire Science

Miramar Community College, San Diego, California - 30+ Credits
- Undergraduate Studies - Major Emphasis: Fire Science

Palomar Community College, San Marcos, California - 20+ Credits
- Undergraduate Studies - Major Emphasis: Fire Science

Santa Ana College, Santa Ana, California - 20+ Credits
- Undergraduate Studies - Major Emphasis: Fire Science

Santa Ana College Fire Academy, Santa Ana, California
- Honor Graduate: Certificated Fire Science Course

California State Department of Education
- Fundamentals of Radiological Monitoring, 1991
- Oil Fire School, 1983
- Surviving Hazardous Materials Incidents, 1989

California State Board of Fire Services
- Fire Apparatus Driver Operator I, IA, IB, 1988
- Firefighter I & II, 1985 and 1986

California Specialized Training Institute (CSTI) Courses
- Building Collapse, 1991 •Fire Investigation IA, 1991
- Firefighter Safety, 1991 •Fire Management I, 1994
- Fire Hydraulics, 1983 •Flammable Liquids Fire Control, 1988
- Fire Instructor IA, 1992 •First Responder Operational, 1989
- Fire Instructor IB, 1992 •Pipeline Safety, 1987

California State Fire Officer Certification Program
- Fire Prevention IA & IB, 1988 and 1989
- Fire Command IA & IB, 1986 and 1986

MEMBERSHIPS, AFFILIATIONS, ASSOCIATIONS

California Firefighters Association (CFA), Sacramento, California
Fallbrook Firefighters Association (FFA), Fallbrook, California

CREDENTIALS, CERTIFICATIONS, LICENSES

- American Heart Association - CPR Certificate
- California State Certified Fire Officer
- California State Class B Commercial License
- San Diego County, Emergency Medical Services, License: EMT-D
- State Certified Driver Operator

Appropriate personal and professional references are available.

---

ella brookstone

108 Paradise Harbour Boulevard, Apt. 405
Fallbrook, California 92028
Phone: (760) 555-1212/Cell: (760) 555-2323
email@email.com

FLIGHT ATTENDANT—FOR A MAJOR AIRLINE
Customer Service/Problem Solving/Organizational Expertise
10 Years of Impeccable Flying Experience

Outstanding Interpersonal and Rapport-¡uilding Skills
Recognized as a Team Player/Leader

A hardworking, service-oriented professional recognized as an enthusiastic team player dedicated to enhancing organizational goals and objectives. More than 15 successful years in fast-track service environments.

CORE STRENGTHS

Policy and procedure enforcement	Regulatory compliance
Crisis management	Organizational leadership/team building
First Aid and CPR training	Communication skills (verbal/written)
Training and development	Flexible and adaptable
Creative and innovative	Quality control

PROFESSIONAL EXPERIENCE

WINGS OF MAN EXECUTIVE TRANSPORT, San Diego, California   1992 to Current
Lead Flight Attendant

- Ensure outstanding customer service and that all guests safely enjoy their flying experience.
- Train and develop new hires over the 3¹/₂ years as senior employee with the airline.
- Developed policy and procedures manual leading to improved efficiency and substantial cost savings.
- Successfully maintained calm and order during two emergency landings.

IBIS GOLF & COUNTRY CLUB, La Jolla, California   1988 to 1992
Assistant Manager

- Consistently meet/exceed club-member expectations while managing main dining room.
- Hired, trained, and supervised a staff of 34 people, including eight chefs and four supervisors.
- Managed and coordinated banquets ranging in size from 15 to 650 people.

EDUCATION

University of Maine, Portland, Maine
Bachelor of Science: Psychology and Pre-Med, 1982–1986

Johnson & Wales College, Providence, Rhode Island
Food & Beverage Management, 1986–1988

ACTIVITIES

Volunteer: Make a Wish Foundation
Volunteer: Special Olympics
Marathon Runner and Fitness Instructor

References Furnished upon Request

ARTHUR C. PARKERTON

2344 Shoreline Drive
Boca Raton, Florida 33433

email@email.com
(407) 555-5337

FOOD & BEVERAGE / HOSPITALITY EXECUTIVE
- DIRECTOR OF CATERING & CLUB MANAGEMENT -

OVERVIEW:

A highly experienced, profit-oriented professional with an impressive record of accomplishments in high-volume, upscale dining environments. A management professional recognized for integrity and competence. Areas of expertise include:

Growth & Revenue Enhancement
Personnel Management
Provide High-Quality Service
Deliver Solid ROI to Stockholders

Profit Attainment
Member/Guest Relations
High-Volume Catering
Increasing Club Membership

PROFESSIONAL
HIGHLIGHTS:

Y **Fine Dining Management Experience:** Employed by distinguished establishments, including Premiere Club of the Palm Beaches, Governors Club at Phillips Point, and Coleman's Catering Corporation. A strong list of accomplishments and fine references.

Y **Caterer For President's Dinners:** For President Reagan and Vice President Bush, Washington, D.C., Convention Center, 1985. Served 5,600 honored guests.

Y **Caterer:** New York Harbor Independence Day Celebration, dedicating the restoration of the *Statue of Liberty*. Served 11,500 guests aboard yachts.

Y **Governor's Ball, New Jersey:** Directed all catering operations (seven consecutive years) for the largest black-tie political dinner held under a tent (5,000 guests).

PROFESSIONAL
EXPERIENCE:
1991 - Present

Premiere Club of the Palm Beaches, Silver Tower Plaza, North Palm Beach, Florida
GENERAL MANAGER / DIRECTOR OF CATERING - Direct all F&B and catering operations for this exclusive private dining club. Recognized for maintaining high-quality food and service during major growth period.

Successfully managed growth as club grew from 345 to 845 members. Stabilized all key positions and significantly reduced turnover.

Reduced membership sales payroll two-thirds, while exceeding growth projections. Simultaneously improved employee productivity and morale.

Directly reported to Club Owner and C.E.O.

Delivered a 26% return on investment to shareholders and owners.

(Continued)

Arthur C. Parkerton

EXPERIENCE
(Continued):
1989 - 1991

<u>Governors Club At Phillips Point</u>, West Palm Beach, Florida
DIRECTOR OF CATERING - Directed all catering operations for this upscale private dining club with over 1,200 members. The club was affiliated with *Country Clubs of America (CCA)*, a worldwide network of renowned establishments.

Ignited catering revenues from $600,000 to $990,000 the first year and $1.2 million the second season. Catering revenues contributed 50% of total sales—a 25% increase achieved in less than 24 months.

Awarded *Catering Director of the Year*, receiving recognition from CCA, for strong pioneering efforts in promoting catering within the private club industry. Trained Catering Directors throughout the region.

1977 - 1988

<u>Ballard's Catering Corp.</u>, Morristown, New Jersey
PRESIDENT - Over 11 years, owned/operated three successful catering firms targeting specific markets, including affluent clientele and government officials.

Built business from ground zero to a highly profitable $6.5 million organization employing over 600 people.

Directed formal black-tie affairs for Presidents Nixon, Ford, Carter, and Reagan (5,600 guests/function). Catered major events including the Governor's Ball (NJ) and Independence Day Celebration (NY Harbor).

Began <u>Associated Catering</u>, 1979 (midprice catering). Began <u>Catering by Albert K</u>, 1980 (Jewish clientele). Restored a historical railroad station to a 175-seat restaurant. All ventures were profitable and sold.

1964 - 1977

<u>Coleman's Inc.</u>, Newark, New Jersey
VICE PRESIDENT / GENERAL MANAGER - Joined in an entry-level capacity and ascended to positions of increasing responsibility over 13 years. Positions held: Sous Chef; Steward; Food & Beverage Manager; Director of Purchasing; Director of Operations; Vice President/General Manager.

EDUCATION:

<u>Adelphi University</u>, Long Island, New York
BACHELOR OF SCIENCE DEGREE
Major: Hotel/Restaurant Management; Minor: Personnel Management

INTERESTS:

Skiing, HO trains (hobby), and gardening. Member: International Geneva Association, Confrerie de La Chaine des Rotisseurs, and Ordre de la Mondial

REFERENCES:

Furnished upon request.

MARCUS H. COLEMAN
5437 East 42nd Street • New York, New York 10012 • Phone (212) 555-5421 • MColeman@email.com

---

MULTISITE FOOD & BEVERAGE OPERATIONS MANAGER

Dynamic 10+ year professional career leading daily operations of fast-paced, F&B operations within the entertainment, hotel, restaurant and contract food service industries. Strong qualifications in personnel development, team building and team leadership. Effective motivator, trainer and mentor. Dedicated to continuous improvements in quality, productivity, efficiency and customer service. Core competencies:

Operations Management
Scope of responsibility is diverse and includes planning, budgeting, expense control, recruitment, staffing, scheduling, procurement, inventory control, menu planning/pricing, facilities management, and customer service/guest relations. Direct and decisive with "hands-on" management style. **RESULT: Contributed to solid cost reductions and revenue/profit growth.**

Customer Relations
Manage ongoing relationships with key customer accounts. As on-site liaison to client management, coordinate the planning, development and delivery of customized service programs. Advise regarding customer contract negotiations and the allocation of personnel, budgets and resources. **RESULT: Recognized throughout career for outstanding customer service and relationship management skills.**

Human Resources & Training
Direct staffs of up to 80 responsible for food preparation and service delivery. Plan staff schedules to ensure adequate manpower coverage, coordinate employee training, and design/implement incentives and other motivational programs to enhance customer service competencies. **RESULT: Consistently improved and strengthened customer relations/retention.**

Purchasing, Vendor Relations & Inventory Management
Plan, budget and manage all purchasing, inventory planning and stock replenishment programs. Concurrently, source and select vendors, negotiate terms and conditions, and implement vendor quality standards. **RESULT: Consistently maintained costs at or under budgeted projections.**

Budgeting & Financial Affairs
Participate in the planning, development, administration and management of annual operating budgets valued at up to $300,000 annually. Evaluate personnel, supply, equipment and material requirements to assist in budget planning and forecasting for multiple operating locations. **RESULT: Consistently managed operations to within 97% of budget.**

PROFESSIONAL EXPERIENCE

Manager – AT&T World Headquarters, International Food Management Services (1996 to 1998)
Recruited to manage $750,000 annual contract providing cafeteria and vending services for 1500 employees at AT&T World Headquarters. Challenged to improve menu selection, introduce professional service delivery and provide operations expertise to enhance client relations where previous management had failed.

Banquet Captain / Maitre'D, Waldorf Astoria Hotel (1990 to 1995)
Directed special event and banquet affairs for this prestigious hotel. Managed an average of 60 events per month, including the "Mayor's Breakfast," a benefit for 200 regional business leaders who played a key role in bringing new business opportunities to metro New York.

Assistant Manager, Sands Hotel & Casino (1983 to 1990)
Fast-track promotion through increasingly responsible operating management positions from Cook to Supervisor to Assistant Manager. Directed the operations of up to five locations with supervisory responsibility for 80+ employees serving more than 2500 clients daily.

EDUCATION

B.S. in Fine Arts & Business Management, Culinary Institute of America (1983)
Apprentice Chef under Chef Garrett Winchester

JENNIFER D. SOMMERS

8400 Industrial Parkway
Dublin, OH 43016

Home: (614) 555-2484
email@email.com

EDUCATION/TRAINING

Bachelor of Science, Natural Resources, Ohio State University, 1995
> Major: Urban Forestry
> Honors: Cum laude with distinction in **Forest Resource Management**
> National Golden Key Honor Society, **Gamma Sigma Delta**

Certified Arborist, International Society of Arboriculture, 1995
Ornamental Plant and Shade Tree Pest Control, Ohio Public Operator's License, 1995
Conferences: Ohio Nurseryman's Conferences, 1994-95, 1996-97;
> Urban Forestry Conference, 1994-95, 1996-97
Accounting Certificate, Columbus Business University, 1982
Bachelor of Arts, Psychology, Ohio University, Athens, 1978

PROFESSIONAL HIGHLIGHTS

- Skilled project coordinator and team supervisor; effective in prioritizing, delegating, and motivating; effective problem solver with ability to maximize resources
- Experienced working with municipal agencies and local governments
- Educated in the infrastructure between urban forestry and city
- Assigned by Horticulturist to maintain large perennial beds in eight city parks
- Experienced crew leader, ensuring all street sites were marked by OUPS (Ohio Utilities Protection Service) before planting of street trees; oversaw planting and maintenance of street trees and public gardens
- Implemented Landmark Tree Program:
  - Sought and gained approval from City Council to initiate a Landmark Tree Program in Marysville, Ohio
  - Researched and documented large tree criteria of surrounding communities and states
  - Established guidelines to certify Landmark Trees

WORK EXPERIENCE

CITY OF MARYSVILLE — Marysville, OH
Park Tree Inventory Specialist — 1997-Present
- Locate, identify, and perform health assessment of all park trees; record and later input into in-house tree inventory computer program

Assistant City Forester — 1994-1997
- Supervised and maintained city street trees. Entailed planting, mulching, pruning, watering, staking, fertilizing, and the ability to operate machinery and small power equipment as well as the use of hand tools. (Tree population - 5,000)
- Participated in the following activities:
  - Pruning approximately 1,950 trees (increase of 76% over previous year)
  - Fertilizing approximately 460 trees (increase of 150% over previous year)
  - Managing citywide tree planting by various landscape contractors and the City of Marysville Parks crews: Established street tree locations; followed up on tree inspections; initiated verbal and written correspondence with developers and landscape contractors; and notified homeowners of tree plantings
  - Organizing City of Marysville, Tree City USA Program

OHIO STATE UNIVERSITY — Columbus, OH
Full-Time Student — 1992-1995
- Gained valuable horticulture field knowledge experience
- Volunteered for campus tree planting program

CITY OF MARYSVILLE — Marysville, OH
Account Clerk, Finance and Mayor's Court — 1989-1992

BENNETT & BENNETT, INC. — Columbus, OH
Bookkeeper — 1983-1989

The creation of a thousand forests is in one acorn.
— *Ralph Waldo Emerson*

COURTNEY BRUELL
18 Brookshield Drive
Las Vegas, Nevada 70623
(505) 555-1212 / email@email.com

Seeking Position as...

FORKLIFT OPERATOR
WAREHOUSE SUPERVISOR

Recognized for 100% Perfect Safety Record—and Strong, Team-Spirited Work Ethic
11 Years' Experience

More than 11 years' experience as forklift operator, four years as warehouse supervisor in charge of six warehouse employees. Excellent work experience supported by verifiable letters of reference.

AREAS OF STRENGTH

Forklift and heavy-equipment operations	Shipping & receiving operations
OSHA regulations and code compliance	Traffic management and control
Inventory management—JIT systems	Cycle and perpetual inventory control
Employee training and supervision	Documentation and record keeping
Quality control	Customer service

EMPLOYMENT

Las Vegas Beverage and Distribution Center, Las Vegas, Nevada   1993 to Present
Forklift Operator/Warehouse Supervisor

- In charge of all forklift operations for 55,000 square-foot warehouse distributing beverages to businesses throughout Las Vegas and the neighboring communities.
- Began as stock clerk and worked way up to warehouse supervisor and lead forklift operator in charge of six employees.
- Train all new employees and ensure all new hires are cleared for safe work.
- Maintained a 100% safety record—reducing liability claims/losses by hundreds of thousands of dollars.
- Helped build morale and reduce employee/warehouse turnover.
- Outstanding technical/mechanical aptitude—repair most forklift trucks on premise.

EMPLOYMENT (Prior to 1993)

Bartender:

Sloop John B's	Las Vegas
Happy Harold's	Las Vegas
The Ace in the Hole	Las Vegas

EDUCATION/TRAINING

OBERTON COMMUNITY COLLEGE, Toronto, Ontario
A.A. Degree: Electronics, 1987

Continuing Education
Warehouse Management
Just-in-Time (JIT) Inventory Seminar
Computer Classes: Word, Excel, and Internet

References and Supporting Documentation Furnished upon Request

Brett Spears

7000 N. Mopac • Austin, Texas 78749 • 512.555.5555 • brett@bigfoot.com

E X E C U T I V E   S U M M A R Y

Dynamic Internet Technology executive with over 12 years experience in Webcasting, broadcasting, online community development, and Internet Engineering for major online, telecommunications, and software organizations. Recognized pioneer in emerging Internet technologies and applications for B2B and B2C content marketing strategies. Visionary developer of corporate online strategies and portal alliances. Highly skilled in functional and technical aspects of online venture creation and launch. Excellent communicator able to achieve goals and motivate team members.

C A R E E R   H I G H L I G H T S

- ❑ **Industry pioneer in Internet Virtual Community Development and Strategic Online Alliances**

- ❑ **Codeveloper of "simulchat" concept combining radio and online communications**

- ❑ **Nationally recognized expert on Online Health and Self-Help portal services**

- ❑ **Key player in start up and initial public offering stages of dot.com and software organizations**

- ❑ **Astute multimedia producer with strong knowledge of program development, strategic planning, alliance creation, and online marketing**

I N T E R N E T   E N T E R P R I S E   E X P E R I E N C E

drkoop.com, Inc.   Austin, Texas
DIRECTOR OF FORUM COMMUNITIES   1998-present

Played key role as creator of most diverse set of online health communities on the Internet during enterprise start-up and launch. Coordinated with Web designers, content developers, public relations specialists, and sales representatives to create award winning health content communities. Negotiated and settled contracts with key health and media organizations for development and delivery of content-rich, customized online health portal services. Produced special events that included special guest chat events, audio/video simulcasts, and cause-based programs. Designed effective incentive programs and managed departmental budget of over $1 million. Instrumental in achieving success in broadband positioning. Managed department of over 80 employees, successfully maintaining morale and motivation despite insecure corporate direction.

America Online, Inc.   Vienna, Virginia
FORUM MANAGER   1993-1998

Managed the National Public Radio and Online Psychology forums for AOL. Originated and deployed content using proprietary AOL publishing software. Directed all events and managed both forums as independent business units. Produced special online events and coordinated with NPR and mental health organizations to produce value-rich content delivery. Broke new ground through launch of simulchat effort, successfully integrating radio and online communications. Initiated thrust for AOL health focus.

HealthDesk, Corp. • elasticMEDIA, Inc.   Berkeley and Walnut Creek, California
ONLINE STRATEGY DIRECTOR/WEBMASTER   1995-1996

Masterminded corporate Internet strategies for both organizations — companies involved in design and deployment of healthcare industry software. Defined e-business strategies from scratch during the infancy stages of the Internet and ecommerce. Led online marketing program and convinced corporate leadership of importance of having online presence.

(Continued)

ONLINE SERVICES CONSULTING

Provided expert consulting and expertise on start-up phases of online healthcare-oriented communities and services for several entities. Spearheaded and defined online strategies and outlined marketing plans for content/service deliverables. Advised on market conditions and consulted during online launch phases of sites and portals.

RadioDigest.com, Inc.	1999-present
MediaLinx Interactive, Inc. • Healthyway.ca	1996
Kaiser Permanente Interactive Technology Group	1996
AT&T Personal Online Services Division	1996

TECHNICAL EXPERIENCE

Exodus Communications, Inc.   Seattle, Washington
NETWORK ENGINEER   1997-1998

Built and managed Network Operations Centers for outsourced network services, serving top 50% of Internet traffic sites. Troubleshot servers and connectivity as Tech Support Specialist and won promotion to Lead Engineer due to work performance. Planned, built, and managed new $20 million data center in Seattle. Supervised installation of servers, creation of security procedures, and buildout of infrastructure. Wrote procedures, hired engineers, and trained on operations to provide 24x7 support.

CORE Communications, Inc.   Fremont, California
CATV ENGINEER   1989-1995

Engineered cable television connectivity and planning of services. Managed daily operations of main office and coordinated with offices in DC, Chicago, and the Bay Area on service provision.

NOTED AWARDS AND ACTIVITIES

National Speaker
HealthFinder.gov Launch Department of Health and Human Services, Washington, D.C. • 1997

National Speaker
Online Consumer Health Conference Fred Mutchinson Cancer Research Center, Seattle, Washington • 1996

Distinguished Achievement Award – Online Health • 1996

Cited as Internet health community pioneer by:
  Health Online   MSNBC
  The Self-Help Sourcebook   The New York Times
  eHealth Strategy & Trends   USA Today

EDUCATION AND TRAINING

Bachelor of Science – Broadcast Engineering
  University of California, Berkeley, California

Training:
  Cisco Router Training • America Online Forum Management • TV Production – TCI Cablevision

Complete Technical Skills Addendum Attached

Matt Wajda

5471 Straight Road, Columbus Ohio 32147 • (111) 555-5555

Legal Consultant

AREAS OF EXPERTISE

- Mediation/Negotiations
- Litigation Management
- International Business
- Proposal Development
- Budgeting & Cost Reduction

- Contract Drafting/Review
- Compliance/Regulatory Reporting
- Large-Scale Project Management
- Marketing/Advertising Regulation
- Public Relations Management

- Dispute Resolutions
- Federal/State Legislation
- Risk Management
- SEC Rules & Regulations
- New Business Development

GENERAL CORPORATE EXPERIENCE

International Law

o Develop, direct, and prioritize international business initiatives and utilize resources to meet existing needs.

o Review various legal agreements and international legislation; prepare presentations from a legal prospective for use in business initiatives.

o Communicate universal model functionality, priorities, and versioning process to staff in international locations. Utilize global perspective to convey relevant corporate activities, priorities, and decisions.

o Establish and maintain business relations with international staff, particularly host country leadership.

o Research products/services from local target markets, select operating sites, and help set up resident infrastructure. Procure equipment/supplies, resolve connectivity issues, conduct lease negotiations, obtain insurance, and assist in recruitment/hiring of in-country staff.

o Lead and coordinate administrative and IT teams to successfully integrate new business abroad. Oversee and direct procedures, controls, testing, and training initiatives for operating business locations.

(Continued)

Matt Wajda

Project Management

o Instrumental in resolution of major class-action lawsuit. Coordinated project management, litigation management follow-up and dispute resolution activities; trained, supervised, and administrated staff performance and astutely leveraged project team to successful settlement.

o Designed, developed, and implemented scoring guidelines/adjustment criteria, evidence analysis/review guidelines, a comprehensive scoring matrix, and other legal assessment instruments to streamline claims review and valuation processes and to establish relief for an anticipated 18,000 class-action lawsuit claims.

o Formulated, drafted, and structured a comprehensive appeals package for the purpose of contesting dispute resolution determinations.

o Prepare/implement project charters and administrative portion of country work plans. Identify/coordinate resources to achieve business objectives in local operating companies. Analyze issues of international law and coordinate resolution and compliance activities.

EMPLOYMENT HISTORY

1987 to 2004
Worthington Financial (www.worthingtonlife.com) – Cincinnati, OH
$96.5 billion holding company for Worthington Insurance Services, and its major operating subsidiary, Worthington Life Insurance Company.

o 1995-present **Country Integrator**
o 1987-1995 **Attorney, Project Development & Dispute Resolution**

EDUCATION

Juris Doctorate, Capital University College of Law, Columbus OH; 1997. Top 3% of Legal Research and Writing class. Admitted to practice law in Ohio and Federal District Court for the Southern District Court of Ohio.

Bachelor of Arts, Human Resources Administration, Saint Leo College, Saint Leo, FL; Honors Graduate — GPA 3.95. 1992

Lindsay Kubeck

21 East 39 Street, Apt. #3
New York, NY 10016

voice ■ 212-555-5555
fax ■ 212-555-1111
e-mail ■ ColeK@aol.com

Senior-level General Management ■ Modular Manufacturing Processes

---

Executive Profile

■ Over ten years of senior-level experience in astute business analysis and profitable management of 20 million dollar custom manufacturer. Forecast sales trends, enhance revenue streams, turn around troubled operations, and achieve profitability in down-trending markets. Administer all manufacturing, marketing, and environmental control functions. Supervise staff of up to 25 direct and indirect reports.

■ A hands-on manager and critical thinker who can learn quickly, develop expertise, and produce immediate contributions in systems, analysis, business operations, and motivational team-management. Possess a valuable blending of leadership, creative, and analytical abilities that combine efficiency with imagination to produce bottom-line results.

Proven Areas of Knowledge

■ business planning / development	■ operations management	■ operational troubleshooting
■ revenues and margins	■ multiple project management	■ task analysis
■ modular manufacturing architecture	■ facilities management	■ capital / consumable purchasing
■ trend and competitive analysis	■ crisis management	■ high-expectation client relations
■ joint venture formation	■ environmental management	■ training and development

---

Executive Highlights

■ Produced exceptional company growth, increased gross margin, enhanced productivity, and set new quality standards through the proactive design of innovative programs, sales techniques, and manufacturing methodologies as well as the imaginative use of unique suppliers.

■ Doubled company's accounts and quadrupled sales by design and implementation of profitable value-added services. Division generated unit sales per employee that were 1.5 times those of the industry's largest independent service bureau. Produced division turnaround time of 10 to 12 weeks vs. industry average of 13 to 18 weeks.

■ Created an innovative in-house service bureau, the only one of its kind in the industry. Produced new revenue streams representing 12.5% of sales through proactive marketing of new service bureau as a quasi-independent operation that gained new cross-industry, nonprinting accounts.

■ Avoided purchase of multi-million-dollar computer graphics system through inventive utilization of offset and reprographic service bureaus, reducing expenses even further by scheduling projects in bureaus' down times.

■ Designed and directed company's strategy to prevent major losses from 40% erosion of customer base during late 80's recession. Spearheaded production of proprietary nationally distributed wallcovering collections, advertising, and collateral materials. Developed manufacturing relationships with large furniture producers and cosmetics firms. Marketed color separation and film services to competitors.

■ Prevented massive disruption in service by assuming immediate control of all manufacturing operations in crisis response to key administrators' mismanagement and subsequent departure.

Lindsay Kubeck page two

Employment History

Distinction Printing, Ltd., Long Island City, NY   1980 to present

Company manufactures custom wallcoverings, decorative laminates, large-scale graphics and point-of-purchase specialties, with a peak sales volume of $20 million and a number two ranking in this specialized industry of twenty contract wallcovering printers in the United States.

Vice President and General Manager   1995 to present

Assumed control of all manufacturing operations following departure of two key managers. Situation required immediate action to position company to recover from mismanagement. Downsized staff, slashed overhead, cross-trained personnel, instituted strict housekeeping controls to curtail waste, and reduced inventory — all with no reduction in quality.

Increased margins by 60% on four existing customer collections, signed with two new national distributors, and developed high-margin accounts. Increased business without increasing expenses through the use of vendors' salespeople as a de facto sales force to market company's services to noncompeting screen-print industries.

Manage facility operation and safety/environmental coordination. Supervise all facility functions, including hiring of contractors for maintenance and renovations. Administer vital hazardous materials program for entire corporation, including training, compliance, documentation, and reporting. Directed all repairs, contractors, and insurance affairs after partial roof collapse and flooding in 1996.

Sales and Operations Manager   1987 to 1995

Held full P&L responsibility. Increased division sales by 30% between 1987 and 1990 and steered company through the recession of the late 80's / early 90's, when fully 40% of the industry's customer base was lost through consolidation and bankruptcy. Researched and developed new markets, created new opportunities as outsourced producer for competitors' small runs, and positioned company as fast-turnaround specialist.

Pre-Press Manager   1980 to 1987

Planned production, scheduled, procured consumables, capital equipment, and outsourced services. Created value-added services that directly contributed to doubling of company's account base and quadrupling of sales from 1980 to 1987. Ran division turnaround times typically 30% less than industry standard, with no decline in quality.

Education and Development

Masters of Business Administration, New York University, New York, NY, 1990

Bachelor of Arts in Business Administration, State University of New York at Stony Brook, 1979

Technology

Use PC word processing, database and spreadsheet software (MS Office), the Internet and e-mail.

Easily learn specific industry systems and software. Familiar with Mac, especially graphic arts software.

REBECCA SAMUELSON

555 West 45th Street • New York, New York 10001
Home: 215-555-5555
samuelson@email.net

SUMMARY OF QUALIFICATIONS

Results-focused performer with 10+ years' accomplishments in the areas of **Operations, Procurement, Materials, Contract Manufacturing and Supply Chain Management**. Experienced managing complex projects involving diverse stakeholders to secure timely, quality-focused results. Genuine talent for identifying supplier and company needs to effect profitable, long-term win-win solutions. Proven team member/leader contributing to high-growth/start-up situations through strategic planning, organizational efficiency and systems development. Focus on customer retention, cost reduction and revenue generation.

☑ Strategic Procurement Initiatives/Alliances
☑ Supplier Contract Negotiation
☑ Technology Installations/Upgrades
☑ New Product Development/Introduction
☑ Staffing, Development and Training

☑ Materials Management in Multiple Facilities
☑ Relationship Development/Management
☑ MRP/ERP
☑ Standard Operating Procedures (SOPs)
☑ Interpersonal Communication Skills

CAREER PROGRESSION

CONTROL EQUIPMENT, New York, New York   2002 to Present
(A subsidiary of Control Holdings, a $200M global, publicly traded manufacturer of replacement parts/service for air pollution control equipment. Control Equipment's focus is the design and manufacture of ABC membrane products.) [www.controlequipmentny.com]

Global Product Supply Manager

Challenged with global supply chain system development for a high-growth start-up operation. Purchased and scheduled component delivery, lamination operations and product movements across 5 product categories driving $4.2 million in revenues. Instituted procurement procedures that boosted productivity and grew revenues. Supervisory and hiring responsibilities. ***Key Accomplishments:***

- **Led team of operations/technologist professionals** in establishing Extranet Global Planning System (GPS) to link global supply partners and improve customer relationship management.
- **Spurred a 4-fold increase in new product trials at USA laminators** by originating a paperless distribution system, while concurrently fulfilling ISO 9001 certification requirements.
- **Devised product supply chain** for 2 new product lines predicted to boost 2003 sales $1.3 million.
- **Cut material purchasing costs an average 15%** on annual contracts totaling $375,000.

LINTON EXCHANGE, New York, New York   2000 to 2002
(Operates world's largest exchange center for limited-edition collector's china.) [www.linton.com]

Operations Manager

Directed global purchasing, scheduling, collectible manufacturing operations and product movements for 5 corporations with a combined $280 million sales. Supervised 9 employees and was authorized to purchase up to $25,000 in assets in a single purchase order. Held joint P&L responsibility with the director for $40.5 million purchasing budget. ***Key Accomplishments:***

- **Spearheaded product design process improvement**; formulated spending goals and facilitated price negotiations for 43 unique product categories, saving a cumulative $620,000/year.
- **Captured over $1 million in cost savings** by originating out-of-the-box strategies: 1) Yantain export discount saving $90,000; 2) China component inventory reduction saving $2.12 million; 3) Domestic china outsourcing to Japan, saving $200,000.

Continued on Page Two

REBECCA SAMUELSON, Page Two
Home: 215-649-5555 • rsamuelson@email.net

MANDIS CORP., Westchester, New York   1998 to 2000
($20 million private-label pharmaceutical company.)

Director of Operations/Purchasing Manager
Reporting directly to the CEO/owner, supervised 7 employees and oversaw manufacturing, inventory control, processing, production line capacity and initial equipment purchasing. Scope of diverse responsibility included processing, filling, packaging, warehousing and product distribution. Served as operations contact for nationwide retailers.

Key Accomplishments:
- **Engineered third-party contract services** for product manufacturing for The Dove Corporation and Medical Laboratories.
- **Boosted line speeds 60%** on company's major drug product category by separating filling and packaging lines to enhance equipment/resources/operational efficiencies.
- **Saved between $30,000 and $180,000** in annual operating expenses.

THE DOVE CORPORATION, New York, New York   1994 to 1998
($700 million chemical and consumer products company with 2,500 employees.) [www.dovecorp.com]

Manager of Contract Packaging/
Specialist—Contract Packaging/Production Manager & Team Leader
Challenged with a series of rapid advancements leading to Manager of Contract Purchasing, charged with scheduling, purchasing and operations management of 5 contract manufacturing companies producing Liquid Dove products. Subcontracted 610,000 cases of Liquid Dove to outside contractor. Innovated long-term win-win strategies between the suppliers and Dove.

Key Accomplishments:
- **Curbed manufacturing costs by 15%** ($2 million/year) by assessing contract needs and strategizing long-term financial solutions.
- **Instrumental contributor to the successful roll-out** of a 30-product bath and body line. Forged contract manufacturer relationship in London, England, and managed the entire supply chain through product introduction, meeting a tight time frame and budget.
- **Achieved a 99% quality rating,** highest ever rating in facility's history.
- **Captured 2 "Whatever It Takes" President's Awards.**

THE BRANDIX COMPANY, Philadelphia, Pennsylvania   1987 to 1994
(Leading manufacturer and marketer of consumer products with FY2002 revenues of $5 billion.) [www.brandix.com]

Production Manager/Maintenance Manager/Project Manager
Brought on board to participate in specification/purchase/installation effort of a $3.2 million molding/filling bleach line. Succession of promotions involved project installation, preventive maintenance and employee supervision initiatives, leading to Production Manager. Led a 17-person molding/filling technician team and oversaw operations and budget.

Key Accomplishments:
- **Saved $2.2 million/year** through installation/management of molding/filling bleach operation.
- **Innovated and achieved buy-in to solution that expanded a "land-locked" department** to accommodate processes to produce 75% of the USA's needs for new Brandix Plumbing product.
- **Drove several six-figure savings efforts** via effective vendor negotiations, materials recycling and systems enhancements.

EDUCATION

MBA in Strategic Management
B.S. in Production Technology Management
New York University, New York, New York

LEE F. STRINGER, PGA GOLF PROFESSIONAL

2344 Wallace Way
Palm Beach, Florida 33418
Phone: (561) 555-1211/Email: email@email.com

A strong, high-energy and proven **PGA Golf Professional** offering twelve-plus years of successful, verifiable experience for a number of America's most prestigious clubs. **A bottom-line focused professional** with outstanding interpersonal skills. Recognized as a top instructor.

CAREER HIGHLIGHTS—*Old Marsh Golf Club*

OLD MARSH GOLF CLUB, Palm Beach Gardens, Florida   1990 to Current
Director of Golf
Director of Golf for prestigious 18-hole facility (rated one of top private golf clubs in country by *Golf Digest*) designed by Pete Dye. The club boasts 255 members playing 20,000 rounds annually. Direct and manage entire golf operations.
• Prepare and administer $390,000+ annual budget—meeting/exceeding all financial goals.
• Recruit, train, and manage a professional staff of 14—to ensure delivery of premiere service.
• Reorganized and direct a caddie program of 30 professional caddies—rated top 50 in United States (*Links Magazine*).
• Incorporate state-of-the-art video/computer technologies to enhance the quality of member instruction.
• Ignited golf-shop sales from $387,000 to $479,000 through improved operational and sales efficiencies.
• Increased golf-shop profit margins 12% by improving staff productivity and customer service.
• Assist with membership sales and conduct new-member orientations.
• Plan and conduct seven major golf tournaments per year—(concept through awards presentations).
• Personally facilitate 340+ private lessons (in season).
• More than 50 of my students either won or placed in club tournaments.
• Work closely with Director of Instruction (1996–97), Todd Anderson (*Golf Digest* Instructor).
• Organized and conducted Mark Calcavecchia Golf Exhibition.
• Utilize Event Man Software for premiere tournament presentation.
• Conduct four-day men's invitational, including a skills contest and shootout.
• Manage inventory in excess of $150,000 with sales of $479,000 annually.
• Expert club fitter—leading to a 30% increase in golf-club sales.
• Increased dollars-per-round from $19.83 in 1996 to $23.95 in 2000/2001.

CAREER HIGHLIGHTS—Prior to 1990

Head Professional   HATHERLY GOLF CLUB, North Scituate, Massachusetts
First Assistant Professional   JUPITER HILLS CLUB, Tequesta, Florida
Assistant Golf Professional   PEMBROKE GOLF CLUB, Pembroke, Massachusetts

FORMAL EDUCATION/TRAINING

SALEM STATE COLLEGE, Salem Massachusetts
Bachelor of Science: Sports Fitness, 1987

PGA Business School I, II, III; David Leadbetter Retreat; Chuck Hogan Expert School; PGA Advanced Teaching and Playing Seminar; Jim McLean Training School; Rick Smith Golf School; Florida State Golf Association Rules Seminar

PLAYING ACHIEVEMENTS

Contestant, Anhueser Busch Classic PGA Tour; Southeast Chapter Assistant's Champion; Placed 3d on South Florida Section PGA Money List; Inducted into Salem State College Athletic Hall of Fame, 1993; Low Last Round South Florida Open (66); Hogan Tour and Mini Tour Participant 1991–1995; Placed 2d in the Rhode Island Open

References and Supporting Documentation Furnished on Request

72—GOVERNMENT—FAA

Mark Hinzman

7759 Ace Drive • Baltimore, Maryland 21203
(410) 555-1212 / emeial@email.com
SS#: 000-00-0000 / Veteran Status: N/A / US Citizen

Department of Transportation – Federal Aviation Administration
Applying for: Civil Aviation Security Investigative Officer
Investigative Specialist – Maintenance Expert
GD-111-222-33/4

Licenses / Credentials

Top Secret Security Clearance
Private Pilot's License
Level 4 Investigative Grade

US Army Maintenance Certification - L12
Advanced Navigational Training
Aviation Regulations 76, 88, FR6, and RR52

Education

GEORGE WASHINGTON UNIVERSITY, Washington, DC
Bachelor of Technical Science: Aviation Management, 2000
Aviation Planning
Aviation Technology
Aviation Disaster Investigation I, II, III

Aviation Safety and Security
Aviation Crisis Management
Aviation for Future Generations

Internship: Dulles Airport – Security Officer/Investigator, Small Aircraft
- Inspections
- Evidence Gathering
- General Security

Computer Skills: SourceBook, AviatePro, NavSystems 6.0, Simmod, Office, and Internet

Professional Experience

AVIATION CONSULTANTS INTERNATIONAL, Baltimore, Maryland   1995 to Current
Aviation Investigator / Assistant to Lead Investigator

- Hired on a part-time basis while attending school to assist and support Lead Investigator in aviation and aviation-related accidents / incidents. Utilized extensive technical and mechanical experience to fit the pieces of the aviation puzzle back together, including crashes, near misses, callbacks, and airline mechanical records and reports. Most assignments are requested by the FAA through Aviation Consultants international.

- Advanced to Aviation Investigator upon complete of BTS degree in Aviation Management in 2000. In the past eight months, successfully investigated six private aircraft crashes, nationwide, developed three comprehensive reports for FAA regarding maintenance records of two major airlines for an eight-month period.

- Trainer of new recruits hired on as Assistants to Lead Investigators. Developed comprehensive orientation program that significantly reduced overall "break in time."

Affiliations / Activities

American Pilots Association
National Aviation Association of America

National Association of Aviation Investigators
Aviation Mechanics Association

References Furnished upon Request

T.J. ZEKE

610 DeVosta Grade Road
Upperville, Virginia 20184
Phone / Fax: (540) 555-1212 / email@email.com

HIGH-LEVEL CORPORATE / GOVERNMENT RELATIONS
State and Federal Congressional / White House Liaison

Increasing Corporate Growth & Exposures through Governmental Access and Influence

High-Level Government Access / Strong Media Alliances
Incorporating Strong Private Sector Partnerships

A well-connected, achievement-driven Public Relations/Communications Executive with outstanding qualifications in all phases of corporate/governmental communications with particular emphasis on strategic crisis management. Spearheaded the public relations efforts for national and international crises, including:

• **Tylenol Crisis**   • **Three-Mile Island Crisis**   • **Teamsters / Government Takeover**

HIGHLIGHTS OF EXPERIENCE

- Spokesperson for International Union representing more than 2 million members and affiliate members
- Director of Public Relations and Congressional Liaison for the American Revolution Bicentennial Administration
- Presidential Appointment, Vice Chairman, National Parks Advisory Board, 1991 to 1995
- Appointed Vice Chairman, Presidential Inaugural Committees, 1969, 1981, and 1989
- Nominee, National Mediation Board, 1995
- Featured guest on *Nightline*, *The Today Show*, *Dateline*, and all network news, including CNN
- Speechwriter (White House and three U.S. Senators).; best-selling author of *"Devil's Pact: Inside the Teamsters"*

PROFESSIONAL EXPERIENCE

VIRGINIA THOROUGHBRED ASSOCIATION, Warrenton, Virginia   1995 to 2000
Executive Director

- Developed programs to enhance breeding of native thoroughbred industry while promoting racing in Virginia. Created and implemented high-impact programs and interfaced closely with industry leaders, breeders, government officials and the legislature to meet association goals and mandates.

- Oversaw budget processes, administered state breeder's fund, directed educational seminars, spearheaded fund-raising activities, and serviced association members – all in an effort to enhance Virginia's stature as a nationally recognized centers for thoroughbred nurseries.

- Coordinated and initiated activities with the Virginia Racing Commission – writing newsletters, brochures, and press releases; developing high-impact advertising, marketing, and promotional programs, including the Virginia Derby and the annual Thoroughbred Hall of Fame Awards Banquet.

WASHINGTON ASSOCIATES INTERNATIONAL, LTD., Washington D.C.   1992 to 1997
Vice President / Government and Public Relations

- Directed marketing, economic development, public relations, and communications consulting services to international and national clientele – from both public and private sectors. Assisted clients in seeking joint venture or strategic alliance partners and provided economic planning and marketing counsel for new ventures.

- Created coalitions for large grassroots advocacy campaigns and supervised media strategies to support objectives. Contracts included economic planning audits, communications and special events management, lobbying, and community relations efforts. Wrote speeches, produced promotional films/videos, and fund-raising management.

(Page one of two)

T.J. Zeke
Page two

PROFESSIONAL EXPERIENCE

INTERNATIONAL BROTHERHOOD OF TEAMSTERS, Washington D.C. 1978 to 1992
Director of Communications / Executive Assistant to the President

- Served as international spokesman and was fully responsible for all communications and media relations efforts for the two million member union and its affiliates. Managed a staff of 20 in producing all publications, educational and policy material, and other pertinent collateral information for the membership.

- Spearheaded logistical efforts for national conventions. PR responsibilities included developing retiree programs, international trade, media relations, and economic development programs. Served as Executive Assistant to the President and Director of Government Relations including White House Liaison for international union activities.

AMERICAN CAUSE, Washington D.C. 1976 to 1978
Assistant Director / Vice President

- Established efforts to promote U.S. international policies, commerce, and trade to enhance targeted causes with government, industry, and business leaders. Wrote speeches and directed press/communications efforts.

- Directed policy development and communications on domestic and international policy for national think tank organization founded by Senators George Murphy, John Stennis, and others, including the late John Wayne.

AMERICAN REVOLUTION BICENTENNIAL ADMINISTRATION, Washington D.C. 1971 to 1976
Director of Public Relations / Congressional Liaison

- Contributing leadership role in developing and implementing all aspects of communications and public relations, including promotional planning, for the National Bicentennial Celebration. Liaison with Congressional members relative to administration and federal development and planning for national observance.

- Chief of the News Bureau, responsible for all press relations, publications and media development, marketing, and high-level speech writing.

HILL AND KNOWLTON PUBLIC RELATIONS, INC., Washington D.C. 1967 to 1971
Vice President / Account Executive

- Directed government liaison activities and public relations campaigns for several major accounts, including Ernest & Ernest, American Airlines, The Wine Institute, Gillette, Owens Illinois, Miles Laboratories, Proctor and Gamble, Continental Can, Zenith Radio Corp., and The New York Times.

- Developed crisis management strategies for the Tylenol Crisis and the Three Mile Island Crisis.

ASSISTANT TO MINORITY SECRETARY OF THE U.S. SENATE, Washington D.C. 1962 to 1967
Administrative / Executive Assistant

Served as personal liaison to then Minority Leader of the U.S. Senate, following four years as a U.S. Senate Page.

EDUCATION

Bachelor of Arts: Communications, Journalism	George Washington University	1966
Associates Degree: Political Science	Dartmouth College	1962
International Law and Foreign Relations Studies	Georgetown / Catholic University	1966-67

AFFILIATIONS

Virginia Society of Association Executives Public Relations Society of America
National Press Club Who's Who in American Politics

REFERENCES

Senator John W. Warner (202) 224-2023 Congressman Tom Davis (202) 225-1492
Lawrence J. Brady (603) 623-2829 Richard Quinn (714) 993-3075

DOREEN SCHMIDT '
Am Gries 1287
R-85935 Regensburg, Germany
Telephone: (49) 555-23456/Mobil: (49) 555-7654321
Email: EMAIL@EMAIL.COM

GOVERNMENTAL/CORPORATE INTERFACE

Vacancy Announcement: A-0687-77-TRT

20 Years of Successful Entrepreneurial Business Experience in Europe

Enhancing Revenues and Profits in Global Markets
Multilingual Marketing Expert/MBA

High-profile career spanning 20+ years—enhancing growth and profitability in international arenas. Fluent in English, German, and French, with a strong working knowledge of Spanish. Highly competitive and driven in exceeding organizational growth and profit objectives via governmental interface and influence.

CORE PROFESSIONAL STRENGTHS

Strategic Visioning/Planning	Brand Development and Management
Corporate/Business Development	Product and Service Development/Enhancement
Resources Management—Physical and Labor	Senior-Level Project Management/Leadership
Building Key Strategic Alliances and Partnerships	Training—Curriculum Development/Enhancement

CAREER HIGHLIGHTS

- Grew business from start-up position to a thriving enterprise employing 80 people with DM 8,000,000 in sales
- Leadership role in developing/expanding the lucrative German fitness market (Germany, Austria, Switzerland)
- Trained over 3,000 woman and men as health trainers/instructors—enabling them to make their hobby their career
- Special Awards: *Business Person of the Year* for the German Fitness Industry
- Successfully introduced Evian Mineral Water to the German fitness market —penetrated more than 600 new clubs
- Spearheaded successful development of high-impact program—*Personal Performance Center*—for Life Fitness
- Coproduced with 20th Century Fox Germany 7 Fitness Videos

PROFESSIONAL EXPERIENCE

Foliatec Gmbh—a Publicly Traded German Company, Nürnberg, Germany   1992 to Current
Marketing and Sales Consultant

- Worked closely with the owner/managing director in developing new "branding" strategies for automotive retailers, internationally. Successfully created new product names as well as the packaging and accompanying displays. Formulated the concept and led production team in developing a high-impact marketing campaign to promote one of the main product lines—Auto Glass Films—to U.S. government and state agencies.

- Established new sales tool,creating 90-page Website to enhance prospect ' s decision-making and eventual ordering techniques for over 300 products.Worked closely with the graphic artist for the final conception and directed the photo shoots.Produced several different (in size and shape)complete "Shop-in-Shop "concepts for the site.Included in this project was the complete ad campaign presentation for this program.

- Results were sensational.Travel to Washington,D.C., and work closely with U.S.governmental officials for past five years.Improved company sales and revenue stream by 22%.

Adrienne Schmidt Group, Regensburg, Germany   1982 to 1992
Managing Director/General Manager/Business Development

- Conceptualized an idea and created the business concept—active in day-to-day activities in leadership roles. The first company was involved in high-end fitness wear, having developed and managed the brand *"Forever Fit by Doreen Schmidt."*

- Designed the completed product line, sourced and contracted with key manufacturers in France, Portugal, and the Czech Republic. Developed "catalog distribution concept," as well as the "new" wholesale distribution channel of fitness clubs. During the second stage, expanded sales to a retail mail-order business.

(Page 1 of 2)

DOREEN SCHMIDT
(Page 2 of 2)

PROFESSIONAL EXPERIENCE

Doreen Schmidt Group,Regensburg Germany (Continued)

- Founded Fitness School Division that initially offered courses in basic and advanced education/training to aerobic instructors.Developed the concept and the "brand " name,*"Training for Trainers by Adrienne Schmidt "* Created course programs,accompanying manuals,and all marketing and collateral materials.

- Grew business at "double digit" rate in the midst of tremendous competition. Maintained industry-leadership role, expanding programs to include specialized training using state of the art fitness equipment for select target markets, and offered management and marketing seminars for fitness club personnel.

- Created the next growth component the distribution of "small" aerobic fitness equipment. Identified emerging trends—for example, **"The Step,"** and hence acquiring exclusive distribution rights for Germany, Austria, and Switzerland. Sourced other fitness products in the Far East and marketed them under the **"Forever Fit"** brand. When no feasible deal could be consummated with reputable U.S. spinning-bike manufactures, developed own superior product in Taiwan.

- Rounded out the fitness group with the opening of the club *"Forever Fit Performance"* in 1989. Catering to the high-end fitness member, offering cutting edge in fitness equipment/programs to 1500 prominent members.

- Developed fitness-evaluation and training programs for the "Baby Boomer" market segment specifically designed to employ a cutting-edge product line for **Life Fitness**. Instrumental in assisting Life Fitness launch successfully and to sell new fitness product line.

Sport Insel, Regensburg Germany   1981 to 1989
Aerobic Director and Fitness Boutique Owner

- An Aerobic Director on a consulting basis. Responsible for developing an aerobic program that soon became the largest in Germany. Personally trained all instructors, developed class curriculum/formats, and taught classes. Responsible for all advertising and marketing for the club over an eight-year period.

- Started a fitness boutique within the club, offering fashionable and fast-selling products that were unavailable at that time in Europe. Initially did the buying in the United States from the top brands. Became an exclusive distributor for Germany, Austria, and Switzerland for the leading American brand at the time, *Dance France*.

PROFESSIONAL EXPERIENCE (1973–1981)

Pilot, Flight instructor and Aerobic Instructor
Free-Lance Flight Instructor, Freiburg, Germany
Free-Lance College Instructor
Part-Time Language Instructor

EDUCATION/TRAINING

MBA, 1975   BOSTON UNIVERSITY, Boston, Massachusetts
(Completed in Europe)

Bachelor of Arts: International relations, 1973   SCHILLER UNIVERSITY, Germany and France

Licenses/Certifications

Commercial Pilot SEL and MEL; Certified Flight Instructor (CFIAII) SEL, MEL, Instrument

PERSONAL

SS#: 000-00-0000
Citizenship: Dual: American/German

- References and Supporting Documentation Furnished upon Request -

DOUG ZOTT

610 DeVosta Grade Road
Upperville, Virginia 20184
Phone/Fax: (540) 555-1212/email@email.com

HIGH-LEVEL CORPORATE /GOVERNMENT RELATIONS
State and Federal Congressional/White House Liaison

Increasing Corporate Growth &Exposures through Governmental Access and Influence

High-Level Government Access/Strong Media Alliances
Incorporating Strong Private-Sector Partnerships

A well-connected, achievement-driven Public Relations/Communications Executive with outstanding qualifications in all phases of corporate/governmental communications, with particular emphasis on strategic crisis management. Spearheaded the public-relations efforts for national and international crises, including:

- **Tylenol Crisis**
- **Three-Mile Island Crisis**
- **Teamsters/Government Takeover**

HIGHLIGHTS OF EXPERIENCE

- Spokesperson for International Union representing more than 2 million members and affiliate members
- Director of Public Relations and Congressional Liaison for the American Revolution Bicentennial Administration
- Presidential Appointment, Vice Chairman, National Parks Advisory Board, 1991 to 1995
- Appointed Vice Chairman, Presidential Inaugural Committees, 1969, 1981, and 1989
- Nominee, National Mediation Board, 1995
- Featured guest on *Nightline*, *The Today Show*, *Dateline*, and all network news, including CNN
- Speechwriter (White House and three U.S. Senators).; best-selling author of *Devil's Pact: Inside the Teamsters*

PROFESSIONAL EXPERIENCE

VIRGINIA THOROUGHBRED ASSOCIATION, Warrenton, Virginia   1995 to 2000
Executive Director

- Developed programs to enhance breeding of native thoroughbred industry while promoting racing in Virginia. Created and implemented high-impact programs and interfaced closely with industry leaders, breeders, government officials and the legislature to meet association goals and mandates.

- Oversaw budget processes, administered state breeder's fund, directed educational seminars, spearheaded fundraising activities, and serviced association members—all in an effort to enhance Virginia's stature as a nationally recognized center for thoroughbred nurseries.

- Coordinated and initiated activities with the Virginia Racing Commission—writing newsletters, brochures, and press releases; developing high-impact advertising, marketing, and promotional programs, including the Virginia Derby and the annual Thoroughbred Hall of Fame Awards Banquet.

WASHINGTON ASSOCIATES INTERNATIONAL, LTD., Washington, D.C.   1992 to 1997
Vice President/Government and Public Relations

- Directed marketing, economic development, public relations, and communications-consulting services to international and national clientele—from both the public and private sectors. Assisted clients in seeking joint-venture or strategic-alliance partners, and provided economic planning and marketing counsel for new ventures.

- Created coalitions for large, grass-roots advocacy campaigns and supervised media strategies to support objectives. Contracts included economic planning audits, communications and special-events management, lobbying, and community-relations efforts. Wrote speeches, produced promotional films/videos, and managed fundraisers.

(Page 1 of 2)

Doug Zott
Page two

PROFESSIONAL EXPERIENCE

INTERNATIONAL BROTHERHOOD OF TEAMSTERS, Washington, D.C.   1978 to 1992
Director of Communications/Executive Assistant to the President

- Served as international spokesman and was fully responsible for all communications and media-relations efforts for the two-million-member union and its affiliates. Managed a staff of 20 in producing all publications, educational and policy material, and other pertinent collateral information for the membership.

- Spearheaded logistical efforts for national conventions. PR responsibilities included developing retiree programs, international trade, media relations, and economic development programs. Served as Executive Assistant to the President and Director of Government Relations, including White House Liaison for international union activities.

AMERICAN CAUSE, Washington, D.C.   1976 to 1978
Assistant Director/Vice President

- Established efforts to promote U.S. international policies, commerce, and trade to enhance targeted causes with government, industry, and business leaders. Wrote speeches and directed press/communications efforts.

- Directed policy development and communications on domestic and international policy for national think-tank organization founded by Senators George Murphy, John Stennis, and others, including the late John Wayne.

AMERICAN REVOLUTION BICENTENNIAL ADMINISTRATION, Washington, D.C.   1971 to 1976
Director of Public Relations/Congressional Liaison

- Contributing leadership role in developing and implementing all aspects of communications and public relations, including promotional planning, for the National Bicentennial Celebration. Liaison with Congressional members relative to administration and federal development and planning for national observance.

- Chief of the News Bureau, responsible for all press relations, publications and media development, marketing, and high-level speech writing.

HILL AND KNOWLTON PUBLIC RELATIONS, INC., Washington, D.C.   1967 to 1971
Vice President/Account Executive

- Directed government-liaison activities and public-relations campaigns for several major accounts, including Ernest & Ernest, American Airlines, The Wine Institute, Gillette, Owens Illinois, Miles Laboratories, Procter and Gamble, Continental Can, Zenith Radio Corp., and *The New York Times*.

- Developed crisis-management strategies for the Tylenol Crisis and the Three-Mile Island Crisis.

ASSISTANT TO MINORITY SECRETARY OF THE U.S. SENATE, Washington, D.C.   1962 to 1967
Administrative/Executive Assistant

Served as personal liaison to then Minority Leader of the U.S. Senate, following four years as a U.S. Senate Page.

EDUCATION

Bachelor of Arts: Communications, Journalism	George Washington University	1966
Associate's Degree: Political Science	Dartmouth College	1962
International Law and Foreign Relations Studies	Georgetown/Catholic University	1966 to 1967

AFFILIATIONS

Virginia Society of Association Executives	Public Relations Society of America
National Press Club	Who's Who in American Politics

REFERENCES

Senator John W. Warner (202) 555-1212	Congressman Tom Davis (202) 555-1212
Lawrence J. Brady (603) 555-1212	Richard Quinn (714) 555-1212

JANE LAWLESS

12A Ridgepointe Drive
Telephone: (717) 555-1212
Bedford, Pennsylvania 32343
Email: email@email.com

Position: Marketing Researcher Grade 9
Department of Consumer Affairs
SS #: 000-00-0000
Citizenship: US
Federal Status: N/A

MARKETING RESEARCHER / CUSTOMER ANALYST
"Voice of the Consumer" - Designing Programs to Enhance Customer Satisfaction

Market Intelligence / Survey Design & Management / Senior-Level Project Management
Strategic Planning & Implementation / Secondary Research & Analysis

Highly experienced, accomplished and creative professional with extensive experience in analytical research and assessment. Recognized for developing high-impact programs aligned with customer and market needs / projections. Bottom-line-oriented strategist with a verifiable record for igniting sales, improving productivity of sales staff, and maximizing available resources - physical and labor.

CORE PROFESSIONAL STRENGTHS

Survey design / questionnaire development	Database design
Direct mail marketing	Competitive analysis
Resource estimating	Vendor management
Customer service and retention management	Quality control management

PROFESSIONAL EXPERIENCE

Horowitz Consulting Group, Ltd., Bedford Falls, Pennsylvania   1999 to Current
MARKET RESEARCH ANALYST
Directed the complete overhaul and manage customer service database and data acquisition for this sales and marketing organization. Monitor the market place for any development relative to past, present, and future customers. Profile existing and prospective customers and industries. Conduct ad hoc research on people, places, and things.

- Improved database efficiency by reducing the number of entries by more than 60%.
- Moved database orientation from corporation to the individual, allowing for tracking movement of individuals.
- "Pushing" marketplace information resulted in meetings with customers for the sales force.
- Customer and industry profiles provided a clear road map for targeted marketing campaigns.

BellTower Marketing., Bedford, Pennsylvania   1994 to 1999
MARKETING ANALYST
Conducted all market intelligence and research activities for corporation. Developed marketing databases and designed sales territories. Provided demographic profiles of prospective markets.

- Database structure allowed for the creation of potential customer lists for the sales forces.
- Designed the sales territories that added structure to the sales organization and led to more efficient sales management.
- Managed direct mail marketing campaign that increased customers by both direct response and product awareness.
- Created customized presentations integrating both company and potential customer information that paved the way for securing national accounts.
- Recommended the most efficient locations for depots.

(Continued)

Jane Lawless
Page two

PROFESSIONAL EXPERIENCE

<u>IBM Corporation</u>, Springfield, Pennsylvania   1988 to 1994
FINANCIAL ANALYST (1992-94)
Directed all financial and resource activity for $11 million operating budget of Information Development organization. This involved tracking labor resources expended by product each month in addition to planning future labor expenditures by product. Led all sizing efforts for new products and planned changes.

- Developed proposal to save $400 thousand a year in contracted labor cost.
- Designed financial model and process to recover revenue for division.
- Devised creative ways to optimize headcount in budget-cutting situation.

STRATEGIC PLANNER (1990-92)
Developed and managed customer/market requirements strategy for an Information development organization. Managed customer/developer meetings. Functioned as adviser for the organization on measuring performance (six-sigma).

- Moved documentation evaluations up to par with other product attributes.
- Customer strategy was singled out as organizational high point during independent reviews.
- Led first-ever customer review of unannounced information products.
- Developed metrics for use in quality control and product improvement.
- Managed research project designed to explore product issues.

MARKET RESEARCH ANALYST (1985-90)
Assumed lead role in getting monthly customer survey up and running. Survey measured customer attitudes and tracked product quality on a monthly basis. Worked with multiple internal areas (service, sales, manufacturing) and external vendors.

- Set new standards for IBM survey methodology by probing customer responses.
- Utilized customer feedback as quality control by helping to drive engineering changes in products with repair issues.
- Structured survey to allow for "question of the month" capability which aided product planners in determining future product specifications.

PROCUREMENT ANALYST (1988-85)
Purchased semiconductors for personal computer manufacturing. Managed worldwide supply/demand forecast.

- Supervised supplier interaction with IBM Engineering.
- Constructed database of personnel information.

EDUCATION & SOFTWARE SKILLS

University of Pennsylvania, Philadelphia, Pennsylvania, Campus
Master of Business Administration (Concentration on Quantitative Management), 1987
Bachelor of Business Administration (Major: Management - Quantitative Analysis), 1985

SOFTWARE SKILLS

Lotus 1-2-3	MS Access	MS Word
Lotus Freelance	MS Excel	BusinessMap Pro
Lotus Approach	MS PowerPoint	MarketPlace
Lotus Notes	MS Publisher	Maximizer

References and Supporting Documentation Furnished upon Request

Matt Morris
50 Trouble Drive
Fairview Heights, Illinois 62208-2332
(618) 555-8228
email@email.com

Graphic/Visual Arts Specialist

Seventeen years experience managing and coordinating visual arts projects from concept to completion. Accustomed to working on multiple projects with short notice, little or no instruction, and total creative judgment for quality and details of finished product.

- Well-rounded business management skills, with proven ability to match customer needs with a wide variety of graphics, visual arts tools, and approaches.

- Effective at communicating ideas and capturing the interest of the intended audience.

Professional Experience

Visual Information Specialist   1989-Present

(self-employment under contract to the Defense Information Technology Contracting Office, a full-service telecommunications and information systems procurement office with 400+ employees supporting the entire DoD and 56 non-DoD organizations)

Managed all operations of a $100,000 business supporting telecommunications, information systems, administrative, financial, and management staff. Responsibilities included record keeping, accounting, budgeting, and inventory control.

- Prioritized customer requirements and assigned workload to meet changing contract specifications and customer deadlines.

- Provided detailed instructions to employees for new, difficult or unusual requirements. Ensured quality of completed products prior to delivery to customers.

- Served as a concept consultant to assist and advise customers on colors, content, and size of finished products.

Additional Experience (1979-1989): Held the same title of Visual Information Specialist as a contract employee without the business management responsibilities.

Education

Graphique Commercial Art School, 1978-1979
St. Louis, Missouri

General Coursework, Belleville Area College, 1976-1978
Belleville, Illinois

Everett Morris - Page 2

Creative and Technical Skills

Paste-Up

Designed and produced paste-ups and artwork for illustrative slides, viewgraphs, and charts used in formal presentations, static displays, cover brochures and posters used for briefings to senior military and civilian personnel, static displays at trade shows, and various reports.

Engraving/Signmaking

Designed and produced plastic and metal engraved signs and plates used for organizational awards, plaques, and other recognitions. Designed and produced vinyl/plastic signs for badges, nameplates, name tags, cubical identification, and hallway directories.

Audiovisual Displays

Maintained audiovisual equipment library, including the distribution, setup and operation of video and still cameras, audio recorders, overhead transparencies, 16mm and 35mm projectors for presentations and training sessions.

Computer/Graphic Design

Designed and produced slides, charts, and graphs for weekly staff meetings and formal presentations using various software packages such as Harvard Graphics, Freelance Graphics, and PowerPoint. Manipulated color and size of clip art with software packages such as Arts and Letters. Produced forms, flyers and publications using PageMaker and Corel Draw software.

Presentation Planning

Provided expert consulting service to assist customers in presentation planning for the various types of media used to market, publicize and document the organization's goal and services. Used Harvard Graphics and Microsoft PowerPoint extensively.

Photography/Video

Provided video/audio and still photographic coverage of formal ceremonies, training, presentations, and satellite downlink training broadcasts. Produced working copies for approval by the customer and master and distribution copies of all materials. Provided photographic darkroom development of film, photo enhancement of prints in both black and white and color.

CAROLYN BARRINGER
23423 Avenue K, Fallsbrae, California 92081 ● 555 555-1212

● HEALTHCARE EXECUTIVE ● PATIENT SERVICES MANAGER ● ADMINISTRATOR ●

Competent, confident, and compassionate healthcare executive with considerable management experience refined by a formal education and specific expertise in Federal and State employment laws. Proven record of success in recruiting, interviewing, selecting, and training healthcare professionals. Strong background in initiating and implementing leadership techniques that significantly improve employee morale and effectiveness, increase productivity and decrease employee turnover rates. Excellent communications and problem-solving skills have dramatically reduced numbers of incident reports, improved relations within hospital departments, increased personnel productivity, improved service levels, favorably impacted customer service, and markedly increased overall quality assurance.

RELEVANT COMPETENCIES

- Compensation & Pay
- Computer Literate
- Staff Coordination
- Department Budgets
- Employee Counseling

- Employee Orientation
- Employee Relations
- Long-Range Planning
- Organization/Scheduling
- Policies/Procedures

- Performance Standards
- Program Development
- Program Management
- Recruitment/Interviews
- Staff Development

PROFESSIONAL EXPERIENCE

BAY CITY MEDICAL CENTER, Bay City, California - 1988 to present

Human Resources Coordinator responsibilities include review and coordination of all Human Resources Department policies, systems, and procedures. Coordinate Human Resource activities with all other medical center departments. Conduct research and analysis of current policies, identifying areas for improvement. Develop and recommend policies revisions and maintain procedure manuals. Perform systems and procedures analyses to support internal control programs. Provide support for periodic evaluations, special services, and programs relating to Human Resources functions. Participate in hospital CQI projects and TCMC division meetings, representing the Human Resources Department. Gather and analyze data from other departments and outside services to assist in the development of new programs or the improvement of existing ones.

Phlebotomy Supervisor responsible for adequate staffing of all positions and completing all administrative and human resource activities required for interviewing, hiring, counseling, motivating, disciplining, and terminating members of the department. Maintained, coordinated, and implemented new programs, protocols, and policy changes. Provided support, advice, guidance, and education to the center's staff. Maintained effective employee relations as well as liaison and communications with the public, physicians, and hospital staff. Reviewed and revised department protocols and standards, updating policies and procedural manuals as needed. Developed performance standards and performed yearly merit performance evaluations. Ensured Phlebotomy Department services were provided and contained within budget constraints. Coordinated expanded phlebotomy staffing at an off-site Clinical Services Center.

LMNO HEALTH CARE CLINIC, Milford, Michigan - 1985 to 1988

Patient Services Manager responsible for management and supervision of patient services department. Oversaw all phases of recruiting, selection of medical and technical

(Continued on next page)

CAROLYN BARRINGER

personnel, hiring, training, counseling, and staff development. Facilitated patient care from start-up for this multiphysician practice through ongoing clinic development. Developed and maintained policy and procedure manuals. Coordinated medical and patient services with physicians, nurses, and department personnel. Liaised with Hidden Valley Hospital and community. Ensured services were performed within budget guidelines and constraints.

PRIOR PROFESSIONAL EXPERIENCE

Laboratory Technician, Hidden Valley Medical Center, Monterey, California
Clinical Technician, Carlinad Osteopathic Health Care, Monterey, California
Laboratory Technician, CHAMPUS Medical Center, Lakeland, Texas

EDUCATION AND PROFESSIONAL TRAINING

National University, San Diego, California
Bachelor of Arts in Behavioral Science - Emphasis: Human Resources Management
Graduated **Magna Cum Laude**

Carlinad Center, Monterey, California
Interpersonal Skills - 1,475 contact hours

Carnegie Institute, Detroit, Michigan
Lab Technician Certificated Course of Study

PROFESSIONAL ACHIEVEMENTS

- Developed and implemented JCAHO proficiency testing procedures to enhance customer service and ensure quality trained personnel.
- Served on hospital task force committees improving performance standards, mandating hourly rounds by phlebotomy personnel, and armband compliance for patient identification augmented by a performance standard for hospital personnel.
- Implemented staff cross-training to ensure expanded coverage and eliminate overtime.
- Restructured staffing decreasing employee requirements and lowering salary costs by more than 20 percent.
- Developed the Phlebotomy Orientation Program, introducing a three-phase, goal-oriented training program; increased overall efficiency and competency of the staff.
- Participated in planning and developing an off-site draw station; as well as an alternate draw station within the hospital; ensured timely, convenient, professional service levels.
- Established a training program for College Paramedic Interns and Bay City Home Health Nurses to learn phlebotomy techniques, resulting in phlebotomy proficiency and quality work performance.
- Participated in new clinic start-up, which involved equipment purchases, supplied inventory medical safety precautions, room layout, and setup.

RELATED PROFESSIONAL ACTIVITIES

- Member, Advisory Board, Regional Occupational Program (ROP), Monterey, California
- Commencement Speaker, Community Colleges, Monterey, California

Appropriate personal and professional references are available.

79—HEALTHCARE ADMINISTRATION

KARL BRITTON, MHSL
1124 West Anandale ■ Long Island, NY 10055
(212) 555-8876
email@email.com

PROFESSION, QUALIFICATIONS

SENIOR HEALTHCARE ADMINISTRATOR with significant experience in managed care environments. Initiated and inspired management and clinical teams to achieve measurable successes in administration, marketing, MIS, physician relations, and patient care. Strengths include:

- Business Management, Operations, Organizational Restructuring
- Strategic Planning, Positioning in Anticipation of Industry Trends
- Marketing, Advertising, Sales Strategy Development
- Community, Physician, Employee & Industry Relations

MANAGEMENT EXPERIENCE

ADMINISTRATOR — Imaging Associates, New York, New York   8/88-Present
Direct accountability for full scope of operations for New York's premier freestanding radiology center.

Administration, Finance
- Increased net profit in excess of 350% within 2-year period.
- Controlled $10+ million operating budget and $1 million capital equipment acquisition budget.
- Negotiated radiology equipment service agreements, realizing savings of $900,000 over 5-year period.
- Engineered organizational restructuring, developed new service lines, and facilitated transition from top-line to bottom-line organization, addressing recent nationwide decline of imaging center services.
- Handled complex and highly sensitive physician-related matters with malpractice liability insurance company, patients, and legal counsel.

Marketing, Public Relations
- Led effort in collaboration with marketing/communications consultant toward design and execution of Center's first Strategic Marketing Plan.
- Involved in industry at national level as Past President of Board of Directors for American Imaging Association; fought successfully against onerous federal and state legislative efforts.
- Developed successful sales strategies to address influx of competition and control major market share.

Information Systems
- Implemented Center's first computerized patient scheduling and registration network.
- Involved in decision processes to ensure information resource architecture is consistent with strategic goals.
- Participated on national task force to survey advancing technology (Picture Archival & Comm. Systems).

Human Resources
- Managed hiring and patient-focused training for management, clinical, and support staff.
- Introduced flexible benefits plan and 401(k) retirement plan for staff of 65.

PRIOR CAREER SUMMARY
- Manager, Syracuse County Health Department, Syracuse, New York   10/87-7/88
- Associate Director, Allied Ambulance Service, Syracuse, New York   8/84-10/87
- EMS Instructor, County General Hospital, Rochester, New York   2/81-8/84

EDUCATION, CERTIFICATION

Masters in Health Systems Leadership, University of Chicago   1987
Bachelor of Science, Organizational Behavior, University of San Francisco   1983

220

CHRISTOPHER YOST, M.D.

3925 DanLynn Drive
Canfield, Ohio 44406

dochris@mpd.com

Home: (330) 262-8522
Office: (330) 799-6666

SENIOR-LEVEL HEALTHCARE EXECUTIVE
Chief Executive Officer...Chief Operating Officer...Consultant

Proven leader in recognition and implementation of current and future healthcare industry trends ...
Accomplished "outside the box" thinker with more than two decades of progressively responsible and diversified administrative and clinical experience directing medical facilities. Diverse background in financial management, strategic market penetration, technology procurement, and staff development. Extensive negotiating skills with insurance and government healthcare contracts to optimize reimbursement status. Broad experience directly interfacing with high-level physician specialists, boards of directors, and executive leadership. Highly skilled in evaluating and implementing mergers and acquisitions focused on regional expansion and cost-effective integration of new business entities. Proven ability to consistently position organizations ahead of the curve in an industry with ever-shrinking margins.

AREAS OF EXPERTISE

✓ Strategic Planning & Analysis
✓ Cost-Benefit Analysis
✓ Project Management
✓ Medicare Guidelines
✓ Contract Negotiations
✓ Operations Management

✓ Financial Funding Strategies
✓ Financial Budgets/Forecasting
✓ Resident Staffing/Training
✓ Community/Media Relations
✓ Presentations & Public Speaking
✓ Integrated Healthcare Delivery

CAREER PROGRESSION

RUTHERFORD HEALTH, Franklin County — Delaware County, Ohio
[*Combined resources of area hospitals, medical centers, ambulatory campuses, home care agencies and other clinical services with approximately 5,000 employees in nearly 30 locations. Rutherford Health is the third largest integrated healthcare delivery system in northeast Ohio.*] **www.rutherfordhealth.com**

Division Chief of Podiatry (1999 – Present)
Tasked to engineer strategic visions for podiatric department, including budget forecasting, community program development, media outreach, and services and technology procurement. Act as mediator between physicians and hospital administration, addressing issues related to pay scale increases, tenure retention, and various related issues. Member of several steering committees directing long-term plans focusing on utilization of future needs and services and preparation of cost-benefit analysis of multiple facilities, including a hospital concentrating on heart development/ailments and orthopedic ambulatory surgery center.

Founding Residency Director of Podiatric Medicine and Surgery (1995 – 1999)
Amid turbulent and volatile market conditions, realized potential for new graduate medical education division. Successfully presented concept to CEO and Department of Surgery Chairman resulting in "go-ahead"' from executive staff. On first attempt, favorably spearheaded appropriate tasks to receive required credentials comprised of providing HFCA guidelines and petitioning the Council of Graduate Medical Education. Secured **$1.3 million** annual funding for resident salaries and education expenses for twelve residents.

(Continued)

CHRISTOPHER YOST, M.D.

✓ **Accountable for hospital and clinic related curriculum design, assignments to instructing physicians, and staff evaluations.** Oversaw and steered resident publications, weekly journal clubs, and staff development meetings. Ultimately responsible for graduate residents' performance focused on patient care.

✓ Promoted community relations campaigns by providing residents and founding director as judges in city science fairs and assisting in "help-hotlines" for healthcare organization outreach programs. **Recognized as 'Outstanding Program Director' by Department of Surgery and Institution Chairman.**

MORGAN STEVENS RESERVE SYSTEM, EAST SIDE HOSPITAL – Youngstown, Ohio
[Combined 300+ bed campus of inpatient and outpatient care serving acute, chronic, and rehabilitative services. Provider of multiple medical and surgical clinics focusing on society's less fortunate. Education programs include dental, podiatry, family practice, pediatrics, internal medicine, and general surgery with more than 120 residents.]

Podiatric Clinic Director (1987 – 2000)
Served as podiatry department chief responsible for managing daily operations, meeting budget parameters, strategic marketing and planning, patient and staff education, technology purchases, contract negotiations, and staffing and development of 12 residents. Manages seven associates, including nursing, billing, and ancillary personnel while overseeing patient caseload of 30-40 per day. Positioned as Medicare Peer Review Physician to interpret and uphold Medicare guidelines. Actively participated in all aspects of Porter model, including analyzing, buying, selling and substituting in clinic implementation and management. Executed multiple presentations to vascular symposiums.

✓ **Clearly visible leading community support promotions and fund-raising campaigns while simultaneously participating in telethons and public service television to raise public awareness and acquire donations and grants to meet $200,000 annual operating budget.**

✓ **Published in the American Podiatric Medical Association Journal with surgical case presentations.**

CONSULTING PROJECTS

TELECARE PHARMACEUTICALS
Hillsborough, Ohio
Managing Project Consultant (October 2000 – Present)

Appointed to identify international pharmaceutical companies attempting to penetrate markets within the United States. Evaluate and research existing product lines and create marketing strategies to capture a desired market share. Steer through federal approval process to ensure fast results.

✓ **Led major push to assist Canadian pharmaceutical firms to fill supply void created by high-priced medicines. Push was successful in increasing stock availability to target population through reduced rates as well as creating a viable position for incoming firms.**

WORTHINGTON PHARMACIA INC.
Somerset, New Jersey
Managing Project Consultant (September 2000 – Present)

Positioned to define and evaluate goals relative to corporate visions. Scrutinize feasible research data to verify goals, development, or alternative scenarios related to vision.

✓ **Most recently supported efforts to identify pertinent data utilized in offering platform of safer tobacco by creating and offering products with fewer carcinogens. Efforts proved positive and led to 15% sales growth through aggressing marketing.**

EDUCATION

Seton Hall University – South Orange, New Jersey
Masters in Healthcare Administration, 2002

Ohio College of Podiatric Medicine – Cleveland, Ohio
Doctorate of Podiatric Medicine, 1986
Winner of Baird-Johnson Award
Kent State University, Warren, Ohio
Bachelor of Science, 1982

Youngstown State University – Youngstown, Ohio
Associate Degree in Applied Science – Nursing, 1982

LESTER E. BRANDON
5706 Grand Circle * Golden Bridge, New York 10526 * (914) 555-1212 * email@email.com

---

HEALTHCARE / NURSING HOME ADMINISTRATOR / CEO / COO
Driving Growth & Profits in Competitive / Fluctuating Markets

Multi-Site & Single Facilities Management / Organizational Leadership &Empowerment
Start-Up & Turnaround Management Expertise

Dynamic operating/management professional offering 15-plus years of successful leadership positions in healthcare environments. Expertise in Medicare administration and protocol. Outstanding business development skills.

AREAS OF EXPERTISE

Personnel team-building; union avoidance
Regulatory compliance management
Public speaking; community relations
Finance management, budgeting, expense control

Customer service/quality control management
Building strategic partnerships and alliances
Cross-cultural new business development
Profit center realignment/reorganization

PROFESSIONAL EXPERIENCE

INTEGRATED HEALTH GROUP, Westin, New York   1993 to Current
Administrator - Directed total operations for 120-bed skilled nursing facility managing 130 employees for healthcare center specializing in both short-term rehabilitation and long-term care for managed care, Medicare, Medicaid, private pay, and insurance residents. Developed and administered a $9.7 million annual operating budget. Accountable for regulatory compliance, business development/retention, quality customer service, and bottom line/profit attainment.

- Increased average daily census from 71% to 96% in six months via aggressive, high-impact marketing techniques
- Enhanced contribution margin from 5% to 19% by controlling costs and improving management team
- Developed new profit center, a highly successfully outpatient therapy program

NORTH CENTRAL MANOR NURSING CENTER, Boynton Bridge, New York   1987 to 1993
Administrator - Managed total operations for 167-bed skilled nursing facility, directing more than 145 employees for healthcare center specializing in both short-term rehabilitation and long-term care for managed care, Medicare, Medicaid, private pay, and insurance residents. Develop and administer annual operating budget of $10.2 million. Accountable for regulatory compliance, business development/retention, quality customer service, and bottom line/profit attainment.

- Received two Superior Ratings – JCAHO Accreditation
- Significantly reduced turnover and lowered Worker's Compensation cases
- Proactively blocked union signing and campaign while dramatically improving employee morale and productivity
- Negotiated and implemented new managed care contracts

EDUCATION & LICENSES

Bachelor of Science: Biology, GPA: 3.58 (Top 25%)   ELIZABETHTOWN COLLEGE
- New York Nursing Home Administrator License

PROFESSIONAL AFFILIATIONS

Member: American Health Care Association (Former Voting Delegate)
Member: American College of Health Care Administrators

References and Supporting Documentation Furnished upon Request

NANCY FOWLER

555 Levittown Road, New York, NY 11717 • 631-555-9090 • NFowler@caresupport.net

---

SENIOR HEALTHCARE MANAGEMENT REPRESENTATIVE

Customer Support / Administrative Services

Knowledgeable, articulate communicator with thirteen years of customer care experience across healthcare, travel, hospitality, and retail sales industries. Maintain strong decision-making and problem-solving abilities, as well as excellent time-management, data research, sales reporting, and situation analysis proficiencies. Effectively train employees in network-based data management systems and departmental procedures.

– Customer/Member Support	– Staff Training and Supervision	– Information Systems
– Relationship Building	– Problem Analysis & Reporting	– Committee Involvement
– Workflow Management	– Sales / Client Presentations	– Investigative Research

Professional Experience

HEALTHCARE MANAGEMENT

Senior Intake Coordinator / Customer Care Representative   1990 – Present
Health Care Services of New York (HSC), Brentwood, New York

Department Management

- Encouraged a structured, teamwork environment that promoted customer care solutions through the appropriate, compliant use of employee resources and management of data information systems.
- Assisted the Utilization Review Department in the close examination and verification of members' prior medical authorization requests submitted by physicians and a multidisciplinary group of vendors.
- Recruited, trained, and supervised Customer Service Representatives and Care Management staff on regulatory documentation, referrals, inpatient hospital authorizations, precertifications, and correspondence.
- Conducted on-site training sessions for client groups, providing an explanatory and benefits-driven overview on a range of available group healthcare plan options.
- Served as liaison between management, service providers, vendors, and staff to maintain open lines of communication and ensure the delivery of quality customer care services.
- Collaborated with information technology teams and managers on the beta testing of newly implemented software releases and enhancements to ensure the integrity of system functionality and data conversion.
- Responded to a daily influx of telephone-based and written communications from members and providers pertaining to benefit plans, claim payments, reimbursements, referrals, and notices.
- Represented HSC at open enrollments and health fairs throughout the medical community to generate new and repeat business; followed up on viable leads by telephone and correspondence, providing answers to key questions concerning coverage, policies, contracts, provisions, and fee schedules.

Committee / Taskforce Involvement

- Selected to participate in company taskforces to investigate, identify, and develop work plans designed to expediently track and resolve complaints issued by concerned and anxious plan members.
- Convened with committee heads to discuss pending appeals (verbal/written) presented by providers and plan members concerning reimbursement issues, referrals, claim payments, fee schedules, and denial of benefits.

— Continued —

NANCY FOWLER
Page 2

Professional Experience
— Continued —

TRAVEL & HOSPITALITY

Travel Agent, National Travel, Inc., New York, New York   2001 – 2002
- Developed and managed a corporate and leisure portfolio of customers seeking cost-effective, knowledgeable travel consultation specifically in the areas of flight arrangements, hotel accommodations, car rentals, train tickets, cruises, resorts, tour packages, restaurants, and excursions.
- Contributed to the workplace administratively from new employee training to billing disputes and collections, authorized competitive price adjustments, and negotiated exclusive wholesale arrangements with vendors.
- Coordinated standard/electronic customer and vendor communications to promote packages, close sales, confirm reservations, generate itineraries and correspondence, process payments, and issue tickets.

Reservations Coordinator, Holiday Inn, New York, New York   2000 – 2001
- Handled front-desk reservations for this leading chain's 139-room hotel located one mile from the airport with accommodations that included a conference room and business center.
- Managed computerized bookings and reservations, corporate and private account management, credit card authorizations, billing, and discrepancy resolutions.

RETAIL SALES

Sales Associate, City Style, New York, New York   1998 – 2000
- Provided floor sales assistance and product consultation to a diverse customer population, consistently meeting and exceeding sales goals for this high-volume store location.
- Managed sales counter activities encompassing purchases, returns, exchanges, layaways, credits, special orders, and service agreements.
- Implemented visual changes and thematic window displays to model a sleek, metropolitan store format and culture that attracted consumers within a highly competitive shopping mall environment.
- Monitored inventory levels as part of a Loss Prevention program to track and thwart incidents of product theft.

Education

Bachelor of Science in Healthcare Management
Long Island Community College, Brentwood, New York, 1998

Associates of Arts in Business Administration
State University at Stony Brook, Stony Brook, New York, 1993

Computer Skills

Windows NT; Microsoft Word, Outlook; Internet research

Laura G. King
88 West Avenue
Winston, Missouri 59812
(406) 555-1212
Email@email.com

*"A progressive thinking professional
Striving to Make a Difference"*

Seeking Position as DIRECTOR OF HEALTH SERVICES
Academic / Educational Environment

SPECIALTIES:
General and Family Practice – Community Health Subspecialty
Health Disorders in Elementary School Children
Health Issues Affected by Socioeconomic Variables

EDUCATION:
Harvard University, Cambridge, Massachusetts
M.D. 1988 Program in Medicine
  Clerkships:
  - Acute Care, Massachusetts General Hospital
  - Pediatrics, Salem Hospital

Colby University, Waterville, Maine
Bachelor of Science: Biology and Chemistry (Dual Majors) 1984

Licenses:
  - Medical License, State of Maine
  - Medical License, State of Massachusetts
  - Medical License, State of Missouri

PROFESSION EXPERIENCE:

Hope Center University, Powell, Missouri		1999 to Present
Director of Health Services		
Wilkins Community College, Springfield, Missouri		1992 to 1999
Assistant Director of Health Services		
Private Practice, Upshaw, Missouri		1988 to 1992
Physician – Family Practice		

AFFILIATIONS:
American Medical Association
Missouri Medical Association
National Association of Health Services Professionals

PUBLICATIONS:
New England Journal of Medicine
- Youth Development in Economically Deprived Populations, 2002
- Downward Health Trends in Upscale Communities, 2001

Harvard Medical Review
- Declining Health on American Campuses, 2003
- Drinking and Drug Abuse and its Affect on Education, 2003

References and Supporting Documentation Furnished upon Request

ROSE EVERET

2300 Rollings Avenue • Baltimore, Maryland 21228 • (410) 555-1212 • email@email.com

---

HOME COMPANION/HOME HEALTH AIDE/HOME MANAGEMENT
Patient Advocate—Senior Populations

Unparalleled Quality Patient Care—Senior Populations

Housekeeping/Meal & Nutrition Management/Financial Management
Medication & Healthcare Oversight/Transportation Coordination
Personal Care & Activity Organization
Family& Social Liaison

Education/Training/Certifications

University of Maryland, Baltimore, Maryland
Bachelor of Arts: Education, 1985

Post-Graduate Studies and Professional Training

Business Curriculum—College of Business, University of Maryland, Baltimore, Maryland	1985 to 1987
Financial Accounting—College of Business, University of Maryland, Baltimore, Maryland	1988 to 1990
Life-Support Skill Training—Baltimore Emergency Medical Group, Baltimore, Maryland	1998 & 1999

Certification

Home Healthcare Companion Specialist (HHCS)	Current
CPR and Advanced First Aid	Current
Advanced Cardiac Specialist	Current

▪ Strong Computer Skills: MS Office

Work Experience

Confident Companions, Inc., Baltimore, Maryland   1994 to Current
Lead Companion
Home companion and health aide for well-respected couple in the D.C. area. Responsible for staff recruiting and management (cooking staff, lawn-maintenance crew, and transportation team). Major emphasis on medical care, including physical therapy, medication and nutrition management, and physician visits and follow-up.

* Exceeded all household financial budget projection while exceeding quality of care
* Received two letters of appreciation from client's physician for exceptional medical attention in emergency situation
* Significantly improved staff morale and teamwork, resulting in higher productivity and overall production

Military Service

Healthcare Specialist, United States Navy, U.S. and Germany   1986 to 1994

* Achieved rank of Major—directing healthcare operations, central division (serving 17 bases and 40,000 soldiers)
* Received seven letters of commendation for outstanding work performance

References Furnished upon Request

GREG FROST

19986 U.S. Highway Ten
Roswell, GA 30075
email@email.com

Home: (404) 555-6077
Fax: (404) 555-0588

MANAGEMENT EXECUTIVE
COUNTRY CLUB, RESORT, & PRESTIGIOUS COMMUNITY DEVELOPMENTS

EXECUTIVE PROFILE

Twenty years experience directing high-caliber properties nationally and internationally.

▼ **Operational Management:**
   * Manage Large-Scale Properties
   * Direct Multiple Profit Centers
   * Establish Quality Standards
   * Maximize Operational Assets

▼ **Recreation Facility Management:**
   * Golf & Country Club Properties
      Course Management
      Golf Academy
      Membership Development
      Tournament & Event Coordination
   * Yacht Club & Marina Operations
   * Tennis & Swimming Facilities
   * Clubhouse Operations

▼ **Financial / Budget Management:**
   * Budget Analysis & Strategies
   * Financial Objectives
   * Asset Evaluation & Enhancement
   * Payroll and Cost Controls
   * Inventory Requirements
   * Systems and Data Processing

▼ **Personnel Management:**
   * Develop "Team Spirited" Organizations
   * Perform Employment Needs Analysis
   * Review Policies and Procedures
   * Multinational Staff Recruitment
   * Manage Over 350 Employees

▼ **Specialized Management Experience:**
   * Turnaround Situations
   * Workouts / Reorganizations
   * Start-Up Operations
   * Equity Conversions

PROFESSIONAL EXPERIENCE

Executive Manager
Dubai Creek International Golf & Yacht Club
Dubai, United Arab Emirates (1992-Present)

Competitively selected from over 800 candidates worldwide to manage the preopening (final design review and changes) and opening of international resort. Full management responsibilities for an 18-hole championship golf course, 9-hole Par 3 floodlit course, golf academy, and golf club. Recruited multi-national staff and senior executives. Coordinated European PGA Tournament on opening day. Directed yacht club operations (115-slip marina) achieving 60% occupancy in first 9 months.

Presold 50% of Club memberships prior to grand opening. Created zero-based budgets, projecting a first year profit of $1.2 million.

Vice President: Hospitality
Bald Head Island
Bald Head, North Carolina (1991-92)

Recruited to the Executive Board, in charge of formulating new development plans and budgets for 1,800-acre Planned Unit Development (PUD). Managed final design and opening of Bald Head Island Golf & Tennis Club. Directed golf & recreational operations, mainland & island marinas, ferry operations, island cafe, and chandlery.

Increased income by constructing a new club and expanding Food & Beverage facilities. Acquired third ferry (secluded island—no access by car) to accommodate growth projections. Remodeled pool and tennis facilities. Reorganized property management division for 105 units. Established quality standards for entire resort operations, enhancing overall resort experience.

228

GREG FROST
Page Two

Professional Experience (Continued):

President
B.K. Nelson Associates
Tequesta, Florida (1988-91)

Point man for various assignments focusing on organizational development, design review, operations analysis, budgeting, and financial evaluation of community development and resort properties. Restructured and repositioned country club and other service industry concerns in meeting growth objectives.

Executive Manager
Mountain View Associates
White Field, New Hampshire (1987-88)

Recruited by majority owner to staff and direct a 235-room hotel facility on 80 acres with golfing, dining, and "carriage trade" related services. Worked on preliminary plans in developing an adjoining 259-acre parcel with single and multiunit residences, including an additional 18-hole golf course.

President: Club & Recreational Division
Heathrow
Orlando, Florida (1986)

Responsible for division—a multiunit PUD residential/commercial property. Hired to enhance design and establish a "world-class" operational philosophy. Redesigned facilities, recruited senior management staff for the Club, 18-hole golf course, 10 tennis courts, and aquatic facility. Staged Heathrow International Tennis Grand Prix.

Vice President: Operations
John's Island, Inc.
Vero Beach, Florida (1983-86)

Directed operations for this 3,500-acre PUD (3 golf courses, 20 tennis courts, a 105-unit hotel, golf & beach clubs, & 4 dining areas) directing over 350 employees. Established progressive management systems and personnel. Reversed Food & Beverage division to a profitable status.

Reduced payroll ($1 million to $675K) in 7 months while revenues increased 190%. Assisted

John's Island, Inc. (Continued):

in multi-million-dollar equity conversion from developer to membership-owned status. Achieved asset appreciation of $22 million in 36 months.

General Manager
Hobe Sound Company
Hobe Sound, Florida (1979-83)

Executive manager for the Hobe Sound Company and two subsidiaries: Jupiter Island Club (one of the most exclusive resort communities in the U.S.) and Hobe Sound Water Company. Formulated a well-managed organization establishing business goals, incorporating strong financial, operating, and maintenance programs for the island:

- 18-hole golf course
- 10 tennis courts
- Health spa
- 4 dining rooms
- 3 club houses
- 60-slip marina
- Movie theater
- Island services

Proactive marketing yielded a 26% increase in hotel occupancy. Reduced pension expenses by $32K. Realized a 100% increase in water plant production. Turned F&B around ($99K loss to $139K profit). Reversed a $300K negative cash flow to a $1.1 million surplus.

Manager
Topnotch at Stowe
Stowe, Vermont (1975-79)

Created and directed dynamic growth ($162K to $4.2 million) for this emerging world-class New England resort. Built solid management team in developing facilities and services to accommodate rapid development. Established quality standards (Mobil Four Star Award) and "award-winning" dining facilities (recognized through membership in the *Leading Hotels of the World*).

EDUCATION:

University of Hawaii, Honolulu, Hawaii, 1970
Business Administration
(Foreign Trade, Management, Economics)

SHANNON E. BRIGGS, PHR

12 Your Street, Any Town, New York • (845) 708-5555 • e-mailaddress@internetserviceprovider.com

---

HUMAN RESOURCES MANAGEMENT • IT RECRUITMENT

A seasoned HR manager with extensive expertise in recruiting high-level information technology professionals. Demonstrated skill in organizational development, change management and strategic design of marketing and recruiting efforts. Strong background in management planning, budgeting, staffing and facilities designed to enhance productivity and profitability. Core competencies include:

- ➤ **Program Development**
- ➤ **Benefits Administration**
- ➤ **Preventive Labor Strategies**
- ➤ **HR Policy Design & Administration**
- ➤ **Succession Planning**
- ➤ **Union Negotiations & Mediations**
- ➤ **Employee & Labor Law**
- ➤ **Compensation & Benefits Design**

PROFESSIONAL EXPERIENCE

FAB Associates, LLC – New York, New York   1991 - Present
SENIOR HUMAN RESOURCES CONSULTANT

- ➤ Recruited as Lead Consultant to standardize organizational structure for an IT Department with 500 employees of an e-commerce company with a subsequent rollout to 6,000 employees nationwide.
- ➤ Led team in analysis of existing operations and development of an action plan.
- ➤ Worked with Senior Management to gain support of new strategic design proposals.
- ➤ Created cost justification of a $2.5 million budget based on savings from retention and retraining expenses.
- ➤ Examined market and recruiting efforts, role and level descriptions as well as lines of communication.
- ➤ Developed a standardized organizational model, which clarified authority, relationships and responsibilities within the department.

Manhattan University Hospital – New York, New York   1983 – 1991
HUMAN RESOURCES MANAGEMENT • 1987 – 1991

- ➤ Responsible for union contract interpretation, grievances, regulatory compliance, personnel files, performance appraisal system and management of worker's compensation programs for the 6,500 employees.
- ➤ Supervised direct staff, development of policy recommendations, and preparation of implementing procedures and served on numerous operating committees.
- ➤ Served as the key player for the institutional authority on state and federal regulatory requirements.
- ➤ Managed complex worker's compensation program with a high volume of claims, including hearings and litigation on challenged decisions.
- ➤ Reorganized problem departments, established stability, and installed procedures and systems to maintain quality of operations.
- ➤ Established improved relationships with ten unions, which reduced adversarial attitudes and labor stoppage threats
- ➤ Substantially reduced worker's compensation costs and subsequent litigation.

(Continued)

SHANNON E. BRIGGS, PHR • PAGE TWO
12 Your Street, Any Town, New York • (845) 708-5555 • e-mailaddress@internetserviceprovider.com

---

TRAINING AND DEVELOPMENT MANAGER   1983 – 1987

➢ Supervised human resource functions for designated units and chaired Institutional Committee for development of employee policy and procedure manuals.
➢ Prepared budgets and coordinated planning with other department managers. Programs included: Compliance with Americans with Disabilities Act, Sexual Harassment Prevention, Labor Relations, Management Development Training, Workplace Literacy, and New Employee Orientation. Additionally, the department selected and installed specialized software systems for tracking training.
➢ Managed JCAHO accreditation process in areas of Orientation, Training, and Education
➢ Appointed to Strategic Design team to participate in broadening Quality Management programs throughout the hospital.

Swiss-American Insurance Group – New York, New York   1980 – 1993
CAREER DEVELOPMENT SPECIALIST

➢ Managed training programs, career database system, and career development promotional programs.
➢ Developed, published and managed wide-ranging programs to promote professional growth of current employees.
➢ Designed career planning concepts, analyzed data on career mobility, and managed departmental administrative operations.
➢ Developed the Company's first video promotion and multimedia career planning programs, participated in customization of career planning software package and served as Internal Consultant to the company's ten operating divisions.
➢ Joined the company as Senior Supervisor, managed training for the U.S. Headquarters and national staff. Chaired Corporate Committee for Career Development, organized high-level review courses for the American Society of Actuaries certification examinations and led curriculum development for the Roosevelt University inauguration of an Insurance degree major.

EDUCATION

➢ **National College of Education**
  MASTER OF ART • EDUCATION AND TRAINING CONCENTRATION
➢ **University of Wisconsin**
  BACHELOR OF ART • HISTORY

PROFESSIONAL AFFILIATIONS

➢ **Member of the American Society of Training and Development (ASTD)**
➢ **Member of the Society of Human Resources Management (SHRM)**
➢ **Adviser in the Chicago Chapter ASTD Human Resources Development Institute**

MARISSA FRANKOS
151 W. Passaic Street
Rochelle Park, New Jersey 07662
(201) 555-3772
frankos@msn.com

HUMAN RESOURCES & TRAINING PROFESSIONAL

- Strong HR generalist experience with a proven talent in the development and implementation of training programs for exempt and non-exempt personnel; proven ability to develop material, impart knowledge and update programs as needed.
- Strong research and analytical abilities; notable experience in the management and reduction of costs related to liability and insurance.
- Recruiting activities included all aspects of screening, interviewing, hiring and orientation for union and nonunion staff
- Continuously updates knowledge relevant to workers' compensation, ADA, EEO, Family Medical Leave Act, OSHA, D.O.T., etc; develop and implement new procedures to ensure compliance.
- Benefits administration experience includes program development, maintenance of costs through negotiations and the development/implementation of alternative benefit programs.
- Assets in collective bargaining activities; successfully administers benefits to assist in successful negotiation.
- Generates ongoing bottom line savings through the introduction of various cost cutting programs.

MAJOR PROJECTS & ACCOMPLISHMENTS:

♦ **Reduced corporate liability insurance costs by 1/3; restructured liability insurance management program to facilitate savings.**

♦ **Reduced annual costs by $250K by establishing an effective self-insured plan for supplemental disability.**

♦ **Facilitated a 33% reduction in medical benefit costs by implementing an HMO as an integral part of benefits plan.**

♦ **Reduced annual paid claims by 45% by developing and implementing aggressive claims handling procedures.**

♦ **Increased parent company revenues by $185K in 6 months by reinstituting billing of subsidiary companies for healthcare coverage.**

♦ **Played an integral role in 12 different collective bargaining agreements - assisted the Senior V.P. by providing benefit guidance.**

♦ **Attained a 50% conversion from indemnity to managed healthcare through the creation and implementation of a successful managed care program.**

(continued...)

MARISSA FRANKOS   -Page Two-

(201) 555-3772

PROFESSIONAL EXPERIENCE:

GLATT AIR TECHNIQUES - Ramsey, New Jersey   1992 - Present

Human Resources Manager • 1994-Present
Direct staff in daily HR operations including employee recruitment, new hire orientation, coordination of COBRA, administration of Federal regulations, collective bargaining, benefits administration and procedure development. Maintain OSHA recordings. Coordinate payroll for 150 employees, interfacing with key intradepartmental personnel. Provide assistance with employee problems and serve as the first line in resolving issues. Team member of the Safety Committee. Revised Company Handbook and implemented organizational policy. Attended comprehensive ADP training program.

Administrative Director/Office Manager • 1992-1994
Managed all office activities - created and administered office procedures. Implemented new accounting software; handled all training.

PILGRIM GROUP, INC. - Fort Lee, New Jersey   1986-1992

Manager of Special Projects
Trained and supervised three staff members in various interdepartmental projects, preparation of monthly trade reports and purchasing activities.

EDUCATION:

Union College - Cranford, New Jersey
A.A.S. in Human Services

Additional Training:
Society of Human Resource Management:
Courses in Employment Law, Disability, Workers' Compensation

MICHAEL P. DYER
27 Hanover Street
South Portland, Maine 04106
(207) 555-1212 / email@email.com

HUMAN RESOURCE MANAGEMENT
Recruitment Specialist—Recruiting Productive and Contributing Team Members

Strategic Planning / Policy & Procedure Development / New Program Conceptualization & Implementation
Personnel Training / Benefits Management / Regulatory Compliance

Solid experience in human resource management, encompassing personnel recruiting, training, and supervision, benefits coordination, policy development/enforcement, office administration, training curriculum development/facilitation, and financial management/budgeting. Contributing to bottom line objectives through enhanced efficiency and labor resources.

CORE STRENGTHS

Program development; enhancing existing programs
Working with governmental agencies/policies
Turning around underperforming operations/departments
Career management and design (internal and outplacement)

Organization and administration - time management
Building key local/national alliances and partnerships
Reengineering and functional change management
Personnel recruiting and job placement

PROFESSIONAL EXPERIENCE

UNITED STATES NAVY
San Diego, California - 1989 to 1998

Administrator / HR Specialist
Responsible for the training and performance reporting of individuals in administrative ratings. Provided administrative services to more than 1,800 enlisted and retired personnel. Coordinated shipboard activities with auxiliary service and nonservice agencies, including the American Red Cross, Navy Relief Society, Navy Drug and Alcohol Rehabilitation Centers, and local community resource centers.

Trained and experienced in such contemporary issues as sexual harassment, personnel administration, wage and salary administration, administrative discharge, as well as solid knowledge of E.E.O regulations and guidelines. Experienced in policy and procedure development/enhancement.

- Developed training resource materials and presented seminars in Human Resource Management.
- Recipient: Navy Achievement Medal for "Excellence in Administration."
- Played significant role in Naval Reserve Centers Portland SELRES retention figures while conducting RESFIRST system.
- Recipient of SOQ/SOY Award for building/maintaining "vibrant morale" and maximizing command productivity.
- Saved more than $1.7 million in training costs over five-year period by developing in-house training programs.

EDUCATION

Bachelor of Science: Public Administration, 2004
(High Honors)

University of Maine at Augusta, Augusta, Maine

Workshops and Seminars
Management by Objectives
Work-Flow Management
Time Management
Cultural Expression

Human Resource Management
Equal Opportunity
Supervisory and Leadership Training
Evaluation/Performance Systems

■ Computer Skills: Word, Excel, Access, PowerPoint, and the Internet

References and Verifying Documentation Furnished upon Request

JANE McGLYNN

221 Hermitage Drive • Nashville,Tennessee 37167 • 615-555-5555 • Jane@yahoo.com

---

- Senior Systems Designer/Information Architect with over 15 years' progressive experience in analysis, design, implementation, and conversions of systems and client/server environments.
- Top-notch professional with proven ability to design solutions, implement new processes and programs, and manage information operations on a large scale.
- Outstanding expertise in systems analysis, program design, system conversions, and software implementation.

_____EXPERIENCE_____

Deloitte & Touche LLP • http://www.dttus.com
Client Service & Information Technology • Hermitage, Tennessee
1990-present

INFORMATION ARCHITECT

Teamed with world-class client service teams in numerous in-house MIS implementation projects, system developments, and training processes. Scoped and planned projects, developed needs assessments, and provided specialized training for implementation teams. Assisted teams through detailed business and functional knowledge application to systems analysis and design. Provided technical guidance to CABS Development Team, Solution 6 software vendor, Financial Control, Firm Accounting, and other teams involved in legacy data conversion and interfaces for CABS. Supervised efforts of 12 implementation team members.

Project Team Lead – SAP Capital Expenditures Implementation
Internal Consultant – CABS Global Practice Management Implementation
Lead Implementation Coordinator – ATSW Client/Server System
Software Implementation Internal Consultant

- Successfully led implementation of Automated Timesheet System for Windows (ATSW) for 26,000+ users in over 120 sites globally in less than 10 months
- Teamed on Accounts Receivable System (ARS) development/implementation to successful completion under tight deadlines throughout entire project life cycle, resulting in back office implementation in over 85 sites in less than 9 months
- Led system conversions to migrate DPS6 minicomputer platform to new ATSW and ARS client/server systems (PowerBuilder, ORACLE, and SQL Server) within 11 months, saving Deloitte & Touche over $400,000 annually by eliminating hardware maintenance costs
- Achieved Lead Analyst position for 3 major systems on Honeywell Bull mainframe, DPS6 minicomputer, and client/server systems

Analysts International Corporation
Contel Information Systems • Washington, D.C.
1990

SENIOR SYSTEMS CONSULTANT

Special Project Consultant retained to lead system conversion from Honeywell Bull mainframe platform to IBM.

- Investigated corruption of E911 Database through analysis of data received from South Central Bell; designed and developed data comparison system to report all discrepancies for immediate correction
- Consulted on Customer Billing System revision project with acquisition of new long-distance carriers (AT&T, Sprint, and MCI)

(continued)

Jane McGlynn • (615) 555-5555

_____TECHNICAL SKILLS_____

LANGUAGES

PowerBuilder	COBOL	DML
PowerScript	JCL	
SQL	ECL	

OPERATING SYSTEMS

GCOS6	SR 4020, SR 4500	Novell 4.11
CGOS8	UNIX, AIX	
HVS 6 Plus	Windows 95, 98, NT	

HARDWARE

DPS6+	IBM 3090, 4030	Compaq Proliant
DPS90	IBM RS/6000	
DPS9000	IBM SP2, S70	

SOFTWARE, TOOLS, AND UTILITIES

PowerBuilder	VFORMS	Lotus Notes EPN
PL/SQL Developer	VISION	MS Office Suite
ORACLE SQL*Plus	SCORPEO	MS Project 98
Transact-SQL	FSTE-6	Express
COBOL-74	EDIT 8	Visio Professional
COBOL-85	FRED	Vantive
GCOS Utilities	ACES	SourceSafe
UTL2	FSE	SnagIt
UTL8	EASY-FORM	WinZip
TSS	TOSC1/PFMS	Ultra-Edit 32
MAGNA8	Lotus cc:Mail	
VDAM	Lotus Notes	

DATABASES

MS SQL Server	DMIV-IDSII	TP8
ORACLE	DVIV-TP	MS Access

_____SPECIALIZED TRAINING_____

Deloitte & Touche LLP

MS SQL Server 6.5 & 7.0	Structured Systems Analysis & Design
MS Project 98	ORACLE
PowerBuilder 5.0	SAP R/3 3.0 Business Process
Object-Oriented Systems Design	

_____AFFILIATIONS AND INVOLVEMENTS_____

Nashville ORACLE Users Group
Music City Powersoft Users Group
Association of Information Technology Professionals

JODY BARRINGER

555 Meadowlark Lane, Los Angeles, CA 90049
(310) 555-1234 • JBarringer@email.com

Senior-Level Insurance Reimbursement Specialist

Offering:

- 10+ years experience including 8 years healthcare reimbursement auditing.
- In-depth knowledge of Medicare issues as well as generally accepted accounting and auditing principles.
- Strong research and analytic skills.
- Excellent training, supervisory and leadership skills.
- Highly organized and skillful project manager.
- Effective written and verbal communications, including presentations.
- Experience with appeals and administrative resolution process.

PROFESSIONAL EXPERIENCE

BLUE STAR OF CALIFORNIA, Los Angeles, CA   1995 to Present
Senior Auditor, 1997–Present
Staff Auditor, 1995–1997
Coordinate audits of healthcare providers, encompassing acute hospitals, psychiatric hospitals, home health agencies, hospices, and skilled nursing homes to ensure compliance with government and industry regulations and directives.

- Direct team of five auditors, with responsibility for 100+ health care facilities representing Medicare reimbursement of $225 million; schedule, monitor and supervise field work and desk audits.
- Conduct exit conferences with providers and representatives.
- Review and approve cost settlements including audit adjustments, interim payments and lump-sum settlements. Ensure ratio of over/under payments comply with regulatory and quality standards.
- Train team members in Medicare regulations and procedures, audit protocols and health care accounting practices.
- Respond to investigative inquiries; perform legal research; work on appeals and position papers.
- Selected for special projects and major assignments including:
  - Directed and supervised $700+ million audit of Los Angeles County General/USC Hospital.
  - Represented company at Washington, D.C., and state of California hearings.

ARONSON, ARGUELLA & STERN, CPAs, Los Angeles, CA   1987 to 1989
Staff Accountant/Auditor

EDUCATION

B.S. in Business Administration • CALIFORNIA STATE UNIVERSITY, Los Angeles, CA

ADDITIONAL INFORMATION

Computer Skills: Windows, Microsoft Suite (Word, Excel, PowerPoint, Access), proprietary applications
Foreign Languages: Bilingual English/Spanish

Marianne Newman

Available for Relocation

555 Lincoln Avenue
Tuckahoe, NY 55555

914-555-1111
man@online.com

Interior Designer

Inspired professional experienced in residential and commercial design. Keeps within budget and within time frame. Employs a client-centered approach to incorporating resources, purpose, and design preferences to maximize usage of space. Speaks English, Spanish, French and Portuguese

Talents

Design

Visually enhances interiors creating harmony with color, texture and textiles. Artistically employs fabric for window treatments and furnishing solutions. Practiced at period and interior décors, including Victorian Georgian, art deco, and postwar modern.

Marketing

Creates winning marketing strategies, product development and referral resources attributed with sharp revenue growth.

Technical

AutoCAD 14, Rendering, Construction Documents, Measured Drawings, MS Office 2000

Administrative

Coordinated vendor deliveries with project schedules, ensuring 100% compliance to deadlines. Maintained a strict accounting of expenses incurred and payment schedules, adhering to set budget.

Professional Experience

SPACIOUS LIVING, New York, NY   **2001 – Present**
Interior Designer
Launched this design and renovation service firm to affluent residents in the tristate area with a focus on functional and comfortable space planning solutions for interiors and home-based offices.

- Introduced line of space-saving furnishings for small apartment living with 35% boost in revenues.

BIZHAN, New York, NY   **1998 – 2001**
Assistant Interior Designer
Initially retained as a project manager and advanced to Assistant Interior Designer with six months for this restoration firm providing design solutions for town houses, country homes, loft space and city living. Contrasted product lines costs in selection of fabrics. Showroom design projects include Yves St. Laurent and Nine West.

- Delivered $500,000 in new business within one year through forging an alliance with a leading paint contractor.
- Introduced decorating elements and fabric lines responsible for increasing revenues by 25%.

Education

UNIVERSITE PARIS – SORBONNE, Paris, France   Bachelor of Arts: Fine Art

Michele A. Jacob

172 River St., Douglaston, NY 11363 ➤ 516-555-4201 ➤ MAJ@aol.com

Residential and Showroom Interior Designer

Over ten years of experience in the planning and coordination of $10 million, 55,000+ square foot fine furniture showrooms for retailers including Macy's Furniture Store and The Place Furniture Galleries.

Plan and implement total showroom design from inception to grand opening. Showrooms have been recognized by industry representatives as some of the best in the tristate area.

Manage complete customer design assignments for Macy's, Ethan Allen, Classic Galleries, Georgetown Manor and Levitz in home, office or retail environments.

Expert in trend analysis, merchandising and management. Highly creative, capable and motivated; readily inspire confidence of clients.

Areas of Expertise

- ➤ residential / commercial design
- ➤ retail showroom design
- ➤ home furnishings trend analysis
- ➤ floor plans / space planning
- ➤ construction planning
- ➤ vignette / color coordination

- ➤ manufacturers' representative interface
- ➤ commercial shoot consulting
- ➤ accessories purchasing / placement
- ➤ faux painting / stenciling
- ➤ themes / holiday displays
- ➤ staff management / budget oversight

Career Highlights

Managed design studio as in-store designer for Macy's 45,000-square-foot Farmingdale Furniture Store's showroom and customers. Worked with high-expectation clientele and a range of fine furniture, accessories and floor coverings. Developed a cohesive and distinctive showroom that became one of Long Island's premier locations for fine furniture.

Totally redesigned and opened The Place Furniture Galleries' new 55,000-square-foot furniture showroom in Farmingdale, Long Island. Independently planned space for grouping of galleries, drafted floor plans, and interfaced with store management and buyers. Purchased accessories to complement vignettes and created elegant look to enhance moderate furniture collections.

Designed The Place Furniture Galleries' new children's area, leather area, and motion area. Determined design strategy, colors, furniture placement and accessory selections.

Achieved second place award in eleven-store display competition; participated in interior design showcases. As Nassau Coliseum Home Show designer, developed and set up 20'x40' vignette.

(Continued)

Michele A. Jacob   *2*

Professional skills

➤ Conceive and draft floor plans and designs for homes, offices and commercial space. Determine all components of interiors—color schemes, furnishings, lighting, accessories, window treatments, etc. Emphasize client needs assessment; relate well to all types of people.

➤ Develop and implement retail client design service programs. Determine client needs; draft plans and create design proposals. Recommend merchandise necessary for fulfillment of goals. Provide home visits, in-store consultations, and coordinate finalization of projects.

➤ Plan and arrange complete furniture store room settings. Make quick and intuitive decisions for placement and floor coordination of unexpected stock arrivals. Redo vignettes and accessories on a daily basis in response to new shipments and constant rotation of furniture.

➤ Buy accessories and work with a semiannual budget. Supervise furniture store operations and handle customer service, sales supervision, opening and closing of building, security, cash vault. Sell on floor when needed.

Experience

Interior Designer, Showroom Designer, Accessories Buyer   1995 to present
The Place Furniture Galleries, Farmingdale, NY

Interior Designer, Design Studio Manager   1993 to 1995
Macy's Furniture Store, Farmingdale, NY

Interior Designer, Showroom Designer   1991 to 1993
Levitz Furniture, Garden City, NY

Interior Designer, Sales   1990 to 1991
Ethan Allen, Hicksville, NY

Interior Designer, Sales   1989 to 1990
Classic Galleries, Huntington, NY

Interior Designer, Sales   1986 to 1989
Georgetown Manor, Westbury, NY

Education

Interior Design Certificate   1986
Metropolitan Institute of Interior Design, Plainview, NY

A.A.S. in Design   1975
Fashion Institute of Technology, New York, NY

93—INTERNET CONSULTANT

Laura M. Fitzpatrick
49 Trillium Blvd. - Traverse City, Michigan 49686
Phone: 231.555.4949 - *Facsimile:* 231.555.0049
emailaddress@emailaddress.com

INTERNET MARKET STRATEGIST & CONSULTANT
creative maverick, heady visionary, industry revolutionary

eStrategist and innovator who motivates, inspires, and expresses opinions to advance Internet dynamics. Right brain / left brain strengths in multifaceted roles of strategy development, project management, budget administration, and creative idea generation. Exceptional interpersonal and communication skills to clearly present concepts with pizzazz, while managing client relationships.

Proven track record in managing interactive online projects B concept through launch B with a thorough understanding of emerging technology and how it can be leveraged. Experience using sophisticated Internet tools; excellent computer and project management skills.

Summary of Attributes

- entrepreneurial drive • multitasking strengths
- easily able to shift from high-level strategic thinking to detail-oriented work
- ability to work in a fast-paced, dynamic environment, collaboratively and under critical deadlines
- excellent verbal and written communication skills
- strong tactical and creative abilities

PROFESSIONAL EXPERIENCE

SENIOR eMARKETING STRATEGY DIRECTOR, 1999-current

NOVO B Detroit Michigan

Play the lead role in developing the company's online strategy. Serve as liaison between the IT, sales, and marketing teams. Direct and coordinate all Internet and intranet activities, including strategy formulation, strategic plan execution, site design and maintenance, data management, budget forecasting and administration, business development, strategic alliances, and ongoing operations. Drive vision, strategic guidance, and leadership on all online business projects in the automotive channel.

- Develop full understanding of the clients' business goals to develop long-term purpose.
- Integrate all areas of eMarketing (research/strategic planning and media).
- Facilitate integration of the various agency partners (seamlessly to client).
- Explore new and innovative ways to add value to clients' online goals.
- Continually mine for new business opportunities.
- Build relationships within client and partner groups.

Successes:

- Accelerated development of online technology to keep pace with regional and national competition.
- Forged strategic alliance with Sierra Systems to deliver technology innovations corporatewide.

(Continued)

BUSINESS DEVELOPMENT MANAGER, 1998-99

DESTINY, INC. — Chicago, Illinois

Challenged to develop and prequalify new business and obtain an initial high-level managerial audience in order to communicate corporate value for a leading provider of eBusiness solutions to the world's premier financial institutions.

- Negotiated all financial, legal, scope, and engagement timing issues to expand relationships for an extended, mutually beneficial, long-term relationship.

- Maintained a pipeline to accurately represent both current business and the extensions of business as well as future opportunities.

Successes:

- Established Internet presence firmly in the eConsulting market; developed a strong clientele base.

- Generated follow-on business by identifying new opportunities with existing clients.

DISTRICT MANAGER — Agency Marketing, 1985-98

WORLDSPAN — Detroit, Michigan

Scope of responsibility encompassed the management of advanced electronic information in a major market area for the third largest travel information service corporation in the nation. Managed departmental budget and administrated technology life cycle. Set guidelines that ensured profitability and retained customer loyalty.

- Oversaw all marketing strategies for comprehensive computer reservations system/package, including LANs, back-office accounting products, and unique functionality.

- Conducted technical and financial negotiations that satisfied customer requirements and met corporate needs.

Successes:

- Achieved 118% of sales goals and increased overall market share by 5% in 1998.

- Fast-track promoted from Manager B Market Planning and Forecasting (Atlanta, Georgia) responsible for overall planning objectives, including market share and revenue forecasting, business planning, analysis of market trends. Managed annual budget of more than $100 million. Prior: Project Manager — Marketing Programs (Atlanta, Georgia).

EDUCATION / PROFESSIONAL DEVELOPMENT

MASTER OF BUSINESS ADMINISTRATION, 1992 — *UNIVERSITY OF DETROIT-MERCY*; Detroit, Michigan

BACHELOR OF SCIENCE DEGREE — Marketing, 1985 — *INDIANA UNIVERSITY*, Bloomington, Indiana

Computer skills/tools/competencies: Web Applications, Resource/Material Tracking Intranets, Contact Management, Distributed Reporting Systems, Web Sites, Computer Based Training, Form Automation, Interactive Benefits, Time Tracking/Timesheets

JULIE STOKES

565 North Avenue • Los Angeles CA 92009 • 619.555.9874 (AH) • jstok@hotmail.com

INVESTIGATOR/CUSTOMER SERVICE SPECIALIST

Credit Card/Check Fraud ♦ Loss Aversion ♦ Fund Protection & Recovery ♦ Problem Resolution

<u>15-year veteran within the banking & finance industry.</u>

QUALIFICATIONS PROFILE

High-performance, results-focused professional with extensive experience and outstanding accomplishments within the banking and finance industry delivering customer service excellence to drive revenues, market growth and overall bottom-line performance. Exceptional insight and experience into the investigation of credit card / check fraud implementing initiatives to minimize loss while optimizing the recovery and protection of funds for bank and clientele.

➢ Distinguished record in achieving organizational goals and objectives while maintaining a long-term vision of continuous improvement.

➢ Comprehensive insight into and full compliance with Code of Banking Practice, Privacy Act, and Discrimination and Harassment; sound knowledge of banking products, policies and procedures.

➢ Strong interpersonal and communication skills with proficiency to promote confidence and build strategic business/client relationships on all levels. Expert problem solver.

QUALIFICATIONS & TRAINING

Code of Banking Practice ♦ Privacy Act ♦ Discrimination & Harassment
♦ Introduction to Legal Aspects of Banking ♦ Consumer Affairs & Trade Practices

Bachelor's Degree in Law ♦ NORTHEASTERN UNIVERSITY, Massachusetts

Computer Expertise: CAPS, Control D, CICS, Vision, Microsoft Office Suite

SELECTED CAREER HIGHLIGHTS

Circumvented Ombudsman/media involvement, and averted losses through incisive investigative, negotiation and arbitration competencies, and insight into distinguishing genuine from fraudulent claims, while executing strategic initiatives to secure successful outcomes without incident.

♦ Isolated and impeded numerous inaccurate claims for compensation against credit cards, merchant customers and the bank by unscrupulous and often reoffending parties; investigated and interfaced with various departments/organizations to ascertain accurate occurrences; and executed strategic resolutions with full compliance to set guidelines and protocols.

♦ Prevented cashing of stolen checks; optimized banks' profile with large corporate client.

♦ Five-years' experience within Fraud & Forgeries Department in a banking environment; gained exceptional understanding of operational methodologies/protocols and the establishment and maintenance of profiles for suspicious customers and account transactions.

Developed key alliances with law enforcement authorities, local community representatives and cross-functional internal/external banking departments to facilitate achievement of goals and objectives in the prevention of fraudulent activities.

♦ Interfaced with local crime prevention groups in the establishment and coordination of fraud profiles on suspicious entities, patterns and behavior, with meticulous input into comprehensive database, while remaining abreast of fraud activity trends.

♦ Provided pertinent credit card and other information to police to facilitate investigations and subsequent arrest of fraudulent credit card suspects.

♦ Collaborated with law enforcement authorities to ascertain and document associated crime statistics, which enhanced and optimized crime prevention within the local community.

Continued…

JULIE STOKES

Problem-solved and diffused numerous customer complaints and concerns without incident, executing strategic customer relationship management techniques to secure client satisfaction, retention and repeat business, while upholding the bank's reputation and professional profile.

- Arbitrated diverse cases, minimizing loss/claims through tactical investigation, sound judgment, and ability to devise and implement mutually acceptable solutions; renowned for expertise in resolving issues fairly, often called upon by clients to mediate and offer advice concerning arising banking issues.

- Researched, advised and arranged suitable banking products for customers unaware of best options to suit their needs; established rapport and trust, and recognition for banking product knowledge and expertise.

- Placated displeased client after they discovered double insurance premiums being deducted from their account over a two-year period; investigated and implemented corrective actions that successfully appeased and prevented customer from taking further action.

PROFESSIONAL EXPERIENCE

NATIONAL BANKING GROUP   1991 – Present
National Customer Liaison Officer (1995 – Present)
Restore relationships with disgruntled customers over products/services, or unresolved long-term issues as a "last port of call" prior to Ombudsman contact. Establish and maintain strategic alliances with cross-functional departments to facilitate speedy resolution of client concerns. Maintain scrupulous records and detailed accounts of customer contact, conversations and reactions to impede possible future claims alleging improper handling of concerns. Minimize and reduce risks for customers and the bank through remaining current with credit risk procedures in order to identify trends in fraudulent activity and subsequently expedite necessary steps.

- Achieved stringent weekly targets of finalizing 24 cases requiring outstanding research, analysis and resolution competencies to achieve realistic win-win outcomes, thus circumventing potential costs of legal action.

- Frequently awarded *Certificates of Recognition* for exceeding 100% of targets.

- Distinguished from peers by receiving the majority of formal customer compliments for going "above and beyond" the call of duty.

- Entrusted by management to present induction training programs to new recruits due to extensive retail banking and credit card knowledge. Coaching encompassed standard protocols, role expectations, and methods to balance the art of customer service with diplomatic conflict resolution.

Customer Service Officer, Head Office Contact Center (1991 – 1995)

Fast-track appointment to Acting Team Leader role; supervising, training and mentoring 30 staff to maximize team performance within a complex, high-pressure customer service environment.

- Recognized for outstanding performances, possessing a record of achievement that remains unbeaten to present day for exceeding call targets and selling most banking products.

- Enhanced and revitalized call center staff performance through provision of on-the-job training in product sales and customer needs analysis; crafted scripts of suggested responses to "brick walls" or rejection. Created environment that encouraged staffs' continual knowledge growth.

- Pioneered comprehensive list of "*dos and don'ts*" to standardize telephone protocols, improve workflows, and drive revenues and market growth.

UNITED BANKERS NOMINEES   1988 – 1990
Data Entry Operator - Settlements Department
Meticulous data-entry into computerized mainframe system with pressure for rapid delivery output to achieve time-critical deadlines.

- Instrumental in capturing significant reduction in error rates, with virtual elimination of rekeying labor and overtime costs, through strategic monitoring of entries for anomalies.

LORENCE BASS
1420 Heatherley Drive SW
Farmington Hills, Michigan 48335

248.555.5776
emailadddress@emailaddress.com

PROFESSIONAL OVERVIEW

Information Technology Professional. Hands-on visionary with advanced technical expertise. Strong skill set in developing, analyzing, and implementing complex network environments. Extensive product knowledge in hardware/ software deliverables. Successfully meets the challenge of remaining current with new and developing technology.

Excellent qualifications in general management, human resources, client relations, training, and communication in a cutting-edge environment.

Demonstrated leadership with customers and consistent quality in the technical development of colleagues/subordinates. Confident in abilities and committed to performance excellence, providing stability and growth in computing environments.

KEY STRENGTHS

- Exceptionally advanced technical knowledge with an ability to manage complex disciplines and circumstances. Provides competence under pressure in highly complicated situations.

- Well-developed organizational skills; identifies work plans, considers priorities, forecasts problems, and envisions solutions. Follows up efficiently.

- Generates a positive impression while interacting with and supporting customers, as well as cultivating a secure corporate impact to ensure project success.

- Clear and convincing oral communication skills; maintains logic and clarity in pressure/intense situations. Extremely clear, succinct, and thorough writing skills; well prepared in routine or complex subjects.

- Proven training/development abilities in cultivating talents within highly complex environments; adapts style to recipient.

- Industry and environment knowledge includes aerospace, healthcare, automotive, manufacturing, wholesale/retail, and finance.

RECENT EXPERIENCE

COMPUWARE CORPORATION   Farmington Hills, Michigan
Specializing in computer information systems management.
PROFESSIONAL STAFF CONSULTANT, 1994-current
Provide leadership in project management through planning, developing, implementing, and managing system and subsystem strategies for Fortune 100 companies.
- Analyze, design, present, and implement effective computer system methods that increase corporate productivity.
- Work closely with clients to assess individual needs and support effectively.
- Train network teams to work cohesively; maintain contact for ongoing instruction.
Achievements:
- Top-ranked consultant in the company nationally.
- Redesigned money transfer processing for a major retailer which ensured stability of the system, increased efficiency of the work flow, and improved system operating efficiency by 400%.
- Drafted and implemented networking standards that provided reliability and growth to computing environments.
- Project managed a national, multisite network upgrade (including proposals, forecasts, and submissions) encompassing more than 2000 end users, on time and within budget.

PREVIOUS EXPERIENCE

INTELLIGENCE NETWORK SYSTEMS, INC.   Bloomfield Hills, Michigan
MANAGER — Technical Services, 1992-94
Responsible for the direction and management of technical services for value-added reseller activities, including installation, support, maintenance of products and service contracts. Supervised a staff of 20 technical specialists.
- Evaluated new and projected technologies for company growth.
- Interacted with clients and acted as liaison between executive management for customer support, conflict resolution, design specifications, quality, and project/program progress.
- Provided training and ongoing support to technicians and customers.

SIERRA MAGNETIC SYSTEMS COMPANY   Ypsilanti, Michigan
NETWORK/OPERATING SYSTEM SPECIALIST, 1990-92
Traveled extensively throughout the nation supporting the large computer manufacturing firm. Led training assignments for the top 140 VARs in the nation.
- Provided technical support, training, and consultation to corporate clients, internal technical staff, marketing and sales groups.
- Attended trade shows; furnished technical information on company product lines.
- Successfully resolved 100% of all internal/external assignments.

COMPUTERWORLD — **SERVICE MANAGER/TECHNICIAN**, 1987-89

SELF-EMPLOYED — **CONSULTANT/INFORMATION BROKER**, 1984-current

EDUCATION / PROFESSIONAL DEVELOPMENT

SCHOOLCRAFT COLLEGE   Livonia, Michigan
   Concentration: Computer Science

DALE CARNEGIE — Effective Speaking and Human Relations

IBM Training Certified: PS/2 Hardware Services; OS/2; DOS Networking; LAN Server, Quality Service Skills

Novell Training Certified: NetWare System Manager and Advanced System Manager; NetWare Service and Support

Microsoft: Windows Technical Certification

Synoptics Certified: Ethernet Connectivity; Token Ring Connectivity; TCP/IP Fundamentals; LattisNet Manager

Netframe: VAR Service Certification; Advanced Application Processor; Advanced Benchmark & Network Tuning

TECHNICAL ADDENDUM

OS Platforms: NetWare; OS/2; Windows 3.x, 95, 98, NT 3.x & 4.x; DOS; Macintosh; SCO UNIX; Xenix; Linux; Solaris; A/IX; HP/UX; LAN Manager; LAN Server; Banyan Vines

Hardware Platforms: AST; Compaq; Dell; Gateway; HP; IBM; Macintosh; NCR; Netframe; Sun

Topologies: Ethernet; Token Ring; FDDI; ISDN; T1; ATM; Frame Relay

Protocols: TCP/IP; IPX/SPX; AppleTalk; Netbeui; Netbios

General: routers, bridges, concentrators, switches; project analysis, deployment and management; remote access gateways; specification of hardware/software; development of documentation for operations and enduser; backup strategies; disaster recovery; performance measurement and tuning; network and information security; network analysis, administration, architecture, design, migration, and troubleshooting.

LORENCE BASS
1420 Heatherley Drive SW — Farmington Hills, Michigan 48335 — 248.555.5776

Sharon L. Whelan
510/555-1212
email@email.com

12345 Mission Blvd., Apt 678
Hayward, CA 95303

◆ ◆ ◆ ◆ ◆ ◆ ◆ ◆ ◆

<u>STRENGTH</u>: Law Firm Accounting Clerk

<u>SKILLS SUMMARY</u>
- Highly proficient in Elite Law Office Billing System.
- SQL; Lotus 1-2-3; Excel; Microsoft Words, Windows, DOS.
- 10-key by touch.
- Effective problem solver; prioritize and manage heavy work flow without direct supervision.
- "Can do" attitude; work very cooperatively with legal and nonlegal staff.
- Excellent working relationship with billing attorneys.
- Additional skills include customer service, general office support.

<u>PROFESSIONAL EXPERIENCE</u>

Accounting Clerk   3/90 to Present
<u>Law Offices of Mason & Matlock</u>, Sun City, CA
- Facilitate conversion of client accounts from manual to computerized billing using Elite Billing System.
- Generate SQL reports; assist in month-end processing.
- Manually post and reconcile checks; backup and assistance for A/P.
- Process and distribute daily checks, review check requests.
- Interaction with and response to 13 partners, 3 associates, and clients regarding A/R matters.
- Assign attorney numbers; maintain rate changes; maintain safe contents.
- Maintain monthly employee postage charges; petty cash backup.
- Train new accounting staff on accounting procedures.

Accomplishment
- Increased the effectiveness of the Elite Billing System by determining a more efficient way to do rebills, resulting in significant savings in time, money, and billing errors.

Assistant Store Manager   4/88 to 2/90
<u>Wilson's House of Suede and Leather</u>, Sunnyvale, CA
- Opened and closed store; supervised sales staff.
- Bookkeeping; payroll; bank deposits.
- Supervised shipping/receiving and inventory control.

Accomplishments
- Increased store sales from 35% to 60%.
- Positive evaluations from secret shoppers increased from 30% to 90%.

<u>CERTIFICATES OF COMPLETION</u>
Sun City Legal Secretary's Association (SULSA), May 1991
Computer Applications, <u>Regional Occupations Program</u>, Newark, CA

DORIS C. FLANNERY

810 Clear Water Avenue
Palm Beach, Florida 33401
(561) 555-1234/email@mail.com

LIBRARY POSITION

"A retired elementary school principal seeking to conclude her educational career contributing to the growth and organizational enhancement of a state-of-the-art library."

Qualifications

Chairperson:	West Palm Beach Library Board, 1995–1997; Active Member, 1983 to current
Active Member:	West Palm Beach Library Long-Range Planning Ad Hoc Committee, 1994–current
Delegate:	To the Florida Governor's Conference on Library Information Services, 1995, 1997, 2000
Delegate:	To the White House Conference on Library Information Services, 2000
Librarian:	Five years as Pharmacy Librarian, Florida A&M University, School of Pharmacy, 1977–82
Change Agent:	Change leader for Palm Beach County School

Professional Experience

PALM BEACH COUNTY SCHOOL SYSTEM
Palm Beach County, Florida
1970–Current

Principal	**1991 to Current**
Assistant Principal	**1983 to 1991**
Reading Consultant/English Teacher	**1976 to 1983**
Reading/English Teacher	**1970 to 1976**

- One of 55 educators selected from DE US to participate in U.S.A. Reading Revival Program
- One of 35 educators selected to participate in State of Florida's Summer Read for Fun Program
- Selected to analyze, evaluate, and redesign reading and studying environment for Florida's libraries
- Principal of one of Palm Beach County's largest elementary schools—The JB Darren Elementary School—720 students and a faculty exceeding 19 professionals.

Education

M.A. in Education:	University of South Florida, Tampa, Florida, 1969
B.A. in Education and Library Science:	University of South Florida, Tampa, Florida, 1968

Certified:	State of Florida
CRI:	Certified Reading Instructor
CSET:	Certified: Special Education

Computer Skills:
PC/Mac; Windows, Office, Internet applications, and a host of Teacher/Student Proprietary Software

Portfolio of References Furnished on Request

Sandra Caneblum

4477 Bay Drive ♦ Boynton Beach, FL 33437
Tel: 561.555.7733 ♦ Cell: 561.555-9911
email@email.com

REFERENCE / SERIALS LIBRARIAN
Academic or Public Library Environment
Bilingual Spanish and English

A high-energy, self-motivated, and committed worker with a solid record for enhancing library experience for all patrons. Combine academic and work experience to exceed all library goals and objectives.

Strengths / Skills

- Comprehensive knowledge of professional library principles and techniques
- Mastery of computerized integrated online circulation systems – excellent research skills
- Knowledge of current literature and emerging trends/developments in library science
- High-impact training (English and Spanish) in electronic databases, Internet, and electronic catalog system

Education / Honors

UNIVERSITY OF WISCONSIN, Milwaukee, Wisconsin
Master of Science: Library & Information Services, 1999

UNIVERSITY OF VERMONT, Burlington, Vermont
Master of Science: Communication Science & Disorders, 1993

WASHINGTON UNIVERSITY, St. Louis, Missouri
Bachelor of Science: Spanish, 1984

Education/ Training Other:
- Teaching certificate – Georgia State University, Atlanta, Georgia
- Microsoft Word; Medical Reference on the Internet; Art Reference on the Internet; Legal Reference Sources
- Attained 1st level of completion for Medical Library Association

Professional Work Experience

PALM BEACH COUNTY LIBRARIES, Palm Beach County, Florida   1999 to Current
Reference Librarian - SW County Regional Library, Boca Raton, Florida (2001-Current)
Librarian – Net County Regional Library, Palm Beach, Florida (1999-01)

Library Internships

VON BRIESEN, PURTELL AND ROPER, Milwaukee, Wisconsin   1998 / 1999
Law Library Assistant - Legal Research Using Westlaw, Lexis, and Dialog

MILWAUKEE LEGAL RESOURCE CENTER, Milwaukee, Wisconsin   1999
Law Library Intern - Legal Research Using Westlaw and Lexis; Patron Assistance

Activities

Big Sister in the Big Brother, Big Sister Program
Member of Hospitality Committee – Palm Beach County Libraries
Former Member of Editorial Board - Palm Beach County Libraries

REFERENCES AVAILABLE UPON REQUEST

CHARLES B. WHITCOMB

440 E. Princeton Palo Alto, CA 95555
(510) 555-7006

LOSS PREVENTION MANAGER

Safety ✦ Loss Control ✦ Workers' Compensation
Hazmat ✦ Environmental ✦ Fire Suppression

QUALIFICATIONS SUMMARY

LOSS PREVENTION MANAGER with impressive 14-year career highlighted by contributions in the areas of:

♦ **Risk Management:** Developed safety, loss control, workers' compensation, hazmat, environmental, and fire suppression programs for commercial and industrial accounts that resulted in a 60-80% reduction in losses.

♦ **Operations Management:** Turned around departmental operations with poor performance history to rank first in the nation. Developed and implemented TQM programs that reduced losses by approximately 33%.

♦ **Marketing:** Instrumental in developing new business valued in excess of $57 million.

EDUCATION, CREDENTIALS

Bachelor of Science, Microbiology
University of California, Los Angeles

Registered Environmental Assessor
California Environmental Protection Agency

Certified Health & Safety Technologist
American Board of Industrial Hygiene

PRESENT EMPLOYMENT

EXECUTIVE OFFICER

Sierra Medical, Richmond, CA — 6/95-Present

Manage medical clinic with $26 million budget, including supervision of 54 professional and technical staff.

PROFESSIONAL EXPERIENCE

V.P., SAFETY MANAGEMENT
American Insurance, Los Angeles, CA — 1996-2003
($900MM workers' compensation and liability carrier)

Managed loss control department providing customized service for approximately 60 accounts totaling $125 million in premiums. Surveyed accounts for workers' compensation, general liability, products, completed operations, and auto/fleet coverage. Prepared and administered $350,000 departmental budget.

♦ Reversed department's poor internal audit ratings from #13 (lowest division in the nation) to #1; awarded "Department of the Year" in 1999, 2000, and 2001.

♦ Active member of business development team; increased revenue from $18 to $125 million in a 4-year period and met premium renewal goal of 100% renewals for four consecutive years.

♦ Recommended risk management programs for high-tech, construction, agriculture, distribution, and manufacturing accounts that yielded a 60-80% reduction in losses within the policies' first year.

LOSS CONTROL REPRESENTATIVE

World Insurance, Los Angeles, CA — 1992-1996
($200 billion property and casualty carrier)

Surveyed and recommended loss control programs for national accounts throughout the US and Asia. Investigated and analyzed loss trends.

PROFESSIONAL AFFILIATIONS

American Industrial Hygiene Association
American Society of Safety Engineers
National Fire Protection Association

Lynn Diaz

45 Fox Crossing ♦ Florissant, Missouri 63034 ♦ (314) 555-3333 ♦ diaz@email.com

Make-Up Artist		
Motion Picture	Commercials	Print Makeup
Television	Stage Performance	Special Effects

"Lynn is an extremely knowledgeable, versatile, and gifted make up artist. Our performers and models requested her for all their difficult makeup needs, and Lynn came through every time with professionalism and creativity. You can count on Lynn for superb artistry!"

Tom Jennings, Director
John Casablancas Modeling Center

Commercials

- **PDQ/3 Spots**
  Cast 20/12-92 Years-Old, Burdeau-Pechin Productions
  Directors/Chris Pechin & George Burdeau, North Hollywood

- **KY-98 FM Radio/3 Spots**
  Director/Al Crane - St. Louis

Films

- **CBS "CLASS ACT"**
  Director/Jon O'Brien; Producer/Brian Winter - LA

- **ABC "ABC ROCKS"**
  15 Nationwide Network Shows
  Director/David Jackson; Producer/Gary Benz - LA

Print & Fashion

- **Fashion Show & Showcase**
  Cast 30 Models
  Producer/Tom Kemp; Publisher/Hollywood Magazine

- **Model's Portfolios & Black/White Color Print**
  Instructor/Beauty Makeup, John Casablancas Modeling Agency

- **CPI Photo Finish; Southwestern Bell Telephone Company**

(Continued)

Print & Fashion (cont.)

- **Casting Party & Model Showcase**
  25 Models - Head Makeup Artist
  Producer/Tom Kemp; Publisher/Hollywood Magazine

- **Pure Sweat Fashion Show**
  Head Makeup Artist/Instructor
  Sponsors/Monty's Steak House, John Casablancas, Pure Sweat Clothing

- **Character & High Fashion Head Sheets**
  All Talent - Players and Others; President/Alona Perez - St. Louis

- **General Sales Catalog**
  Photographer/Rick Meoli

- **Still Photography**
  Alishe Tamburri; Photographer/Susan Ioata

- **Still Photography/Headsheets**
  Photographer/Dan Dreyfuss

Theater

- **Emmy Awards 1984**
  Makeup/Wardrobe Carol Lawrence, Fox Theater - St. Louis

Training

- **Joe Blasco Makeup Center**, Hollywood, CA
  Graduated 1984; Continuing Education 1996-Present

- **Certified Aesthetician**
  American Institute of Aesthetics

References

- Joe Blasco, Joe Blasco Makeup Center   (213) 555-2222
- Baron Von Mock, Enrollment Director, Blasco Studio   (213) 555-2222
- Kelcey Fry, Professional Makeup Artist   (213) 555-2222
- David Langford, Professional Makeup Artist   (714) 555-2222
- Tom Kemp, Publisher, Hollywood Magazine   (213) 555-2222
- Richard Dashut, Producer (Fleetwood Mac)   (213) 555-2222
- Jack Fisher, Photographer   (314) 555-2222
- Alona Perez, President, Players & Others   (314) 555-2222

Video and Portfolio Available upon Request

MAXWELL S. SMART

119 Old Stable Road
Lynchburg, Virginia U.S.A.
Phone (804) 555-4600 Fax (804) 555-4700
email@email.com

SENIOR OPERATING & MANAGEMENT EXECUTIVE
Building & Leading Start-Up, Turnaround, & Fast-Track Growth Corporations

Talented, creative, and profit-driven executive recognized nationally for pioneering efforts in product development and industry leadership. Expertise in sales/marketing, global business expansion, manufacturing, corporate finance and business process development. Harvard University Graduate. Distinguished honors and credentials include:

- "Person of the Year," *Printing Magazine*'s highest award in the Promotional Products Industry (1985). Honored as the founder of a billion-dollar consumer products market.

- U.S. Delegate to the 1987 People-to-People Economic Conference in Beijing, China. Long-term career in developing cooperative business ventures with Pacific Rim partners.

- Well-respected public speaking career at national and international trade associations, universities, and professional industry conferences.

- Impressionist painter with works in private and corporate collections in 15 countries worldwide. Earned prestigious designation as a Signature Member of the National Oil & Acrylics Painters Society (N.O.A.P.S.).

- State Masters Racquetball Champion. Ranked #6 in the U.S.

CAREER HISTORY:

Executive Marketing & Management Consultant   1991 to Present

Senior Associates, Inc., Lynchburg, Virginia

Consult with U.S. and Asian companies to provide top-flight expertise in strategic business planning, product development, global marketing, sales promotion, and marketing communications.

- Identified joint venture partners and researched international trade/tariff regulations for diversified Asian manufacturer seeking expansion into the Latin American market.

- Guided insurance company in the preparation of 5-year business plan and capital funding request.

- Orchestrated successful introduction of well-established U.S. mail order company into the promotional products market. Developed budget, defined infrastructure requirements, and designed product promotions (e.g., catalogs, literature, customer communications).

- Currently consulting with premier U.S. supplier of holographic products to provide situational analysis and market development strategies and for successful product positioning.

Chief Executive Officer   1972 to 1991
Graphics International, Lynchburg, Virginia

Senior Operating Executive of this printed apparel and textile manufacturing company supplying the promotional products, premium, department store, and mass merchant markets nationwide. Initially directed operations from Lynchburg-based headquarters. Subsequently directed company's start-up of subsidiaries in Columbus, Georgia, and Kowloon, Hong Kong. Chaired the Board of Directors.

(Continued)

MAXWELL S. SMART - Page Two

Held full P&L responsibility for the entire corporation, all design and production operations, key account sales and business development programs, human resource affairs (staff of 350), technology acquisition, capital improvement, materials sourcing and the complete finance/accounting function. Directed a four-person senior management team, on-site plant and production management staff, and Managing Director of Hong Kong trading company.

- Built company from $600,000 in annual revenues to $17.8 million and ranking as the fifth largest screen printer in the U.S. Produced over 22,000 orders annually.

- Pioneered development of industry-leading products, technologies, and production methods currently the foundation for a multi-billion-dollar industry. Achievements included development of the first 10-color textile printing presses in the U.S., introduction of original packaging standards for major activewear mills and, most significantly, the first multicolor textile apparel printing processes.

- Launched the successful introduction into the global market through development of both import and export operations (combined annual revenues of $1.5+ million).

- Identified tremendous market opportunity for the efficient design and production of small custom orders virtually ignored by major competitors. Developed innovative printing techniques, captured millions of dollars in sales, and won dominant market positioning nationwide.

- Built a nationwide network of 2200 distributors that generated over 50% of total company revenues. Personally directed and negotiated sales programs direct to major accounts including Sears ($2 million annually), Walmart, Target, J.C. Penney, and Wards.

- Introduced sophisticated technologies into the manufacturing, administrative, and financial departments that consistently enhanced quality, productivity, and profit performance.

President   1968 to 1972
Perkins Promotions, Inc. (Subsidiary of Mitchell & Associates), Lynchburg, Virginia

Senior Operating Executive of sales promotion firm servicing its parent advertising agency and major national accounts. Worked in cooperation with teams of advertising executives and creative staffs to plan, design, and produce (via contracted manufacturing) theme-based promotional and internal incentive products in concert with national ad campaigns.

- Completed projects for major U.S. corporations, including Anheuser-Busch, McDonald's, Cadillac, Ralston Purina, and Southwestern Bell.

(NOTE: Established Perkins Promotions, Inc. in 1966 and sold to Mitchell & Associates in 1968. Subsequently purchased it back in 1972 as the foundation on which Graphics International was founded.)

EDUCATION:

HARVARD UNIVERSITY GRADUATE SCHOOL OF BUSINESS ADMINISTRATION
Graduate, OPM Program

UNIVERSITY SCHOOL OF FINE ARTS

Three EURAM International Marketing Conferences (Amsterdam, London, Paris)
Five AMA President Association Programs
Certified Advertising Specialist (C.A.S.) Designation

102—MANAGEMENT CONSULTANT (E-MAIL RESUME)

Renee Tressle
2724 Cameron Street
Washington, DC 20008
W (703) 555-1212, H (202) 555-1212
renee.tressle@mail.argi.net

EXPERIENCE

A.T. Kearney - EDS Management Consulting Services
Washington, DC
Principal, 1996 - present
Senior Manager, 1994-1996

Specialized in the development of business plans for emerging wireline and
wireless telecommunications companies. Responsible for client relationship
management and sales into preexisting client base. Responsible for managing
large (up to 30 people) work teams. Provided advice to senior management on a
broad variety of strategic and operational subjects, including:
-Business strategy and planning
-Financial modeling
-Competitive assessment
-Market segmentation
-Operations design and optimization
-Mergers and acquisitions
-Implementation assistance
-Churn management

Deloitte & Touche Management Consulting
Washington, DC
Manager, 1993-1994
Senior Consultant, 1991-1993

Primarily focused on developing market-entry strategies for telecommunications
clients. Developed very strong financial modeling skills. Responsible for
managing smaller projects and developing client deliverables.

EDUCATION

B.S. in Physics, Montana State University, 1989
MBA in Finance, Carnegie Mellon University, 1991

PUBLICATIONS / SPEECHES

"An Ice Age Is Coming to the Wireless World: A Perspective on the Future of Mobile
Telephony in the United States," 1995
Thought Leadership Series, EDS Management Consulting

"Analysis of the FCC's Order Regarding Ameritech's Application to Provide InterLATA
Toll Services within the State of Michigan," A.T. Kearney White Paper, 1997

Presented at over two dozen industry conferences, workshops, and panels

JENNIFER SCOTT

555 Belle Street
Novi, MI 55555

Jennifcott@yahoo.com

Residence: 248-555-1289
Cellular: 248-555-3378

SENIOR-LEVEL MANAGEMENT PROFESSIONAL
Operations . . . Manufacturing . . . Engineering

Accomplished professional with over 17 years of comprehensive large-scale management and engineering experience in diversified project design. Strong background in product development and quality assurance with an outstanding history of managing projects from initial conception, through development, to launch. Unexcelled record of bringing mission-critical projects in on schedule and within budget. Especially skilled at strategic planning, financial controls, and problem resolution. Outstanding communication talents with proven ability to build and lead highly efficient teams, to train technical personnel, and to convey complex concepts in understandable terms. Extensive international experience, including Europe, Japan, and Mexico. Ford PTPB European division's first minority member as well as Chesterfield's first minority area manager.

AREAS OF EXPERTISE

- **Executive Leadership & Motivation**
- **New Business Development**
- **Systems & Process Improvement**
- **Recruiting, Hiring, Training, & Supervision**
- **Project Design & Management**
- **Trends Analysis & Forecasting**

- **Strategic & Tactical Planning**
- **New Product Development**
- **JIT & Lean Manufacturing Strategies**
- **Strategic Alliances & Partnerships**
- **Team Building & Leadership**
- **Troubleshooting & Problem Solving**

CAREER PROGRESSION

FIBERFILL INTERIORS / MOSBACH AUTOMOTIVE COMPANY (www.mosbach.com) – Troy, MI
Leading independent supplier of instrument panels, plastic interior/exterior trim and functional components for North American and European-made cars/light trucks. Employs 25,000 and yields $4 billion.

Director, Systems Integration Engineering (2000 – Present)

Accepted challenge to maintain competitiveness in cockpit business by creating unique design. Lead team of 30-40 engineers to strengthen systems capability and direct research/product development of cockpit/door applications (stamping, welding and electronics) for 2005/2006 programs. Recruit, hire, train, motivate, and evaluate all engineers and program managers in cockpit program. Direct and supervise $5.5 million budget. Currently heading steering team and providing leadership to 4 other teams.

Tasked to work initially with manufacturer to engineer and sell complete cockpit system (first ever). Led 20-30 development project presentations to 120 different personnel, including Executive Vice President of Product Development and staff. Assure cockpit product designs meet all federal (FMVSS), European and Japanese safety rules and regulations. Developing similar concepts for Chrysler, General Motors, and several European and Asian partners.

Performance Highlights:

- **Initial targets are 30% assembly time reduction, 40% quality enhancement, and 20% cost improvement.**
- **Filed 2 invention disclosures in last year** (pending determination from corporate lawyers).
- **Currently leading cockpit product commercialization program** (directed toward Ford) expected to be finalized second quarter, 2002 with **winning $300-$400 million proposal**.

COCKRELL MOTOR COMPANY/VISIONAIRRE (www.cockrell.com) – Dearborn, MI   **1984 – 2000**
One of the world's leading vehicle manufacturers. Employs 346,000 and yields $171 billion. Visionairre Automotive Systems, a $17 billion component supplier, was spun off June 2000.

(Continued)

JENNIFER SCOTT

COCKRELL MOTOR COMPANY/VISIONAIRRE (Continued)

Engineering Manager (1999 – 2000)
Led cockpit systems engineering pursuit team with mandate to design and win cockpit business for Visionairre's Interior Systems division and oversaw $6 million yearly budget. Directly supervised team of 25, including 5 program managers, and presided over recruiting, interviewing, hiring, training and performance review processes. Ensured cockpit designs met all federal, European, and Japanese safety rules and regulations. Made numerous cockpit development presentations for internal vice presidents and to directors, managers, and vice presidents from Toyota, Honda, Nissan, Hyundai, and Mitsubishi.

Performance Highlights:
- **Led program team that won $350 million cockpit contract** from Nissan (starting in 2005), first non-Ford program ever awarded to Visteon.
- **Reduced cockpit system cost 10%** versus cost of individual components.
- **Saved $50 per unit (5% of total cost)** by recruiting tier-2 suppliers to work on Nissan program.
- **Played key role on teams** that developed $600 million Honda Accord and $250 million Hyundai Sonata programs

Area Manager, Chesterfield Trim Plant (1993 – 1999)
In charge of manufacturing, engineering, operations, and maintenance of $230 million Chesterfield Plant I. Recruited, hired, and evaluated 400 plant personnel and delivered performance reviews on 7 direct reports. Trained and assigned quality representatives to customer plants. Forecasted departmental budgets and maintained oversight of $200 million operating and $5 million capital budgets. Served as direct customer contact for plant managers of Wayne and Michigan Truck. Ensured compliance with all manufacturing safety standards (OSHA, EPA, etc.). Participated in UAW contract negotiations.

Performance Highlights:
- **Slashed labor costs $1 million annually** by leading engineering team that launched first "lean" manufacturing cell to support 2000 Ford Focus seat build.
- **Reduced downtime 45%** in foam-area by working closely with preventive maintenance team.
- **Developed and implemented 8% plant cost-reduction plan.**

PRIOR SERVICE:

Program Manager – Vehicle Interior Systems Engineering – Basildon, Great Britain (1992 – 1993)

Unit Supervisor & Program Manager -- New Model Assembly Engineering – Saline, MI (1991 – 1992)

Project Manager -- Instrument Panels and Consoles – Saline, MI (1990 – 1991)

Product Design Engineer – Redford, MI (1987 – 1990)

Manufacturing Process Engineer/ Production Supervisor – Saline, MI (1984 – 1986)

PROFESSIONAL PROFILE

EDUCATION:	- MS / Engineering Management; University of Detroit (1992) - MS / Mechanical Engineering; University of Michigan (1987) - BS / Mechanical Engineering; University of Michigan (1984)
AFFILIATION:	- National Society of Black Engineers - Society of Automotive Engineering
SEMINARS / TRAINING:	- Consumer-Driven 6 Sigma Program – Green Belt (2001) - Lead Program for High Potential Managers (1999) - Principles Of Emergency Management (1999)

CHRIS DURSO
11601 Fir Street • Columbus, Ohio 43211
(614) 555-1212/email@email.com

MANUFACTURING OPERATIONS EXECUTIVE

Driving Growth & Profits in Industrial/Manufacturing Environments

Product Development & Enhancement/Start-Up & Turnaround Leadership
Market & New-Business Development/P&L Responsibility

Dynamic operating/management professional offering extensive and successful leadership positions in industrial and manufacturing arenas. Successfully integrate solid management, business development, personnel leadership, and technical expertise in pursuit of bottom-line goals and objectives. Additional areas of expertise include:

Strategic planning and logistics management	**Regulatory compliance oversight**
Budget/expense control—financial reporting	**Efficiency/productivity enhancement**
Customer-service and quality-control management	**Sales, marketing, and business expansion**

PROFESSIONAL EXPERIENCE

Walters Coatings, Inc., Columbus, Ohio   1996 to Current
Director of Operations

Direct all aspects of the Columbus facility ($3.2 million operation) for a recognized leader in the application of industrial coatings—serving a diverse clientele as a Dupont-licensed applicator of Teflon® finishes. Company also applies specialized coatings from other manufacturers of liquid and powder coatings. Oversee daily production by coordinating activities with plant manager to assure production meets deadlines, quality standards, and customer/sales requirements. Spearhead sales and new-business activities—identifying and capitalizing on new and emerging market opportunities. Full charge P&L responsibility—ensuring proper pricing, expense control, and systems/technology integration.

- Built up and service more than 300 accounts, exceeding $3 million in sales.
- Turned around an unprofitable operation ($100,000/yr. loss) to a profitable operation ($336,000) in 23 months.
- Maintain an average net operating profit of 13%—some 5% above industry standards.
- Closed and manage key accounts, including Motorola, Ford, Heinz Food, and Panasonic.
- Developed and introduced new coating technologies resulting in $450,000 in added revenue per year.

Coat-Up, Inc., Chester, Pennsylvania   1983 to 1996
General Operations & Sales Manager

Company specialized in custom industrial finishing and coating (liquid and powder fluorocarbon coatings—Teflon, Kynar, Halar, PFA, etc.) serving diversified industries, including equipment manufacturers, electronics, chemical, petrochemical manufacturers, plastic molders, and aerospace. Directed day-to-day operations and sales/marketing activities, hired, trained, and supervised employees, oversaw production efforts, and ensured regulatory compliance. Full P&L responsibility.

- Orchestrated all sales and marketing efforts for start-up company, resulting in $750,000 in new business.
- Closed and managed key accounts, including Polaroid, IBM, Litton, and Boeing Corp.
- Oversaw production activities—optimized both labor and physical resources to achieve projected profits.
- Developed new and highly unique coatings/processes to maintain competitive edge and meet customer needs.

EDUCATION & LICENSES

Penn State University, Springfield, Pennsylvania
Bachelor of Science: Business Administration, 1982

References and Supporting Documentation Furnished upon Request

MARK PORTO

897 Village Drive
Springfield, VA 22150
Home: (703) 555-4387 - Fax: (703) 555-0843
E-mail: email@emailaddress.com

E-MARKETING / ON-LINE MARKETING DIRECTOR
Award-Winning Pioneer and Expert in Web / Internet / New Media Marketing

CAREER PROFILE

Web-savvy marketing professional accomplished in creating and leading high-impact marketing campaigns that consistently meet aggressive e-business goals. Initiated groundbreaking programs and delivered large revenue gains. Excel in both start-up and mature corporate environments. Strong leader known for tenacity and positive "can-do" attitude. Fully fluent in interactive and Internet technologies and tools.

AREAS OF EXPERTISE

- Web, Print, & Broadcast Advertising
- Business Development Initiatives
- Community Building & Customer Loyalty
- E-Business Strategies & Technologies
- Product Launch Strategy & Execution

- Partnership & Alliance Building
- Online Relationship Marketing
- Market Awareness Building
- User Acquisition & Retention
- Staff Development & Leadership

PROFESSIONAL HISTORY

ComputerTrends.com   **1998 - Present**
Dynamic start-up e-business offering PC-related sales, service, and support in the business-to-business (B2B) and business-to-consumer (B2C) markets.

E-MARKETING DIRECTOR

- Led development and execution of marketing strategies and new business initiatives that drove rapid growth, from the ground floor to $8.2 million.

- Pioneered a fully functional marketing department infrastructure, including policies and procedures, streamlined business processes, and a talented marketing and communications team.

- Created and deployed unique advertising campaigns proven successful in positioning the company with a competitive distinction. Won national attention for innovative and edgy ads that piqued interest in the target markets.

- Delivered 54% ROI from marketing efforts by employing a shrewd balance of Internet and traditional print and broadcast medias to maximize results.

- Negotiated and structured 8 major business partnerships and alliances; built and led successful win-win programs through cost-effective comarketing initiatives.

Real Estate Sales, Inc.   **1994 - 1998**
Leading national real estate brokerage company with more than 4000 offices and 50,000 sales associates in 50 U.S. states.

SENIOR MARKETING MANAGER

- Guided strategic planning, development, and leadership for all marketing and external communications strategies. Managed a 25-person team and $20 million annual budget.

- Coordinated creation and implementation of all print and broadcast advertising, image building, collateral sales support materials, direct mail, special events, relationship marketing, and electronic marketing.

- Conceived and launched the most extensive real estate Website on the Internet with over 1.2 million listings, generating 770,000 unique visitors each week and fortifying sales with more than 2500 customer leads each month.

(Continued)

MARK PORTO

PROFESSIONAL HISTORY CONTINUED

National ISP, Inc.   **1988 - 1994**
One of the nationwide largest Internet service providers, known for consistent positioning as a leading-edge provider of online services to consumers and businesses.

MARKETING & COMMUNICATIONS MANAGER

- Spearheaded strategy development and implementation, growing revenues more than $15 million by launching the company's online services within the retail environment.

- Revitalized languishing member acquisitions; conceived and initiated a special "Member get a Member" online promotion that was credited with consistently generating 68% of total membership.

- Negotiated and contracted against the competition for the company to be the sole online service exhibitor at Disney's Epcot Center, a position that ramped membership by 135,000 users the first year.

- Directed an 8-person staff; resolved challenging performance, ethical, and employee issues through aggressive corrective actions and a leadership style that inspired top performance.

Omni Advertising   **1984 - 1988**
Large advertising agency serving a diverse B2C and B2B clientele, overseeing the creation and execution of multi-million-dollar campaigns.

ACCOUNT EXECUTIVE (1985 - 1988)
ASSISTANT ACCOUNT EXECUTIVE (1984 - 1985)

- Planned strategies and repositioned a major cable network from a vertical sports network to a horizontal family channel; guided all consumer and affiliate marketing on both the local and national level.

- Conceptualized, developed, and implemented advertising and marketing programs for a portfolio of 10 major accounts. Personally designed and produced 3 critically acclaimed, award-winning television spots.

- Played an instrumental role in driving the most successful new cable network launch in history, topping over 60 million subscribers in two years despite a highly competitive market with limited channel space.

EDUCATION & TRAINING

M.B.A., Marketing and Communications
Boston University, MA (1990)

B.S., Business Administration
University of Kentucky, Lexington (1984)

Recent Continuing Education:
- 7 Habits of Highly Successful People, Stephen Covey Leadership
- Delegation & Team Effort, Boston University, Executive Education
- Building Customer Loyalty, The Duncan Group

PROFESSIONAL ACTIVITIES

Building your Digital Business - Featured speaker, BMA conference, 1999
High-Impact Marketing - Keynote speaker, NAFME conference, 1999
Preparing your Business for a Digital World – Keynote speaker, IAPM conference 1998

ASSOCIATIONS

Business Marketing Association – Current Board of Directors, Past President
Power Marketing Association – Current Board of Directors
American Marketing Association – Current Member

DONNA MARZETTI
DONNA MARZETTI

Director of Media Integration - Executive Web Producer

e-mail@e-mailaddress.com

503-555-5030

❖ Six years of success in promoting the strategic vision of e-commerce sites through Web design, architecture, and content.

❖ Serve as the nexus among all Web disciplines, interactive/design agencies, external partners, internal designers and developers, hosting providers, and content providers.

❖ Demonstrated skill in managing production work flow from brainstorming phase through award-winning implementation in a variety of media, capitalizing on the core competencies of technical and creative teams.

❖ Expert project management, effectively identifying and managing milestones, dependencies, and bottlenecks by creating production standards, gathering initial user requirements, collecting user feedback, generating and refining specifications for the development cycle.

❖ Innovative design of user interfaces and site navigation features, cocreating and managing the logical flow of content. Exceptional knowledge of copy writing, editing, graphic design, typography, and film/video production.

❖ In-depth knowledge of Web usability, cross-browser environments, navigation, content management, technical development, hosting, site metrics, and databases.

❖ Proficient in HTML, dHTML, JavaScript, Cold Fusion, ASP, PhotoShop, Dreamweaver, NT, IIS, SQL-Server, Illustrator, Fireworks, ImageReady, GoLive, PageMill, FTP, MS Office, and MS Project.

EXPERIENCE

CyberShoppingMall.com, Seattle, WA   1998-Present
Director of Media Integration

❖ Support the corporate mission of delivering the fastest, most effective merchandising and display technology systems to maximize sales and advertising for clients of this provider of next-generation e-commerce sites and 3D applications.

❖ Direct a team of 12 in the ongoing development and exploitation of core and complementary technologies on company and client Websites.

❖ Provide project leadership for Website production,including:budget control,production schedule,status reporting, deliverables definition and accomplishment,client/project team coordination,and quality assurance.

❖ Team with executive producer and art director to implement HTML and graphics, guiding all facets of content development.

❖ Collaborate with product managers to develop long-term strategic objectives, product specifications, and implementation tactics. Devise and implement new Web solutions in partnership with the JSP/ASP/database development team.

❖ Develop and execute annual plan outlining Web projects and budgets, as well as online marketing campaigns and budgets. Build and maintain relationships with interactive Web service agencies and Internet service providers.

❖ Execute, monitor, and continually improve e-commerce programs. Collaborate with IS, Distribution, and Brand teams to gather and deliver content in line with marketing and e-commerce objectives.

❖ Manage project and production schedules as necessary to meet deadlines and budgets.Generate Website reports, analyze data and utilize information for online marketing decisions.

CONTINUED NEXT PAGE

DONNA MARZETTI
DONNA MARZETTI

Page 2 ~ e-mail@e-mailaddress.com ~ 503-555-5030

EXPERIENCE
CONTINUED

NaturoHealth.com, San Francisco, CA   1997-1998
Media Integration Consultant

❖ Redesigned architecture and content for leading natural health e-commerce/portal site. Created structure, organization, and navigation for multiple customer-focused channels.

❖ Implemented interactive features, banner ads, affiliate programs, and links. Supervised HTML and graphic design teams. Interfaced with engineering, database management, merchandising, marketing, and business development departments.

❖ Completed project a month ahead of schedule and $25,000 under budget.

NetsMakeADeal.com, Los Angeles, CA   1996-1997
User Interface Project Manager

❖ Managed front-end development for a high-traffic e-commerce Website.Coordinated efforts with back-end team for integration of site functionality.

❖ Sourced writers, designers, and technical specialists and supervised production process. Recruited and managed HTML/JavaScript developers. Motivated staffs and fostered positive, productive team environment.

❖ Designed graphical elements, including logos, layout, ads, and icons. Managed/maintained server files using PCAnywhere and FTP protocols, and ad-rotator middle-ware.

❖ Provided guidance on development of shopping cart and transaction interfaces.Balanced long-term projects with bi-weekly releases,fixes,and site updates.

❖ Served as Customer Advocate, identifying and organizing customer focus groups and online feedback. Solved user and site problems by translating important functional issues into technical solutions.

❖ Generated site activity reports, analyzing data from multiple perspectives. Utilized information for online marketing decisions as well as ISP accountability for uptime, latency, and connectivity.

The New Media Group, Inc., Los Angeles, CA   1994-1996
Producer

❖ Produced high-end Web applications for entertainment, e-commerce, B2B, and consumer organizations. Managed high-profile clients, including AOL, Discovery Online, PBS Online, Intel, and the World Bank.

EDUCATION & AFFILIATIONS

❖ Certified Web Administration & Development Professional, Certified Intranet/Internet Professional, 1999, Learning Tree International.
❖ Bachelor of Arts, Communications and English, University of Washington, 1990
❖ Member, Association for Internet Professionals
❖ Member, Association for Multimedia Communications

MARGARITA GONZALES

6767 Ryan Ave., Apt. 22
North Hollywood, CA 91400

(818) 555-1234
MargaritaGonzales@email.com

MEDICAL ASSISTANT (BACK OFFICE)

- Self-motivated and enthusiastic professional with a strong work ethic and verifiable record of dependability, punctuality and low absenteeism.
- Ability to put patients at ease and explain physicians' instructions clearly.
- Well liked and respected by patients and coworkers.
- Consistently demonstrates a caring attitude toward patients.
- Well organized and efficient, with excellent follow-through on problems and inquiries.
- Works well in a fast-paced environment with ability to remain calm in a crisis.
- Professional in appearance and work habits.

—Certifications—

California Certified Medical Assistant, Phlebotomist
Red Cross First Aid and CPR Certified

PROFESSIONAL EXPERIENCE

Medical Assistant • 1998 to Present
GREGORY KRAMER, Beverly Hills, CA
- Provide high level of back-office support for OB/GYN practice, including taking and recording vital signs, preparing patients for examinations, performing routine laboratory tests, maintaining supplies inventories and assisting with office procedures.
- Heavy patient interaction in person and on telephone.
- Maintain supply inventories; interface with pharmaceutical representatives and vendors.

Medical Assistant • 1996 to 1997
PETER ROBINSON, M.D., Beverly Hills, CA,
- Provided back- and front-office support for plastic surgery practice.
- Offered position after demonstrating superior abilities while serving externship.

EDUCATION

NATIONAL EDUCATION CENTER, Los Angeles, CA
Medical Assistant Certificate; 1996

LOS ANGELES CITY COLLEGE, Los Angeles, CA
Course work in General Education; ongoing

LANGUAGES

Bilingual English/Spanish

IDA R. MENESES
402 Hope Sound Lane
West Palm Beach, Florida 33415

(561) 555-1212
email@email.com

MEDICAL BILLING PROFESSIONAL
Electronic Claims Specialist
Expert in Accurate Claims Submission, Coding and Updates, & Collections
FAST, ACCURATE COLLECTIONS

INTRODUCTION

Highly experienced in all phases of medical billing—Medicare, Medicaid, Champus, HMOs, PPOs, and private insurance carriers, including secondary insurance claims. Outstanding record with Worker's Compensation, auto, and personal-injury claims. A professional who respects the fact that *"accurate billing and prompt collections are paramount to the physician."* A verifiable record of success in managing billing operations—leading to enhanced collections and cash flow in ever-changing environments.

Trained in computer hardware/software,electronic data transmission,and health-care-claim reimbursement.A resourceful,solution-focused individual recognized for lowering receivables,troubleshooting billing problems,and addressing challenges due to a lack of payment for insurance claims.Verify that billing codes are current and accurate.Additional areas of strength include:

* Business start-up and expansion
* Skilled negotiator
* Research and analysis
* Employee management and supervision
* Follow up; detail oriented

* Telephone communication skills
* Patient relations—professional/courteous
* Powerful writing skills
* Training and development
* Integrity; maintain high ethical standards

PROFESSIONAL EXPERIENCE

GTR Medical Billing Service, West Palm Beach, FL   1995–Present
Billing &Collection Agent/Manager —Start-up management and supervision for new billing office.Marketed services to local physicians and medical practices —preparing oral/written presentations.Directed all phases of billing service.Implemented a successful system for intensive and comprehensive follow-up for all nonresponsive insurance companies approaching the 30-day limit for payment.Improved practice 's collections/cash flow;organized record keeping and aging reporting,and significantly reduced bad-debt write-offs.

- Significantly reduced outstanding accounts receivable over 90 days by 77%—wrote off the balance
- Reduced returned claims from Medicare/Medicaid by nearly 95%
- Collected $49,000 of monies scheduled to be written off
- Maintained an above-average billing ratio of 73/27

PROFESSIONAL EXPERIENCE (Prior to 1995)

Glendale Federal Savings & Loan Association, Delray Beach, FL   1985–1995
Loan Officer

Nationwide Insurance Companies, Palm Beach Gardens, FL   1983–1985
General Insurance Agent

EDUCATION

Associate's Degree: Business Administration	Palm Beach Community College, Lake Worth, Florida, 1982
Insurance Billing for 3d-Party Billing	Palm Beach Community College, Lake Worth, Florida, 1992–1994
Medicare Guidelines	Medicare Guidelines & Billing Seminar, Tampa, Florida, 1996
Advanced Electronic Billing	Synaps Introduction to Insurance Billing, St. Petersburg, Florida, 1999

References and Supporting Documentation Furnished upon Request

KENNETH D. COLE

6663 Laverne Court
Jupiter, Florida 33458
(407) 555-9921
email@email.com

MANAGEMENT / OPERATIONS / AUTOMATION / LOGISTICS

OVERVIEW: Over 23 years of successful management and leadership experience with a reputation for meeting the most challenging organizational goals and objectives. A pragmatic and focused individual recognized for *"making seemingly impossible situations work."* A proven and *VERIFIABLE* record for:

- Producing higher performance standards and **enhancing productivity during a period of shrinking budgets.**

- Automating departments. As head of the Resources Department for a 14,000 personnel installation, automated major control system, **increasing the effective resource utilization rate from 46% to 97.6% in less than 12 months.** This resulted in a cost savings of over $101 million.

- Controlling growth management - **able to motivate and maximize productivity and employee morale** *without* **financial incentives.** Took a division with the lowest performance level (out of 54 divisions) and improved to #1 ranking in less than 12 months.

- **Developing and implementing highly successful strategic plans (short and long term).** Established inventory/purchasing control systems that gained accountability for millions of dollars in equipment, thus reducing inventory purchases by $1.1 million.

PROFESSIONAL EXPERIENCE:

United States Army, 1990 - 2003

CAPTAIN - Completed 23-year career with the U.S. Army. Gained upper-level manager status. Participated in the complete revitalization and overhaul of the U.S. Military in general - and the U.S. Army specifically - from the low status perceived in the 1970s to the most powerful and effective military in history.

An active participant in the swift/forceful turnaround of the armed forces that led to the U.S. victory in Operation Desert Storm. Part of the management team that proved that the military could be managed like a well-tuned corporate machine (same size as Exxon Corp.). A successful record for managing complex organizations, supervising thousands of people through hundreds of line-management personnel, responsible for millions of dollars in assets. Specific duties and achievements include:

MANAGEMENT: Led the Army's largest armor company consisting of 14 tanks, 10 APCs, an Engineer Squad and Maintenance Platoon. Managed testings of 14 high-tech, multi-million-dollar products that, in less than 12 months, went from conception to production. These systems were highly instrumental in the success of the Desert Storm operation. Upgraded training curriculum and methods, cross-trained personnel in job duties resulting in lower supervision requirements and a significant cost savings in overtime.

Kenneth D. Cole

**Experience
(Continued)**

*OPERATIONS &
LOGISTICS:* Was the primary logistical adviser to the Commander for 250 men, responsible for $25 million of equipment. Managed a $719,000 budget. Responsible for controlling the procurement of durable and expendable items under the budget. A recognized expert in planning and executing complex operations with 100% accuracy and success, including the scheduling and movement of thousands of personnel and the timely transfer of millions of dollars worth of equipment to support and maintain operations.

*AUTOMATION &
COST CONTROL:* Managed and automated the Resource Department on a 14,000-person installation responsible for budgets, materials, and resources. Improved the effective resource utilization rate from 46% to 97.6% in less than 12 months, saving over $101 million in cost with no change in personnel. A highly skilled technical individual, computer-literate, able to maximize Management Information Systems to increase profitability.

*TRAINING &
DEVELOPMENT:* Spent the last two years as an Assistant Professor of Military Science (Delta State University, Cleveland, Mississippi). Redesigned comprehensive management training program (regarded by superiors as the "most aggressive training program within the Brigade"), resulting in subordinates' excelling in all evaluated areas. Developed programs comprising 67 qualifications skills, 19 professional education subjects, and OJT training-leadership curriculum.

EDUCATION: Ohio University, Athens, Ohio
BACHELOR OF SCIENCE DEGREE, 1992
Business Management

* **Combined Armed Services Staff School**, Leavenworth, Kansas
  Effective Management, Public Speaking and Briefings, 2001

* **Company Leaders Course**, Monterey, California
  Management, Leadership & Administrative Procedures, 1999

* **Officers' Advanced Management Level Course**, Ft. Knox, Kentucky
  Advanced Leadership, Management & Problem Solving Analysis, 1996

* **Motor Officers' School**, Ft. Knox, Kentucky
  Equipment Maintenance, Management & Record Keeping, 1992

INTERESTS: Enjoy deep sea fishing, reading (History, Science, & Technology), gardening, cultural activities, and travel.

- References & Supporting Documentation Furnished upon Request -

GOLDIE BENJAMIN

7759 Eisenhower Drive • Naval Air Station #123455-BT • Madrid, Spain TF-10523
555-122-1233/email@email.com
SS#: 000-00-0000/Veteran Status: Active—Military Police Team Leader/U.S. Citizen

Objective:
Lead Officer—Operations & Logistics
Department of Military Affairs, U.S. Navy Command 201—Spain
MP-111-222-33/4

"Protecting and Serving Military Personnel, Guests, and Dignitaries"

SUMMARY

- Five years as senior law-enforcement officer III; Naval Police Team; Madrid, Spain—responsible for 33 officers and a staff of five. Ensure total safety and security for an air station comprising 3,000 people.

- Three years as military police officer I, II, and III—in charge of access control and escort, and emergency-response team member in enforcing U.S. Navy/Military codes/standards.

- Awarded seven commendation medals, including three Silver Stars for significantly exceeding job standards. Recognized for strong organization, administration, and time-management skills. Recipient of eight consecutive Merit Awards from superior offers for top job performance.

U.S. MILITARY SERVICE

UNITED STATES NAVY
Naval Air Station, Madrid, Spain
1994 to Current

Senior Law Enforcement Officer III	1999 to Current
Military Police Officer III	1997 to 1999
Military Police Officer II	1996 to 1997
Military Police Officer I	1994 to 1996

Top Secret Security Clearance (Level Six)
Expert/Certified Weapons Specialist—Trainer IV
Private Pilot's License

EDUCATION

AMERICAN UNIVERSITY, Madrid, Spain
Bachelor of Science: Criminal Justice and Law-Enforcement Management, 2000
GPA: 3.73

Key Course Work:

Law and the Judicial Process in the Military	Leadership in a Global Community
Terrorist Detection and Prevention	Access-Control Management
Facilities Safety and Protection Management	Crisis and Emergency Planning

Computer Skills:
Windows, PC, Mac, Office, QuickBooks, PhotoShop, and Internet Applications

STEPHEN N. LONDON

120 Cambridge * Berkley, Michigan 48072 * 248.555.1212 * email@email.com

DIRECTOR MIS

Manager in BigS Consulting Firm
Successful Manager of People, Process, and Technology
eCommerce Expertise in Growth and Profit Generation

A motivated, innovative, growth-oriented IT Consultant with positive, contagious energy who builds teams, creates relationships, and earns trust. Strategically and tactfully resolves and troubleshoots problems. A high-impact, multidimensional IT professional respected by his peers/superiors with a verifiable record of achievement of exceeding expectations.

CORE STRENGTHS

Information systems issues, risks, development, implementation	Business process analysis and improvement
Vision, strategy, and assessing market opportunities	Product development and enhancement
Teaching, leading, and empowering team members	Business and technical acumen
Relationship development skills; building strategic alliances	Web design and e-commerce technology

PROFESSIONAL EXPERIENCE

ERNST & YOUNG, LLP, Detroit, Michigan   1997 to Current
MIS Director

MIS Director for the Information Systems Assurance and Advisory Services (ISAAS) practice. A history of success delivering measurable value to a myriad of clients in multiple industries, from Fortune 1000 to small, high-growth companies. Extensive experience managing risk as organizations apply technology to complex internal and external business processes. Strategically focused in eProcurement, Internet security, venture acceleration, business process analysis/design, and IT strategy. Helped Ernst & Young develop eProcurement and eCommerce methodologies and build market share. Creates teams, empowers people, and delivers results. Innovative thinker. Pursuit leader on sales efforts. Delivers measurable value on every project.

- Lake Erie region ISAAS eProcurement and eCommerce leader.
- Selected to deliver eCommerce presentation at the annual national Ernst & Young accounting update meeting.
- Selected as ISAAS leader on Ann Arbor territory expansion and pursuit team.
- Increased revenue streams through demonstrating value to clients' IT organization and business processes.
- Successfully managed client expectations on all projects, resulting in additional work/favorable client referrals.
- Instrumental in building the ISAAS practice, trained staff/senior consultants in successful client service delivery.
- Industry expertise includes healthcare, insurance, manufacturing, and banking.

Listing of Ernst & Young Major Projects:

Project Name	Description
Venture Acceleration	Accelerated venture business plans to first round of funding. Activities include business modeling, revenue modeling, content sourcing, value chain analysis, competitive analysis, and product definition and design.
Business Plan Assessment	Assessed start-up business plans.
eProcurement	Managed and led strategic eProcurement ROT and diagnostic assessments
Internet Security	Implemented Axent's Technologies NetProwler and Intruder Alert host and network-based intrusion detection software.
Internet Security	Assessed online systems security of B2B transportation provider.
Business Process Analysis	Defined business process improvement opportunities for a myriad of clients in multiple industries.
IT Strategy	Conducted an IT departmental budget assessment.
Due Diligence	Assessed ASP internet start-up as due diligence for potential Venture Capitalist.
Systems Consulting	Defined and assessed technical and functional requirements.

(Continued)

Stephen N. London Page two
PROFESSIONAL EXPERIENCE

BLUE CROSS & BLUE SHIELD OF MICHIGAN, Southfield, Michigan   1994 to 1997
Workflow & Imaging Consultant, Contract through Computer Methods Corporation
Assisted Blue Cross Blue Shield in the design of the dental claims imaging system. Was the only consultant on the business side of the imaging project. Led client teams in defining business process and system requirements for various automated work flow queues. Defined detail process flows for work flow and imaging system design. Codeveloped system reporting requirements with client management team.

- Selected by users/management to facilitate business process improvement initiatives with orthodontic work team.
- Defined and established benchmark criteria for the Dental Imaging System to measure overall project success.
- Designed, developed, and implemented dental claim appeals-tracking database that is still in use today.

COMPUTER METHODS CORPORATION (CMC), Livonia, Michigan   1987 to 1994
Project Manager (1992–94)
Employed with CMC for over five years as a Project Manager, Account Executive, and Business Analyst for this $30 million software consulting firm. Reported directly to the President and CEO for three years. Selected in 1997 to lead the Imaging Technologies business unit after much employee turnover, customer dissatisfaction, and lack of organizational structure. Instrumental in achieving stability, increasing revenues, cutting costs, consolidating customer confidence.

- Directed Imaging Technologies business unit operations, responsible for $1.2 million in annual revenues.
- Successfully negotiated new business and renewal contracts with small and Fortune 1000 clients.
- Consistently increased group profitability on a quarterly basis.
- Comanaged implementation of OCR technology integrated with custom-developed claims adjudication software.
- Successfully managed department's staff of 30+ people (programmers, network admin, and administrative staff).
- Responsible for business unit financial planning and budgeting.

Account Executive (1990–92)

- Responsible for high-growth, middle-market clientele sector, successfully increased annual sector revenue.
- Sold client/server solutions, wrote and presented comprehensive proposals for custom application development, established new revenue streams.
- Main liaison between customer and development team, managed customer expectations.
- Selected as sales and marketing contact for Microsoft's Solution Provider program.

Business Analyst (1987–90)
- Defined user, business, and system requirements for scope and design documents.
- Identified & tracked corporate quality measurables, lead contributor to Ford's on-site Q1 quality audit.

EDUCATION / TRAINING

Bachelor of Arts Degree, 1993   **ALBION COLLEGE, Albion, Michigan**

Dual Majors: **Mathematics**, GPA: 3.8 / 4.0; **Economics**, GPA: 3.8 /4.0
Concentration: Carl A. Gerstacker Professional Management Program; Business Study Exchange, Germany, Summer, 1993

Training: Certified Document Imaging Architect (expected 2/2001); Commerce One eProcurement Technical Training; PeopleSoft Application Controls Training

ACTIVITIES

Junior Achievement High School Economics Teacher and Consultant
Troy High School, Volunteer Football Coach
Albion College Class Agent, Class of '93; Albion College Leadership Campaign Committee Member

GARY RICARDO

15 Marshwood Road, Brightwaters, NY 11706
voice ● 516-555-5555   e-mail ● gr@aol.com

Senior-Level Information Systems Group Manager

- Bottom-line-oriented executive with over fifteen years of comprehensive experience in profitable oversight of teams *and* technology. Produce consistent achievements in cutting-edge information systems management, team management, contract negotiations, purchasing logistics, and expense reduction. Utilize an anticipatory management style to drive results in a rapidly changing industry.

- Manage information systems group supporting production and business operations for Newsday, the nation's seventh largest newspaper. Supervise 48 direct reports and control $5 million+ operating budget. Research, assess, and approve technology purchases. Implement system improvements to maintain profitable, competitive, and quality-driven production processes.

Key Management and Technology Abilities

- Advanced Technologies
- Resource Management
- Project Planning/Budgets
- Project Management
- Expense Reduction
- Team Building/Motivation
- Presentations
- Capital Expenditure Planning

- Technology Needs Assessment
- Technology Rightsizing/Upgrades
- Win-Win Negotiations
- RFP Development/Review
- Vendor Partnerships
- Network Administration
- Project Lifecycle
- UNIX, SUN, LAN, WAN

- Systems Configuration
- Systems Implementation
- Parallel Systems Operation
- Intranet Development
- Technology Integration
- Disaster Recovery
- Systems Security
- Year 2000 Solutions

Summary of Major Accomplishments

- Reorganized entire Newsday Business Systems operation and hardware for 20% productivity improvement and a $230 thousand savings against operating expenses. Reduced footprint, allowing department's relocation to main building, freeing old location for lucrative commercial rental.

- Recruited and led team of volunteers to independently develop Information Systems Department's Intranet Server. Program was so successful that it was adopted companywide and became part of Information Systems Department's long-range strategic plan.

- Led project team that planned and implemented Newsday $4.8 million pagination project representing cutting-edge production technology. Project delivered ROI in only two and one-half years.

- Increased productivity and reduced expenses by purchase of new Tivoli system, replacing "manual" monitoring/installation method which provided fast-response central network monitoring, asset management, and LAN central software distribution to 1,200 desktops and 35 servers.

- Developed and implemented $680 thousand network project that replaced old copper Ethernets with a fiber-optic backbone and Cat5 10baseT wiring to the desktop utilizing dynamic switching hubs.

(Continued)

GARY **RICARDO**   page two

Network, Client Server, and Software Technology

- Fiber-Optic Backbone
- LAN and WAN
- Wide Area Networks Through T-1 lines
- Class B Internet license
- TCP / IP
- Firewall One, Hub Watch
- Wellfleet and Cisco Routers
- Dial and Dedicated Remote Communications
- Frame Relay
- DEC 900 Dynamic Switching Hubs
- Switched and Shared Ethernet Circuits

- Tivoli LAN Management system
- UNIX Operating Systems
- SUN Solaris and Raid Disk Technology
- Sybase Relational Database
- WinFrame Syntrex for Thin Client/Fat Server
- NT Alpha Server with Microsoft Mail
- Windows 3.1, 95, NT (Client and Server)
- Microsoft Office
- Norton Anti-Virus
- Microsoft Project and Support Magic
- Total Intranet Development and HTML Code

Career Development

NEWSDAY, INC., MELVILLE, NY   1982 to present

Director, Information Systems Group 1995 to present
Publishing Systems Manager 1984 to 1995
Editorial Project Manager 1982 to 1984

Manage 48 employees and oversee a $5.6 million budget to research, plan, install,integrate, and maintain hardware, software and networks to support 2,000 internal and external customers at Newsday's New York, Long Island, and Washington DC facilities. Areas of responsibility include:

- **Publishing Group** handles all support for print functions of publication :software, hardware, operating systems, desktop installations, upgrades, repairs 24 X 7 365 days.

- **Business Systems Group** the actual operations team. Includes systems programmers and data center staff for *Newsday* and the *Baltimore Sun*. Team also handles testing and implementation of the business systems disaster recovery plan for 24-hour data center catastrophe recovery.,

- **Networking Group**—the technical team. Designs, implements, installs, monitors, and repairs LAN and WAN systems in New York City, Long Island,and Washington, DC.

Conduct strategic planning including system upgrades, and capital, operating and line item budgets. Develop RFPs, execute ROI analysis, and negotiate/review contracts. Control departmental purchasing and resource management. Track expenses and maintain budget integrity. Produce management and staff reviews, determine salary increases and payroll budget.

Lead project teams, and manage projects using Microsoft Project and Support Magic to direct teams handling internal and client hardware and software installations. Perform system reliability analysis and cost justifications on system replacements.

Education

Certificate in Information Systems Management, Hofstra University, Uniondale, NY 1994

Bachelor of Science in Business (Magna Cum Laude), Hofstra University, Uniondale, NY 1980

ELIZABETH VERDERSO

10680 Avenue of Americas • Miami Lakes, FL 33356
(305) 555-1212 • Cell: (305) 555-9393
email@email.com

INTERNATIONAL MODEL

Recipient of 12 International Awards, Including *The Randall Award*, Milan, Italy, 2001
12 Years' National & International Experience as a Successful Fashion Model

Highly disciplined, results-driven, and outgoing professional seeking magazine and print media assignments in Miami and South Florida area.

PERSONAL

Height: 5'9"	Eyes: Blue	Hair: Blonde, Natural
Size: Six	Weight: 123	Complexion: Fair
Hips: 36	Waist: 25	Bust: 36

EDUCATION/TRAINING

MIAMI SCHOOL OF MODELING, Coral Gables, Florida
4 Years of Study with World-Renowned Trainer, Madame Bubois Liliac, 1996–2000

FLORIDA ATLANTIC UNIVERSITY, Boca Raton, Florida
Bachelor of Arts — Dual Degrees: English and Communications, (Cum Laude/Honors), 1994

PROFESSIONAL EXPERIENCE

International Fashion Model, Based out of Seattle, Washington   1987 to Current
Worked: ***Milan, Paris, Vienna, London, Barcelona, Madrid, Tokyo, New York City, Seattle, and Miami***. Developed key strategic relationships with agencies in each city and utilized their contacts to land jobs and establish client relationships for future business.   Assignments included:

Estee Lauder Campaign	Gelati Ice Cream	Polaroid
Camera Calendar	Honda	Nike
PepsiCo	Procter & Gamble	Élan Skies
Ferrari of Italy	Sports Illustrated	TWA

SELECTED AWARDS

The Randall Award, Milan	2001
The Green Diamond, Madrid	2000
The Edgar Snelling Award, London	1999
Model of the Year Award, *Fashion Trend Magazine*	1999
Jacque Denefe Recipient, Paris	1998
The Manhattan Award, New York	1998

AFFILIATIONS

International Modeling Association
Mothers' Connection — Editor for 15-page newsletter, with 350-person circulation

References Furnished upon Request

PATRICIA GOODMAN
pgoodman@email.com

12345 Ventura Boulevard, Suite 555   (818) 555-1234
Sherman Oaks, California 91423   Fax (818) 555-5432

MORTGAGE INDUSTRY SALES & MANAGEMENT PROFESSIONAL
Expertise in A Paper, Nonconforming, Subprime and Home Improvement Loans

Dynamic 12 year career in high-energy sales and loan production management. Expert qualifications in identifying market opportunities to accelerate expansion, increase revenues and improve profit contributions. Strong background in underwriting and new product development.

Equally strong qualifications in training and development, administration, strategic planning, team building and leadership. Proven ability to function in a dynamic and changing environment and interact effectively with all levels of support staff and management as well as successfully developing long-term profitable business partnerships. Maintain up-to-date knowledge of industry and governmental policies and regulations.

Licensed California Real Estate Broker

PROFESSIONAL EXPERIENCE

Wholesale Account Executive 1999 to Present
FIRST CAPITAL INC., Studio City, CA
Hired to head up business development for previously unprofitable branch. Provide full-range of service including prequalifying borrower and preunderwriting files. Oversee entire lending process to ensure timely and seamless closing.

- Turned branch around within first month; tripled revenues by third month, funding $2.5+ million in business.
- Acquired and developed a solid, profitable base of broker/correspondent relationships throughout Los Angeles and Orange counties, becoming consistent top producer in Western Region.
- Attained #1 Volume Producer in Western Region, 2000, 2001, 2002.
- Set Western Region record of $4.1 million, 2002.
- Consistently exceeded aggressive company income and volume goals.
- Achieved #1 Profitable Branch in country three consecutive years: 2000, 2001, 2002.
- 2001 recipient of company's highest award.
- Set all-time volume high in a California office, 2001.

Wholesale Account Executive/Sales Manager 1995 to 1998
GOLDEN STATE FINANCIAL RESOURCES, INC., Los Angeles, CA
Mortgage Division, Corporate Headquarters
Reported directly to company president in managing day-to-day operations of wholesale/retail division of sub-prime residential/construction lender during high-growth cycle. Consistently increased production volume and contributions to bottom line profits. Charged with full responsibility for hiring, training, motivating and managing sales and support staff.

- Achieved highest revenues and profits in company's 10-year history.
- Created new major profit center by targeting and developing contracting industry.
- Developed and implemented strategic marketing plans including first ever direct mail campaign to construction industry.
- Member of loan committee responsible for underwriting, structuring, pricing and issuing final approval for sale of loans to private and institutional investors.

(Continued)

PATRICIA GOODMAN
Page Two

Loan Origination Representative   1991 to 1995
BLUE RIBBON LENDING, Encino, CA
Gained valuable experience with well established sub-prime mortgage lender specializing in B through D residential loans. Developed/managed wholesale broker/lender relationships. Originated loans and managed detailed files from inception through funding.
- Consistent top producer 1986-1988
- Tracked aging loans for two branches becoming #1 in state for rewriting loans

Previous experience in retail sales concurrent with community college studies.

EDUCATION

COLDWELL BANKER SCHOOL OF REAL ESTATE, 1991

LOS ANGELES VALLEY COLLEGE, Valley Glen, CA
A.A. in General Studies

COMPUTER SKILLS

Windows; Microsoft Word, Excel, WordPerfect, Lotus Notes, ACT! and Mortgage Industry Software

PROFESSIONAL AFFILIATIONS

California Association of Mortgage Brokers

Jennifer Capizzi
892 #B Rose Bud Lane, San Diego, California 92131 ● 858 555-1234
jcapizzi@hotmail.com

SENIOR NETWORK ENGINEER ● SENIOR SYSTEMS ENGINEER

PROFILE

Competent, confident, client-oriented information technology professional with considerable experience augmented by a graduate-level education in Computer Science and refined by specialized, industry-related training. Flexible and focused, with unique analytical problem-solving ability. Exceptional knowledge of and expertise in hardware, software, and applications for defense and industry. Global perspective based upon life, travels, and work abroad. Significant software engineering analysis expertise, including software design and development. Bilingual/Bicultural: Farsi. Expertise includes competence in:

- Cost Estimating/Controls
- Customer Interface/Liaison
- Global Business Development
- ISO 9000 Standards
- Operations & Maintenance
- Performance Improvements
- Performance Monitoring
- Process Improvements
- Proposal Development
- Staff Training & Development
- Systems Enhancements
- Technical Marketing Support

STRENGTHS

- Design, Implementation, and Maintenance of LAN/WAN Network Infrastructures
- Computer Systems Design, Development, and Installation
- Customer Service and Technical, On-Site Field Support
- New Business Development, Proposals, and Negotiations

PROFESSIONAL EXPERIENCE

CUBIC CORPORATION, San Diego, CA - 1996 to present

Senior Network/Systems Engineer reporting to the Manager, Systems Engineering Department. Provide technical, marketing, and engineering support for the future Combat Training Center/Instrumentation Systems (CTC/IS) developed by CDS. Analyzed systems requirements, customer interface and presentations, proposal development, cost estimating, and, system and software design for international CTCs, including Sweden, Norway, and England.

Oversaw activities of Operations and I.S./UNIX departments. Managed implementation of several key projects, including installation of NetApp, upgrading production of the mail server, and redesign and reimplementation of the companywide Legato Networker installation. Resolved difficult and persistent technical issues arising on-site, specializing in back-end database servers and in high availability.

Performed trade study analysis and conceptual design for the Small Unit Operations - Situation Awareness System (SUO+SAS), based on the leading-edge secure cellular/wireless communications and robust networking technologies. Analyzed requirements; developed system specifications and architecture.

Conducted extensive research and development related to the future generations of Combat Training Systems and their interoperability based on the Distributed Interactive Simulation (DIS) protocols, the High Level Architecture (HLA) standards, and the ATM networking technology. Research included: Object Oriented Analysis and Design based on the UML standards, feasibility study for software development based on Common Object Request Broker Architecture (CORBA) and Java.

Orchestrated activities of 12-person team during transition, operation, and maintenance of a large instrumentation system at the Combat Maneuver Training Center (CMTC) in Germany.
- Led ongoing prototype design and development for the next generation of Analyst Workstations based on distributed object technology using Java Development Kit (JDK) Swing set and CORBA products.

(Continued on next page)

PROFESSIONAL EXPERIENCE (Continued)

INTERNATIONAL COMPUTER SCIENCES CORP. (ICSC), San Diego, California - 1990 to 1996

Computer Scientist. Responsibilities included: System software security and product support, software evaluation and selection, networking and system performance monitoring of a VAX cluster environment.

- Designed and developed software utilities to support software sizing and performance measurements of a large financial system, developed for the Department of the Navy.

I-NET E-BIZ CORPORATION, San Jose, California - 1986 to 1990

Senior Programmer Analyst. Designed, programmed, operated, and maintained multiprocessing Tactical Aircrew Combat Training Systems (TACTS). Developed software packages providing executive control functions for the Ocean View Measurement and Debriefing Systems (OVMDS).

- Developed and provided direct software support for the Automatic Fair Collection Systems.
- Designed, developed, and installed software to provide an executive control function and capability for real-time recording and retrieval of data from a multiple-disk system.

EDUCATION

Pacific West University, Los Angeles, California
     Master of Science - Computer Science and Technology
     Master of Science – International Business Management

Tehran University, Tehran, Iran
     Bachelor of Science in Business and Economics

COMPUTER TECHNOLOGY

Data Acquisition	Online System Administration	Systems Administration
High-Level Architecture	Real-Time Applications	Systems Engineering
Networking	Research & Development	Systems Security
Object-Oriented Analysis	Software Design	Systems Software

SOFTWARE

Cicso GSRs, BGP, SNMP, RMON, RMONII, EIGRP CISCO, IOS, HSRP, EtherNet Switches, Network Design, LAN/WAN Analysis, Multiplatform Web and Object-Orientated Systems, X-Window, UNIX, JAVA, CORBA, OOAD, OODB, TCP/IP, DIS, HLA, Informix, Oracle, SQL, DCL, Ada, FORTRAN, C, Assembly, Rational Rose, DOORS, RTM, JFC, JDBC, IDL, JBuilder

HARDWARE

Sun Microsystems:	Solaris, NFS, NOS
Silicon Graphics:	IRIX, System and Network Administration
Digital Equipment:	VRM, DECNET, NCP, SPM
Concurrent (MPS3200):	OS/32, System Programming
Personal Computers:	Windows-95, Windows-NT, MS-Office

LICENSURE, CREDENTIALS, AND CLEARANCE

- MCSD:Windows Internal Architecture 1 & 2
- Professional Certificate in Systems Engineering, UCSD Extension, 1998
- U.S. Government Final Top Secret Security Clearance based upon December 1989 BI

KEITH MORRANO

15869 Calle Mazatan • Morgan Hill, California 95037 • (408) 778-5555 • kmorrano@isp.com

CAREER OVERVIEW

A results-oriented **Network Operations Manager / Professional** with progressive career in information systems for both domestic and international environments. Decisive and goal-oriented, able to set realistic priorities to coordinate and complete multiple complex projects simultaneously. Demonstrated ability to adapt readily to new situations while maintaining consistently superior levels of productivity. A proactive leadership style which instills confidence in peers and staff. Broad-based exposure to all aspects of information technology strategies with proven strengths in devising and implementing improved approaches to internal technology auditing.

AREAS OF STRENGTH

- *Information Systems*
- *Worldwide Audit*
- *Coordination Information*
- *Application Development*
- *Communications*
- *Network Information Technology*
- *Asset Security*
- *Internal Controls*
- *Team Building*

PROFESSIONAL EXPERIENCE

I.B.M. Inc. • 1969/Present
Chief Information Officer, Network Systems Storage Division - United States
San Jose, CA • 1996/Present
- Manage day-to-day operations and overall $142 million budget of SSD Network Information Technology investments.
- Develop team and management system and implement effective controls to achieve communications to division through extended team and sitewide employee presentation.
- Negotiate agreements and service contracts for data center services, applications development, and maintenance of $75 million contract.
Selected Accomplishments:
- *Reduced IT division spending by $23.5 million, improving productivity by 18%.*
- *Designed division Lotus Notes development strategies for the deployment to 3000 end users worldwide within 3 months, including upgrades for employee workstations.*
- *Developed and implemented division approval for containment of applications development expenditures to fund Year 2000 project and strategic systems development.*

(Continued)

KEITH MORRANO

(Page 2)

Manager, Information Processing Audit Competency Group Corporate Internal Audit
Armonk, NY • 1990/1996
- Directed information system audits worldwide, including information asset security, system service and application development.
- Managed operational audits of ISSC and Advantis.

Selected Accomplishments:
- Coordinated and managed multiple audits conducted concurrently worldwide.
- Reduced duration of on-site field work and improved customer satisfaction by 18% year to year.
- Completed coursework and received Bachelor's degree while on 100% worldwide travel assignments.

Senior Internal Auditor, Corporate Internal Auditor
Stamford, CT • 1988/1990
- Led and performed various types of information-processing audits worldwide.

Technical Assistant to Site Director of Business Support Systems
Bethesda, MD • 1987/1988
- Supervised administrative and personnel support, site issue management.
- Directed the preparation of reports and coordination of executive visits and staff meetings.

Senior Project Manager, Purchase Billing Business Administrative Systems
Bethesda, MD • 1986/1987
- Acted as second-line manager responsible for application ownership, requirements, definition, application development/maintenance and function testing of customer purchase billing systems.

CICS Function Test Manager
Bethesda, MD • 1985/1986
- Managed stability and reliability of application change top CICS production environments.
- Established function test environments and formal testing procedures.
- Maintained code library management systems.

Inventory and Billing Development Manager
Bethesda, MD • 1983/1984
- Oversaw the development and maintenance of billing and inventory systems for OP heritage systems.
- Developed consolidation projects and coordinated management and system support personnel.

EDUCATION

- **Syracuse University** - Syracuse, New York
  Bachelor of Science • Business Administration/Finance • 1996
  Magna Cum Laude • GPA 3.6

LONNIE H. FRANKLIN

142 Glendale Court
Palm Beach Gardens, Florida 33418
Phone: (561) 555-1212 / Email: email@email.com

CEO / COO / DIRECTOR
John D. & Catherine T. MacArthur Foundation

Grants Management Specialist
* Foundation Resource * Community Resource * Fundraising

A highly organized, results-driven individual with professional qualifications in strategic planning, long/short-term goal setting, finance and budget management, program development, and personnel team building and leadership. Equally effective in needs evaluation and identification, implementation, and outcome assessment. Recognized for outstanding lobbying skills, fundraising expertise, and resource utilization. Successfully blend experience in the private sector with nonprofit and volunteer service. Solid writing and presentation/public speaking skills.

AREAS OF EXPERTISE

* Creative, visionary thinking and strategic planning
* Program/grant evaluation and enhancement
* Research, analysis and assessment
* Intradepartment/agency cooperation
* Policy and procedure development
* Networking - building key alliances/partnerships

* Grant making on contemporary issues
* Performance review and improvement
* Organizational leadership
* Cross-cultural training/supervision experience
* Volunteer recruitment, training, and supervision
* Integrity - maintaining high ethical standards

PROFESSIONAL EXPERIENCE

FLORIDA MEDICAL ASSOCIATION ALLIANCE, INC., Palm Beach Gardens, Florida   1994 - Present
First Vice President / Member Board of Directors

♦ Supervise and direct vice presidents in provision of resources, training, and support to enhance operations of county medical alliance on a statewide basis. Served as District Vice President, Health Projects Chair, Annual Convention Chair/Cochair, Coordinator of Idea Fair, Membership Summit and S. District Workshop.

♦ Promoted optimal functioning of alliances in areas of public relations, fundraising, health project administration, membership, and leadership development. Developed guidelines for implementation of Action Resource Team program to consult with alliances throughout the State of Florida. Developed/implemented $29,000 convention budget. Member of Finance Committee.

♦ Write in-depth, comprehensive reports. Developed state membership brochure, Health Projects Guide, and written guidelines for implementation of A.R.T. Program. Oral presentations.

♦ Selected as Grassroots Lobbyist to represent FMA/Alliance on key legislative health/safety issues. Spearheaded fundraising efforts for County Alliance resulting in raising $80,000 in 1999 and $105,000 in 2001.

♦ Recipient of "Presidential Service Award," 1997-2001. Appointed to represent alliance on critical FMA committees.

EDUCATION

Bachelor of Arts in Social Work, 1985   DAMON UNIVERSITY, Orlando, Florida
Leadership Conference, 1998   AMERICAN MEDICAL ASSOCIATION ALLIANCE, INC.

SELECTED VOLUNTEER AND COMMUNITY SERVICE WORK

PALM BEACH COUNTY MEDICAL SOCIETY AUXILIARY, West Palm Beach, FL   1990 - Present
Parliamentarian / Member Board of Directors
- Former President, Treasurer, Assistant Treasurer
- Chaired Charity Review, Finance, Legislation, and Long-Range Planning Committees
- Recipient of Palm Beach County Medical Society Outstanding Service Award, 1995
- Recipient of FMA Alliance Membership Award, 1994, 1995, 1996, 1997, 1998, 1999, 2000, 2001

Professional Refereences and Supporting Documentation Furnished on Request

JOAN LEEMAN

800 Bates Toad
West Palm Beac, Florida 33405
(561) 555-5604
email@email.com

FUND-RAISING PROFESSIONAL

A dynamic top-performing **Development Professional** experienced working with high-net-worth individuals, corporations, and the general public to secure major/planned gifts since 1990. Successful in donor prospecting, cultivation, and recognition.

AREAS OF STRENGTH

Organizational/time management skills	Presentation/public speaking skills
Leadership skills	Networking/partnership building
Media relations	Strategic planning
Volunteer training and development	Budgeting management
Key donor development/management	Writing/detailed report generation

PROFESSIONAL EXPERIENCE

HOSPICE OF PALM BEACH COUNTY, INC., West Palm Beach, Florida   1994 - Present
Director of Development
Full responsibility for all aspects of fund-raising, including planned/major gifts, direct mail, special events, and grant writing management. Chair Research and Development Project. Appointed to and serve on Marketing, Communications, and Outreach Committees. Member of Senior Leadership Council. Named Alternate Spokesperson for the agency.

- Increased annual fund-raising efforts from $1.4 million to $2.1 million, a total of $6.8 million in a 48-month period
- Conceptualized/implemented innovative and successful direct mail marketing program - raised $400,000 in 4 years.
- Managed/directed three auxiliary revenue-generating guild, resulting in an additional $500,000 in revenue.
- Restructured Development Department, increasing efficiency in donor relations, recognition, and, acquisition.
- Spearheaded and administered FundMaster software program - trained all staff members (20+ people).
- Grew donor base file from 20,000 to 68,000 between 1994 and 1998.

ECCLESTONE ORGANIZATION, West Palm Beach, Florida   1993 - 1994
Director of Community Relations
Authored comprehensive community relations plan to position the company for enhanced public exposure and maximize business development and growth opportunities.

- "Executive on Loan" to the Economic Council of Palm Beach County for Operation Headquarters (9/93-1/94).
- Developed procedural guidelines for Operation Headquarters project, including special events and publicity.
- Identified national CEO prospects interested in Corporate Headquarters' relocation to Palm Beach County.

REPUBLICAN PARTY OF PALM BEACH COUNTY, West Palm Beach, Florida   1990 - 1993
Executive Director
Executed political visitation/press conferences for members of the U.S. Senate and House of Representatives, Florida Congressional Delegation, Federal/State Cabinet members, and other ranking political leaders. Liaison to the Secret Service, FBI, White House, State and House Legislatures, Constitutional Officers, County Commissioners, and Gubernatorial Candidates.

- Managed daily operations of 100,000 member organization and created/directed annual member drive.
- Developed student intern program and training program for volunteers.
- Received Special Recognition Award for outstanding contributions - 1992 and 1993.
- Spokesperson for organization. Coauthored county political plan.

Melanie Olsen, CRNA
1555 Main Street • Charleston, WV 25302 • (304) 555-8443 • email@email.com

"... exhibits high degree of intelligence and readily grasps new concepts ... has an affable charm ... interacts well with patients, colleagues ... even in the most stressful of situations."

James McCroskey, MD
General Anesthesia Services
Charleston, WV

"... reliable and responsible team player ... willingly shares the workload ... level-headed and competent in an emergency ... proficient and knowledgeable in anesthetic skills and techniques."

Barb Schmitt, CRNA
CAMC-Memorial Division
Charleston, WV

"... an excellent anesthetist who remains calm under pressure ... highest integrity ... exhibits excellent leadership ... has been a tremendous asset to our organization."

Lee Ann Smith, CRNA, BA
Instructor, CAMC School of
Nurse Anesthesia
Charleston, WV

"... a very responsible employee ... always volunteering for additional assignments ... prompt and punctual ... has a positive attitude ... a valuable asset to our staff."

Tamy L. Smith, Charge CRNA
CAMC-Memorial Division
Charleston, WV

Professional Profile

- Certified Registered Nurse Anesthetist
- Bachelor's degree and four years CRNA experience
- Clinical instructor with over 1,000 hours experience
- Outstanding clinical expertise and proficiency
- Attend weekly continuing education meetings
- Excellent problem solver who works well under pressure
- Reputation as a team player with superb people skills
- Upbeat, personable, and highly energetic

Licensure & Professional Affiliations

- Certified Registered Nurse Anesthetist, Certificate #22250
- Registered Professional Nurse, License #0556500
- Member, American Association of Nurse Anesthetists
- Member, West Virginia Association of Nurse Anesthetists
- Professionally involved with local Women's Health Center

Professional Experience

CHARLESTON AREA MEDICAL CENTER MEMORIAL DIVISION
Charleston, West Virginia   1984-Present
- ☐ **CRNA** - **Cardiovascular Center** - 1993-Present
  Surgeries include arterial bypasses, hearts, amputations, gallbladders, mastectomies, biopsies, major orthopedics
- ☐ **RN** - **Medical Surgical** - 1984-1993
  RN and charge nurse duties on a 40-bed med/surg unit, included adolescent ward and peritoneal dialysis

Education

- **Certificate of Anesthesia,** Charleston Area Medical Center School of Anesthesia, Charleston, WV, 1989
  ☐ Received Josephine A. Reier Memorial Scholarship Award
- **Associate Degree in Nursing,** University of Charleston School of Health Sciences, Charleston, WV, 1983
  ☐ Received Nursing Student Achievement Award
- **Bachelor of Fine Arts Degree,** *magna cum laude,* Arizona State University, Tempe, Arizona, 1977

JACQUELYN A. DAVIDSON, RN, CNOR
7402 Field Park Drive South
Athens, OH 45701

(614) 555-9019
jackie@aol.com

CERTIFIED REGISTERED NURSE - OPERATING ROOM
Training, Supervision, and Leadership Skills

A highly skilled Nursing Professional with qualifications in management and expertise in OR nursing. A hospital advocate, promoting the hospital by providing high-quality nursing care and unparalleled patient service. A cost-containment professional through quality management and inventory control. Provide total backup and support to physicians and surgeons.

STRENGTHS & SKILLS

OR Specialty; Vascular, General, Thoracic, Renal
Scrub Experience
Experienced Circulator
Organization and Time Management
Adhere to High Ethical Standards; Professional Integrity

Personnel Training and Supervision
Assessment Skills
CPR Certified
Educator to Patient, Family, Peer Group
Communicating Skills - Verbal / Written

PROFESSIONAL EXPERIENCE

KENT COUNTY MEMORIAL HOSPITAL, Shade, OH   1990 - Present
Circulating Nurse Coordinator (Staff OR Nurse rotating to all specialties)
♦ Developed organizational system for effective management of cases, personnel, and surgeon start time
♦ Reduced operating suite turnover time from 35 minutes down to 8 minutes
♦ Participant on Cost Containment Committee; reduced expenses without compromising quality of care

SOUTH COUNTY / ROGER WILLIAMS HOSPITALS, Athens, OH   1988 - 1989
OR Nurse - Per Diem (While attending school at Ohio University)

THE PLAINS OHIO UROLOGICAL ASSOCIATES, The Plians, OH   1986 - 1988
Registered Nurse (Office / OR)
♦ OR Coordinator; pre /post-op educator; post-op visitations from lithotripsies (ESWL)

ROGER WILLIAMS GENERAL HOSPITAL, Athens, OH   1978 - 1986
Registered Nurse / Specialty Nurse
♦ RN in pilot project; primary patient care, providing continuity of pre/post op care; charge experience
♦ Specialty nurse responsible for orientation and staff development; coordinated daily schedule of OR

WOMEN & INFANTS HOSPITAL, Athens, OH, RI   1974 - 1978
Registered Nurse / Managerial Position - 30 beds / 30 newborns
♦ Hired for pilot project: Family centered care; expanded project to entire postpartum unit
♦ Educated parents / staff with hands-on demonstration care of newborns; nursing and nutritional guidelines

EDUCATION & TRAINING

Newport Hospital School of Nursing, Newport, RI   **Diploma, 1974**
University of Rhode Island, Providence, RI   **BSN/Masters Program, Currently Enrolled**

AFFILIATIONS

Member / Board Member: AORN
Delegate to National Congress - AORN, 1996
Member / Supporter of MADD

Member: National Kidney Association
Century Club Contributor: AORN Foundation
Active in HCFA - Campaign to oppose rule changes

LYNN GREEN, R.N.

rngreen@email.com

5555 Balboa Boulevard • Encino, California 91356
Residence (818) 555-3131 • Mobile (818) 555-3232

REGISTERED NURSE

- ❖ Team-oriented nursing professional committed to providing the highest quality of patient care.
- ❖ Flexible in accepting assignments and responsibility.
- ❖ Possesses excellent teaching skills, with the ability to make complex information understandable to patients and families.
- ❖ Reputation for establishing and maintaining exceptional relations with coworkers and patients.
- ❖ Well organized with ability to prioritize and delegate as appropriate.
- ❖ Detail-oriented and meticulous in record keeping.
- ❖ Extensive experience and special expertise working with diabetic patients.
- ❖ Ability to communicate with Spanish-speaking population.

LICENSES/CERTIFICATIONS

California RN License #xxxxx
CPR Certification
IV & Blood Withdrawal
PALS, NALS Certification
Hospital Fire & Life Safety Training

PROFESSIONAL EXPERIENCE

Registered Nurse • 1995 to Present—*Concurrent Per Diem Position*

UCLA MEDICAL CENTER, Pediatric Unit, Los Angeles, CA (1996–Present)
- Work with diverse patient population, performing multiple procedures, including patient isolation, ventilators, tracheotomy, NG, TPN, central IV lines, PCA pumps, dialysis, chest tubes, etc.
- Diagnoses have included cystic fibrosis, sickle cell anemia, HIV/AIDS, transplants (liver, kidney, heart), diabetes, tuberculosis, RSV, multiple traumas, surgeries (plastic, reconstructive, orthopedic, otolaryngology, genitourinary), cardiac, renal, gastrointestinal, neurological, psychosocial and genetic disorders.
- Conduct patient/family teaching and education.

WESTLAKE COMMUNITY MEDICAL CENTER, Thousand Oaks, CA (1995–2000)
- General pediatrics, newborn nursery, noncritical neonatal ICU.

VALLEY MEDICAL CENTER, Los Angeles, CA (1995–1999)
- General Pediatrics.

(Continued)

Registered Nurse • 1995
Nursing Attendant • 1993 to 1995
VALLEY VIEW MEDICAL CENTER, Northridge, CA
- Pediatrics, Pediatric ICU, Pediatric ER

Nursing Aide • 1991 to 1992
VALLEY PRESBYTERIAN HOSPITAL, Van Nuys, CA

EDUCATION

Continuing Education (partial list):
Chemotherapy… TB Standards… Medical Management of Adolescent Eating Disorders… CHLA Care Delivery Model Education Program… Scoliosis… Pediatric Developmental Issues… Fluid & Electrolytes in the Pediatric Patient… Computers for Health Care… Acute Hyperglycemia & Hypoglycemia… Nutrition… Skin Breakdown… Enteral Nutrition Formulary… Pediatric Emergency Nursing… Chronically Ill children: How Families Adjust… Neonatal Resuscitation…

LOS ANGELES PIERCE COLLEGE, Woodland Hills, CA
A.A. in Registered Nursing Program; 1993

PROFESSIONAL AFFILIATIONS

American Diabetes Association
California Nursing Association

COMMENDATIONS

My volunteers had nothing but praise for her and her care of the patients… I was impressed by her sensitivity and the quality of work she showed.

Mike Alvarez, Director of Child Development

Lynn was a godsend to us, both in the comfort she provided to overly concerned parents as well as in the care and sensitivity she showed to our infant son… she displayed such professionalism and went so beyond the expected that we felt compelled to make sure her supervisors were aware of her job performance.

John and Melinda Ellis

Laura Haus, RNC

555 Fairview Avenue E, Seattle, WA 55555
lh@comcast.net

(206) 555-8521 Residence   (505) 555-6392 Cell

Women's Health Care Nurse Practitioner

Professional Summary

Dedicated women's health care nurse with 10+ years' experience providing positive, high-quality nursing care. RNC in Inpatient Obstetrics with experience working all four areas: labor and delivery, nursery, postpartum, and recovery. Proven ability to care for high-risk antepartum and postpartum clients and gynecological surgical patients. As IBCLC, possess high level of expertise in lactation consulting. Hardworking, dependable.

Key Accomplishments

- **Achieved 98% success rate** in assisting any mother/infant pair to breastfeed in 5–10 minutes while offering breastfeeding expertise during underserved shifts at Northwest Hospital & Medical Center.

- **Increased profits** of University of Washington Medical Center **by $20K per year** when acknowledged for submitting idea to the Value Improvement Program (VIP). Idea eliminated system inefficiency.

- **Achieved 4.0 GPA** in completing Women's Health Care Nurse Practitioner certificate program while working twelve-hour shifts as PRN.

- **Mentored new graduates** in all aspects of women's health care, including sharing expertise with patient breastfeeding challenges.

Education

Women's Health Care Nurse Practitioner Certificate, University of Washington Medical Center, Seattle, WA, 1999 GPA: 4.0

ADN, RN, Linfield College, McMinnville, OR, 1990
GPA: 3.9 Graduated with Honors

Licenses and Certifications

Licensed in Washington, Registered Nurse
Active RN licenses in California, Colorado, Idaho, Oregon, and Washington

Women's Health Care Nurse Practitioner, National Certification Corporation (NCC)

RNC, Inpatient Obstetric Nursing, NCC

IBCLC, Internationally Board Certified Lactation Consultant

NRP, Neonatal Resuscitation Program Provider

(Continued)

Professional Experience

Sacred Heart Hospital & Regional Medical Center, Seattle, WA **RNC, Women's Care Unit**	2003–Present
Northwest Hospital & Medical Center, Seattle, WA **RNC, Family Birth Center**	1999–Present
University of Washington Medical Center, Seattle, WA **RN, Labor and Delivery**	1993–1999
Harborview Medical Center, Seattle, WA **RN, LDPR, Postpartum, and Nursery**	1991–1993
Good Samaritan Hospital, Portland, OR **RN, Labor and Delivery, Nursery, and Postpartum**	1990–1991

Recent Professional Development

Contraceptive Technology Seminar, Washington Nurse Practitioner Council, 2004

Dialogues in Contraception (Lunelle), National Association of Nurse Practitioners in Women's Health Conference, 2003

Managing Uterine Fibroids, CME Resource, 2003

Breastfeeding: Challenges and Successes, CME Resource, 2002

Inevitable Menopause, North American Menopause Society, 2002

High-Risk Obstetrics, University of Washington Medical Center, 2002

Professional Associations

National Association of Nurse Practitioners in Women's Health (NPWH)

North American Menopause Society (NAMS)

Washington Nurse Practitioner Council (WANPC)

Computer Skills

MS Windows, Internet, e-mail, familiar with computerized charting

◆ ◆ ◆

SHEA O'REILLY
11479 Eagle Mountain
San Antonio, Texas 78200
(210) 555-4371
email@email.com

PROFESSIONAL SUMMARY:
Registered Nurse

- ◆ Highly skilled career professional with over 20 years practical experience in hospital, home health, and **primary care** environments.

- ◆ Established in **STD** and **AIDS patient support**, including assessment, counseling, education regarding medications and treatment, lab work, documentation with care plan for diagnosis, and administration of treatment procedures.

- ◆ Computer skilled, managing heavy daily patient volume, including telephone triage, appointment scheduling, and patient referral. Proficient in all documentation/record maintenance/paperwork to ensure accuracy and patient confidentiality.

- ◆ All areas of major and minor surgical procedures performed in hospital environment.

CREDENTIALS:

Board Examination, 1981
License, State of Texas, 1985

EXPERIENCE:

1993-2003	Office/Surgical Nurse, Lisa Rouse, MD, Kerrville, Texas
1989-1991	Supervisor - Home Health Aides, VNA Private Care, Fort Worth, Texas
1986-1989	OR/PACU Nurse, Harris Methodist Hospital, Fort Worth, Texas
1985-1986	ICU Supervisor, Twin Oaks, Fort Worth, Texas
1983-1985	Office/Surgical Nurse, Thomas Virgin, MD, Montgomery, Alabama
1982-1983	Clinical/Classroom Instructor - LVN/EMT/NA, Health Care Institute

EDUCATION:

Associate, Nursing, 1981
Troy State School Of Nursing, Montgomery, Alabama, *St. Margaret Scholarship Student*

AFFILIATIONS:

Texas Nurses' Association, 1985-Current
American Nursing Association, 1981-Current
Alabama Nurses' Association, 1981-1985

COMMUNITY SERVICE:

1989-1991   **AIDS Counselor,** Community Outreach Center, Ft. Worth, Texas

Launched volunteer system and food bank with two other professionals. Provided counseling, information regarding available housing, SSI, food stamps, and other services. Coordinated transportation for medical appointments, personal errands, and outings. Promoted daily activities to sustain positive attitude and quality of life for full-blown AIDS clients.

REFERENCES ON REQUEST

124—NURSE ADMINISTRATOR

MARY FRENCH, R.N., B.S., C.A.C.

555 Carol Drive
Brentwood, NY 11717
(631) 555-5555
nadmin@health.com

SENIOR NURSE ADMINISTRATOR

Accomplished Career Path

THE ISLAND SHORE HEALTH SYSTEM, Great Neck, NY   1990 – Present

The Island Shore Medical Center at Bethpage DIRECTOR, QUALITY MANAGEMENT	5/97 – Present (On call)
The Island Shore Health System ASSISTANT DIRECTOR, QUALITY MANAGEMENT	2/96 – 5/97
The Island Shore Medical Center at Syosset DIRECTOR, REGULATORY AFFAIRS DIRECTOR, RISK MANAGEMENT DIRECTOR, MEDICAL STAFF CREDENTIALING	10/90 – 2/96 (On call)

Quality Management / Performance Improvement

- Directly responsible for hospital-wide quality management and performance improvement encompassing
  - **Utilization Review**
  - **Risk / Quality Management**
  - **Performance Improvement**
  - **Social Services and Physical Therapy Departments**
  - **Regulatory Agencies**
  - **Medical Staff Credentialing**

- Ensure staffs focus on individual, departmental, and hospital-wide initiatives, as well as team concepts.

- Guide the process of root cause analysis to identify, track, and resolve adverse events encompassing the development, implementation, and monitoring of corrective action plans.

- Prepare and process monthly statistical reports and analysis of hospital-wide operations.

Program Development and Implementation

- Direct the planning, development, implementation, and monitoring of case management (Care Guide®).

- Guide the development, implementation, and monitoring of healthcare practices to assess, identify, maintain, and improve the community standard of care.

- Initiate the development and analysis of hospital-wide studies to track and monitor specific patterns and trends.

Regulatory Affairs

- Coordinate and direct the multidisciplinary education and compliance of the New York State Department of Health Codes and the Joint Commission standards.

- Maintain staff development, program objectives, and risk management oversight.

- Develop programs designed to reduce liability and increase staff awareness, education, and reporting activities.

— Continued —

288

MARY FRENCH, R.N., B.S., C.A.C.

Page 2

Medical Staff Credentialing

- Develop and initiate the implementation of system-wide medical staff credentialing, allowing for a concise and expeditious application process.
- Ensure full compliance with New York State and Joint Commission regulatory requirements.

Presentations

- The Island Shore Health System, Medical Staff Credentialing Presentation, 2004
- The Island Shore Health System, Medical Staff Credentialing Presentation, 2004
- The Island Shore Health System, Quality Management Presentation, 2003
- The Island Shore Health System, Medical Staff Credentialing Presentation, 2002
- The Island Shore Health System, Department of Quality Management Presentation, 2002

Earlier Chronology

Nurse II, Alcoholism Recovery Center, Brentwood, NY — 1985 – 1990

Inventory Manager, The Pharmaceutical Company, Hauppauge, NY — 1982 – 1985

Staff Registered Nurse, Sachem Hospital, Sachem, NY — 1980 – 1982

Staff Registered Nurse, St. Jude Medical Center, Roosevelt, NY — 1974 – 1980

Education & Training

Certificate of Completion, JCAHO, 2004
CONSULTANT'S CLINICAL CENTER, Brentwood, NY

Bachelor of Science in Health Administration, 1997
SAINT JOHN'S COLLEGE, Patchogue, NY

Alcoholism Counseling, 1989
INSTITUTE of ALCOHOLISM STUDIES, SOUTH OAKS HOSPITAL, Amityville, NY

Associate of Applied Science in Nursing, 1974
NASSAU COMMUNITY COLLEGE, Garden City, NY

Licenses & Certifications

New York State Certified Alcoholism Counselor #5555, 1989

New York State Licensed Registered Nurse #555555-1, 1974

Professional References and Portfolio of Over 75 Letters of Recognition Available upon Request

GLENDA L. NORMAN, M.D.

Curriculum Vitae

555 SE Taylor Street
Portland, Oregon 55555
normanmd@yahoo.com

(503) 555-5621 Residence

(503) 555-2131 Fax

EXPERTISE

Obstetrics and Gynecology

PROFESSIONAL SUMMARY

Compassionate, capable medical doctor with 10+ years' experience providing outstanding patient care. Excellent diagnostician with strong skills in endometrial ablation and laparoscopic surgery. Good listener, excellent communicator, diligent in providing counseling in preventive medicine. Strong time management and record keeping skills with proven ability to relate well with both peers and employees. Strong ability and willingness to learn new things. Conscientious, dedicated, problem solver.

EDUCATION

| Medical | University of Oregon Medical School, Portland, Oregon
M.D. | 1987 |
| Undergraduate | University of Oregon, Eugene, Oregon
B.S., Pre-Med | 1983 |

MEDICAL TRAINING

| Fellowship | University of Oregon Medical School, Portland, Oregon
Obstetrics and Gynecology | 1989 to 1990 |
| Residency | University of Oregon Medical School, Portland, Oregon
Obstetrics and Gynecology | 1987 to 1989 |

RECENT PROFESSIONAL DEVELOPMENT COURSEWORK

Latest Techniques in Uterine Fibroid Management, American Medical Association, 2004

Contraceptive Technology Seminar, Oregon Health & Science University, 2003

High-Risk Obstetrics, Oregon Medical Association, 2002

Breastfeeding Challenges, Oregon Health & Science University, 2002

Nutrition for New Moms and Babies, Medical Society of Metropolitan Portland, 2002

Managing Menopause Naturally, National College of Naturopathic Medicine, 2001

Obstetric Breakthroughs: Latest Information from the AMA, American Medical Association, 2001

Laparotomy without Hysterectomy: Latest Techniques, Oregon Medical Association, 2001

(Continued)

GLENDA L. NORMAN, M.D.

LICENSURE AND CERTIFICATION

Oregon State Medical License #MD9852269

Board Certified, Obstetrics and Gynecology

PROFESSIONAL EXPERIENCE

Private Practitioner, Obstetrics and Gynecology   1995 to Present
Lake Oswego, Oregon

Clinic Practitioner, Obstetrics and Gynecology   1990 to 1995
Rose City Women's Clinic, Portland, Oregon

VOLUNTEER EXPERIENCE

Volunteer Medical Officer   1995 to Present
Mercy Corps International, Portland, Oregon
Completed humanitarian projects in Iraq, Afghanistan, and Ethiopia

Medical Volunteer
American Red Cross, Portland, Oregon   1996 to 2000
Taught variety of medical programs for lay volunteers.

HOSPITAL AFFILIATION

St. Vincent Hospital, Portland, Oregon, 1990 to Present

Committee Memberships: Medical, Obstetrics and Gynecology

PROFESSIONAL AFFILIATIONS

American Medical Association

American Society of Obstetrics and Gynecology

Medical Society of Metropolitan Portland

Oregon Medical Association

Physicians Committee for Responsible Medicine

ROLANDO P. WYNN

230 Pennsylvania Avenue
Liberty, Iowa 45372
(333) 555-1212/email@email.com

OCCUPATIONAL-SAFETY ENGINEER/LOSS-CONTROL MANAGER
Contributing to Organizational Growth/Profits via Safety & Loss-Control Management
16 Years' Experience in Diversified Environments

Construction & Facilities Safety Management/Regulatory Compliance Expertise
Program Development/Organizational Leadership & Training/Claims Management

---

A dynamic, team-spirited and bottom-line-oriented Safety Engineer/Loss-Control Specialist offering outstanding qualifications in and a verifiable record of, reducing work-related injuries and the severity of work-related accidents. Contribute to growth and profitability by significantly reducing liability exposure and claims.

A solid track record for successful leadership in staff/personnel training, development, and empowerment. Recognized for strong Worker's Compensation claims management, investigative/inspection aptitude, and meeting and exceeding regulatory compliance mandates.

CORE STRENGTHS

Reducing work-related injuries (severity of injuries)
Claims management and control
Staff training, development, and empowerment
Efficiency and production-improvement management

Program development and enhancement
Presentation and public-speaking skills
Complex problem solving/troubleshooting
Quality-control assurance/management

ACADEMIC HIGHLIGHTS

EMBRY RIDDLE AERONAUTICAL UNIVERSITY, Daytona Beach, Florida
Master's in Aeronautical Science, 1991

SOUTHERN ILLINOIS UNIVERSITY, Carbondale, Illinois
Bachelor of Science: Industrial Technology, 1988

COMMUNITY COLLEGE OF THE UNITED STATES AIR FORCE, Maxwell AFB, Alabama
Associate in Applied Science: Safety Technology, 1986

Certified Environment Compliance Manager
United States Air Force Safety Specialist Course
Triple A Driver-Improvement Instructor

OSHA 500 Basic Instructor's Course
United States Air Force Supervisor's Safety Course
CPR Instructor—National Safety Council

PROFESSIONAL EXPERIENCE

THERMA SEAL ROOFING, INC., Liberty, Iowa   2000 to Current
Safety Manager
Direct Occupational Safety Program for high-volume roofing contractor with more than 200 employees throughout the state of Iowa. In high-risk work environment, proactively develop/implement policies, procedures, programs, and systems, to reduce work-related injuries and the severity of such mishaps. Establish strategies to limit Worker's Compensation claims, develop one-on-one/group training to reinforce safety issues, and take aggressive action to ensure a drug-free work environment. Coordinate accident investigations, conduct thorough site/workforce inspections, and spearhead all regulatory compliance matters.
- Significantly reduced numbers of and severity of injuries.
- Wrote company's comprehensive Safety Manual and a Subcontractors Training Manual.
- Developed a highly effective disaster/hurricane preparedness action plan.

(Page one of two)

PROFESSIONAL EXPERIENCE (Continued)

NU-TEC ROOFING CONTRACTORS, INC., Johnson, Iowa   1997 to 1999
Safety Administrator
Directed the Occupational Safety and Worker's Compensation programs for the seventh largest roofing contractor in the United States—program encompassed more than 200 employees in Florida. Performed accident investigations and daily jobsite inspections to ensure program/regulatory compliance. Conducted preinspections of all new projects and submitted pragmatic recommendations to project managers. Created and employed Employee-Safety-Training program, spearheaded the Return-to-Work program, and developed modified work responsibilities for injured employees. Maintained all safety records.

- Identified the requirements for, approved, and procured personal protective equipment for employees exposed to safety and occupational health hazards—significantly reducing liability and injury probability.
- Developed and managed Drug-Free Workplace program and associated training curriculum.
- Authored and initiated company's Safety Manual and established a new Bilingual Employee Manual.
- Reduced Worker's Compensation costs by $500,000-plus via aggressive claims management and in-house training.

FRSA/SIF, Winter Park, Iowa   1990 to 1997
Loss Control Consultant/Manager
Provided professional, high-tech risk-management services to more than 500 policyholders throughout the state of Iowa. Assisted policyholders in the prevention and reduction of risk and losses—with emphasis on safety, health, and Worker's Compensation-related issues. Hired and trained loss-control consultants and safety engineers. Responsible for budget management and contributing to the bottom line via safety/loss-control management.

- Dramatically reduced the number of injuries and severity of majority of policyholders.
- Reduced loss ratio by 30%—and improved account retention considerably.
- Author of monthly safety column for the *Iowa Forum Trade Association Magazine*, 1990–1997.

MILITARY SERVICE

UNITED STATES AIR FORCE   1981 to 1990
Ground Safety Technician
Contributing team leader in planning, development, and execution of the Occupational Safety Program for the 56th Tactical Training Division (F-16 Fighter Pilot Training Unit). Program encompassed more than 8,000 personnel, including on- and off-duty mishap-prevention programs. Prepared annual operating budget for the Occupational Safety Program. Maintained liaison with federal, state, and local safety organizations and officials. Conducted comprehensive investigations entailing all classes and categories of mishaps/accidents, including fraud and workplace safety risks.

- Selected as *Tactical Air Command's Exceptional Performer in Ground Safety*, 1988.
- Awarded *Air Force Commendation Medal*, 1986 and 1990.
- Author of monthly safety column for the *Mac Dill Air Force Base Newspaper*, 1985–1990.

COMPUTER SKILLS

MS Windows, Word, Publisher, Excel, PowerPoint, Access
Internet applications

AFFILIATIONS

Member: American Society of Safety Engineers
Volunteer/Participant: Youth Soccer

References and Supporting Documentation Furnished upon Request

MARY JO BENNING

3205 Brook Street • Charleston, West Virginia 34552 • (304) 555-1212 • email@email.com

OFFICE MANAGEMENT/EXECUTIVE SUPPORT
15 Years' Successful Experience in Responsible, High-Visibility, and Multitask Environments

"Solving Problems and Taking the Initiative"

**Organizational & Personnel Leadership/Sales Support/Event-Planning Expertise
Excellent Computer Skills/Assignment & Project Management**

A positive-thinking, results-oriented, and team-spirited Administrative/Executive Support Professional recognized for proactively exceeding organizational mandates over past 15 years in diverse work environments.

CORE STRENGTHS

Communications skills (verbal & written)
Sales and marketing support
Staff training, development, and empowerment
Document control—information processing

Project and assignment management
Interpersonal and relationship-building skills
Time management—deadline-sensitive
Customer service and client retention

Computer Skills: Windows, MS Office 2000 (Word, Excel, PowerPoint, Outlook), Publisher, and Internet research

PROFESSIONAL EXPERIENCE

GE Medical Systems Clinical Services, Charleston, West Virginia   1996 to Current
Human Resources Assistant
Provide support to the Human Resources Department with various duties, including preparing benefits binders. Update spreadsheets, prepare offer letters, follow up on necessary paperwork and procedures. Update policy and procedure manuals, screen prospective new hires and follow up on employment interviews, set and coordinate training schedules, and assist in all areas of EEO and regulatory reporting.

- Assisted with special programs—Diversity Training, EHS Quality Training, and Employee Recognition Awards.
- Designed flyers and invitations for the Young Executives Division and assisted with the implementation of their community programs, including *"Teens Speak Out," "Aspiring Youth,"* and *"Minority Outreach."*
- Member of the computer help group, "WIZARDS"—designed to assist coworkers with software questions/problems.
- Promoted to Document Control Administrator after one year as document specialist.
- Participated in the formation of policies in the area of traditional engineering documentation and compliance.

STATE BAR OF WEST VIRGINIA, Charleston, West Virginia   1989 to 1996
Executive Secretary to the Director of West Virginia Center for Law-Related Education
Assisted the Director in preparing and monitoring annual reports, fiscal budgets, departmental budget packets, grant applications, and other reports and surveys. Handled renewals for dues, subscriptions, and memberships. Processed management requests for conference and educational seminars. Assisted with assignments and special projects for the Bar Foundation Board of Directors and other bar associations, organizations, and attorney and nonattorney groups.

- Coordinated with Director on *Project Citizen* and *We the People*—statewide civic education programs. Designed program booklet, handled registrations, reserved rooms at the state capitol, and recruited volunteers.
- Helped plan the *Civitas Bosnia Teachers' Delegation* visit to West Virginia, including hotel and meal arrangements. Designed itinerary booklet and welcome packets. Accompanied the delegation on visits.

EDUCATION & TRAINING

Courses in Liberal Arts and Computer Networking, Broward Community College, Charleston, West Virginia, 1985–89

Continuing Education—Seminars—Workshops
Seminar—"Management Skills for Administrative Assistants and Support Staff"   Fred Pryor Seminars, 2001
Seminar—"Meeting Planning and Contract Negotiation"   WVSA Executives, 2000

References upon Request

OnlineCareerFolio...

John Wang

Silicon Valley Region
(555) 555.5555
E-mail ~ johnwang@mediaone.net
E-folio ~ http://www.careerfolios.com/johnwang

SUMMARY

E-Commerce Executive with substantial record as a leader and manager of new-economy initiatives. Envisioned tactics that capitalized on Internet opportunities, launched core e-initiatives, and achieved first-to-market status in Web and traditional markets. Enterprise planning, P&L, and management skills reflect strengths in Web marketing, business development, strategic alliance development and negotiations, global sales, and technology product development and management. Career highlights:

➤ **General Management:** Authored marketing, fiscal, and operating strategies that drove e-sales from start-up level to $23 million in less than one year, with conservative predictions of $77 million in recurring revenue by next year end.

➤ **Business Development, Alliance Initiatives:** Structured and negotiated watershed deal with **America Online**, gaining valuable cobranding leverage for company.

➤ **Product / Brand Management:** Conceptualized innovative Internet device—marketed and managed product that shipped 200,000 units in less than 1 year.

➤ **Fiscal Management:** Owned division balance sheet and P&L responsibilities (up to US$80 million). Undertook reengineering initiatives that captured hard-dollar savings of $18 million.

➤ **High-Profile:** Invited speaker at national and international technology summits. Interviewed by **CBSmarketwatch.com**, **CNBC**, **CNN**; quoted in **_Fast Company_** and tech publications regarding emerging technology. (Click links for reprints.)

EDUCATION

MBA ~ Entrepreneurial Management: Duke University Fuqua School of Business, Durham, North Carolina.

BS Degree ~ Finance: University of California, Santa Barbara

Click on Link to Review ...

Summary

Education

Experience

Technology

Affiliations

References

Contact

Rita Rouse

rbrouse@aol.com □ 8800 West 18th Street, Denver, CO 80201 □ 303-555-1819

Profile

- Capable and creative **Senior Online Editor** with eight years of progressive experience in journalism seeking promotion to Director of Publications.

- Outstanding ability to develop innovative "look and feel" of online information while establishing and maintaining high editorial standards. Dedicated to driving the development of new strategies for a new medium, continually pushing the envelope of print and broadcast forms.

- Key strength in networking and collaborating cross-functionally to build the business of a national media company, setting strategy with other local managers.

- Highly productive and organized, balancing multiple projects under extremely demanding deadlines. Well-versed in developing editorial calendars, organizing production schedules, managing budgets, and coaching staffs of up to 20.

- Articulate, persuasive communicator, with excellent public relations and writing skills. Frequent presenter at national journalism conventions on the topic of Web publishing.

Experience

CitySearch.com, Denver, CO   1996-Present
Publisher of Comprehensive Local City Guides on the World Wide Web
Editor-in-Chief, Denver.CitySearch.com

Guarantee accurate and up-to-date coverage of all CitySearch topics, including news, sports, weather, arts and entertainment events, community activities, recreation, shopping, and professional services in the Denver metropolitan area.

- Collaborate extensively with business groups and marketing staff to site enhancements, continually reviewing content to ensure meeting the mission and business requirements of the company.

- Incorporate a standard approach and consistency in AP style, grammar, and voice. Establish and improve content update processes across all departments.

- Motivate and train an online publishing team of 20. Provide coaching to enhance reporting, writing, fact-checking, and editing skills, as well as building editorial judgment.

- Develop and maintain a broad network of industry contacts. Review and publish wire-service news stories to online news site throughout each business day.

- Frequently represent CitySearch.com as an invited speaker at national and regional journalism conventions on the topic of the evolution and future of New Media.

CompuServe, Inc., Columbus, OH   1993-1996
Online Editor

- Developed and reorganized content for interactive communities and online editions of PC Week, Inter@ctive Week, and Computer Shopper magazines.

- Functioned as liaison between the newspaper's online and print staffs, facilitating multiple daily updates of the Internet edition.

- Coordinated efforts of marketing, technical, and editorial content providers. Directed a graphic design team to improve menu graphics, logos, and icons. Identified internal and external resources for ongoing community management. Drove development of multimedia elements, opinion polls and forums.

■ Continued Page 2

Rita Rouse
Page 2 □ rbrouse@aol.com

Experience, continued

The Ohio State University, Columbus, OH   1989-1993
Editor-in-Chief, The Bulletin - OSU's student newspaper, 1991-1993
Assistant Editor, Student Reporter, 1989-1991

- Wrote and edited copy for each weekly edition. Assisted with layout and paginating of 5-10 pages per issue. Determined and assigned story ideas to staff writers and stringers.

- Instrumental in the paper's achievement of a #3 ranking among American college newspapers (1992) by the Journalism Education Association.

Technical Proficiencies

- In-depth knowledge of the World Wide Web, including all aspects of site design, creation, and server management.

- Working knowledge of Perl, JAVA, Flash, and VBScript/ASP.

- Highly skilled in graphic design and layout to give locally produced online news stories effective and innovative multimedia elements, using PhotoShop, Illustrator, RealAudio and RealVideo media delivery systems, Premiere, SoundEdit, PhotoVista and Apple QuickTime VR.

- More than five years of experience with QuarkXpress.

- Proficient with DOS, Windows, Windows95/98, NT, MacOS, and UNIX operating systems.

- Extensive experience using HyperText Markup Language (HTML) and Web-page design techniques.

Education

Bachelor of Arts, Journalism, with minor in English, 1992
The Ohio State University, Columbus, OH

Charter member of The Ohio State University's student chapter of Society of Professional Journalists.

Professional Organizations

Society of American Business Editors and Writers

Association of American Publishers

International Webmasters Association

Kathy Hillary

143 Hillside Lane • Belleville, Illinois 62223 • (618) 555-7770
• email@email.com

Paralegal/Legal Administration
Legal Investigations...Personal Injury...Family and Criminal Law

Solid training and experience in legal administration and paralegal studies involving research, writing, investigation, litigation support, mediation/arbitration techniques, rules of evidence, and dissolution of marriage proceedings. Familiar with word processing, spreadsheet, docket control, and database applications. Key responsibilities included:

- Drafted and filed motions, interrogatories, initial and responsive pleadings.
- Tracked client employment records and other information, using various sources.
- Helped clients fill out income, expenses, and property statements.
- Assisted with research for preparation of briefs.
- Prepared settlement agreements and other closing documents.

Education

ST. LOUIS COMMUNITY COLLEGE AT MERAMEC
Certificate in Paralegal Studies, DECEMBER 1998

BELLEVILLE AREA COLLEGE, BELLEVILLE, IL
Associate of Science Degree, Business, DECEMBER 1994
Associate of Arts Degree, Psychology, MAY 1993

Legal Experience

U.S. ATTORNEY'S OFFICE, SOUTHERN DISTRICT OF OLLINOIS, SEPTEMBER-DECEMBER 1998
- Completed a 100-hour internship under the supervision of a paralegal supporting 40-50 attorneys in both criminal and civil cases.
- Observed and studied legal proceedings associated with the recent Venezia trial. Took detailed notes; organized exhibit list.
- Summarized depositions, videotapes, and medical records.
- Reviewed docket cards and prepared trial notebooks.

LORRI MOTT, ATTORNEY, JULY 1997-SEPTEMBER 1998
- Worked extensively with clients in person and via telephone.
- Drafted pleadings, affidavits and prepared discovery requests.
- Initiated and organized files for trial.
- Typed correspondence and billing information.

ADDITIONAL EXPERIENCE: Waitress, various locations, 1992-Present; Lab Assistant, Streiter Laboratory, Collinsville, IL, 1991-1992; Sales/Customer Service, Sears Roebuck & Company, Fairview Heights, IL, 1989-1991; Fitness/Sales Consultant, Living Well Fitness Center, Belleville, IL, 1987-1989

References Available upon Request

MAUREEN BENSON, R.P.

3620 Williamsburg Court ▪ Woodbury, MN 55125 ▪ (651) 555-3337 ▪ mbensonlawsupport@email.email

REGISTERED PARALEGAL / LEGAL SECRETARY

Committed to providing superior support services that enhance legal practice, professionalism and profitability.

VALUE OFFERED

✓ Highly proficient in word processing, data entry, Internet research and dictaphone transcription; noticed for maintaining consistently superior levels of accuracy. Typing rate is 85 WPM.
✓ Outstanding record of performance, reliability, confidentiality and ethical business standards.
✓ Thrive in performing under stress and taking pressure off superiors and peers; maintain flexibility to multitask and meet deadlines.
✓ **Technology Skills include:** NILS, LEXIS-NEXIS, Westlaw, CCH applications, MS Word, Excel, Access, PowerPoint, Project.
✓ **Legal Experience:** Civil Trial/Settlement, Personal Injury, Contract & Property Disputes, Debtor-Creditor, Product Liability, Immigration, Legal Aid, Public Benefits Programs, Administrative Law, Probate, Estate Planning, Construction/Real Estate, Criminal Litigation.

EXPERIENCE

CITY ATTORNEY'S OFFICE – Arden Hills, MN   2001 – present
Paralegal
▪ Draft resolutions, contracts, leases, deeds, permits, public bid/construction documents, and other legal documents and instruments.
▪ Coordinate the gathering of information from various departments in the preparation of contracts and other legal documents; review contracts and legal documental to ensure the inclusion of necessary provisions.
▪ Perform manual and computerized cite checking, shepardizing and legal research. Utilize technical information to make independent decisions and recommendations to the City Attorney. Digest and summarize depositions and legal documents.
▪ Serve as City liaison with the general public. Respond to citizen complaints and inquiries.
▪ Prepare reports, correspondence and memoranda of law and other documents.
➢ Formerly recognized for superior performance in conducting city survey related to real estate development and expansion activities.
➢ Consistently commended by legal staff for precision and expediency in producing quality documents for complex cases.

BENSON & PRATT, P.A., ATTORNEYS AT LAW – St. Paul, MN   1999 – 2001
Paralegal / Legal Assistant
▪ Researched state statutes and municipal codes to support client cases in civil and criminal litigation.
▪ Interviewed witnesses and prepared declarations. Reviewed case files in preparation for settlement negotiations.
▪ Communicated extensively with clients, health care providers and insurance adjusters.
▪ Drafted summons, complaints, wills, trusts, deeds, petitions, pleadings and wills.
➢ Acknowledged by Senior Partner for "exceptional case investigation work" involving legal service clients.

GRIFFITH, BURNS & NOBLE, ATTORNEYS AT LAW – Fargo, ND   1998 – 1999
Paralegal / Legal Secretary Intern
▪ Interviewed client, researched the law and wrote brief for an immigration case.
▪ Researched statutes regarding Limited Liability Companies and Writs of Attachment.
▪ Procured public records from state agencies, filed and served court documents, served processes and drafted affidavits.
➢ Rapidly entrusted with daily delivery of confidential materials.

EDUCATION, CREDENTIALS & PROFESSIONAL ACTIVITIES

MINNESOTA STATE UNIVERSITY – Moorhead, MN
Paralegal Department approved by the American Bar Association
Bachelor of Science Degree in Paralegal, Public Interest and Civil Litigation Concentrations, *Magna cum Laude*, 1998
Paralegal Advanced Competency Exam, achieving designation PACE Registered Paralegal, 1998

▪ Minnesota Paralegal Association (MPS), 1998 – present
▪ National Federation of Paralegal Associations, Inc. (NFPA), 1998 – present
▪ Lambda Epsilon Chi, national honor society for paralegal students, 1996 – 1998
▪ Minnesota State Paralegal Association Moorhead (MSPAM) and Red River Valley Legal Assistants (RRVLA), 1998
▪ Mock Trial competition, sponsored by MSUM's Pre-Law Club, 1998

Sara Groffton

email@email.com
330 Greenough Place • Newport, RI 02840 • (401) 555-2801

CERTIFIED PARALEGAL
Strong Performance in Fast-Track, Deadline-Sensitive Environments

- **Exceptional litigation support**
- **Accurate and thorough research using cutting-edge tools**
- **Superior writing skills – meticulous attention to details**
- **Advanced PC knowledge, including Internet, NILS, LEXIS-NEXIS**
- **Provide extraordinary client service – and professional relations**
- **6 years professional experience – exceeding all performance standards**

Education / Honors

BROWN UNIVERSITY, Providence, Rhode Island
Bachelor of Arts: Sociology, (GPA 3.75), May, 1996

BAYLOR SCHOOL FOR LEGAL SERVICES, Providence, Rhode Island
Paralegal Certificate, 1997

COMPUTER PROFESSIONAL, Providence, Rhode Island
Paralegal Advanced Computer Training Certificate, 1998
- NILS
- LEXIS-NEXIS
- MS Word, Excel, Access, Outlook, PowerPoint and Project
- Advanced Internet Research and Legal Applications

Work Experience

WALTERS, BUTTS, CRASTON, AND JINKS, PA, Newport, Rhode Island   1997 to Current
Paralegal

- o   Promoted to paralegal following two summer Internships.
- o   Conduct in-depth research and summarize depositions, medical documents, and employment records.
- o   Provide comprehensive litigation support by assisting case investigators.
- o   Assist in all phases of trial preparation.
- o   Work with clients from case initiation through final adjudication – liaison between attorneys and clients.
- o   Review all writing communications – proofread, edit, and approve final documents prior to formal signoff.
- o   Consistently received high marks at annual reviews — and above-average promotions due to performance.

Internship

WALTERS, BUTTS, CRASTON, AND JINKS, PA, Newport, Rhode Island   Summers 1996 / 1997
Paralegal Intern

- o   Performed legal research and provided written summaries of research papers, documents, complex agreements, and case law. Assisted in case investigations, drafted pleadings, declarations, and memoranda of law.
- o   Completed and successfully passed Paralegal Certification program.

REFERENCES AVAILABLE UPON REQUEST

JESSICA WOJICK

45 Yacht Club Drive, #202
Chicago, Illinois 60662
(312) 555-1212/email@email.com

Seeking Position as...

PHARMACEUTICAL SALES/ACCOUNT MANAGER

"Six Consecutive Years of Enhancing Growth and Profits"

Lead Generation/Customer Service & Referral Management
Start-Up &Turnaround Management/New Product Launch

CORE STRENGTHS

Strategic marketing and goal setting
Communication skills (verbal/written/listening)
Presentation/public-speaking skills
Relationship/consultative sales techniques

Building/maintaining key strategic alliances
Direct mail/marketing expertise
Research and intelligence gathering
Negotiation, persuasion, and closing skills

HIGHLIGHTS OF PROFESSIONAL EXPERIENCE

PITNEY BOWES, INC.
Chicago, Illinois/1995 to Current

Major-Account Representative (1999 to Current)
Senior Sales Associate (1995 to 1999)

Develop and maintain large/corporate accounts through strategic/targeted marketing efforts and high-impact relationship-building skills. Enhance revenue stream by increasing customer base, improving average transaction value, and increasing customers' frequency of purchase.

Accomplishments/Contributions

- ❑ Leadership role in pioneering virtual office concept—utilizing expertise to help grow clients' businesses
- ❑ Closed and managed 600+ accounts contributing $3.94 million in sales over past six years
- ❑ Averaged $970,000 in annual revenues over past two years with a stunning 81% closing ratio
- ❑ Recognized for strong mentoring abilities—assisted six new representatives, achieving $900,000 in production
- ❑ Pacemakers Club; Member: President's Roundtable; First Honors Club

DELMAR TITLE COMPANY
Chicago, Illinois/1990 to 1995

Real-Estate Title/Transaction Closer
Responsibilities included closing real-estate transactions on a daily basis, utilizing research and customer-service skills and abilities. Evaluated projects, prepared written reports, addressed customer inquiries, and trained new employees.

Accomplishments/Contributions

- ❑ Recognized as the center's primary training facilitator—able to inspire top levels of production
- ❑ Average 39 closings per month—14 closings above industry average
- ❑ Elevated to Senior Closer—coordinating activities of four Junior Closers

EDUCATION/TRAINING/CERTIFICATIONS

B.A. Degree: Sociology, 1989, State University of Illinois, Chicago, Illinois
Computer Skills: Microsoft certified, Windows, Word, Excel, and Pathfinder, Internet applications and research

References and Supporting Documentation Furnished upon Request

MARY BETH BRISSETTE

34 Main Street
Swampscott, MA 01907
(781) 555-1212 / email@email.com

LICENSED PHARMACIST

13 Years Successful Experience with Walgreen and CVS

A highly competent and accomplished pharmacist combining strong professional skills with outstanding customer service skills to meet pharmacy and patient needs and objectives in a high professional manner. Areas of skill include:

* **Excellent knowledge of pharmaceuticals and applications**
* **Excellent liaison between patient/customer and physicians**
* **Excellent knowledge of insurance company / HMO / Medicare-Medicaid protocols**
* **Excellent skills in quality control and regulatory compliance**

Education

UNIVERSITY OF SOUTH FLORIDA, Tampa, Florida
Bachelor of Science: Pharmacy, 1990

- Licensed Pharmacist
- Pharmacy Internship: Tampa Regional Hospital
- Pharmacy Internship: Quest Medical Center
- Pharmacy Advanced Internship: St. Petersburg Medical Hospital

Professional Employment

CONSUMER VALUE STORES, Swampscott, Massachusetts   1997 to Present
Lead Pharmacist

- Dispense prescription orders for small town pharmacy (filling approximately 700 prescriptions daily). Direct four-person staff, communicate with nursing home staff/management relative to drug-related issues and concerns including order clarifications, drug interactions, and therapeutic recommendations, assist in the training and evaluations of newly recruited pharmacists and pharmacy technicians, and specialist in pharmacokinetics, IVs, and TPN prescription orders.

- Contributing team member in improving company's sales by providing outstanding customer service, seeking customer referrals, and seeking physician referrals as well. In-depth knowledge of billing procedures to improve customer service, billing, and collection efforts.

WALGREEN, Tampa, Florida   1990 to 1997
Pharmacist

- Processed prescription orders for high volume pharmacy – 5,500+ prescriptions per week. Interfaced with physicians, hospital staff personnel, nurses, and other medical professionals to ensure accurate and timely filling of prescriptions. Worked closely with lead pharmacist to meet high demands and assure customer satisfaction.

Activities

Member: Massachusetts Pharmacy Association
Member: Essex County Pharmacy Association
Volunteer: March of Dimes and American Heart Association
Enjoy: Health and fitness activities, computers, chess, and mountain climbing

References and Supporting Documentation Furnished upon Request

135—PHARMACIST

MANNY HERSHKOWITZ

2021 West Drive
Orono, Maine 17461
(261) 555-1212

LICENSED / CERTIFIED CONSULTANT PHARMACIST
Solid Contributor to Organizational Goals and Objectives
Combining Nursing, Health Policy, Clinical Information, and Management Expertise

Efficiency and Productivity Management / Organizational Leadership
Cost Containment and Expense Control / Process and Technology Specialist
Fluent – English and Spanish

A dynamic, customer-service-oriented Licensed Pharmacist / Certified Consultant Pharmacist offering six years of successful experience in fast-track, high-volume environments.

CORE STRENGTHS

Regulatory compliance management
Personnel training, development and empowerment
Customer service management

Communication skills
Problem solving/conflict resolution
Quality control management

EDUCATION / TRAINING / LICENSURE

Bachelor of Science: Pharmacy, 1994
Licensed Pharmacist - PS 0029548
Pharmacy Internship: Jacobi Hospital

LONG ISLAND UNIVERSITY, Brooklyn, New York
Consultant Pharmacist - PU 0004605
Pharmacy Internship: Pathmark Supermarket

PROFESSIONAL EXPERIENCE

PHARMERICA (Formerly Pharmacy Corporation of America), Bangor, Maine   1985 to Current
Staff Pharmacist

- Process/dispense prescription orders for high-volume pharmacy (filling up to 1,200 prescriptions daily). Manage pharmacy staff of up to 14, including pharmacists, pharmacy technicians, and data entry personnel.
- Communicate with nursing home staff/management relative to drug-related issues and concerns including order clarifications, drug interactions, and therapeutic recommendations.
- Assist in the training and evaluations of newly recruited pharmacists and pharmacy technicians.
- Specialist in pharmacokinetcs, IVs, and TPN prescription orders.
- Increased company's gross revenues by more than $98,000 through a special project.
- Contributor in the development and implementation of a system to handle narcotic CII prescriptions.
- Expertise in online Medicaid billing.

Consultant Pharmacist for Pharmerica

- Supervise narcotic and medication utilization for local medical facilities. Inspect and supervise all procedures and counts concerning controlled and noncontrolled drugs. Ensure all medical records for accuracy and compliance. Review Adverse Drug Reaction reports.

PROFESSIONAL AFFILIATIONS / COMMUNITY SERVICE

Member: Florida Pharmacy Association
Member: Palm Beach Pharmacy Association
Volunteer: Landmark Education Corporation

References and Supporting Documentation Furnished upon Request

Trent Looke
4635 Montgomery Road, Cincinnati, Ohio 45211 (513) 555-7777 email@email.com

PROFILE

- Strong foundation in photography, commercial art, and computer applications complemented by knowledge of business operations and the need for customer-focused service.
- Track record of initiative and achievement — seeking out freelance projects, expanding job description boundaries, volunteering and being selected for positions of responsibility within chosen field.

EDUCATION

Xavier University • College of Design, Architecture, Art and Planning • Cincinnati, Ohio
Bachelor of Fine Arts, 1995

EXPERIENCE

Commercial Photographer • Freelance

Successful completion of commercial photography assignments requiring planning, follow-through, and results that meet client objectives.

- *Project:* Marketing brochure for independent producer of specialized archery equipment (Fall 1995). *Scope:* Worked with client to select and position products; shot and developed photos; made brochure layout recommendations and gave technical input regarding reproduction of photographs.

- *Project:* Real estate catalog for Architectural and Design Services, Xavier University (Fall 1994). *Scope:* Met with client to determine project goals; selected shots and photographed University-owned properties from numerous perspectives; working with strict budget limitations, researched developing options and selected vendors based on quality and price; organized and presented finished photographs.

Night Manager • Starlight Restaurant, Cincinnati, Ohio (1994-Present)

- Train and supervise employees.
- Promote positive customer relationships by focusing strong attention on meeting customers needs and ensuring their enjoyment.
- Coordinate and book entertainment; develop and place related advertising.
- Introduce new product lines following analysis of current operations and growth opportunities.

Lab Monitor • Xavier University, Photography Department (1993-1994)

- Supervised and provided expert assistance to beginning photography students.
- Operated and maintained darkroom equipment.

Exhibit Assistant • Images Center for Photography, Cincinnati, Ohio (1994)

- Participated in the installation of exhibits for photographic-art gallery.
- Monitored gallery shows and provided information to visitors.

COMPUTER SKILLS

Macintosh Systems
Applications: Adobe Illustrator, Adobe Photoshop, Sculpt 3D, Authorware

ADDITIONAL SKILLS

4x5, 2 1/4, 35mm cameras
Black/white and color film processing and printing

EXHIBITS

Student Works • College of Design, Architecture, Art and Planning (1994, 1995)
Undergraduate Ceramic Exhibit • 840 Gallery (May 1994)
Undergraduate Painting Exhibit • 840 Gallery (May 1993)

Portfolio and references available on request.

JACQUELINE NEWTON, A.T.C.

444 Derby Circle
Louisville, KY 86342

email@email.com
(880) 555-7202

CERTIFIED ATHLETIC TRAINER
Offering Solid Credentials in Athletic & Injury Rehabilitation

CREDENTIALS:

* Certified Athletic Trainer, experienced working in rehabilitative environments with *547 hours of clinical practice and 2,125 hours of internship as Trainer.*
* Averaged in the *90th percentile* on the Allied Health Professions Admissions Test. Completed additional courses in *Vertebrate Anatomy, Physics, Chemistry and Biology.*
* Highly competent in evaluations, injury management, rehabilitation, and administration. Successfully work with top college varsity athletes on timely and effective rehabilitation programs.
* Certified *Water Rehabilitation Trainer.* Have clocked over 179 hours of water rehabilitation training to fellow trainers (NATA Program).

EDUCATION:

Marshall University, Huntington, KY   (Currently Enrolled)
Master of Science: Health & Physical Education

University of Kentucky, Louisville Campus, Louisville KY   1992
Bachelor of Science: Exercise & Sport Sciences, GPA: 3.62

RELATED WORK EXPERIENCE:

Marshall University, Huntington, KY   1993-Present
Graduate Assistant Athletic Trainer (All Sports)

Louisville Rehab Center, Louisville, KY   1991-93
Athletic Trainer / Exercise Instructor

Caldwell High School, Caldwell, KY   1989-91
Assistant Athletic Trainer, (Internship), Football

VOLUNTEER WORK: Westerman Rehabilitation Center, Louisville, KY   1989-Present
Post-Op Hip Replacement Therapy

Hendersen Nursing Facility, Caldwell, KY   1990-95
Senior Citizen Injury Rehabilitation

AFFILIATIONS:

* National Athletic Trainers' Association
* Athletic Trainers' Association of Florida
* American College of Sports Medicine

- References Furnished upon Request -

LORRAINE KREMER, MPT

555 Union Terrace Lane North
Maple Grove, MN 55777

(763) 555-2485
lorrainekremer@email.email

PHYSICAL THERAPIST
SKILLED-NURSING AND COMMUNITY HOME-BASED SETTINGS FOR GERIATRIC POPULATIONS …
12-year career of positively impacting older adults' abilities to gain or improve physical function

Extensive physical therapy management and practice in aiding geriatric patients' independence. Talent for dealing with the aging population in a sensitive and professional manner. Dedicated to promoting the healing process to maximize life quality.

Expertise

- Conservative Pain Management Techniques ▪ Osteoarthritis ▪ Nutrition ▪ Family Issues ▪ Strength Training
- Ventilation & Respiratory Dysfunction ▪ Functional Training ▪ Incontinence ▪ Prosthetics
- Remedial & Therapeutic Exercise ▪ Manipulation ▪ Massage ▪ Managed Care/Medicare/Medicaid Reimbursement
- Treatment Planning and Implementation ▪ Program Development and Management ▪ Service/Patient Liaison.
- Staff Training & Development ▪ Community Physical Therapy Advisory Leadership ▪ Budgets ▪ Charting/Documentation.

PROFESSIONAL EXPERIENCE

NORTHWEST HEALTHCARE & RETIREMENT CENTER – Brooklyn Center, MN   2000 – present
259-bed skilled nursing home facility.
   Director of Rehabilitative Services / Physical Therapist
- Direct 11 therapists and activities for an inpatient/outpatient setting, while providing primary patient treatment.
- Led the planning, development and implementation of a new physical therapy department.
- Originated and set up preemployment and postinjury screenings (functional assessment) for staff.
- Established Rehab Rounds, multidisciplinary meetings to discuss and coordinate patients' treatments.
- Recruited to serve on the Anoka Vocational Technical College's Advisory Board on PTA program outreach.
- Serve as Rehab Services' liaison with administration, government agencies, insurance companies and the public.

HEARTLAND HOME CARE & HOSPICE – Golden Valley, MN   1991 – 2000
Network of home health and hospice care comprising 80 offices in 22 states.
Physical Therapist / Geriatric Specialist
- Recruited for Heartland's first home-site geriatric specialist team, visiting clients to assess and treat motor function.
- Utilized rehabilitative techniques of exercise, gait training, prosthetics and heat to restore the client to his/her highest functional level of strength, range of motion and mobility.
- Collaborated with multiple service providers: physicians, speech, nursing, occupational therapy, social services, psychologists, therapeutic recreation, dietary, orthotists, prosthetists, medical supply and insurance companies.

UNIVERSITY OF MINNESOTA CLINICALS & AFFILIATIONS – Minneapolis and St. Paul, MN   1989 – 1991
   Adult Rehabilitation / Acute Care Facility: University of Minnesota Hospitals – Minneapolis, MN
   Children with Mental and Physical Disabilities: Burnett School – St. Paul, MN
   Private Outpatient Sports Injury Specialization: Quinlin Physical Therapy Associates – Minneapolis, MN
   Acute Care Facility: Hennepin County Medical Center – Minneapolis, MN

ST. LOUIS PARK PLAZA HEALTHCARE CENTER – St. Louis Park, MN   1988 – 1991
   Certified Nursing Assistant: Evening Shift
- Checked on patients and assisted them with mobilization, hygiene and basic needs.

EDUCATION

UNIVERSITY OF MINNESOTA – Minneapolis, MN
Master of Science in Rehabilitation Science (1999)
Thesis: *Item Analysis of the Physical Therapist Clinical Performance Instrument*
Bachelor of Science, Physical Therapy (1991)
American Physical Therapy Association Scholarship recipient

AFFILIATIONS

American Physical Therapy Association (APTA)
American Academy of Orthopedic Manual Physical Therapists (AAOMPT)

ROBERT A. GARALD, MD

136 11st Lane North
Palm Beach Gardens, Florida 33418
Phone: (561) 555-9515 / Cell: (561) 555-0237
email@email.com

HEALTHCARE LIAISON / PROJECT LEADER / CONSULTANT
Combining Clinical and Business Expertise to Enhance Financial / Operational Performance

Operational and Logistics Management / Billing & Collections
Regulatory Compliance Issues / High-Tech Integration
Revenue Enhancement & Profit Center Development

More than 38 years experience in medicine and business/corporate management; recognized for pioneering growth and profit-building concepts in highly competitive markets, including medical practices. Outstanding interpersonal and staff management skills in successfully navigating business through fluctuating economies to enhance revenue and income.

CORE STRENGTHS

Strategic planning and practice assessment review
Production and efficiency optimization
Personnel/staff training and development
E&M code utilization review and analysis
Quality utilization management

Building strategic alliance and partnerships
Finance and budget management
Merger and acquisition management
Internal controls and operational evaluation
MIS integration and coordination

EDUCATION / HONORS

Medical Doctor   Iona College, New Rochelle, New York
MS/PhD – Biology   New York University, New York, New York
Bachelor of Science: Biology   Iona College, New Rochelle, New York

Honors:
- Fellow American Association for the Advancement of Science (AAAS)
- Tri Beta Biological Honor Society
- Aesculapius: The Medical Arts Honor Society

HIGHLIGHTS OF PROFESSIONAL EXPERIENCE

- Directed $15 million operation consisting of 15 locations, 250 employees with full charge P&L accountability.
- Oversaw warehouse operations (warehouse manager and assistant warehouse manager) consisting of 125,000 SF with $2 million in inventory. Implemented a Just-in-Time system (converting from manual to automated system) for 25,000 sku's.
- Increased warehouse productivity by 25% while decreasing personnel by 50%. Enforced OSHA and safety regulations.
- Initiated a strong educational program of products/sales techniques resulting in significant increased sales and sales force production. Transformed customer service department from one of reaction to proactive/preventative service.
- Project leader/liaison between retail store chain and the consulting firm of Booz, Allen, and Hamilton during major expansion and computerization undertaking (MIS / POS).
- Teaching Assistant for New York University Biology Department.
- Actively participated in research studies of melanoma under the direction of world-renowned ichthyologist Dr. Alfred Perlmuter at New York University.
- Expertise in bioinformatics and biotechnical approaches for application in pharmaceutical development and treatment.

CHRONOLOGY OF EMPLOYMENT (1961 to Current)

Medical Consultant – Billing and Collections   TRANSWORLD SYSTEMS, INC., West Palm Beach, Florida
Vice President, Special Operations   GOLDSMITH BROTHERS, New York City, New York
Business / Medical Consultant   Arthur Anderson Medical Consulting Div., New York, New York
Physician – Private Practice   Robert A, Garold, MD, New York and Florida

References and Supporting Documentation Furnished upon Request

LANCE PORCO, P.A.-C.

15392 78th Drive North
Fort Lauderdale, FL 33401-7319
(407) 555-7722 (Home)
(407) 555-8698 (Cellular)

PHYSICIAN ASSISTANT
Specializing in... Orthopedic Surgery

OVERVIEW: A high-energy, peak-performing *Physician Assistant* with 17 years of above-average success in the medical field. Manage full caseload, providing high-quality professional care. A reputation for strong rapport-building skills and for contributing to the growth of a successful medical practice. Areas of expertise include:

- Pre/postoperative management
- Performing initial evaluations
- First Assistant
- Setting fractures
- Total hip & knee procedures

- General orthopedics
- Hand surgery
- Arthroscopic surgery
- ER calls
- Teaching & training

EDUCATION:

SURGICAL INTERNSHIP / RESIDENCY
General Surgery House Staff   1978 - 1980
Orthopedic Surgery House Staff   1980 - 1982

    Montefiore Hospital and Medical Center, Bronx, NY
    Associated Hospitals:
    - Hospital of Albert Einstein College of Medicine
    - Bronx Municipal Hospital
    - North Central Bronx Hospital

ASSOCIATE IN APPLIED SCIENCE   1976 - 1978
Cincinnati Technical College: Physician Assistant Program, Cincinnati, OH

PRE-MEDICINE   1969 - 1971
University of Missouri, Columbia, MO

LIBERAL ARTS / ENGINEERING   1962 - 1963
Syracuse University, Syracuse, NY

PROFESSIONAL
EXPERIENCE:
Ben C. Cotter, Jr., M.D., Palm Beach Gardens, FL   1987 - Present
PHYSICIAN ASSISTANT - Orthopedic Surgery; Private Practice

George P. Gonzalez Ergas, M.D., New York, NY   1982 - 1987
PHYSICIAN ASSISTANT - Orthopedic Surgery; Private Practice

TEACHING:
Ongoing *shadowing experience*   1991 - Present
For budding PA and high school students contemplating careers in medicine and health-related fields.

University of Florida, Gainesville, FL
Preceptor-Externship; Physician Assistant Program   1994

Barry University, Miami Shores, FL
Guest Lecturer - Occupational Therapy   1991

SIMON HENSEL

555 North 555 Place • Tulsa, Oklahoma • 74155
Residence: 918-555-5555 • Cell: 913-555-5551 • E-mail: shensel@email.net

---

PLANT MANAGER / PRODUCTION MANAGER – ADMINISTRATION & OPERATIONS

Experienced Management Professional with a process-oriented leadership approach and proven diligence implementing the required resources to achieve cradle-to-grave product management. Equally comfortable participating in an executive board meeting discussing strategies and performing on the front line applying the strategies. Employ an organized approach in creating simple, cost-effective and resilient systems that stand the test of time. Build productive teams that work toward shared objectives. Detail-oriented and highly organized in authoring procedures, establishing flows and tracking methods. Leverage technology to create user-friendly databases for practical production purposes. **Areas of Strength and Skills Sets include:**

• Manufacturing Processes	• Cost Reductions / Controls	• Operations Start-Up
• Inventory / Materials Management	• Manufacturing Technology	• Quality Management
• Production Scheduling	• Operating Procedures	• Team Leadership
• Process Redesign / Reengineering	• Performance Improvement	• Safety / OSHA
• Personnel Management	• Product Commercialization	• Vendor Negotiations

— CAREER HIGHLIGHTS —

ABC PRODUCTION, Tulsa, Oklahoma   *1997 to 2004*
($200M global, privately held manufacturer of replacement parts / service for air pollution control equipment. Niche focus is on the design and manufacture of eDBFE membrane products.) [www.abcproduction.com]
Global Supply Chain Manager (2003) / **Production Manager** (1997 to 2004)
Initially brought on board for the start-up production management of a fabric lamination operation and then later directed lamination product outsourcing efforts (scheduling, tracking and coordinating). Charged with start-up production leadership of the new eDBFE membrane product, contributing to a cumulative 650% profit growth (seven consecutive quarters of profitability) despite a sluggish economy. Oversaw day-to-day production operations and administration while supervising 21 employees across two shifts (blending, extrusion, tentering and more). In global supply chain management role, influence methods of tracking business opportunities/supply chain management via international business partners. *Significant Achievements:*

- **Plant Start-Up Growth:** Vaulted capacity of new production operation (eDBFE membrane product manufacture) from 0 to 190,000 yards per month throughput in two years.
- **Plant Start-Up Delivery:** Earned a record of 100% on-time delivery during plant start-up period.
- **Human Resources & Training:** Built a production staff that grew from three to 21 employees during tenure. Contained labor costs using a temp-to-hire strategy to manage the increasing production labor requirements.
- **Process Improvements:** Identified and reversed process deficiencies in the outsourcing procedure for lamination jobs, curbing the exploitation of vendor relationships. Same system also was implemented across customer orders area.
- **Technology Solutions:** Developed and implemented multiple database systems for areas such as supply chain management and product testing. **Results:** Facilitated data sharing (multiple users/multiple databases) to speed product testing. Enhanced abilities in measuring organizational performance through metrics analysis.
- **Product Development:** Collaborated closely with product developers to institute new processes/products on production floor, including follow-up data analysis and commercialization trials.

Continued on Page Two

309

- **Product Introduction:** Instrumental during the production start-up of glove line that delivered 2,500 glove liners a week after only two weeks' operation. Organized initial systems including the origination of CAD files to define glove samples/sizes to the die and platen houses.
- **Subcontractor Communication:** Negotiated with subcontractors regarding lamination production schedules; coordinated material supply for new glove liner product; scheduled and performed on-site management of chemical treating process at subcontractor location.
- **Operating Budget:** Devised a stable cost-per-yard metric during rapid growth phase of plant.
- **Award:** Captured "Record Setter" award for development work on chemical treating process to achieve oleophobic properties hydrophobic eDBFE membranes.

WRAP CORPORATION, Tulsa, Oklahoma   *1993 to 1997*
($17 million, European owned and operated paper converting business. Oklahoma plant comprised 60,000 sq. ft. and eight production centers.)

Assistant Plant Manager (1996 to 1997) / **Production Manager** (1995 to 1996) / **Plant Engineer** (1993 to 1995)

Initially served in a technical role as Plant Engineer, repairing production equipment, and earned succession of promotions to Assistant Plant Manager. In management role, supervised 30+ employees and directed graphics packaging production for make-to-order business. Scope of day-to-day accountability included training, scheduling and technical troubleshooting, as well as inventory control, quality assurance, safety and human resource management (pay and benefits and policy/procedure administration). *Significant Achievements:*

- **Attacked ongoing problem with OSHA recordable injuries** (22 injuries in one year) by expanding dialogue with the employees to identify and address safety hazards. Employed administrative or engineering controls to limit or eliminate the issues and instituted an incentive system to reward staff for incremental accomplishments
  - ✓ **Result:** Slashed OSHA recordables by 75% and achieved 227 consecutive days with zero OSHA recordable injuries, containing insurance rates.
- **Assimilated two departments – production and quality analysis/testing –** reducing flowtime by approximately 4%.
- **Attained double-digit-percentage savings** in production downtime and production scrap without a material cost increase via codevelopment effort with adhesive supplier.
- **Mentored and employed outsource training** for other supervisors.

MAJOR AEROSPACE COMPANY, Oklahoma City, Oklahoma   *1990 to 1993*
Apprentice Electrician (1992 to 1993)/**Electronics Inspector** (1990 to 1991)

- **As Apprentice Electrician,** achieved full-time, hands-on and classroom training for electrical trade in an industrial environment (maintenance and construction).
- **As Electronics Inspector,** handled performance testing and evaluation of purchased electronic components.
- **Instrumental participant** on a cross-functional business reengineering team that reduced product inspection flowtime by 55%.

— EDUCATION —

MBA in Management, 1992
B.S. in Electrical Engineering Technology, 1990
Oklahoma State University, Stillwater, Oklahoma

Computer Knowledge: MS Word, Excel, Access and PowerPoint, AutoCAD LT, AS400

Residence: 918-254-5555 • Cell: 913-230-5551 • 9040 North 85th Place • Tulsa, Oklahoma 74133
shensel@email.net

CAMERON SPERRY

555 Riverside Drive
Brentwood, New York 11111
(631) 602-8866
plantmanager@abc.net

Production Operations Manager / Quality Control

Twenty-five years of senior-level experienced managing Plant Facilities Operations

➢ Ensure the integrity of production, packaging, and distribution operations while maintaining productivity levels, reduced costs and equipment functionality in a multishift manufacturing environment.

➢ Maintain Quality Control standards, processes, and procedures encompassing in-process, incoming, and final inspection; acceptance and testing; scheduling and monitoring; internal and external audits.

➢ Excellent problem-solving and interpersonal communication skills required to effectively interface with engineers, contractors and vendors; union representatives, corporate management and plant personnel.

➢ Demonstrated team management skills in areas of hiring, training, and performance evaluations in accordance with human resources policies and procedures; proven track record for successfully motivating employees.

PROFESSIONAL EXPERIENCE & ACCOMPLISHMENTS

LONG ISLAND LAMPS, Huntington, New York, $80MM annual revenues   1990 – Present

Plant Facilities Manager, 1993 – Present
Quality Control Manager, 1990 – 1993

➢ **Maintenance and Facilities Operations**

- Manage Quality Control Department of major screw machine production facility, ensuring material manufactured is in accordance with internal standards, as well as H-28 and MIL-I-45208.

- Supervise two (2) full-time shifts six (6) days per week, including the direct supervision of day-shift operations and supervision of night-shift operations through night foreman.

- Direct production activities through supervision of individual managers and plant personnel.

- Played an integral role in the comprehensive layout planning and implementation of a second facility.

- *Manage both manufacturing facilities totaling 167,000 sq. ft.:*
  - Oversee production operations of decorative faucets, lamp and lighting fixtures and plumbing components turning in excess of 235,000 lbs. of brass per week.

- Assist Industrial Engineers with time studies on machines to ensure efficiency & productivity levels do not decline below 80%; collect machine downtime logs and time-study reports from individual supervisors.

- Collaborate with corporate management to meet manufacturing objectives with new product assemblies.

- Respond to 24-hour emergency calls for two (2) facilities requiring immediate attention and resolve, including boiler shutdown and/or failure; security alarms; water flow and/or sprinkler system tripping.

- Supervise manufacturing and distribution operations, including washing operations, packaging, and warehousing; shipping, unloading and routing to inspection; plating and polishing.

- Maintain tight production schedules to ensure materials process timely and efficiently preventing the occurrence of bottlenecks.

- Assist with the writing and revisions of proposals to secure qualified contractors.

- Supervise contractors; approve payment for services rendered and maintenance orders.

— Continued —

CAMERON SPERRY

Page 2

PROFESSIONAL EXPERIENCE & ACCOMPLISHMENTS
Long Island Lamps, continued

➢ **Staff Training and Management**
- Reduced annual overhead costs by 35% through elimination of excessive overtime and need for outsourcing as a result of new personnel recruitment and restructuring of assigned personnel.
- Provide general direction to individual managers acting as their liaison to corporate management.
- Delegate assignments based on workload assessment and available manpower, securing need for personnel replacement with in-house floaters.
- Train and educate staff on the proper use of protective gear, and the mandatory need for OSHA compliance; distribute OSHA safety data sheets to staff members during training sessions, itemizing protection gear as part of the required training materials; requisition protective gear as needed.
- As Chair to Safety Committee, investigate and report on injuries, cause and prevention in the workplace.
- Meet with corporate management on a weekly basis to openly address employee-related problems, report findings of productivity efficiency reviews, and discuss gain-sharing issues.

ELECTRO MAGNETIC CORP., Hicksville, New York   1987 – 1990
Quality Control Manager
- Maintained Quality Control standards for all manufactured material; performed internal/external audits.
- Wrote procedures required for all Quality Control areas; reviewed all contracts for Quality requirements.
- Scheduled and monitored quality levels throughout the company.
- Interfaced directly with both local DCAS representatives and customers.

ENVIRONMENTAL SYSTEMS, Bethpage, New York   1983 – 1987
Quality Control Group Leader
- Directed in-process, incoming, and final inspection areas.
- Maintained scheduling and acceptance standards of all materials.

JCA ELECTRONIC DEVICES CORP., Brookhaven, New York   1978 – 1983
Inspection Supervisor
- Supervised acceptance and testing of all mechanical and electrical material.
- Utilized MIL-STD for sampling.

EDUCATION

SUFFOLK COMMUNITY COLLEGE, Brentwood, New York
A.A.S. in Business Administration

RAYMOND DYER
848 Blue Ridge Circle
Clarkston, MI 48829
(810) 555-3824
email@email.com

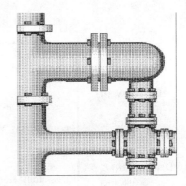

LICENSED MASTER PLUMBER
#CFCO-18290

15 Years Residential & Commercial Experience

Qualifications:

- Leaks
- Fixtures
- Backflow Repair
- Sprinklers & Irrigation
- Lift Stations
- Backflow Certified

- Repairs
- Sewer & Drains
- Cleaning Service
- Septic Tanks
- High-Velocity Water Jetting
- Hot Water Heaters

Highlights of Experience:

Introduced TV Sewer Line Inspection as an additional service, generating 6% more income to company's bottom line.

Have successfully directed over 27 plumbers working on 7-10 jobs simultaneously. Hire, train, and assure quality performance of all workers for all projects.

Completely renovated (plumbing) *The Brewster House*, a 160-year-old historical structure in Dearborn, MI. This $105,000 job was completed 3 weeks ahead of schedule and came in 18% under budget, without losing quality.

Over past 15 years, have done major construction/renovation on 82 restaurants, 14 health clubs, 32 manufacturing facilities, 31 warehouse units, 24 high-rise office buildings, 23 hospitals, and over 360 private residences.

Managed high-volume, high-pressure repair operation in Detroit for French company (SOS Depannage). Directed 18 plumbers in 3-county area responding entirely to emergency plumbing and water heater repairs.

Employment:

Master Plumber for:

Master Rooter, Pontiac, MI	1993 - Present
Dawson Plumbing, Pontiac, MI	1990 - 1993
SOS Depannage, Detroit, MI	1989 - 1990
Pontiac Heating & Plumbing, Pontiac, MI	1981 - 1989

Education:

Wilbur Technical Institute, Norwood, MI, 1979-81
Master Plumber Training and Certification

Interests:

Coach Little League, flag football, and soccer; Executive Board Member: Clarkston Youth Athletic Association; enjoy golf, fishing, and jazz.

PRODUCT
DEVELOPMENT

RESEARCH &
DEVELOPMENT

DEVELOPMENT &
SOURCING

NEGOTIATIONS &
PROCUREMENT

COST-EFFECTIVE
MANAGEMENT

PRODUCT GROWTH &
PROCESSES

NURTURE
LONG-TERM
CLIENT
RELATIONSHIPS

MANUFACTURING
OPERATIONS

SHIPPING &
DISTRIBUTION

BUSINESS PLAN
DEVELOPMENT

PROJECT
MANAGEMENT

SYSTEMS AND
WORK FLOWS

CREATE COMPLEX
POWERPOINT
PRESENTATIONS

WORD, NT,
INTERNET,
QUICKBOOKS,
EXCEL, ACCESS

Martin B. Curtis

3041 Patriot Road * Baltimore, MD 21045
410.555.5244 * MBC@aol.con

PRODUCT MANAGER
- Staying ahead of a warp-speed, forward-moving, high-tech industry -

PROFESSIONAL VALUE OFFERED

Highly creative, profit-driven Product Manager with a proven record of accomplishments, and a keen ability to develop new business opportunities, successfully launching new products into the marketplace. Develop products, introduce product line maintenance, documentation, and integration.

PROFESSIONAL EMPLOYMENT

Technical Product Specialist
e-Entertainment, Inc., Reston, Virginia   **1995 to Present**
e-Entertainment, Inc., specializes in the complete production of electronic entertainment products, including technical design, engineering, component sourcing, manufacturing, assembly, package design and distribution. The company has grown from start up operations to $7.5M volume with national distribution in an extremely competitive high tech market.

SCOPE OF OPERATIONS

- Achieved strong and sustainable revenue for the company through demonstrated knowledge of financial and product management practices. Expertly determine long-range objectives and manage projects within or below established budgets.

- Competent expertise of highly specialized electronic entertainment products. Envision products, work with business development, and marketing to create and execute product strategies. Research industry trends. Review the competitive landscape of the industry and expertly translate market analyses into ongoing product development.

- Gather technical requirements, prepare proposals, and manage the implementation of product features with corporate operations, marketing, and sales efforts. Create and monitor business metrics. Analyze revenue streams, establish and manage costs, draft schedules and product delivery. Keen insight for reviewing processes and advising production and operations.

Selected Achievements

- Instrumental in building a start-up dot.com company from the ground floor to three sites with 65,000 square feet of manufacturing space, millions of dollars of capital equipment, a warehouse with distribution capability, and an annual volume of $7.5M.

- Successfully positioned and marketed a CD game product, clinching the market and doubling annual revenue for the company.

- Improved quality product ratings by 16% by implementing a continuous improvement process. Execute operational aspects of market trials and key customer sampling.

- Planned and drafted a formal, master production schedule for annual and five-year product manufacturing plans based on current and projected trends.

- Expanded vendor sourcing and captured over $500K in material and cost reductions.

(Continued)

Martin B. Curtis, Page 2

Product Manager/Market Segment Manager
Molecular Sciences Company, Baltimore, Maryland　　　　　　　**1990 to 1995**
* Molecular Sciences Company is the world's largest manufacturer and distributor of state-of-the-art research products and electrophoresis apparatus used in gene research—moving toward the Millennium.

SCOPE OF OPERATIONS

- Prepared business and marketing plans to include pricing, market strategy, and forecasting. Designed and implemented numerous marketing plans for several markets—with each market fully exceeding the quota. Monitored competitors—gathered and analyzed competitive market intelligence and determined competitive trends within the market.

- Project Management: Coordinated engineering, marketing and outside vendor tasks for each new product. Established inspection, diagnostic, and installation procedures as required. Assessed processes and designed customer-friendly products. Researched, developed, and implemented policies and procedures.

Selected Achievements
- Assembled a cross-functional team to address productivity, efficiency, product quality, and distribution issues—resulting in improved relations between marketing and business operations in the launch and promotion of a new product line, with a significant increase of 26% in annual sales.

- Controlled over $2.6M in capital plant and equipment assets, engaging the company in new and even more profitable business opportunities. Evaluated molding processes to best suit specific products.

- Envisioned and designed a presentation binder instrumental in closing million dollar plus sale projects, with several essential customers.

- Published a District Brochure, the standard for promoting equipment. Composed operation and maintenance manuals for company equipment.

- Participated in various promotional programs. Created and delivered complex PowerPoint presentations. Displayed and promoted products at trade shows. Conducted customer visits.

- Working with engineers, developed and marketed approximately 40 different genetic research products, creating the benchmark of electrophoresis apparatus used in gene research, with an annual contract of $2.5M. Oversaw design processes, contracting, operations/production, and distribution for plastic medical technology products. Researched and determined best raw materials suppliers to purchase from.

EDUCATION

MBA, Radford University, Virginia, 1990
BS in Economics, University of Maryland, 1988

TRADE ORGANIZATIONS

Society of Product Managers, National Program Chairman, 1999 to 2001

Chad S. Lewis

784 Callaway Drive ● *Kansas City, Kansas 66011* ● *913-555-4416*

Professional Experience

SPRINT CORPORATION
April 1992 to Present

Senior Product Manager, Long Distance Division, 1997 to Present

- Developed and implemented a new network platform called Sprint ION.
- Made sales presentations to 40 of the Fortune 100 list of companies explaining converged network services and how Sprint ION represented this new approach to voice and data networking.
- Developed product implementation process for new platform, including, training, support of the sales staff, and resolution of issues related to implementation.

Manager of Finance Markets, Local Telecom Division, 1992 to September 1997

- Responsible for the development of applications sold to the financial markets in the 19 states in which the Local Telecom division of Sprint operates.
- Developed market strategy to address the finance markets, including the generation of an overall market plan and application marketing plans.
- Made multiple sales and marketing presentations in support of the sales process to customers of the seven regional operating companies.
- Taught training classes for sales and marketing personnel to acquaint them with the consultative sales process within the banking markets.
- Wrote a business case for a new related business for Sprint.

FARM & HOME SAVINGS INFORMATION SYSTEMS
FARM & HOME FINANCIAL CORPORATION
1987 to 1992

Vice President of New Product Development Farm & Home Financial Corporation, 1989 to 1992

- Directed a staff of 34 in the areas of Telecommunications, Operations, and Computer Systems.
- Managed all aspects of software purchase from design, to security, to negotiation of contract and price as well as the implementation process.
- Handled the coordination of all acquisitions and mergers from the data processing perspective.

Vice President, Manager of Information Support, 1987 to 1989

- Managed a staff of 8 people responsible for the sales and marketing of outsource services.
- Responsible for the evolution and implementation of application systems.
- Held primary responsibility for budget tracking and reporting for the company.
- Maintained a business plan and set priorities for enhancement to the system.

(Continued)

Chad S. Lewis   *Page 2*

FINANCIAL INFORMATION TRUST
December 1974 to November 1987

Regional Director of Member Services, 1983 to 1987

- Managed a staff of eleven people, five dedicated to telephone support and six dedicated to sales and on-site support of financial institutions in a six-state area.
- Had expanded duties that included sales and support responsibilities and met or exceeded overall objectives for territory during every year in which I managed region.
- Participated in the analysis of multiple software packages for utilization at the Trust.
- Held responsibility for the direction of field support staff in the areas of sales to existing and potential customers.
- Maintained an action plan and budget with reporting on a monthly basis to senior management.

Account Manager, 1976 to 1983

- Was responsible for the sale, service, and subsequent support of financial institution in a three-state territory.
- Met or exceeded sales objectives during all 8 years in which I had responsibility for the territory.
- Held responsibility as the correspondent banking representative for member institution of the Federal Home Loan Bank of Des Moines.

Account Representative, 1974 to 1976

- Learned financial processing and financial institution management.

ARDAN WHOLESALE
1973 to 1974

Branch Accounting Manager

- Responsible for store accounting staff at corporate headquarters.
- Directed the accounting and auditing function in 8 stores in 5 states.

Education

Simpson College, Indianola, Iowa
Bachelor of Arts in Business Administration, May 1973

REFERENCES
References will be furnished upon request.

EMILIO ROCHE

555 Brighton Straight • Brentwood, NY 11111 • (631) 555-0072 • roche@manufacturing.net

Production Operations Manager

PROFESSIONAL EXPERIENCE

Production Supervisor, PLASTIC PRODUCTIONS, Lake Grove, NY   9/91 – Present

Manage twenty-five (25) plastic injection-molding machines throughout two (2) production facilities, ensuring that all manufacturing practices and procedures are in accordance with ISO 9000 standards. Supervise the production of more than ninety (90) injection molded plastic parts, including caps and compacts, for the fragrance and cosmetic industry, such as Avon, Revlon, Elizabeth Arden, Cosmair-Lancóme, and Loréal.

- Oversee automated injection molding operations, including patented closure systems, high-quality electroplating, vacuum-metallizing, and on-line decorations, flat and contour hot stamping, lining sonic welding, in-house UV lacquer operations, and quality metal components manufacturing processes.
- Direct production activities for three (3) shifts through supervision of two (2) mechanics, (20) production crew members and two (2) foreman per shift, responding to 24-hour emergency calls for both facilities.
- Maintain tight production schedules to ensure the integrity of production and packaging operations, reduced costs and equipment functionality; keep ongoing activity logs to record details of downtimes.
- Interface with quality control inspectors, engineers, contractors, corporate management and plant personnel to ensure manufacturing requirements are met properly and on time throughout three (3) shifts.
- Oversee production crew members' training and performance evaluations in accordance with human resources policies and procedures; proven track record for successfully motivating employees.

Plant Leadman, HCD INDUSTRIES, INC., Brightwaters, NY   8/89 – 9/91

Oversaw fifteen (15) plastic injection molding machines ensuring the on-time manufacturing of bearings, ball screws and motion control technologies for industrial, automotive, aviation, machine tool, medical, office automation, aerospace, government, defense and distribution markets.

- Set up manufacturing processes of custom-engineered, high-precision ball screws and lead screws. Products included linear, anti-friction Ball Bushing bearings; Roundway roller bearings; 60 Case Linear Race (shafting); ready-to-install, RoundRail systems; AccuGlide and AccuMax ProfileRail linear guides.
- Interfaced extensively with quality control inspectors and maintained tight production schedules to ensure on-time production performance and equipment functionality.

Supervisor's Assistant / Quality Control Manager, J & R PLASTICS, Hauppauge, NY   5/86 – 8/89

Monitored thirteen (13) plastic injection molding machines and on-time production of medical and laboratory devices distributed to healthcare facilities. Ensured the integrity of production operations while maintaining productivity levels, reduced costs, and equipment functionality in a multishift manufacturing environment.

- Set up and monitored production activities based on workload assessment and available manpower.
- Maintained quality control in areas of in-process, incoming/final inspection, acceptance, and testing.
- Maintained tight production schedules to reduce the occurrence of bottlenecks; kept time study logs to record downtimes, cause of faultiness and corrective actions.
- Supervised, trained and motivated ten (10) production crew members for three (3) shifts.

CREDENTIALS

Associates in Applied Science, A & P Mechanical, Academy of Aeronautics
Certificate of Completion, UVA Plastic Injection Molding Machines
ISO 9000 — Completed all training requirements

RANDY C. GRECCO, Ph.D.

2345 River Road • Bainbridge, Georgia 31728
(912) 555-1212 • email@email.com

Seeking Position at University Level as...

PROFESSOR
Ph.D. African American Studies
Seven Years Experience in Ivy League Environments

Profile

More than 10 years experience in Ivy League environments meeting/exceeding academic standards and enhancing overall curriculum. A published author of seven books, and hundreds of journal/magazine articles and a reputable speaker on the African American Studies.

Education / Research

YALE UNIVERSITY, Princeton, New Jersey
Master of Science: African American Studies, 1994

UNIVERSITY OF VERMONT, Burlington, Vermont
Bachelor of Science: Sociology and Political Science, 1992

Research Specialty:
- Developed comprehensive psycholinguistic profiles through extensive research of autobiographical antidotes of former slaves of African descent in 18th, 19th, and 20th century America. Created compelling evidence to indicate and support the hypothesis that through anchor-collapsing technologies, conditioned patterns of behavior can be modified to attain equilibrium in 21st century lifestyle advances of the African American population.

Appointments

Professorship	Dartmouth University, Hanover, New Hampshire
Professorship	Brown University, Providence Rhode Island
Professorship	Yale University, Princeton New Jersey

Employment

DARTMOUTH UNIVERSITY, Hanover, New Hampshire **Professor – African American Studies**	1999 to Current
BROWN UNIVERSITY, Providence Rhode Island **Professor – African American Studies**	1996 to 1999
YALE UNIVERSITY, Princeton, New Jersey **Assistant Professor – African American Studies**	1994 to 1996

Selected Publications

- Pubal K, Lasricha S, Bhargava M: African America Challenge, World Today Analg 2003; 72: 257-8
- Chrewstline M, Poteau S: Impoverished Lives of Ex-Slaves by EMGG® Cream. Biography Analg 2002; 86:915
- Gorden, J. Paul, Steven Joshi H: The Obstruction of a Free Society: Modern Analg; 2001, 118:87-129
- Grecco, R. C., Psycholinguistic Profiles of Autobiographical Antidotes of Former Slaves of African Descent in America, McGraw-Hill, 2000

References and Supporting Documentation Furnished upon Request

SETH MARLER

575654 Lane Boulevard, La Mirada, California 91943 ● (858) 555-1946
smarler@aol.com

PROGRAMMER

Competent, intelligent, and personable computer professional with considerable experience developing and programming database and computer support programs. Computer-literate in a wide variety of technology and software applications. Proven record of success in training end-user staffs in technical aspects of computer program products. Developed excellent reputation for creating, designing, presenting, implementing, and evaluating accurate and effective processes. Formal academic studies are reinforced by technological expertise enhanced by specialized professional training. Skills include:

☑ Communications	☑ Program Analysis	☑ Strategic Planning
☑ Computer Languages	☑ Program Development	☑ Support Services
☑ Management Skills	☑ Program Evaluation	☑ Systems Requirements
☑ Organizational Skills	☑ Repair and Maintenance	☑ Telecommunications
☑ Policies and Procedures	☑ Quality Assurance	☑ Troubleshooting

COMPUTER LANGUAGES AND ENVIRONMENTS

C(DOS, Windows, and UNIX), C++ (DOS, Windows, OS/2), DELPHI, Java, Pascal and Turbo Vision (OOPS), Basic (DOS), Visual Basic (Windows), HTML, Perl, JavaScript, CGI, SQL, Prolog, VB for Application, FORTRAN, ASSEMBLY (x86, 8031, VAX, PDP-11), HPL (Hardware Programming Language), Ladder Logic, Continuous Control Chart (CCC)

COMPUTER AND OTHER SYSTEMS

VAX 11/780, Micro VAX, UNISYS, and AS/400. IBM PC SeriesX86, Cicso Routers series 4500, AS5100 Access Server, Process Control and Real-time machines like Honeywell UDC Series 9000, LAN, WAN, PLC Network, and Zworld PLC

OPERATING SYSTEMS, ENVIRONMENTS, DATABASES, AND PACKAGES

DOS, Windows 95/98/NT, NT-RAS, UNIX, LINUX, VMS, ALTRIX, OS/2, PCDM, SCADA, NETWARE, INTERNET, SQL Server, Oracle, Access, FoxPro, MS Project, MS Office, AutoCad, Orcad, Erwin, Casewise

PROFESSIONAL EXPERIENCE

NAVAL FACILITIES ENGINEERING COMMAND, La Mesa, California – 1997 to present

Programmer, Project Management, Analysis, and Development Department. Oversee development and implementation of documentation, security, and formal management systems for command customers. Act as Management Analyst in the Operations and Systems Division, providing technical support of existing program applications aimed at developing and implementing new applications in support of the Public Works community.

- Managed and developed Visual C (Win32), JavaScript and Oracle based billing, inventory, accounts management, and MIS systems.
- Incorporated change in the billing and account management systems by implementing Roaming services by GRIC.

(Continued on next page)

SETH MARLER

575654 Lane Boulevard, La Mirada, California 91943 ● (858) 555-1946

Resume   smarler@aol.com   Page Two

PROFESSIONAL EXPERIENCE *(Continued)*

NAVAL FACILITIES ENGINEERING COMMAND, Coronado, California – 1993 to 1997

Programmer and Computer Specialist in the Information Management Support Section involved in supporting existing applications in the Family Housing Activity Management Information System (FAMIS) program and technical representation to projects aimed at new applications development and implementation.

- Spearheaded creation and development of the FAMIS program, 1995.

HOUSING DEPARTMENT, Marine Corps Base, Camp Pendleton, California – 1990 to 1993

Programmer and Computer Specialist in the Facilities Division, involved in coordinating and integrating technical computer aspects with administrative matters such as standards management, acquisition and configuration management, ADP security, and risk management.

- Oversaw development of commandwide management analysis techniques.

ISMO, 1st Force Service Support Group (FSSG), Camp Pendleton, California – 1988 to 1990

Computer Programmer and Analyst providing Site Coordinator and Database Administrator assistance and production requirements coordination to ensure sufficient scheduling flexibility and equipment capacity to meet peak production needs, maintain accurate automated workload schedules, and processing times. Prepared, designed, and wrote complex computer application programs, procedures, and systems for the military information systems management program.

- Coordinated and simultaneously administered programs for 38 cross-functional, multitiered military organizations in multiple locations.
- Nominated for Navy Achievement Medal for significant accomplishments as a Programmer, Team Leader, and Analyst.

EDUCATION

Southern Illinois University, Carbondale, Illinois
     Master of Science - Computer Information Systems

National University, San Diego, California – GPA: 3.9 Cum Laude
     Bachelor of Science - Major: Information Technology

PROFESSIONAL DEVELOPMENT AND TRAINING

Irvine Training Center, Irvine, California
     Administering ENS for NetWare

David Maibor Associates, Inc. Seminars, Long Beach, California
     Software Development and Documentation: EIA/IEEE J-STD-016 and ISO/IEC 12207

Appropriate personal and professional references are available.

Jennifer Southworth

104 N. Meyers Drive • Hazel Park, Michigan 48030 • emailaddress@emailaddress.com • 248.555.0955

PROFESSIONAL PROFILE

Skilled project manager and savvy Internet steward. Track record of successful product introduction and implementation. Dynamic self-starter with a strong sense of responsibility and positive, aggressive attitude.

Creative problem-solver who applies technical skills and business knowledge to achieve improved results. Able to manage complex programs and multiple projects simultaneously. Productive as both individual contributor and team member. Excellent communication and relationship-building skills.

> *"Jennifer continues to deliver a strong, consistent performance. Her positive attitude and attacking style help keep those around her focused on solving complex problems."*
>
> *"She always takes the initiative, works extremely well on her own, and rarely needs follow-up on action items."*
>
> *"Her professional conduct and technical wisdom have earned her the respect of her peers and management."*
>
> .. C. Laurencelle, Manager

ACHIEVEMENTS

- Recognized for success in the delivery of user training and support programs that *outpaced the competition and provided 24-hour support to internal/external customers worldwide.*
- Conducted an analysis to reduce online search complexity. *Implementation of the design reduced timing issues without affecting the overall design.*
- Integral member of team that convinced management to allow the team to develop a tool that addressed a major Website integrity issue. *Resulted in an improved design and greatly improved customer satisfaction.*

EXPERIENCE

MITSUBISHI TECHNICAL CENTER, U.S.A., INC.   Plymouth, Michigan
INTERNET ANALYST, 1998-current
Interface with IS/IT and outside agencies to develop and implement systems which advance development of comprehensive international Web presence to grow/increase business efforts.
- Pilot new software and technologies which support the Internet site.
- Develop Internet strategy to provide a competitive advantage.
- Define metrics for success, analyze and interpret data, breed Web strategies and tactics and present reasoning to upper management.
MARKETING SPECIALIST, 1996-98

THE DAVIS:MARTIN GROUP   Detroit, Michigan
COPYWRITER/ADMINISTRATIVE ASSISTANT – 1995-96
- Provided design and writing skills for client campaigns in boutique design firm specializing in creating printed materials and Website development.

EDUCATION & PROFESSIONAL DEVELOPMENT

EASTERN MICHIGAN UNIVERSITY   Ypsilanti, Michigan
Master of Arts in Composition and Rhetoric course work

OLIVET NAZARENE UNIVERSITY   Kankakee, Illinois
BACHELOR'S DEGREE IN ENGLISH, 1993 – Minor: Business Marketing

150—PROPERTY MANAGER

GREG MYERSON

555 Morgan Avenue South ☖ Richfield, MN 55555 ☖ (612) 555-3106 ☖ gmyerson@email.email

PROPERTY MANAGEMENT PROFESSIONAL

☖ 10 years of experience managing multiple rental properties, complemented by impeccable credentials.
☖ Relate warmly to diverse individuals at all levels by using a friendly yet confident communication style.

Asset Management & Valuation	Mixed-Use Property Occupancy	Commercial & Residential
Renovation & Turnkey Operations	Capital Improvement	Site Remediation
Tenant Relations & Retention	Collections	Legal Processes

CREDENTIALS & LEADERSHIP

Certified Property Manager (CPM®)
Certified Commercial Investment Member (CCIM®)
Registered Professional Adjuster (RPA®)
Institute of Real Estate Management (IREM®) Minnesota Chapter 45 Secretary

CAREER CONTRIBUTIONS

☖ P lanned and directed the purchase, development, and disposition of real estate on behalf of business and investors for Minnesota s largest privately owned multifamily housing manager.

☖ Recruited as temporary Marketing Director for a distressed, 360-unit market rate housing project with 150 units down, including vacate notices. Spearheaded and led a marketing campaign, reducing a 25% vacancy to 5% in 4 months.

☖ Managed receivable activities for 1,600 units. Successfully reduced large outstanding (1-2 months) debt accounts to 25% above acceptable industry levels; maintained these long term.

☖ Turned the occupancy rate of a 7-building distressed student housing project from 40% to 95% in 3 months.

☖ Consistently achieved a satisfactory (or better) return on owners' investments.

☖ Analyzed property management companies' computer needs and implemented updated systems integrating construction and property management software with word processing and spreadsheet applications.

CAREER HISTORY

Property Manager / Marketing Director ▪ HART MANAGEMENT, INC. ▪ St. Paul, MN   1998 – present
34 buildings comprising 440 residential and retail units, plus 346 mini storage units.

Real Estate Asset Manager ▪ STEVEN BYRON PROPERTY MANAGEMENT ▪ Edina, MN   1996 – 1998
Largest privately owned multifamily housing manager in Minnesota.

Property Manager ▪ BLD PROPERTY MANAGEMENT ▪ St. Cloud, MN   1993 – 1996
15 buildings comprising 300+ residential units.

EDUCATION

ST. CLOUD STATE UNIVERSITY – St. Cloud, MN   Degree: 1996
Bachelor of Science in Real Estate, *Summa cum Laude*   **Minors: Finance and Risk Management**

323

ROBERT S. BOWDEN

4655 Rocky Road West, #123 • Blue Skies, Montana 99877
Phone: (987) 555-1212 • Cell: (987) 555-3232
email@email.com

CONSTRUCTION MANAGEMENT/PROJECT SUPERINTENDENT
PROPERTY MANAGEMENT PROFESSIONAL

"On-Time/On-Budget Management History"

30+ Years' Successful Residential and Commercial Experience
Contributing Team Member for Growth and New-Business Development

---

STRENGTHS

Full charge construction and development management
Multiple-project management and coordination
Project budgeting and expense management
Contract negotiation and administration

Project troubleshooting and problem solving
Project scheduling and deadline management
Quality control and customer/client relations
Residential and commercial property management

PROFESSIONAL WORK EXPERIENCE

MERIDIAN MANAGEMENT CORP., Hopeville, Montana   1998 to Current
Project Manager
Direct day-to-day operation and maintenance of physical plant and mechanical aspects of college campus (FAU, John D. MacArthur Campus, High Fall, Montana). Full-charge responsibility for all human resources vis-à-vis custodial and maintenance staff. A liaison between university officials and corporate offices in Los Angeles. Responsible for all preventive maintenance and computer operations of HVAC system. Gather bids and spearhead appropriate maintenance and repair contracts with vendors.

- o   Recognized by university officials for unprecedented project performance.
- o   Raised systems and operations to peak performance levels through creative, hands-on leadership.

THE GOODMAN COMPANY, Blue Skies, Montana   1990 to 1997
Commercial Property Operations Manager
Liaison between the tenants and owners for several properties, including prime locations—The Esplanade on Royal Avenue and Okee Square Shopping Center in Blue Skies. Provided appropriate staffing and services to ensure smooth facilities operations as it related to mechanical, structural, and landscaping needs.

- o   Assisted in arranging special events, including the gallery opening for Tico Tores (Drummer for Bon Jovi).
- o   Implemented cost-saving, energy-efficient cuts, resulting in cost savings of $47,000.

CUSTOM COMMERCIAL CONSTRUCTION, Hanover, Maryland   1986 to 1990
Construction Supervisor
Coordinated construction projects throughout MO, AR, WA, SN, and ND—from prebid through final inspection and opening. Gathered bids and negotiated and administered contracts for all aspects of the projects. Projects included office buildings, shopping centers, restaurants, and supermarkets.

- o   Successfully managed large-scale multiple projects concurrently.
- o   Projects completed on time and on schedule—exceeded expectations.

TRAINING / CERTIFICATIONS

Associate's Degree: Business, Monroe Community College, Rochester, New York, 1985
- o   Licensed Community Association Manager (CAM), Montana
- o   EPA Certification
- o   Certified Pool/Spa Operator, National Swimming Pool Foundation

MICHAEL BERNARD WILSON, M.D., Ph.D.

2748 Kittbuck Way
Falls Church, Virginia 22132
(703) 555-1212 / email@email.com

Nonpracticing

PSYCHIATRIST / TEACHER / LECTURER / RECRUITER

Combining more than 25 years of medical expertise with outstanding sales, marketing, managerial, and communications skills. Seeking position where qualifications and experience can enhance organizational recruitment, growth, profits, efficiency, resource utilization and employee satisfaction.

Patient-Treatment Evaluation / Hospital Stay Cost Analysis / Pharmaceutical Drug Management
Physician-Patient Consultation / Education & Research / Article Writer & Editor
Insurance Evaluations / Medical Advertisement Writer & Consultant

Highly experienced and accomplished retired physician successfully combining medical expertise with organizational leadership, growth management, and productivity enhancement experience. Able to assist contemporary organizations navigate through a dramatically changing medical environment on all fronts and facilitate reorganization, training, and staff education and updating.

CORE PROFESSIONAL STRENGTHS

Team building and problem solving	Proactive strategic planning
Presentation/public speaking skills	Research and development
Active treatment expertise	Preventive treatment protocols
Expert in drugs (efficacy/side effects)	Advertisement compilation
Project management/coordination	Medical history expert
Working with diverse cultures	Resource utilization (physical/labor)
Patient relations management	Quality control management

Languages: Fluent in English, German, Yiddish; Good Working Knowledge of Chinese, Japanese, and Korean

EDUCATION / BOARD CERTIFICATIONS

Columbia University, New York, New York	1952-56
Bachelor of Arts: Humanities & Science (Geology)	
Harvard University and the University of Chicago, Cambridge, MA / Chicago, IL	1956-59
Ph.D. : Geology and Archeology	
Chicago Medical School, Chicago, Illinois	1959-62
Medical Doctor (MD)	
New Rochelle Hospital, New Rochelle, New York	1962-63
Internship	
Kings Park State Hospital, Kings Park, New York	1964-67
Psychiatry Residency	
New York School of Psychiatry, New York, New York	1967-69
Q.P. (Qualified Psychiatrist) – NY State	

* Board Eligibility: American Board of Psychiatry and Neurology	1971
* Board Certified, American Board of Psychiatry and Neurology (#22892)	1981
* Medical Licenses: NJ, NM, NY, SC, VT (Currently Expired)	1964-76

(Page 1)

MICHAEL BERNARD WILSON, M.D., Ph.D.
Page two.

HIGHLIGHTS OF PROFESSIONAL EXPERIENCE

- ❑ General Practitioner – private practice for 8 years.
- ❑ 10 years as a Staff Psychiatrist in Kings Park State Hospital, Kings Park, Virginia.
- ❑ 10 years as a practicing and well-respected private psychiatrist.
- ❑ Division Psychiatrist in the United States Army Medical Corps (Major), Republic of Vietnam.
- ❑ Medical Treatment Director for Suffolk County Mental Health Board, Narcotic Clinic, Hauppauge, NY.
- ❑ Recruited and worked as Senior Associate Medical Director for Sandoz Pharmaceutical in East Hanover, NJ.
- ❑ National/international lecturer, speaker, consultant and presenter at conferences, conventions, symposiums, and meetings.
- ❑ A published author on various topics for numerous publications (specifics provided upon request).
- ❑ Expert medical consultant/witness on various subjects, including drugs, treatment, preventive medicine, and advertising.
- ❑ Proven experience in the area of change management, new business development, and overall strategic planning.
- ❑ Experience in psychiatric/neurologic drug research and development.

CHRONOLOGY OF PROFESSIONAL EXPERIENCE

Sandoz Pharmaceuticals, East Hanover, Virginia   1986-Current
Senior Associate Medical Director

Private Practice – in association with Dr. Fredrick Apowitz, Smithtown, Virginia   1975-86
Psychiatry (For Suffolk County Mental Health Boards)

Northeast Nassau Psychiatric Hospital, Kings Park, New York   1971-75
Psychiatrist II and III

United States Army Medical Corps (Rep. of Vietnam)   1967-71
Division Psychiatrist

SELECTED MEDICAL ARTICLES / REPORTS

Brain Chemistry, C&EN Magazine, p.79-93, June, 1999
Diet and Brain Function, Nutrition Reviews/Supplement, p.12-15, May, 1996
Management of Adverse Events, a 21-Page Booklet, Sandoz Pharm. Corp., 1995

PROFESSIONAL AFFILIATIONS

American Medical Association
American Psychiatric Association
Association of Pharmaceutical Research Physicians
State Medical Societies - NJ, NM, NY, SC, VT
Chicago Medical School Alumni Association
Far Eastern Study Group of Archeological Association of Long Island NY (Past President)
Stony Brook Museum (Curator of Oriental Art)
Metropolitan Museum of Art (Consultant - Oriental Art)
Drew University, NJ (Curator of Ancient Art)
Archeological Institute of America (Lecturer)
Gemological Institute of America (Certified Gemologist)

References and Supporting Documentation Furnished upon Request

Ariel S. Figuroa

email@email.com
212 · 555 · 5555

10 West 25th Street, Apt. B • New York, NY 10001

Event Planning • Public Relations • Media

High-energy, background in fast-paced corporate event planning, promotion, and media relations / production. Possess outstanding cross-industry skills, superior presentation abilities, a passion for excellence, and a contagious enthusiasm. Tenacious and resourceful; will work any hours necessary and will always find a way to get project done on-time / on-budget.

Summary of Qualifications

- Blend creative and administrative abilities to coordinate unique corporate affairs, and media meeting planning for Dun & Bradstreet, Canadian Imperial Bank (CIB), and Jump-Start Productions.
- Manage budgets; select event venues; handle bookings, travel planning, entertainment, and gift selection. Team with design groups to create event ads and collateral materials.
- Function as associate producer on commercials and as media marketer for Jump-Start Productions, a television/cable commercial production firm. Maintain excellent rapport with producers, clients, and high-profile talent.
- Highly experienced in PC word processing, database / spreadsheet design, and presentation development. Familiar with Mac programs.

Career Highlights

- Helped plan and deliver Dun & Bradstreet's largest and most luxurious special event, a $1 million golf/spa outing at Pebble Beach, CA, that was attended by nearly three hundred top clients, executives, and their guests.
- Coordinated cocktail receptions, luncheons, company tours, and interviewing rounds for D&B's recruiting events. Created sophisticated spreadsheets to organize hundreds of participants into six $100 thousand events.
- Planned high-profile golf and entertainment excursions and closing dinners for CIIB. Coordinated cocktails, dinner menus and locations, transportation, executive suite at Madonna concert, and other entertainment. Purchased amenity gifts, inspected sites and paid invoices.

Professional Development

PUBLIC RELATIONS AND EVENTS COORDINATOR Dun & Bradstreet, New York, NY	1996 to present
MEDIA MARKETING REPRESENTATIVE (freelance) Jump-Start Productions, Inc., New York, NY	1994 to present
SPECIAL EVENTS COORDINATOR / PROJECT ASSISTANT Canadian Imperial Bank, New York, NY	1991 to 1995

Education

Bachelor of Arts in Communications, Queens College, Flushing, NY, 1990

Areas of Expertise

corporate representation

PR strategies

press releases

presentations

conflict mediation

investor relations

consumer relations

event coordination

budget development

travel planning

meeting planning

venue selection

cocktail receptions

luncheons / dinners

entertainment selection

golf outings

theme design

invitations

corporate gift selection

collateral materials

vendor payment

MARGARET P. LEADER, CPM

8745 St. Michael's Way, Baltimore, Maryland 43121
Email: MPLeader@hotmail.com
Home: (410)555-0216

CAREER PROFILE:

- Procurement & Supply Chain Management
- Materials Management & Inventory Control
- Supplier Sourcing & Analysis
- Contract Negotiations & Administration

- Continuous Process Improvement
- Cost Reduction & Containment
- Supplier Relationship Management
- Staff Development & Leadership

Expert planning, organizational, leadership and negotiation skills demonstrated through management of over $150 million in domestic and international contracts throughout career. Innovative in identifying and implementing immediate changes in procurement policies, systems and methodologies to improve performance, capture opportunities, and facilitate positive and profitable change. Excellent communicator and tenacious negotiator with a strong record of reducing costs and enhancing quality of operations. PC proficient with Word, WordPerfect, Excel, Quattro, Internet and Performance Now.

PROFESSIONAL EXPERIENCE:

BUTTE PERFORMANCE MACHINING, INC., Baltimore, Maryland   1984 to Present
(Acquired by Advanced Manufacturing Technologies in January 1998)

Purchasing Manager

Promoted through several increasingly responsible purchasing assignments during a period of rapid growth and market expansion of this $80 million manufacturer with 500 employees. Challenged to link purchasing to corporate vision based on delivering the highest quality product at the lowest cost with the fastest delivery through cost containment, continuous process improvement, technology innovation, supplier relations and team leadership.

Direct the entire purchasing organization accountable for purchases in excess of $40 million annually. Scope of responsibility is expansive and includes procurement of thousands of products from 150+ domestic and international suppliers. Personally manage large dollar purchasing negotiations and major supplier relationships. Recruited, trained and currently direct an eight-person purchasing/administrative staff.

Key Projects & Highlights:

- Played a key role building Butte's purchasing department from start-up to its current $40 million in annual volume. Positioned the purchasing function as a strategic business partner with core operations delivering profit contributions up to 6% annually.

- Achieved strong and sustainable profit improvements through aggressive control of annual purchasing costs. Implemented economic ordering quantity methodologies and JIT purchasing systems. Reduced cycle time on 40% of purchase volume from two weeks to one/two days.

- Spearheaded automation of the entire purchasing function. Worked with IS to create operating infrastructure, automatic supplier stocking programs and corporate-wide procurement card initiative. Significantly improved operating efficiencies, streamlined processes and improved availability/accuracy of key purchasing information.

Temporary Address:
555 East Suffolk Avenue
Brentwood, NY 11111
631-555-5543

DEREK RANDOLF

Permanent Address:
555 Wheeler Road
Juno Beach, FL 33408
561-555-9076

Position of Interest:

Quality Assurance / Quality Control Inspector — Pharmaceutical / Medical Supply

Profile of Qualifications:

➤ **18 years of experience** working in progressively responsible positions for a major stocking **distribution** center.

➤ Ensure **Quality Assurance/Control** standards in broad areas of **product inspection** and **logistical operations.**

➤ **Extensively cross-trained** in **warehousing, shipping, receiving**, and **inventory control** procedures.

➤ Depended upon to provide **supervision, training,** and **coverage** to ensure department-wide efficiencies.

PROFESSIONAL EXPERIENCE

Quality Control Inspector / Assistant Warehouse Manager, Hauppauge, NY   1985 – Present
Hughes Aerospace Parts Corporation   — *annual revenues $42,000,000*

In addition to primary role, hold concurrent responsibility for assuming cross-trained positions as needed within Inventory Control, Shipping, Receiving, Scheduling, Packing, and Return Departments.

• Manage **Quality Control and Inspection** procedures for an **inventory of over 80,000** fasteners and rivets.

• Comanage **shipping and receiving operations** in areas of picking, packing, and inspection of orders with an emphasis on part/lot numbers, quantities, dates, certifications, special labeling, and packaging.

• Ensure the fulfillment of **end-user** and **government contract specifications** in collaboration with Shipping, Receiving, and Inspection technicians within a 50,000-square-foot, state-of-the-art stocking distribution center.

• Assign bar codes ("license plates") to incoming/outgoing shipments for efficient storage and internal tracking.

• Coordinate the daily movement of inventory through **UPS, FedEx, Airborne and Emery** online and manual tracking systems, exercising a knowledge standard/bulk shipping documentation and reporting procedures.

• **Conduct "show and tell" tours** for established and potential customers to demonstrate warehouse and distribution operations that exceed the industry's strictest **material handling and storage** guidelines.

• As a **Security Response Team** member, **remain on call 24/7** to investigate unforeseen facility emergencies.

• Recognized as an in-house **Dymax** system expert, placed in charge of **training others** several times a year on **system operations** and **bar code scanning** procedures.

TECHNICAL PROFICIENCIES

➤ **Technical / Mechanical:** blueprint interpretation, calipers, micrometer, optical comparator, and cage blocks.

➤ **OSHA Certified Forklift Operator:** trained and experienced in the safe loading/unloading of heavy inventory.

➤ **Scanning Technology:** expertly perform multiple functions of a Dymax inventory tracking/bar coding system.

EDUCATION

Associate in Science, Business Administration, 1999

Suffolk County Community College, Selden, NY

JANICE WASHINGTON

• JaniceWashington@abc.com •
• 3596 First Street • Novi, Michigan 48374 • Home: 248-555-1645 •

ASQ CERTIFIED QUALITY ENGINEER
• QUALITY ENGINEERING • NEW PRODUCT DEVELOPMENT • SUPPLIER QUALITY •
• QUALITY SYSTEM AUDITS • PPAP • CUSTOMER LIAISON • FMEA •

Creative and versatile results-oriented quality engineer with more than 15 years' successful track record scrutinizing multiple systems and products within multiple environments. Significant capability to manage all phases of product development, from analysis and requirements definition to scheduling and projects management through final implementation and support. Adaptable and innovative, with ability to balance multiple priorities, manage change, and effectively deal with the most challenging situations. Proficient in Microsoft Office and CATIA (design software for Honda & many other automobile manufacturers). **Member of ASQ – American Society for Quality.**

AREAS OF EXPERTISE

• Digitization • Control Plans • Customer Liaison • Reverse Engineering • New Product Development	• Problem-Solving Methodology • Corrective Action Methodology • Problem Identification/Resolution • Failure Mode Effects Analysis (FMEA) • Production Part Approval Process (PPAP)	• Presentations • Laser Scanning • Precision Measurement • Nondestructive Testing • Computer-Aided Inspection

CAREER CHRONICLE

TIGER INDUSTRIES – Detroit, Michigan   February 2002 to Present
Manufacturer of injection molded plastics primarily to automotive industry; tier-1 direct supplier to automobile manufacturer and tier-2 supplier to supplier of automobile manufacturer. Primary customers including Honda, Isuzu, and Mazda. Number of employees approximately 200. **www.tiger.com**

Quality Engineer
Ultimately accountable for entire scope of internal/external product line quality control serving as customer liaison providing corrective action, manufacturing instructions, problem solving, and continuous improvement; simultaneously responsible for generating reports detailing plant-wide quality system effectiveness via data accumulation and analysis of internal/external sources. Appointed as member of multiple troubleshooting/problem-solving teams responsible for development and implementation of quality and delivery improvements plant-wide. Travel frequently to client operations during preproduction trials to monitor parts performance on completed assembly; as needed implement modifications/enhancements to company/manufacturing process as requests. Position agenda breakdown includes:

- **New Product Team:** Quality representative on new product team responsible for quality related new product activities.
- **Production Part Approval Process (PPAP):** Responsible for all aspects of Production Part Approval Process for new model automotive components & assemblies.
- **Customer Liaison:** Represent quality group to several OEM and tier 1 Automotive Suppliers.
- **Corrective Action/Problem Solving:** Coordinate cross-functional corrective action and problem solving activities; accountable for ensuring timely implementation of corrective action plans into manufacturing process.
- **Continuous Improvement:** Develop and maintain system of tracking key indices relative to product quality for purpose of prioritization and elimination of quality problems.
- **Failure Mode Effects Analysis (FMEA):** Leader of cross-functional FMEA team tasked with development of FMEA plans for new products.
- **Control Plans:** Creation and maintenance of control plans detailing quality control activities and their relationship with the injection molding process.
- **Manufacturing Instructions:** Responsible for creating & implementing step-by-step instructions explaining process parameters & requirements for given product.

Janice Washington   Resume Page 2

Key Accomplishments:

- **Amid complete reform of manufacturing operations satisfied strategic move by management to replace multiple hourly quality department associates with 3 technically advanced associates;** strategy involved reducing staff by 80%, from 30 associates to 4, focused on saving labor dollars.

- **Played pivotal role in support of 2003 Honda Element, successfully transitioning 47 parts from development to mass production over 3-month time span.**

HARMON RESEARCH & DEVELOPMENT – Croy, Ohio   August 1996 to November 2001
Key player in development of Honda automobiles and motorcycles produced exclusively for domestic and export markets; state-of-the-art facility emphasizes product engineering, prototype development, and testing. www.harmonresearch.com

Quality Engineer
Served within *Prototype Parts Quality Group* accountable for quality certification of prototype parts to be placed in new model vehicles. Front line operative accountable for performing "source inspections" on prototype automotive components and systems. Responsible for indirect supervision of 2 contract inspectors. Position agenda breakdown includes:

- **Supplier Quality:** Acted as liaison between supplier and customer, addressing quality-related issues, including disposition of defective parts & components, supplier quality systems audits, parts inspection, source inspection, and review, approval and implementation of corrective action.

- **Quality Engineering:** Reviewed all facets of prototype parts for quality identification, facilitation, disposition, and troubleshooting of defective parts & component issues with results and resolutions being directly reported to management staff of various related departments.

- **Precision Measurement:** Facilitated pre- and posttesting as well as impact analyzing of dimensional verifications and testing of automotive body, chassis and engine components. Fluent with basic metrology tools, FARO ARM and SHEFFIELD coordinate measuring machines.

- **Reverse Engineering/Computer-Aided Inspection:** Digitized automotive components using KREON laser scanning equipment, then using IMAGEWARE software to interpret scan data results.

Key Accomplishments:

- **Designed and implemented articulate communication system** consolidating defective part information and subsequent disposition actions within relative departments, including design, manufacturing, testing, procurement, and supplier. End results increased efficiency and accuracy of commerce and intercommunication. Created and introduced multi-department education program intended to construe combined activities, goals, and expectations.

- **Led multiple revision efforts of supplier quality assurance manual** necessitated by continuous improvement goals and constantly changing scope of responsibilities within *Prototype Parts Quality Group.* Produced presentations made to 100 suppliers in separate roundtable discussions numbering between 5 and 8 participants.

- **Partook in the creation and introduction of Supplier Quality Systems audit program** addressing 150 separate suppliers resulting in insight and modification of internal systems, product quality, and system controls.

EDUCATION • PROFESSIONAL TRAINING

CERTIFIED QUALITY ENGINEER CERTIFICATION, June 2002

TERRA TECHNICAL COLLEGE, Fremont, Ohio
Associate Degree - Technical Studies

ANITA MOREAU

3426 Island Drive • Billings, Washington 55234 • (888) 555-1212

REAL-ESTATE SALES PROFESSIONAL
Residential / On-Site Developer Sales
Outstanding Presentation and Closing Skills

A dynamic, enthusiastic, and highly motivated individual with six+ years' professional sales experience in landscape/real-estate-related environments. A resourceful, solution-focused individual combining solid sales and management skills with landscape background—pursuing a career in real estate sales.

AREAS OF STRENGTH

Prospect development; lead generation
Financing skills—contract administration
Communications skills—verbal/written
Knowledge of Washington laws/regulations

Networking; building strategic alliances
Creative problem solving
Organization and time management
Landlord experience—asset management

PROFESSIONAL EXPERIENCE

ADMIRALS COVE, Jupiter, Washington   1997–Present
Real-Estate Sales
Generate leads and develop book of clients. Assist customers buy/sell homes/property. Market and sell homes in the $125,000–$600,000 range—concentrating on Martin, Granger, and Madison Counties.

- Average a closing every two weeks—with the average home selling for $189,000, or $4.9 million in property/year.
- Member of Million-Dollar Club, President's Club, and Silver Achiever's Club.

GAZEBO LANDSCAPE, INC., Holden, Washington   1992–1997
Sales
Sold landscape design and materials to existing client base. Managed six commercial sites in addition to individual home accounts, supervising two crews consisting of eight people.

- Average commercial contract represents $80,000 in annual revenues. Managed key developments, including Broken Sound and the Office Depot Headquarters in Delray Beach.

RUPPERT LANDSCAPE, INC., Ashton, Washington   1987–1992
Sales
Sold landscape design, materials, and maintenance to commercial and residential clients. Heavy prospecting and cold canvassing—qualifying and closing new prospects.

- Promoted to Manager in 1993 for $50 million commercial landscaper with more than 600 employees. Managed two crews consisting of ten people. Responsible for 13 properties, including Westinghouse and the University of Maryland (Baltimore). Managed annual contracts in the $80,000–$150,000 range.

EDUCATION/LICENSES/CERTIFICATIONS

Bachelor of Arts: Real Estate, 1986
Associate of Science: Turf Management, 1990
Real Estate—Sales Course I

Gordon College
State University of Washington
Gold Coast Real Estate School

- Washington Real Estate License
- Certified Horticulturist
- Computer-Literate

References Furnished upon Request

Barbara Lawrence
147 Middlewood Road
East Brunswick, New Jersey 08816
(908) 555-4113
email @ email.com

Profile	Fifteen years of professional experience in personnel and recruiting for both retainer firms and contingency agencies...background includes applications in operations, business development, and human resources...possess strong organizational and interpersonal skills.
Summary	Broad-based responsibilities in the following areas:

- Recruitment
- Research Analysis
- Screening and Interviewing
- Candidate Development

- Job Development
- Consultative Sales
- Employer Liaison Functions
- Search Plan Development

Experience

- Developed candidates for executive-level positions in the health care industry.
- Worked on Director-Level searches for Marketing and Sales, Business Development, Strategic Planning, Environmental Affairs, and Formulations.
- Wrote search plans for clients, detailing information.
- Extensive experience in recruiting of professionals for engineering and manufacturing environments.
- Create advertising campaigns and develop sources of qualified applicants through an extensive network of referrals and corporate recruiting techniques. Market candidates to fill a variety of positions.
- Perform the following functions: prescreening and collection of candidates, interviewing and reference checks, and employee orientation.
- Work closely with Presidents of companies, Hiring Managers, and Human Resources to assess technical personnel needs.
- Directly supervised a staff of five recruiters. Performed extensive training and development of professionals specializing in technical areas.
- Strong background in business development efforts, including client needs assessments, acquiring new accounts, and cultivating existing relationships.
- Conduct client presentations and negotiate contract terms. Provide ongoing support to promote future business development.
- Responsible for managing projects from start to completion. Staffed entire departments for newly formed corporations.

Employment

1995-Present	**Smith Farrell International,** Princeton, NJ *Associate*
1991-1995	**Lawrence Associates, Inc.,** Iselin, NJ *Recruiter/Manager*
1981-1991	**John Raymond Associates,** Sayreville, NJ *Recruiting Supervisor*

Education	Kean College of New Jersey Degree Program: Psychology

D'Scribe
RESUMES

112 Preston Road, Dallas, TX 75000
Metro 214-555-4000
email @ email.com

Darby Hendricks

OBJECTIVE:
EMPOWER
THE
JOB SEEKER

Professional Credentials:
CERTIFIED PROFESSIONAL
RESUME WRITER
Certified Word Processor

Professional Associations:

A member of

Highlights Of Qualifications

◊ 15 years administrative support in single staff and supervisory positions.

◊ Experienced professional employment counselor.

◊ Intuitive interviewer; employs genuine enthusiasm to discover client's full marketing potential.

◊ Committed to helping clients get the results they want.

Technical Skills

◊ Type 90 wpm.

◊ Packard Bell 486DX2.

◊ Microsoft Word, Microsoft Publisher.

Abilities

◊ Style traditional and nontraditional formats including scannable and theatrical resumes.

◊ Enhance documents with graphics; craft presentations, including brochure layouts.

Professional Experience

Resumes

◊ Design successful resumes—for individuals with diverse career situations—that capture employer interest, generate interviews, increase job offers.

◊ Create impressive cover letters and thank-you letters that promote client throughout hiring process.

Additional Writing & Editing

◊ Originated sales reports, performance reports, and correspondence in the capacity of regional office manager, division office secretary, and executive secretary.

◊ Authored detailed training manual for executive secretaries that became the company standard.

◊ Edited, typeset, and proofed manuscripts and book proposals.

Graphic Design & Layout

◊ Develop information and promotional materials for D'Scribe Resumes that prompt compliments and appreciative comments from printers and clients.

◊ Designed fliers, brochures, door signs, and other promotional materials for Made By Hand craft store chain; endorsed by company vice president.

◊ Created property listing fliers for Spradley Real Estate; endorsed by owner.

KENT CALUKO
915 Lecara Lane
Atlanta, GA 47632
(404) 555-0085
email @ email.com

UPSCALE RETAIL SALES

OVERVIEW: Over nine years working for and managing fashionable boutiques and retail establishments on Atlanta's prestigious *Galt Avenue*. Recognized for delivering unexcelled customer service. A *verifiable* track record of success backed by impeccable references. Areas of expertise include:

- Sales - Exceptional Customer Service
- Merchandising & Display
- Employee Management
- New Location Start-Up Management
- Tri-Lingual (English/Swedish/Finnish)

- New Product Introduction
- Budgeting/Record Keeping
- Problem Solving
- Inventory & Pricing Controls
- Computer/POS Scanning Use

EMPLOYMENT: Max Mara, USA Inc. on Galt, Atlanta, GA
SALES ASSOCIATE

The Village Shop on Galt Avenue, Atlanta, GA
STORE MANAGER / SALES

Gucci on Galt Avenue, Atlanta, GA
STORE MANAGER / SALES

Frances Brewster, Atlanta, GA
SALES ASSOCIATE

The Ritz Carlton Hotel, Atlanta, GA
BOUTIQUE MANAGER

EDUCATION: Kuopion Teknillinen Opisto, Kuopio, Finland
Equivalency: Bachelor of Science in Land Planning & Surveying
- Drafting
- Land Surveying
- Blueprint Development

PERSONAL: Enjoy & Active in:
- Studying Italian
- The Arts & Theater
- Classical Music, Opera
- Ice Skating
- Exercise

- References & Supporting Documentation Furnished upon Request -

Michael Torocco
52 Gerard Street ▪ Bellport, NY 11713 ▪ (516) 555-0074 ▪ email @ email.com

---

Consultative High-End Retail Sales Professional

Career Profile	**Highly experienced retail professional with extensive thirty year background in upscale home furnishings sales, business management, buying, and advertising.**

Areas of Expertise	▪ Upholstery ▪ Broadloom ▪ Computer Use ▪ Bedding ▪ Consumer Education ▪ Advertising ▪ Case Goods ▪ Sales Training ▪ Buying ▪ Leather ▪ Customer Service ▪ Management

Summary of Qualifications	**Over thirty years' experience in furniture and bedding** as business owner, store manager, and furniture consultant. Impressive ten-year track record with furniture department of premier retailer. **Demonstrated track record of increasing revenues** in declining markets. Contributed to high growth rate in sales and productivity of retail activities with personal leadership ability, analytical skills, and sales experience. **Extremely knowledgeable in all areas of furniture, bedding and broadloom** design and construction as well as current trends and traditional styles. **Consistently requested by customers;** have developed loyal customer base and referral network. **Train new hires in all systems and procedures, furniture and bedding knowledge and sales techniques.** Often called upon to answer technical questions of fellow sales associates.

Employment History	**Furniture Sales Consultant** Bloomingdale's, Garden City, NY	1985 to 2003
	Sales and Advertising Sunrise Sleep Shops, Lynbrook, NY	1983 to 1985
	Store Manager Sleepy's Bedding Centers, Syosset, NY	1980 to 1983
	Store Manager Suburban Colonial Shops, Jericho, NY	1978 to 1980
	Operator of Family Business Michael R. Torocco Furniture Co., Bayside, NY	1970 to 1978
Education	**Bachelor of Science Degree in Marketing** St. John's University, School of Business Administration, Jamaica, NY	

ANNA ROWLANDS

HIGH-TECHNOLOGY SALES, MARKETING & NEW BUSINESS DEVELOPMENT

1632 112th Avenue SE, #A203, Bellevue, WA 98005
(206) 555-7150
email @ email.com

SUMMARY

Aggressive, enthusiastic sales professional with proven talent for making new contacts, closing orders, and generating repeat business through effective account management. Leading-edge presentation skills. Experience managing unique marketing initiatives and programs. Mainframe and PC computer skills. B.A. degree.

1995 SALES ACCOMPLISHMENTS

♦ **Generated over $1 million in revenues** by landing key account with a major catalogue distributor, convincing them to switch their air shipping service away from our major competitor.

♦ **Increased average monthly sales volume by 32%** in less than 12 months by continuously strengthening relationships and building value with customers.

♦ Played key role in team multimedia presentation to top Boeing executives; created data show and assisted in delivery of a presentation that resulted in a new multiyear shipping contract worth over $3 million.

KEY SKILLS & AREAS OF EXPERIENCE

♦ **ACCOUNT MANAGEMENT:** Currently manage over 30 senior accounts in the Puget Sound region; consistently exceed revenue goals by actively prospecting for new customers, effectively prioritizing leads, and working with existing accounts to expand business and obtain valuable referrals.

♦ **RELATIONSHIP BUILDING:** Selected to manage the UPS Associations Program, a unique marketing effort designed to sell shipping services through trade and professional associations. Closed $50,000 in new business in the first eight months, signing up five associations when none had been signed in over a year.

♦ **PRESENTATIONS:** Extensive experience designing customized proposals and sales presentations; skilled at listening to client needs and concerns, developing effective solutions, and persuading customers to take action; preference for presenting directly to senior executives and key decision makers.

♦ **TECHNICAL:** Excellent computer skills; strong experience using mainframe (AS/400) and PC-based systems, combined with working knowledge of multiple business software packages. Experience interacting with Logistics Services, Industrial Engineering, and Information Systems departments to clarify account needs, obtain resource commitments, and develop value-added solutions.

♦ **MARKET RESEARCH:** Familiar with modern data collection and statistical analysis techniques; compiled extensive research on shipping companies for inclusion in UPS 1993 Washington District Business Plan.

CAREER EXPERIENCE WITH UNITED PARCEL SERVICE (UPS)—1992–present

Within four years at UPS, demonstrated the skills and sales finesse necessary to move from internship to senior sales position for the Pacific Northwest region. Currently serve as **Senior Account Executive** (1994-Present); past positions include **Account Executive** (1993-1994), **Internship Coordinator** (1993), and **Marketing Intern** (1992).

EDUCATION

B.A. in Communications, University of Washington, 1992.
Currently pursuing M.B.A. degree (marketing emphasis) through Seattle University.
Completion of numerous professional sales, marketing, and technical training courses.

CHRIS HEINZ

78 Lafayette Street	Home: (814) 555-6543
Erie, PA 16508	Office: (814) 555-2109
Email: emailaddress@email.com	Cell: (814) 555-0327

SALES / SALES MANAGEMENT EXECUTIVE
CUTTING-EDGE COMPUTER & INTERNET TECHNOLOGIES

Key Account Management ♦ New Business Development ♦ Direct Sales & Reseller Partnerships
Consultative & Solution Sales ♦ Networking & Relationship Building ♦ Contract Negotiations

PROFILE

Dynamic 14-year sales career reflecting pioneering experience and record-breaking performance in the computer and Internet industries. Remain on the cutting edge, driving new business through key accounts and establishing strategic partnerships and dealer relationships to increase channel revenue.

♦ Expert in sophisticated e-commerce sales models and vast knowledge of both the e-business marketplace and the capabilities and complexities of products.

♦ Outstanding success in building and maintaining relationships with key corporate decision makers, establishing large-volume, high-profit accounts with excellent levels of retention, and loyalty.

♦ Exceptionally well organized with a track record that demonstrates self-motivation, creativity, and initiative to achieve both personal and corporate goals

"David is a dynamic leader and arguably one of the best salespeople that has ever worked on any of the sales teams I have managed. I highly recommend David for a position within any organization."

— *VP of Sales, Millennium Software*

PROFESSIONAL EXPERIENCE

1998 - Present **Web Communications, Philadelphia, PA**

DISTRICT SALES MANAGER

Execute direct and channel partner sales models for advanced e-commerce software applications. Target a broad market, meeting sophisticated e-business needs for customers that include Fortune 500s and emerging dot-coms. Interface directly with top-level executives, negotiate high-dollar contracts, and coordinate implementation. Manage accounts and orchestrate post-sale professional services and resources.

Key Achievements:

♦ Achieved 186% of quota and qualified for "President's Club." Grew sales to $4 million within 6 months and positioned as the top #2 rep in the company.

♦ Established alliances with 10 major integration partners and attained ranking as the top #1 sales producer within just one year, generating $7.6 million annually.

♦ Delivered $2.8 million revenue, selling 2 of the first 5 units in North America of a newly released, cutting-edge e-commerce business solution.

♦ Opened a completely unworked territory, surpassing all sales goals in spite of challenges associated with the sale of a v.1 release product with no reference sites.

♦ Generated the highest volume of new accounts companywide and was recognized with a "President's Achievement Award," the company's most prestigious honor.

(Continued)

CHRIS HEINZ Page 2

1994 - 1998   **Millennium Software, Boston, MA**

AREA SALES MANAGER (1995 - 1998)
SENIOR ACCOUNT EXECUTIVE (1994 - 1995)

Built a territory spanning Maine to Pennsylvania for this $5 billion provider of Web development tools, Web-based applications, and consulting services. Rapidly achieved goals and refocused to resolve challenging sales and personnel issues. Led a 10-person team generating $15 million annually through sales of middleware and application-server solutions in enterprise software space.

Key Achievements:

♦ Transformed an underproducing sales team, immediately resolving long-standing problems and instituting incentives that elevated performance while building morale and motivation. Ramped area sales 550%+ in under 3 years.

♦ Surpassed personal quota, generating more than 200% of license sales goals and 175% of service sales goals. Overachieved area sales objectives every eligible year.

♦ Identified, pursued, and closed the largest license deal in company history, contributing millions of dollars through annually recurring revenue.

♦ Penetrated dozens of profitable B2B accounts, individually valued at up to $2.5 million, with major Fortune 500 customers.

♦ Championed creative marketing initiatives, including seminar series with partners, sponsorship of national Java user groups, and speaking engagements in Internet and e-commerce space.

1991 - 1994   **Multimedia, Inc., Saddlebrook, NJ**

EAST COAST TERRITORY MANAGER

Sold and marketed multimedia, computer-based training, graphics and 3-D design, photo-imaging, sound editing, and Web page development tools to key Fortune 500 and 1000 accounts. Supervised the sales force in all East Coast trade shows and industry events. Drove sales of more than $8 million annually through consumer distribution channels; delivered an average 145% of channel quota.

1986 - 1991   Early career includes inside/outside sales experience with two large computer resellers targeting both consumer and business markets.

EDUCATION & TRAINING

B.S., Business Administration (1986)
University of California, Los Angeles

Extensive professional training in the areas of sales, relationship building, and leadership. Certified for IBM, Apple, and Compaq sales. Completed Novell Network sales training.

TECHNICAL SKILLS

Skilled with MAC OS, Windows 3.11, 95, 98, NT, and NT Server, MS Office (Word, PowerPoint, Excel, Access, Project, and Outlook), Director, FreeHand, Authorware, Soundedit 16, Extreme 3D, Backstage Desktop Studio, CC:Mail, Lotus Notes, Novell GroupWise, ACT, MS FrontPage, and Vivo Active Producer. Advanced Internet skills.

William H. Perrineau
123 Any Ave * Mytown, USA 00000
H 123 456 7890   W 123 456 7890

Summary of Qualifications

* Public Speaking/ Presentation Skills
* Technical Writing
* In-Depth Technical Knowledge of Data Networking, including Frame Relay,
  Managed Network Services,TCP/IP (Dial and Dedicated),Security,ATM,
  Network Design and Implementation,Router Configuration and Emerging
  Technologies

Professional History

Sprint Corporation, Greensboro, NC
September 1999 to Present
Sprint ION Business Development Manager
National Accounts overlay sales manager for Southeast Region. Responsible for
leading Sprint sales in the southeast national accounts region.

Sprint Corporation, Greensboro, NC
March 1998 to Present
Area Consulting Engineer
Area Support for Eastern United States. Reported directly to Director of
Application Engineering. Drove product development issues and disseminated
information to field presales support groups. Delivered presentations to
internal and external customers at all levels. Worked on Sprint ION product
and process development. Responsible for leading Regional ION Support Teams in
the sales cycle for Sprint ION opportunities, including account planning,
network design, customer presentation, and contract negotiation. Contributed in
the development of marketing and pricing strategy for Sprint ION.

Sprint Corporation, Greensboro, NC
1995 to 1998
Regional Consulting Engineer
Senior engineering position provided expert-level consulting, design and sales
support for data networking and emerging technology opportunities. Responsible
for ensuring success of all strategic sales opportunities involving data.
Heavily involved in qualification, positioning, contract negotiation, and
closing throughout the sales cycle. Worked directly with sales management team
during account planning and strategic opportunity review. RCE team leader:
worked closely with management on key initiatives, including product
development and rollout. Supervised Network Engineers in North Carolina.
Responsibilities also included mentoring the sales support field engineers;
developed technical training curriculum and instructed specific courses such
as IP Services, Security Services, and Frame Relay.

Sprint Corporation, Greensboro, NC
1990 to 1995
Network Engineer
Responsibilities included presales engineering of data opportunities.
Completed verbal and written responses to Request for Proposals on all levels,
including executive briefings, technical overviews, solution presentation, and

(Continued)

340

detailed engineering briefings. Performed cost analysis on different network designs in order to provide complete and detailed responses to proposals. Prepared order packages and tracked orders through provisioning process to implementation. Worked with customer to ensure satisfaction of products and services "post-sell." Ongoing life-cycle support of data accounts for growth, redesign, and change management.

Sprint Corporation, Washington, DC
1989 to 1990
Test and Acceptance Engineer
Responsibilities included the supervision of all activity on Sprint's northeast U.S. fiber network related to the actual splicing and testing of the backbone cable. Coordinated work activity with Sprint internal groups, construction contractors, and Sprint field technicians on an as needed basis to complete backbone cable maintenance and repair. Developed career pathing and assisted with merit reviews for Sprint field technicians. Developed annual budgets for backbone cable maintenance and repair.

American Spliceco Inc., Columbia, MD
1985 to 1989
Operations Manager
Responsibilities included personnel acquisition, development and motivation, profit/loss for splicing/testing division, including generation of bid responses and quotes for additional work, capital expenses and operating budget, coordination of work schedule to meet deadlines.

Education
East Carolina University, Greenville, NC, 1984
BS Industrial Technology/ Manufacturing and Management

SIMON DRAX

23541 Old Towne Lane
Westin, Ontario L5P 8B3

Phone: (905) 555 -3321
Email: drax4@aol.com

SENIOR SALES & MARKETING EXECUTIVE
Start-Up & Emerging Technology Ventures

Top-Producing Management Executive with more than 15 years experience in the development, commercialization and market launch of leading-edge technologies worldwide. Combined expertise in strategic planning, P&L management, marketing, tactical sales and client relationship management. Outstanding record of achievement in solutions selling and complex contract negotiations. Diverse industry and multichannel sales experience within the financial services, banking, healthcare, retail and Fortune 500 market sectors.

PROFESSIONAL EXPERIENCE:

Vice President of International Sales   1993 to Present
INTEGRATED SYSTEMS WORLDWIDE (ISW), Toronto, Ontario

Technology: E-commerce & OLTP Applications Delivered on Client/Server, UNIX-Based Open Systems

Recruited as Management Consultant to this venture-funded start-up seeking to launch newly-acquired technology from major U.S. manufacturer. Created corporate vision, strategies and tactical action plans to design/launch a complete platform of network and systems management tools to drive the industry toward integrated enterprise-wide/open system solutions. Identified potential markets, led road show presentations and built the organization from concept into full-scale operation.

Accepted permanent position as the Senior Sales & Marketing Executive challenged to build a global sales organization, expand product offerings and capture emerging technology opportunities throughout the healthcare and financial services industries. Hold full P&L responsibility for strategic planning, new business development, technology development and licensing, and technical service/support. Travel throughout North America, Latin America, Europe, Pacific Rim and South Africa.

- Built ISW's entire network of direct sales and multichannel distributors producing $23 million in annual revenues.

- Delivered annual growth averaging 100% in a highly competitive global market. Played key role in a successful IPO in 1993.

- Championed the development and spearheaded the market launch of several new technologies with cumulative revenues of $2 million annually.

- Guided sales team through several complex contract negotiations and closings. Personally closed $10 million contract in Argentina, $3+ million contract in New Zealand and $4 million contract in France.

Director of Sales   1991 to 1993
TECHNOLOGY SOLUTIONS, INC., Cherry Hill, New Jersey

Technology: HP Systems & Customized Applications Distribution & Service

Member of an eight-person senior management team challenged to launch the start-up of a full-scale distribution, maintenance and service operation as part of joint venture between Hewlett Packard and Techx3. Authored strategic and tactical marketing plans to expand market presence and accelerate revenue growth. Established operating infrastructure, led product development, and recruited/led six-person sales team.

- Played a key role in the company's growth from start-up to $14 million in revenues within two years. Personally generated 50% of total company revenues.

- Spearheaded development and market launch of six new product lines that contributed to $4 million new revenue stream.

- Negotiated a highly profitable corporate licensing agreement with the Bank of New York.

GRACE MATHERLY

578 Frisco Road ◊ Plano, TX 45237 ◊ H)(214) 555-0254 C (214) 555-3604

Summary

- 10 years experience in professional sales within Fortune 500 arena
- Specialty in high-tech industries, including computer software, telecommunications and consumer electronics
- Specialty within sales is "hunting" – new sales acquisition and relationship development
- Excellent presentation skills, good rapport builder with sales support (internal) and generally self-sufficient

Key Accomplishments

- 2002-2003: Took new sales region with $0 in customer base and in 2 years grew that to over $7MM
- Acquired 2 new "logo" Fortune 100 companies in 2003. Developed the account relationship where no previous existed; designed customized solution for client and closed order within 14 months
- President's Club winner in 2003, 1999 and 1997
- Consistently ranked in top 10% of all sales professionals
- Top salesperson in 1997

Professional Experience

AT&T, Denver, Colorado   2001 to Present
Global Account Manager, Mountain Region
- Target Fortune 250 companies in Rocky Mountain region that have no current use with AT&T. Developing customized voice and data solutions for all verticals.
- Won business with third largest corporation in Colorado, representing $4MM in revenue annually for AT&T
- Grew total revenue base of five target accounts from $0 to $7MM in two years.
- President's Club winner in 2003
- Achieved some level of sales penetration in three of five global accounts within 18 months
- 187% of sales plan for 2003; $106% of sales plan in 2002

US West (now Qwest) , Denver, Colorado   1994 to 2001
Sales Representative, Denver
- Representing voice and data solutions for medium size businesses in Denver metro area
- Sales Representative of the Year in 1997
- Specialty was hunting – developing new business where there was previously none.
- Achieved following sales performance:
  o 2000: 163% of sales plan
  o 1999: 112% of sales plan
  o 1998: 210% of sales plan
  o 1997: 230% of sales plan

Education

Southern Methodist University, Dallas, Texas Bachelor of Arts, Marketing, 1992

Patti Coury

555 North 555 Place • Tulsa, Oklahoma 74155 • Residence: 918-555-5555 • Cell: 913-555-5551 • E-mail: pcoury@email.net

Executive Sales

President's Club winning sales professional with 15 years sales experience. Specialty is developing account strategy, sales execution and account management for leading uniform supply company. Verifiable sales performance record with expertise in:

- ☐ Hunting and new account acquisition
- ☐ Account planning
- ☐ Networking with referrals
- ☐ Sales account renewals

Patti is an excellent sales professional. She was aggressive, yet smooth through the sales process. She kept on us, but never turned us off. She developed a solution to meet our needs, and we ended up awarding her 80% of our total share of business for uniform service.

--- Emma Thompson, ABC Company

PROFESSIONAL EXPERIENCE

Regional Manager   ARAMARK Industries, Atlanta, Georgia   1988 to Present

Promoted though a series of increasingly more responsible customer support and sales executive positions with the leading uniform supply and management company in the U.S. Currently specialize in custom uniform and apparel design for large multinational firms in Atlanta area. Have been in direct sales since 1995 and have always been ranked in top quarter of country each year.

As a customer service and later sales executive, many challenges have been overcome. This is a vital attribute of a successful salesperson. Below are four examples of volatile situations faced and the associated resolution:

Situation	☞	Launched new market segment selling corporate signature apparel to a new and unestablished market with no base from which to grow.
Result	☞	Developed strict account plan and executed it through first year. Achieved 23% above sales objective in new market place.
Situation	☞	Increased sales objective in 1999 to reflect need for increased business in response to increased competition.
Result	☞	With sales quota increase over 35%, continued to meet challenge and exceed quota; ranked number one in sales in 1999
Situation	☞	Customer churn increased in 2001 due to increased competition.
Result	☞	Increased customer visits, proactively reviewed contracts, focused on renewals and generally showed more customer interest. Churn decreased in base from 16% in 2000 to 7% in 2001.
Situation	☞	Promoted to Regional Manager in 2002 while still responsible for revenue acquisition in abbreviated sales territory.
Result	☞	Exceeded personal sales objective while also achieving as manager: 0 employee turnover, 100% participation in sales plan and maintaining low customer churn.
Situation	☞	Employee churn and sales rep participation identified as major impediment to successful sales management.
Result	☞	Selectively hired sales reps and focused on their success through training, account management, team-building activities and employee development. Achieved 0 employee turnover and leading sales performance in SE Region.

EDUCATION   Georgia Tech University, Bachelor of Arts, History   1988

Lori Denman

123 Park Place Chicago, Illinois, 12345
312-555-1111

Senior Sales Executive

Experienced National Account Sales in Telecommunications Industry

🦋 summary

Experienced and results-oriented sales professional. Consistently reaching top 25% sales performance nationwide, with highest referral and renewal rate in company. Excellent sales and professional skills. Sales results easily verifiable.

🦋 expertise

- 🦋 Account Planning
- 🦋 Solutions-Based Selling
- 🦋 High Renewal Rate
- 🦋 High Referral Rate
- 🦋 Low Customer Churn
- 🦋 Consistent Top-Ranked Performer
- 🦋 President's Club winner
- 🦋 Business Development

- 🦋 High Technology:
  - o Voice
  - o Internet
  - o Data
  - o Frame Relay
  - o RFP Response
  - o Local Dial Tone
  - o Computer Integration

Lori has been an outstanding National Accounts Manager for over eight years. She has an excellent grasp of the product and is particularly skilled at navigating through the bureaucratic waters of selling to Fortune 250 companies. Her sales support and implementations staff find her easy and reliable to work with, and her customers find her reliable and an extension of their own operation. I would highly recommend her.

- Roberta Alexander, Director of National Accounts, ABC Telecommunications Company

🦋 professional experience

National Accounts Manager,
ABC Telecommunications Company   1990 to Present

Led the Midwest region in national account sales in 1993, 1994, 1997, 2000, and 2002. Grew revenue base by over 30% each year, even while experiencing up to 20% in write-downs some years. Developed detailed account plans and executed groundbreaking approaches to winning new accounts and growing market share.

- 🦋 President's Club winner in 1993, 1994, 1997, 2000, and 2002. .
- 🦋 Grew revenue base from $0 to over $30MM/year
- 🦋 Experienced very little customer churn, maintaining 91% of customer base from 1993 to present
- 🦋 Offered multiple management opportunities but opted to focus on direct sales strengths
- 🦋 Won national accounts such as Ford Motor Company, General Electric and Motorola.

🦋 education

Bachelor of Arts, University of Connecticut   1989

Pete Weldon

50 New England Drive, Garden Grove, New York 10576 (516) 555- 7645

NATIONAL ACCOUNTS SALES PROFESSIONAL

Verifiable track record of exceeding sales objectives and winning "logo" national accounts

2003	2002	2001	2000	1999
186 %	132%	240%	148%	155%

Strengths

- Developing strategic plans based on identifying customer functional needs
- Relationship building at the CXO level
- Working effectively internally with support staff
- Exceeding sales objectives and leading sales organization – winning President's Club!

PROFESSIONAL EXPERIENCE

National Accounts Manager, D'ITALIA, INC., New York, New York (1996 to Present)

Senior Account Manager with this $1 billion global clothing manufacturer. Challenged to plan and orchestrate an aggressive market expansion into key leading retailers nationwide. Scope of responsibility includes strategic planning, competitive assessment, market positioning, customer acquisition and retention.

- Led the successful national market launch of three product lines.
- Target Fortune 250 retail companies nationwide to distribute specialty clothing line.
- Won business with second largest retailer in Northeast, representing $4MM in revenue annually.
- Grew total revenue base of five target accounts from $0 to $7MM in two years.
- President's Club winner in 2001 and 2003.

Retail Manager, SAKINAS, INC. (1988 to 1995)

Recruited to this upscale national retail chain to manage daily operations for start-up and high-growth retail sites throughout the Midwest. Scope of responsibility was diverse and included daily operations management, recruitment, training, scheduling, inventory control, administration and the entire sales, marketing and customer service function. Led a staff of up to 65.

- Led the Chicago store to ranking as the highest-volume operation nationwide.
- Managed the start-up of Detroit store. Recruited 45 personnel, created merchandising displays and coordinated grand opening activities. Built operation to solid first year revenues.

EDUCATION

B.S., Marketing, Syracuse University, New York, 1988

DYLAN PITERA
5555 East Milford Road • Milford, Michigan 48821 • (248) 555-5555 • dp@link.net

CAREER PROFILE

- ❏ 11 years experience in telecommunications industry, both wireless for consumer and businesses and high-end voice and data products for businesses

- ❏ 8 years experience in sales and field management, 3 years in corporate marketing management

- ❏ Full go-to-market responsibility for two Sprint broadband markets and with PrimeCo (PCS) and AirTouch

- ❏ Led B2B sales at major account and national account levels within Sprint and Verizon Wireless, as well as small business sales for Sprint and AirTouch

- ❏ Experienced at sales and marketing execution for various telecommunications services, including large-scale voice and data applications, PCS, broadband Internet services and cellular

PROFESSIONAL EXPERIENCE

Sprint Communications Company   1997 to Present

Sales Performance Coach, GMG, SE Region   2002 to Present

- ❏ Integrally involved in selling to Mastec ($1.5 MM/year), Compass Bank ($8 MM/year), Ashland ($2 MM/year), Humana Healthcare ($2+ MM/year), Hilton Corporation ($4+ MM/year), Morgan Keegan ($1+ MM/year). Leading sales efforts from both strategic and tactical manner.

General Manager, Florida   2000 to 2002

- ❏ Complete launch responsibilities for two Sprint broadband services in Florida, Sprint ION in Miami and Sprint Broadband Direct in Central Florida, including hiring all staff and managing all marketing and public relations

- ❏ Led Central Florida market to 3rd highest customer penetration in 2001 out of 26 markets nationwide

- ❏ Developed sales teams to sell commercially. Direct sales channel was most productive in this Sprint division. Recruited only AE in this Sprint division to exceed quota in 2Q01 or 3Q01. Had 100% participation in plan.

- ❏ Created complete retail network in each market for distribution of Sprint products, (for both national and local retailers), as well as created POP materials, local promotions, co-op and training programs

Market Development Manager, Sprint Business, Dallas, Texas   1997 to 2000

- ❏ Led overall sales channel development for Sprint ION in Sprint Business, in Nationals, and Mid/Major accounts; assumed leadership role in Sprint's sales organization for Sprint ION sales.

- ❏ Work directly with account teams on many customer opportunities, facilitating account team needs by working with other field resources, product management and marketing. Created and managed a very tactical Sprint ION sales process, which increased Sprint ION sales by 53% from February 2000 to September 2000.

- ❏ Established a leadership role and presence within Sprint across the marketing, sales, product management, UE and NIS organizations.

Verizon Wireless, Miami MTA, Boca Raton, Florida   1995 to 1997

Market Manager, SW Florida

❑ Managed full market launch of SW Florida within Miami MTA, area of .6MM population. Areas of responsibility included staffing, developing retail channel, direct sales channel and marketing/local event support.

❑ SW Region achieved higher penetration than any other Florida region for Verizon in 1997.

❑ Created and executed market development plan for new start-up launch of new wireless service.

AirTouch Teletrac, Miami MTA, Fort Lauderdale   1992 to 1994
(wireless vehicle location service provider)

Sales Manager

❑ Managed direct sales team of eight B2B account executives. This AirTouch market exceeded quota for three straight quarters in 1993, the most successful market in the company in 1993.

❑ Directly responsible for creating and managing $2MM budget and achieving best performance to budget in company in 1992 and 1993, including start-up sales growth, gross margin, managing cost of goods and lowest accounts receivable (1993)

Window Works International Inc., Fort Lauderdale, Florida   1988 to 1992
(national franchisor of customer window treatment stores, 120 nationally)

Franchise Operations Manager

❑ Worked with region of franchisees as liaison between franchisor and franchisee, offering business improvement suggestions and extending corporate directives to the field

❑ Developed field market launch program that refined advertising strategies for start-ups. In Minneapolis this resulted in a 27% increased sales volume over other new market launch areas, with slightly below average demographics

❑ Traveled extensively to manage new franchise launches, establish networking contacts and relationships important to the franchise's success, hire and train new personnel and ensure conformity of the franchisee to the franchise agreement

EDUCATION   Bachelor of Arts, Accounting, Michigan State University   1984 to 1988

BRETT JOHNSON

19950 Roe ■ Overland Park, Kansas 66213
913-555-5555 Cell: 913-555-1234 ■ bjohnson@email.net

PROFILE

15+ year business career with excellent qualifications in general management, new business development / strategies, customer relations, project / product management, communications and Internet strategies. Successful in building profitable organizations in highly competitive consumer markets. Strengths in relationship building, with exceptional networking and partnering abilities. Experience in engineering and marketing combined with outstanding people skills contributes to product management / product strategy forte. Analytical, innovative and out-of-the-box thinker with record of securing results. Familiar working in a matrix-managed environment. Tireless, enthusiastic worker.

- **Internet / eBusiness / eCommerce**
- **Competitive Market Position**
- **Team Leadership / Consensus Building**
- **Corporate Image / Branding**
- **Corporate Vision & Strategy**
- **Profit & Loss Management**
- **Customer-Driven Management**
- **Efficiency Improvement**

CAREER HIGHLIGHTS

BUSINESS DEVELOPMENT

- Built eBusiness consulting firm (onlinecommerce.com) from start-up planning to full-scale operation with 12,000 sq. ft and 50 employees.
    - Researched venture capital funding and acquisition opportunities and ultimately negotiated start-up funds through private financial placement.
    - Successfully marketed services to marquee clients, including Greenwood Electric, Farmland Industries, Rockwell International, American Greeting, Party Warehouse and The Jones Store.
- Established key partnerships and alliances with multiple organizations to position onlinecommerce.com as the #1 eCommerce company area-wide.
    - Originated highly profitable alliance with Dell; earned Dell's eBusiness National Partner award.
    - Aligned with cybercash.com to participate in online bill payment program that was rolled out to Greenwood Electric, among others.
    - Forged alliances with MCI, Intel, Smith Gardner and various advertising agencies.
- Key Performance:
    - Grew IBM account 100-fold in 18 months (from $10,000 to $1M).
    - Hammered the competition to secure $275,000 American Greetings account.
    - Doubled onlinecommerce.com revenues year-to-year.

MARKETING

- Spearheaded creative and targeted marketing campaigns utilizing customer-centric themes and Internet-based presentations that secured new business.
- Designed attention-grabbing trade show strategies / displays capturing up to 25% of annual business.
- Enhanced corporate image through publication in media: Associated Press and the *Kansas City Star*.
- Pioneered referral merchant banner network through Java development that automatically managed renewals of online banner, reducing administrative management time by 45%.
- Generated business from food additive manufacturers through convention trade shows, brochure and proposal development at Major Research Institute.

Continued...

PROJECT MANAGEMENT

- Managed wireless Web software development projects and eCommerce / eMarketing projects through teams of 4 to 15 individuals at wireless.com.

- Learned and applied ITPF (wireless.com's private development process) and the new object-oriented RUP iterative development process.

- Lead project manager for high-profile project, an eCRM / mobile portal strategy designed to push "smart" content over the phone through the Web.

- Managed high-profile alliances and key research projects for governmental and private-sector clients at Major Research Institute.

EFFICIENCY IMPROVEMENT

- Collaborated with accounting department to engineer, pilot, and roll out full-scale $80,000 accounting system that slashed billing cycle by 28% and broadened scope of accounting functions.

- Installed intranet-based time / work tracking tool that permitted online time sheets and integrated with accounting package. Result: Saved 50% time in human resource tracking.

- Innovated ROI that connected to Dell's net.commerce package and assisted online sellers in tracking real-time sales statistics.

PROFESSIONAL SUMMARY

wireless.com, Liberty, Missour   1997 to 2003
Independent business unit within Wireless' marketing department
PROJECT MANAGER
Managed wireless Web software development and eCommerce/eMarketing projects through teams of 4 to 15 members. Scope of responsibility included interfacing with management, directing project kick-off / planning meetings, monitoring workflow and budgets. Extensive communication with service delivery and IT groups, security and marketing departments.

onlinecommerce.com, Kansas City, Missouri   1990 to 1997
eBusiness consulting company that designed and implemented online commerce sites
PRESIDENT
Founded eBusiness company that marketed primarily to the retail (eCommerce) industry. Engineered distribution channel strategy, positioning onlinecommerce.com as national partner with Dell and affiliating with organizations like American Greetings, MCI and Rockwell International, among many others.

Major Research Institute, Columbia, Missouri   1985 to 1990
Non-profit research institute with 250 employees
RESEARCH CHEMIST / PROJECT MANAGER
Twice-promoted during tenure with Major Research Institute due to creative research and solutions-building skills. Contributed to major research initiatives for governmental and private-sector clients. Deployed project plans and research strategies. Managed researcher / chemist / technician teams that conducted research, authored and presented reports. Instrumental team member that facilitated landmark alliance with Battelle Columbus Laboratories.

EDUCATION

Master of Business Administration, 1992
University of Missouri, Columbia, Missouri

Bachelor of Science in Chemistry, 1985
Southwest Missouri State University, Springfield, Missouri

THERESA MASCAGNI

17177 Northway Circle
Boston, Massachusetts 01977
Phone: (617) 555-1212 / Cell: (617) 555-3232
email@email.com

SENIOR-LEVEL OPERATIONS / MANAGEMENT EXECUTIVE
Increasing Shareholder Value in Both Publicly Traded and Private Companies

SEC Reporting & Compliance / Start-Up & Turnaround Management
Technology Integration / Business Development & Expansion
P&L Responsibility / Cash Flow Management

A market-driven Senior Executive with outstanding qualifications in directing multi-million-dollar operations in global theaters. Recognized for capitalizing on existing product potential and identifying new growth opportunities.

Core Professional Strengths

Visionary leadership/innovation management	Strategic alliance/partnership development
Production and efficiency optimization	Multiple project/location management
Customer service and retention management	Multichannel product distribution
Business development and expansion	Organizational/team leadership

Professional Experience

HEALTH CARE INTERNATIONAL, INC., Boston, Massachusetts   2000 to Current
Senior Executive

- Business adviser to the President of a NASD Company in the health care industry with annualized run-rate revenue of $220 million. Wrote comprehensive business plan to acquire new company and merge into existing division.
- Directly responsible for filings of past due Form 10 K (fiscal year 1999) and subsequent Form 10 K for the four ensuing periods (through 6/2000). Prepared initial drafts of these filings and coordinated between SEC counsel, CFO, and Board of Directors. Settled more than $250,000 of payables for $45,000 in cash payments. Successfully reorganized an unprofitable division, turning around an operation draining more than $80,000/month in cash.
- The Company was in default on a note of $200,000 that was previously renegotiated. The lender, as part of the note, had obtained a Confession of Judgment, precluding the Company from entering any defenses to the note. Successfully negotiated payment of note with Company stock, not only saving the company $200,000 in cash but transforming a debt into an equity on the Company's balance sheet.
- Spearheaded all litigation with outside counsel and negotiated a fee reduction from $10,000 to $2,000/month. Re-assigned workload of HR department saving $50,000/year while improving output. Coordinated all insurance matters, prepared leases and physician contracts and developed comprehensive analysis for in-house billing/collection efforts.
- Successfully renegotiated a $1.2 million billing contract (far in excess of normal costs) and arranged a contract buyout for $350,000 in stock - and obtained a new contract on more favorable terms.

MACKENZIE CONSULTANTS, Boston/New York
Full-Time Consultant for Multi-Office OB/GYN Practice

- Recruited to restructure and turn around an underperforming, unprofitable high-volume medical practice (six physicians) with operations throughout five South Florida counties - with revenues exceeding $3.5 million.
- Restructured $750,000 fully recourse loan with Merrill-Lynch to a non-recourse loan with more favorable interest and advance rates. Initiated and installed new accounting systems of control to evaluate each office's productivity and profitability. Developed new accounting control systems for in-house certified clinical laboratory.
- Analyzed cost benefits of closing targeted offices without compromising patient revenue or quality patient care. Improved cash flow by reorganizing billings and claims department with a $300,000 reduction in A/R.
- Acquired new medical practice congruent with strategic goals and objectives for seeking marketshare dominance.
- Successfully negotiated contract with state agencies to provide additional sources for new business.

(Page one of two)

Theresa Mascagni
Page two

Professional Experience

KFC - KENTUCKY FRIED CHICKEN – INTERNATIONAL OPERATIONS, Curacao/Aruba   1979 to 1990
Franchise Owner

- Purchased two international franchise businesses in Curacao and Aruba, both of which were losing propositions. Developed strategic business plans (operations/marketing) and initiated core organizational changes and began to consistently turn a profit in less than 10 months.
- Opened three additional stores in Curacao – total combined revenues exceeded $4 million with net earnings between 8% and 18%. These stores were among the highest-volume franchised units in the world.
- Recruited, trained and developed strong management team to contribute to corporate success – with an overall workforce consisting of 120 people. Implemented ironclad financial systems of control – accounting for over 240,000 pieces of chicken per month with less than a 1.4% loss factor.
- Implemented incentive program for employees to enhance sales and operating profit margins. Negotiated long-term supplier contracts at fixed and favorable prices with US companies to provide consistent source of supply and to ensure measurable gross profit margins.
- Returned investor's initial capital investments within 24 months and continued to pay dividends thereafter.

Education / Training

HOFSTRA UNIVERSITY, Hempstead, New York
Bachelor of Arts: Accounting, 1978

Additional / Ongoing Training

- Master's Degree Program Coursework in Taxation, St. John's University
- Real Estate License, Poes Institute
- Computer Courses in IBM RPG Programming and Cobol
- Coursework in Windows, Excel, Lotus, Solomon Accounting Software, Timberline, Word, T-Value
- Sales, Customer Service, and Quality Management Training

BOARD POSITIONS

Board of Governors, St. Andrews Country Club (Three Years)
Board of Directors, NASD Listed Company (Four Years)

References and Supporting Documentation Furnished upon Request

KEN O'BRIEN
7 Sherwood Forest Drive, Ft. Worth, Texas 76114 ● 555 555-1212 ● kennyo@aol.com

CAREER PROFILE

SENIOR EXECUTIVE experienced in the strategic planning, development and management of multi-million-dollar international business operations with specific expertise in manufacturing environments. Proven record of achievement in handling newly formed joint venture corporations from start-up through profitability. Verifiable record of instituting successful "turnarounds" for troubled companies. Consistently successful in analyzing market trends and capitalizing upon market opportunities to create high-profit, high-visibility companies. Particularly adept in developing effective, loyal, and cohesive staffs. Qualifications include:

- Administration
- Communications
- Contract Negotiations
- Cost Controls
- Human Resources
- Labor Relations

- Market Analyses & Trends
- Global Perspective
- Operational Management
- Staff Development
- Plant Management
- Quality Assurance

- Operational Productivity
- Bottom-Line Profitability
- Project Administration
- Resource Planning
- Sales and Marketing
- Strategic Planning

PROFESSIONAL EXPERIENCE

E Network Technologies, Daly City, California - 1997 to present

Project Manager reporting to the Executive Vice President, Engineering and Construction with bottom-line P&L responsibility for $55 million turnkey, design, engineer, and build automatic toll collection project for California Department of Transportation (CalTrans) covering all state-controlled toll bridges. Functional authority includes all aspects of human resources management, engineering, CAD, contract and subcontract administration, warranty administration, marketing plans, quality assurance, inventory control, finance, scheduling and customer relations. Functional responsibilities for systems integration include all technological aspects of RF transponders, infrared vehicle classification devices, antennae, light beams, treadles, computer controllers at each traffic lane, fiber optics, license plate capture system with character generation capability, plaza (bridge) computers including operating and report generating software, a host (central) computer system and report-generating software. Ancillary responsibilities include the operation of 5 customer service centers and development of an accounting system for financial management and auditing.

- *Recruited to assume control of the most complex toll project in the western hemisphere which was over budget, understaffed, behind schedule, and undisciplined.*

- *Orchestrated complete turnaround while generating $3.4 million in project cost savings in first 10 months while simultaneously negotiating schedule changes to eliminate all potential liquidated damages.*

EcoTrans Technolgy, Inc., Los Angeles, California - 1994 to 1997

General Manager reporting to the Board of Directors. Hired and trained the complete staff, using the preliminary business plan, of a joint venture between Southern California Gas Company and EcoTrans Systems, Inc., converting gasoline/diesel powered engines to compressed natural gas (CNG).

- *Perfected the business plan building the company, de novo, in a new, emerging industry.*

- *Achieved profitability within 14 months while capturing an 82% market share within Southern California.*

- *Personally generated actual sales of over $2.3 million with a 1,500+ vehicle order backlog valued at $6 million and options for an additional $3.1 million during first year.*

(Continued on next page)

PROFESSIONAL EXPERIENCE *(Continued)*

Yellow Bird Bus of North America, Mississauga, Ontario, Canada - 1990 to 1994

Vice President, Engineering and Sales (Consultant) reporting to the President and Board of Directors. Oversaw all phases of engineering and sales for an organization averaging $300+ million in annual sales. Responsibilities included design, development, and manufacture of heavy-duty transit buses for both Canadian and American markets. Additional responsibilities included design engineering; methods and manufacturing engineering; management of the service department including technical publications, research and development of hybrid and low floor buses, and handicapped bus design; the computer aided design (CAD) group; sales, contracts, bidding, and proposals; testing and a joint development hybrid vehicle program with G.E.; and alternative fuels (CNG) design.

- *Developed a successful "turnaround" business plan with other consultants. Personally developed engineering and sales and marketing plans.*

Cubic Control Corporation, San Marino, California - 1988 to 1990

International Business Development Director reporting to the General Manager. Responsible for development of both domestic and international new business. Focus was on rail and bus system new business regarding fare collection, data acquisition, and reporting systems. Handled special assignments involving overseeing Program Management, Technical Publications, and Product Support Departments for Farebox Product Line. Coordinated specifications and proposal development with consultants worldwide.

- *Analyzed new market segment (light rail), developed and prepared the proposal strategy and direction to win new job in Hong Kong.*

- *Established a nationwide team of efficient, effective sales representatives.*

- *Captured 80% of Canadian electronic fare box market share.*

Hagen Corporation, Beaumont, Texas - 1986 to 1988

President and Chief Executive Officer. Set up the Sales and Marketing and Engineering Departments for this newly acquired company building patented shuttle buses with optional wheelchair lifts. Established the computerized financial and inventory control systems. Coordinated efforts of the Sales and Marketing, Service, Spare Parts, and Engineering Departments in Western States. Assumed responsibility for operational management of 4 departments of a $375 million corporation including Technical Publications, Contract Administration, Marketing Analysis, Marketing Administration, Public Relations, and Advertising. Prepared near-, intermediate-, and long-range marketing plans.

- *Converted company from loss to profitability within first 14 months.*

- *Increased market share from 12% to 30% while competing with six competitors.*

- *Directly responsible for developing bids and proposals, leading to negotiating 81 contracts and establishing $175 million business backlog of buses to be built to U.S. Government (ADB) specifications.*

EDUCATION

Southwestern Texas Institute of Technology, Alice, Texas
    Bachelor of Science - Industrial Management and International Business

HAROLD R. CONNORS
17177 Northway Circle
Boston, Massachusetts 01977
Phone: (617) 555-1212/Cell: (617) 555-3232
email@email.com

SENIOR-LEVEL OPERATIONS/MANAGEMENT EXECUTIVE
Increasing Shareholder Value in Both Publicly Traded and Private Companies

SEC Reporting & Compliance/Start-up & Turnaround Management
Technology Integration/Business Development & Expansion
P&L Responsibility/Cash-Flow Management

A market-driven Senior Executive with outstanding qualifications in directing multimillion-dollar operations in global theaters. Recognized for capitalizing on existing product potential and identifying new growth opportunities.

CORE STRENGTHS

Visionary leadership/innovation management
Production and efficiency optimization
Customer service and retention management
Business development and expansion

Strategic-alliance/partnership development
Multiple-project/location management
Multichannel product distribution
Organizational/team leadership

PROFESSIONAL EXPERIENCE

HEALTH CARE INTERNATIONAL, INC., Boston, Massachusetts   2000 to Current
Senior Executive

- Business advisor to the President of a NASD Company in the health-care industry with annualized run-rate revenue of $220 million. Wrote comprehensive business plan to acquire new company and merge into existing division.
- Directly responsible for filings of past-due Form 10 K (fiscal year 1999) and subsequent Form 10 K for the four ensuing periods (through 6/2000). Prepared initial drafts of these filings and coordinated between SEC counsel, CFO, and Board of Directors. Settled more than $250,000 of payables for $45,000 in cash payments. Successfully reorganized an unprofitable division—turning around an operation draining more than $80,000/month in cash.
- The Company was in default on a note of $200,000 that was previously renegotiated. The lender, as part of the note, had obtained a Confession of Judgment, precluding the Company from entering any defenses to the note. Successfully negotiated payment of note with Company stock, not only saving the Company $200,000 in cash, but transformed a debt into an equity on the Company's balance sheet.
- Spearheaded all litigation with outside counsel and negotiated a fee reduction from $10,000 to $2000/month. Reassigned workload of HR department, saving $50,000/year while improving output. Coordinated all insurance matters, prepared leases and physician contracts and developed comprehensive analysis for in-house billing/collection efforts.
- Successfully renegotiated a $1.2 million billing contract (far in excess of normal costs) and arranged a contract buyout for $350,000 in stock—and obtained a new contract on more favorable terms.

MACKENZIE CONSULTANTS, Boston/New York   1990 to 2000
Full-time Consultant for Multioffice OB/GYN Practice

- Recruited to restructure and turn around an underperforming, unprofitable high-volume medical practice (six physicians) with operations throughout five South Florida counties—with revenues exceeding $3.5 million.
- Restructured $750,000 fully recourse loan with Merrill-Lynch to a nonrecourse loan with more-favorable interest and advance rates. Initiated and installed new accounting systems of control to evaluate each office's productivity and profitability. Developed new accounting-control systems for in-house certified clinical laboratory.
- Analyzed cost benefits of closing targeted offices without compromising patient revenue or quality patient care. Improved cash flow by reorganizing billings and claims department with a $300,000 reduction in A/R.
- Acquired new medical-practice congruent with strategic goals and objectives for seeking marketshare dominance.
- Successfully negotiated contract with state agencies to provide additional sources for new business.

(Page one of two)

Harold R. Connors
Page two

PROFESSIONAL EXPERIENCE

KFC—KENTUCKY FRIED CHICKEN—INTERNATIONAL OPERATIONS, Curacao/Aruba   1979 to 1990
Franchise Owner

- Purchased two international franchise businesses in Curacao and Aruba—both of which were losing propositions. Developed strategic business plans (operations/marketing) and initiated core organizational changes and began to consistently turn a profit in less than 10 months.
- Opened three additional stores in Curacao—total combined revenues exceeded $4 million with net earnings between 8% and 18%. These stores were among the highest-volume franchised units in the world.
- Recruited, trained, and developed strong management team to contribute to corporate success—with an overall workforce consisting of 120 people. Implemented ironclad financial systems of control—accounting for over 240,000 pieces of chicken per month with less than a 1.4% loss factor.
- Implemented incentive program for employees to enhance sales and operating profit margins. Negotiated long-term supplier contracts at fixed and favorable prices with U.S. companies to provide consistent source of supply and to ensure measurable gross profit margins.
- Returned investor's initial capital investments within 24 months and continued to pay dividends thereafter.

EDUCATION/TRAINING

HOFSTRA UNIVERSITY, Hempstead, New York
Bachelor of Arts: Accounting, 1978

Additional/On-going Training

- Master's Degree Coursework in Taxation, St. John's University
- Real Estate License, Poes Institute
- Computer Courses in IBM RPG Programming and Cobol
- Coursework in Windows, Excel, Lotus, Solomon Accounting Software, Timberline, Word, T-Value
- Sales, Customer Service, and Quality-Management Training

BOARD POSITIONS

Board of Governors, St. Andrews Country Club (Three Years)
Board of Directors, NASD Listed Company (Four Years)

References and Supporting Documentation Furnished upon Request

Devana

18 Elm Street
Anna, Texas 75000
(214) 555-2008—Pager (214) 555-0695
email@email.com

Data

Height: 5'1"	Hair: Red	Age: 24
Weight: 105	Eyes: Blue	Birthday: 5/19/79

Vocal Profile

★ Powerful, wide-range contralto; comfortable in high and low registers.
★ Varied musical styles including Country, Blues, Rock, Top 40, and Classics.
★ Strong live performer, singing with passion and energy in vocal styles ranging from graceful ballads to power-driven blues-rock and hard core honky-tonk.
★ Captures audience with lyric-focused phrasing and emotion that comes from the heart.
★ Has looks, personality, and style for video.

Vocal Performances

Audiences' Reactions:
Shouts, Cheers, Standing Ovations, Requests to Disc Jockey for Encores.

*"I've never heard singin' like that!" **"You ought to be recording."**—Audience*
(A large group of cowboys stood, holding their hats over their hearts in appreciation.)

"Boy, folks, SHE can sing!"—Disc Jockey
"Why aren't you in Nashville?"—Disc Jockey
"You made me cry, little lady."—Audience
"What a show!"—Disc Jockey
"Tremendous power!"—Audience
"Fantastic voice!"—Disc Jockey

2003

Sparky's, Commerce, Texas—***Talent Night***
Songs:
IF YOU'RE NOT IN IT FOR LOVE (artist: Shania Twain)
TOTAL ECLIPSE OF THE HEART (artist: Bonnie Tyler)

Brass Rail, Greenville, Texas—***Karaoke Night***
Songs:
ANY MAN OF MINE (artist: Shania Twain)
DOWN ON MY KNEES (artist: Trisha Yearwood)
JUST AROUND THE EYES (artist: Faith Hill)
IF YOU'RE NOT IN IT FOR LOVE (artist: Shania Twain)

(Continued)

Addendum

Prior to 2003

Lou Hamilton Center, San Antonio, Texas—*Our Part of Town Talent Show—Winner 3rd Place*
McCreeles Mall, San Antonio, Texas—*Our Part of Town Talent Show—Featured Singer*
YWCA, San Antonio, Texas—*Fund Raiser—Featured Singer*
Carlos Kelly's Restaurant, San Antonio, Texas—*Special Guest Singer*

Additional solo performances in San Antonio and Houston.

Professional Associations

Member: **Metroplex Country Music Association (MCMA)**

JEFFREY C. MERIWETHER

1299 West Maple Street
Springfield, Missouri 65802
Residence: 417-555-5555 ➤ E-mail: jmeriwether@email.net

SUMMARY OF QUALIFICATIONS

Bottom-line-focused Accounting Professional with over 10 years' progressively responsible experience in a client relationship management setting. Instrumental in effectively managing pressing client issues and helping retain key clients during employer's change management initiative. Consistently successful in meeting strict deadlines and troubleshooting/solving problems. Equally successful in capturing bottom-line reductions through process redesign, productivity improvement and operations quality enhancement.

➤ Financial Statements	➤ Bank Reconciliations	➤ Depreciation Schedules
➤ Journal Entries	➤ Payroll Taxes	➤ Sales and Use Taxes
➤ General Ledger	➤ Corporate Income Taxes	➤ Individual Income Taxes
➤ Depository Cards	➤ Accounts Receivable	➤ Accounts Payable

"His (Jeffrey's) native intelligence, initiative, diligence, and his ability to grasp new material and learn new skills quickly were responsible for his continually progressive accountabilities..." Jane Schollars, Owner, *Jane Schollars Accounting & Tax Service.*

PROFESSIONAL EXPERIENCE

JANE SCHOLLARS ACCOUNTING & TAX SERVICE, Stafford, Missouri   1992 to Present
Privately held accounting and tax practice focused on individual / corporate income taxes and financial statement preparation for small businesses.

SENIOR ACCOUNTANT
Challenged to manage 9 concurrent account relationships, performing their accounting functions from start to finish: code checks, perform journal entries, process payroll tax returns, monthly sales and use taxes, individual and corporate income taxes, including W-2s and 1099s. Conduct/monitor inventory, complete financial statements/bank reconciliations and create depreciation schedules.

Highlights of Accomplishments

➤ **Challenge:** Perform instrumental role in retaining key accounts following company's split.

➤ **Action:** Stepped up to the plate, assisting ownership in managing the transition/deadline attainment of key accounts.

➤ **Result: Influenced the retention of long-standing accounts** (up to 25-year loyalties) by helping avoid payroll tax penalties of 7% to 29%, while handling other pressing issues/deadlines.

*** *

➤ **Challenge:** Implement new rule that required capitalizing a portion of inventory costs.

➤ **Action:** Examined the literature and sample worksheets, formulated new capitalization method and applied to a client account.

➤ **Result: Ownership rolled out the new method** across other accounts affected by the new ruling.

Continued on Page Two

PROFESSIONAL EXPERIENCE
continued ...

Highlights of Accomplishments, *continued ...*

➤ **Challenge:** Investigate potential employee embezzlement at client site during extremely busy month.

➤ **Action/Result:** Scrutinized deposits/paperwork and successfully calculated amounts stolen.

***

➤ **Challenge:** Provide accounting solutions for customer who had existed two years running without an accountant, and who, during this period, had also experienced extensive technological issues.

➤ **Action:** From scratch, organized multiple accounts, reconciled bank accounts, recovered useful information from computer reports and focused on significant accounts payable issues.

➤ **Result: Identified and corrected cumulative $95,500** of inappropriately handled invoices. Repaired rental fleet tracking issues and, overall, mended the major accounting problems.

***

➤ **Challenge:** Perform quarterly tracking of a large rental fleet for construction equipment company client, tracing fleet from the rental master report to the depreciation schedule.

➤ **Action:** Redesigned procedure by numbering the assets on the depreciation schedule to coincide with the rental master report and designating a group number for individual years.

➤ **Result: 52% reduction** in processing time to track equipment.

***

➤ **Challenge:** Problem-solve key restaurant account's high-volume payroll tax issues that were intensified by constant employee turnover and computer issues.

➤ **Action:** Collaborated with ownership to innovate a methodical plan involving extensive worksheet/reporting initiatives, "backing out" the first three quarters and ultimately calculating a "true figure" for the fourth quarter.

➤ **Result: Prevented potential penalties** caused by underpayment and spurred refunds resulting from overpayment.

EDUCATION/TRAINING

Bachelor of Science in Business, 1992 / Summa cum Laude
Southwest Missouri State University
Member, Accounting Club

Gear-Up Tax Seminars
Easy Accounting Program
DS2-Depreciation Program
MS Word/Internet/Windows

Randy Bailes
1135 Michigan Avenue
East Lansing, MI 48823
(517) 555-0588

QUALIFICATIONS

- Marketing Degree from Michigan State University
- Tom Hopkins Seminar Attendee
- Two years experience selling telephone service and publishing materials
- High level of ambition to begin career

EDUCATION

Michigan State University
East Lansing, Michigan   March 1999
Earned a bachelor of arts in Marketing in under the prescribed four-year
course schedule while financing my own education. My final two years I
was totally self-supportive, working an average of thirty hours per week.

Tom Hopkins Seminar
Detroit, Michigan   February 10, 1999
The seminar "How to Master the Art of Selling" shall improve my
inherent sales abilities. Learning various personnel skills for applicable
situations will be an invaluable asset to my career.

WORK EXPERIENCE

United Parcel Service, Lansing, Michigan   November 1997 to present
Working at UPS enabled me to earn enough to support myself in school. I
earned over $12,000 per year, an impressive accomplishment for a college
student. As well, I maintained the highest production average at our
center.

Sprint Telephone Division, Lansing, Michigan   1996
Sold local telephone feature services to the consumer market in Lansing.
This experience paved the way for my future career path in sales. After
three months at Sprint, I was the sales leader among the part-time college
students and enjoyed the interaction with the customers. The only reason I
left was to move on to UPS, where the part-time earning potential was
greater.

American Collegiate Marketing, Lansing, Michigan   1995
This position was my introduction to sales, where I worked in a call center
selling magazine subscriptions. Though I enjoyed the sales environment,
my desire was to sell closer to customer in a more direct manner.

SKILLS / INTERESTS

Beyond my formal education, I have a working knowledge of MS Word,
Excel, Outlook and Explorer. I also enjoy playing golf, tennis, and fishing.

Kelly Adornetto

124 East 51st Street North
Metamora, IL 61111
(309) 555-1212/email@email.com

"Shannon is one of the sharpest students we've ever had in our office. There is nothing she can't learn!" (Dan Mathers, Operations Manager, Mathers Manufacturing)

Objective

Seeking entry-level **Data Entry/Office Support** position.

Profile

- Proficient office skills include keyboarding (50+ wpm), data entry, customer service, billing, and answering multiple phone lines.
- Diplomatic in relating to coworkers and the public; balances a positive, outgoing personality with professionalism and courtesy.
- Completes assignments with a high level of speed and accuracy.
- Possesses a sound knowledge of the rules of English grammar.
- Computer-literate; knowledgeable in all Microsoft Office products; able to learn and apply new software quickly.

Experience

Data Entry & Customer Service Associate/Student Co-op   3/01 to Present
MATHERS MANUFACTURING—Peoria, IL
Performs a wide range of office support functions, working within a time-sensitive environment. Enters and continually updates account information onto database. Answers phone inquiries and provides direct support to corporate accounts. Cross-trained to enter and retrieve inventory control data for the production department as needed.
- One of two selected to process payments and apply credit for the company's largest account.
- Attended several training classes for both customer service and in-house computer system.
- Cited for completing assignments with a high level of speed and accuracy.

Office Clerk, part time as needed   1/00 to Present
O'REILLY LUMBER—Metamora, IL
Calculates employee vacation and sick time, orders office supplies, and tracks inventory levels.
- Designed and implemented the company's first inventory-control database.

Education

Diploma, METAMORA HIGH SCHOOL—Metamora, IL   5/02

VICTOR C. HOPUS

555 Woodland Terrace, Orangeburg, NY 55555
(845) 555-1212 • (914) 555-9898 Cell
email@email.com

PHYSICAL THERAPIST

A dedicated, results-oriented individual who possesses excellent interpersonal and assessment skills, with the ability to put individuals at ease. Proven planning and organizational adeptness, possessing the skill to maintain superior levels of quality care under all types of circumstances. An able problem solver with the tenacity to complete assignments successfully and the flexibility to adapt to changing situations and requirements. Fluent in Spanish.

EDUCATION

Quinnipiac University—Hamden, CT
Currently Pursuing **MASTER'S DEGREE in Physical Therapy**—GPA 3.75
Expected date of graduation • December 2005
Quinnipiac University—Hamden, CT
BACHELOR of SCIENCE in Health Sciences GPA 3.89 • May 2002

PROFESSIONAL EXPERIENCE

Mercy Medical Center—Lynbrook, New York   2001
Physical Therapy Intern
- Performed initial evaluations of orthopedic and neurological patients for this medical facility.
- Arranged Cybex equipment for exercise protocols, and implemented manual therapy techniques.
- Educated patients on correct body mechanics during exercise, and performed massage.
- Managed and developed care plans for multiple patients simultaneously.
- Selected to perform an in-service for the department on Reflex Sympathetic Dystrophy.

Eddy Cohoes Rehabilitation Center—Cohoes, New York   2001
Physical Therapy Intern
- Handled initial evaluations on stroke, total knee, and hip replacement patients for this rehabilitation center.
- Performed assistive device assessments, neurodevelopmental treatments, and proprioceptive neuromuscular facilitation techniques on patients.
- Delivered an in-service on recombinant tissue plasminogen activator.
- Participated in home visits, interdisciplinary meetings, and community reentry programs.

Good Samaritan Regional Medical Center—Pottsville, Pennsylvania   2000
Physical Therapy Intern
- Performed initial evaluations on total knee, hip and shoulder replacement patients, amputees, and stroke patients at this acute care facility.
- Provided gait training for amputee patients on the use of prosthetic devices.
- Developed and trained patients on individualized exercise programs.
- Taught family members the mechanics of transferring patients to and from wheelchairs.
- Delivered an in-service presentation on the management and care of burn scars.

PROFESSIONAL AFFILIATIONS

- American Physical Therapy Association • **Member**

BRIAN MICHAELS

52 Kirkland Street ✦ Cambridge, MA 02138 ✦ 617-555-1212 ✦ email@email.com

LANDSCAPE ARCHITECT

Seeking to contribute to landscape design that adds value to natural and built sites while minimizing environmental impacts and project costs...

Skills
- Drafting
- AutoCAD 14 and 2000
- Site analysis and planning
- Appropriate selection of plant materials
- Oral/written/artistic communication
- Modeling using collage, sculpture, drawing, video, and multimedia

Academic and Project-Based Knowledge
- Design of gardens, courtyards, parks, and plazas
- Rural, suburban, industrial reclamation, recreational, and urban design
- Designing for compatibility with area architecture, history, natural systems, culture, and landscape

EDUCATION

TEMPLE UNIVERSITY AMBLER, Ambler, PA
Bachelor of Science in Landscape Architecture   2002
   Selected Coursework

- Field Ecology
- Woody Plants
- Site Design Studio
- Landscape Engineering I, II, and III
- Geology
- Soils

- Western Landscape Tradition
- American Land Tradition
- Park Design
- Management & Restoration
- Design Build Studio
- Herbaceous Plants

LANDSCAPE DESIGN EXPERIENCE

DEPARTMENT OF PARKS AND RECREATION, Hamilton, MA   Summers 2000 and 2001
Intern
Participated in the Rails-to-Trails initiative funded by the Massachusetts State Legislature. Worked with two licensed landscape architects to design and model a park area in the town center through which the trail runs.
- Selected five species of trees indigenous to the area and planned their placement.
- Helped design seating areas and select bench materials and style to be compatible with the landscape.
- Researched different natural path materials and made recommendations.
- Used AutoCAD 2000 to help plan the layout for the one-half-acre town center park.
- Selected hardy ground covers for nonpath areas.

THE SUZUKI FAMILY, Hamilton, MA   Spring and Summer 1999
Garden Planner (Volunteer)
Designed and built a small fishpond for a neighbor's sloping land.
- Created a garden with tiered pools bordered by 10 varieties of shade-loving perennials.
- Stocked the lowest pool with Japanese koi and planted water plants.

Portfolio available upon request

Corporate Communications

ANDREW LITTLE
123 SW Madison Street ■ Kewanee, IL 61433
(888) 449-2200 ■ emial@email.com

Public Relations

CORE STRENGTHS
Writing ■ Editing ■ Publishing
Negotiating ■ Public Speaking ■ Training

QUALIFICATIONS SUMMARY

- Accomplished, enthusiastic, and dedicated Communications/Public Relations professional. Solid academic credentials complemented by hands-on experience.
- Polished communicator with excellent negotiation, training, conflict resolution, and written/oral presentation skills; able to relate comfortably and effectively to people at all levels and from diverse backgrounds.
- Advanced computer skills include MS Word, Excel, Access, WordPerfect, Lotus 1-2-3, PowerPoint, Internet, and E-mail.

EDUCATIONAL BACKGROUND

B.A. in Corporate Communications (2002)
UNIVERSITY OF CALIFORNIA—San Diego, CA
A.A.S. FONTAINE COMMUNITY COLLEGE—Lewiston, CA (1990)
Academic Highlights: Warren Johnson Academic Scholarship Recipient ■ Elected Vice President of the University's Student Public Relations Association ■ Served as Chairperson and President of the Association for Student Activity Programming ■ Annual Fund Phonathon participant ■ WXYZ College Radio DJ/News Reporter

PROFESSIONAL EXPERIENCE

Public Relations Assistant Intern (1999 to 2002)
NELSON & BRIGGS COMPANY—Bronsonville, CA
Performed a wide range of PR functions for the company, including research/fact finding on current internal labor negotiations information to include in outside press releases. Posted current company information and employee-related topics on the corporate Internet site and edited existing information. Typed and distributed all press releases to the local media.
- Commended for thorough research and excellent written communication skills during labor negotiations, which had favorable results.

Writer/Editorial Assistant (1987 to 1999)
THE CALIFORNIA PRESS/OBSERVER—San Diego, CA
Served as the main point of contact for resource information and editorial subject matter for this large communications publication with a distribution of 175,000. Researched and wrote articles on various current business topics, prescreened all articles submitted for possible publication, and supported staff members in locating vital resource information.
- Started as company mascot, promoted through the positions of Advertising Sales Representative, Events Coordinator, and then Writer/Editorial Assistant.

EVALUATION COMMENTS

"Andrew Stewart possesses exceptional proficiency at both communications and customer relations. Also, his charismatic personality complements his fine work ethic, which I can assure you is both energetic and assertive. I feel **Andrew has all of the confidence, motivation, courage, and skills necessary to excel at any endeavor in life.**"

—Ed Sims, PR Manager
NELSON & BRIGGS CO.

"Andrew's positive attitude is a great testament to his outlook on life. He is able to find the positive in every situation. I have been in the communications industry for 17 years [and] must say that **Andrew is one of the best professionals I've ever had the privilege of meeting, based on the extra effort he put forth.** He is able to maintain a steady pace in the workplace without having to be prodded, even though the pressures are very great."

—Reese Olson, Editor
THE CALIFORNIA PRESS

"He is flexible and always willing to accept and embrace change."

—Mike Smith, Manager
NELSON & BRIGGS CO.

References Available on Request

365

WILLIAM H. (BILL) JEFFERSON
email@email.com
123 Second Street • Saybridge, Connecticut 55342 • (702) 555-1212

Drama Teacher—Community Theatre Director

FORMAL EDUCATION

Bachelor of Arts—May 1998
Speech and Drama
University of Kansas, Lawrence

TEACHING CREDENTIALS

K–12 Certificates:

Alabama	*Florida*
Colorado	*Kansas*
New York	

PERSONAL PROFILE

- Proven professional in planning, budgeting, coordinating, and scheduling.
- A practical problem solver using analytical, communication, and creative skills.
- Award-winning teacher.
- Experience with comedy, drama, Shakespeare, melodrama, and musicals.
- Intense educator, with the ability to motivate students to achieve their potential.
- Well-organized and goal-oriented director with proven ability to create high-caliber theatrical events.
- Outstanding participant in community affairs, utilizing a fair and balanced approach to the needs of the arts.

PORTFOLIO, PRODUCTION HIGHLIGHTS, AND PUBLISHED REVIEWS AVAILABLE AT TIME OF INTERVIEW

PRACTICAL EXPERTISE

- ➤ Able to achieve major increases in revenues:
  - ➤ Designed marketing plan that increased sales by 47%
- ➤ Community interaction:
  - ➤ Served on the Boards of United Way, County Art Council, and BBB
- ➤ Expense control:
  - ➤ Under expense budget by $22,000 at season end 2001
- ➤ Effective negotiator, moderator, and mediator:
  - ➤ Negotiated first long-term union contract in theater's history

CREATIVE EXPERTISE

- ➤ Directing:
  - ➤ "Colorado's Best Summer Stock Director" - Durango
- ➤ Choreography:
  - ➤ "The finest high school choreographing ever" - Manhattan
- ➤ Writer:
  - ➤ "His work will always play here" - Peoria
- ➤ Actor:
  - ➤ "Even with his Midwest 'twang,' the Globe's best male lead" - San Diego
- ➤ Teaching:
  - ➤ Honored as "Teacher of the Year" 2000–2001

EMPLOYMENT HISTORY

Director
Diamond Circle Theatre, Durango, Colorado   **Summers 2000–2001**
Direct professional actors in "The Tavern" melodrama and oleo skits for this summer stock theater in this mountain tourist community. Manage all marketing and community relations. Negotiated first long-term union contract for stagehands. Direct responsibility for working within an assigned budget.

Theater & Speech Instructor
XYZ High School, Manhattan, Kansas   **September 1998 to Present**
Director and choreographer of three productions per class year. Classroom instructor of Theater and Speech (2 Drama Classes and 2 Speech Classes) with a waiting list of students. Faculty Adviser to Thespian Club and Drama Club. Teacher of the year award.

Guest Director
Joe Jefferson Players, Mobile, Alabama   **2000**
Directed the first musical ever produced by this 85-year-old theater company.

Actor
Old Globe Theatre, San Diego, California   **1998–1999**
Played numerous lead and supporting parts, including comedy, drama, Shakespeare, melodrama, and musicals. Assisted with choreography.

REFERENCES AND FURTHER DATA UPON REQUEST

James Thrasher

email@email.com
265 Charlotte Street, Asheville, NC 28801 • (828) 555-1212

Profile

Successful achievement of academic and project goals in demanding curriculum with high standards, using logical, systematic problem identification and resolution skills.

Self-motivated college student with strong academic record seeks entry-level nuclear engineering position at Atomic Power Company.
- Persistent goal setter with strong analytical, research, organizational, and communication skills. Team participant.
- Computer Skills: C++, Pascal, UNIX, Windows, DOS, Word, WordPerfect, Excel, MS Works, LOGO, Internet research, some experience on Maple. Excellent keyboarding skills.
- Some fluency in German.

Education

Meritor Engineering Scholarship Finalist, Class of 2001 Competition, University Laurels

Class Rank: 8th of 200
Academic Medals for Excellence in Science & Mathematics
Perfect Attendance Award, Senior Year
North Carolina Scholar

COLLEGE OF NORTH CAROLINA—ASHEVILLE
B.S. in Nuclear Engineering   **December 2001**
- GPA: 3.7 / Dean's List
- Phi Eta Sigma National Freshmen Honor Society
- Selected Relevant Courses: Principles & Theory of Nuclear Engineering, Research & Experiment Design, Nuclear Fuel Production & Reclamation, Analytical Models of Research, Thermonuclear Analysis, Nuclear Equipment & Instrumentation, Computer Organization & Microprocessors, Nuclear/Computer Engineering Lab

JAMES B. MADISON HIGH SCHOOL, Asheville, NC
High School Diploma, with Honors   1997
- GPA: 4.21 (on 4.0 scale)
- Beta Club, Computer Club (Treasurer)
- Led team in State Computer Science and Math Competitions
- Member, Tennis Team (Best Doubles Award, 1997), 2 years

Experience

Eagle Scout, 1996

DAVY CROCKETT COUNCIL, Asheville, NC
Boy Scout Troop 46   1989–1996
- Initiated, planned, and coordinated a painting project for large, high-traffic church entrance room. Planned project, securing permission from Board via a written proposal. Recruited, organized, and led a crew of 8; calculated costs and purchased materials; assigned and scheduled crew. Maintained daily log with pictures. Upon completion, wrote and presented report in a final interview to 3-member Board of Davy Crockett Council.
- Additional volunteer work building trails, serving food to the homeless, working at St. Elmo Hospital, and performing a variety of other community services.

Red Cross Certified Lifeguard
Red Cross Certified CPR
Consistently high in service evaluations (and accompanied by raises)

BELLSON COUNTY PARKS & RECREATION, Asheville, NC
Lifeguard, Swimming & Safety Instructor   1996–2000
- Supervised an average of 150 children and adults per day during summers at Elgin Community Pool, as member of team of 8. Maintained and cleaned pool, deck, and bathrooms; watched for potential hazards and rule violators.

References

Major Adviser

Susan B. Anthony
CNCA Director of Nuclear Engineering Programs
728 Wilder Hall, Box 42, Asheville, NC 28800
(828)555-2323

Scoutmaster

Tom L. Fellers
Boy Scout Troop 46
70 Miller Street, Asheville, NC 28800
(828)555-4343

Supervisor

Clam Barton
Benson County Parks & Recreation Services
345 Rains Street, Asheville, NC 28800
(828) 555-2678

brian peavey
email@email.com

6701 Margarita Avenue • Valley Glen, California 91405
(818) 555-5432 • Mobile (818) 555-2345

"Brian stood out in every way. He was courteous, efficient, prompt, professional, highly motivated, and very eager to learn. He also showed a tremendous amount of initiative."

C.R.,
Assistant Director
The Haunted Castle

"I found Mr. Lawrence willing to take the initiative, resourceful, conscientious, and highly motivated."

F.B.,
Vice President
Zebra Spot Productions

"I was very impressed with Brian's student film production. I fully expect to see his name among the credits of tomorrow's blockbuster films."

R.M.,
Director
The Longest Shadow

college senior—experienced in film production & coordination

- Film & Television major with direct experience and in-depth understanding of the production process.
- Skilled in identifying tasks and following through to completion.
- Well organized with proven strengths in handling multiple responsibilities in a fast-paced environment with critical deadlines.
- Possesses excellent verbal and written communication skills; works well with broad range of temperaments.
- Learns quickly and enjoys challenges.
- Proactive in tackling projects and resolving problems.

experience includes:

Script Breakdowns • Production Schedules • Story Boards
Preproduction • Postproduction
Coordinating Production Material • Budget Management
Scriptwriting • Editing (Digital & Linear)

education

CALIFORNIA STATE UNIVERSITY, Northridge, CA
B.S. in Film & Television; May 2002
Dean's List, 5 semesters; 3.5 GPA; 3.8 GPA in major
Teaching Assistant, Film Production; Spring 2001

producer/director credits

Producer/Director
THE CONFLICT
Oversaw all aspects of production on student film from development through postproduction. Hired crew, obtained equipment, cast talent, coordinated shooting schedule, directed actors, managed budget, etc.
- **Received first place in regional student film competition**

(Continued)

brian peavey • page two • (818) 555-2345

internships

Production Assistant, The Haunted Castle (May–Sept. 2001)
ZEBRA SPOT PRODUCTIONS, Los Angeles, CA
- Provided direct assistance to producer on location.
- Facilitated communications between location shots and studio.
- Assisted with coordinating international travel.
- Compiled, summarized, and submitted detailed expense reports including currency conversions.
- Managed executive calendar, scheduled appointments, handled correspondence, directed calls.

Publicity Intern (Feb.–May 2001)
GRANITE PRODUCTIONS, Hollywood, CA
- Assisted publicist and talent with interviews, press, and media.
- Contributed ideas to promotional campaign for popular cast member. Organized appearance on TV news show to promote upcoming film release.

Production Assistant, *The Longest Shadow* (Summer 2000)
SUNSET STUDIOS, Hollywood, CA
- Coordinated voice-over recording sessions, script breakdowns, and updating.
- Scheduled executive and production meetings. Produced and distributed agendas for producer approval meetings.
- Arranged international and domestic travel.
- Maintained business and personal calendars for two producers through all phases of production.

additional work history

Server (Seasonal & Part-Time 1998–2000)
WILD BILL'S GRILL, Sherman Oaks, CA
Provided high level of customer service at popular dining establishment.

computer skills

Windows, Microsoft Word, Excel, PowerPoint, Access, Outlook, WordPerfect, Quicken, QuickBooks, WordPerfect, Lotus 1-2-3, Adobe Photoshop, Telnet, E-mail, Internet, HTML, Web Page Design

Karen D. Black, Esq.

10 Washington Street, Salem, MA 01970 ■ (978) 555-1212 ■ email@email.com

Seeking a position as...
Attorney—General Practice

Juris Doctor committed to generating new and repeat business by providing skilled legal services and building strong client relationships. Four years of varied legal experience. Bachelor of Science degree in Marketing. Polished, professional demeanor. Areas of strength:

- *Research using Westlaw and CaseBase*
- *Legal analysis*
- *Legal strategy development*
- *Negotiation*

- *Interpersonal skills*
- *Public speaking*
- *Written and oral communication*
- *Regulatory compliance*

Education

New England School of Law, Boston, MA
Juris Doctor   2001

Babson College, Wellesley, MA
Bachelor of Science in Marketing   1996

Legal Experience

Law Clerk, The Law Offices of William Shepherd, Attorneys-at-Law, Danvers, MA   1999–2001
Real Estate Mortgage and Conveyance Practices
- Helped generate new business by writing and implementing a new telephone script for use in responding to initial inquiries from potential clients.
- Researched titles and drafted deeds.
- Discharged documents and trust provisions.
- Negotiated lien discharges and conveyance materials with the I.R.S., the F.D.I.C., and municipal tax assessors.
- Assisted attorneys in the administration of home equity mortgage refinance options for a major bank.
- Prepared documents for recording procedures and mortgage closings.

Intern, LOWELL DISTRICT COURT, Lowell, MA   1998
Civil and Juvenile Law
- Directly assisted the 1st Magistrate.
- Conducted research and wrote opinions.
- Interviewed petitioners.

Legal Assistant, SHARON WILLIS, Attorney-at-Law, Peabody, MA   1997
Family Law and Will, Estate, and Probate Law
- Assisted attorneys in drafting documents, pleadings, and outside correspondence.
- Interviewed parties involved and made recommendations.

Licensure and Memberships

Licensed to Practice Law in the Commonwealth of Massachusetts by The Board of Bar Overseers
Licensed Notary Public
Member: Massachusetts Bar Association, Boston Bar Association, American Bar Association
Member: Toastmasters International

MARIA CRUDO

11935 West 9th Street • Sun Valley, Idaho 83404 • (208) 555-1212 •
email@email.com

SPECIAL EDUCATION TEACHER

Highly dedicated, compassionate, patient, and positive professional with
numerous accomplishments working with the handicapped.

SUMMARY OF QUALIFICATIONS

- Current teaching certificate for Elementary Education—endorsement in Special Education.
- Quickly develops rapport with students, employees, and staff.
- Three years' experience (summers) working with handicapped individuals in a Developmental Disabilities Agency and writing programs for handicapped individuals.
- Manages and promotes self-directed work teams and coordination for three employees.
- Experienced with licensure surveys for Developmental Disabilities Agencies.
- Strong leadership, management, and organizational skills; exceptional work ethic.
- Self-motivated, creative, dependable, and patient.

EDUCATION

Current Teaching Certificate valid in Idaho and Washington. 2001.
Bachelor of Science Degree in Special Education, **Idaho State University**, Pocatello, Idaho. 1997.
Developing Capable People Seminar, **Temple Elementary**, Presented by Stacie Smith. 1997.
Managing People with Handicaps Seminar, **Temple Elementary**, Presented by Stacie Smith. 1996.

EMPLOYMENT

AIDE. DEVELOPMENT WORKSHOP, INC., Idaho Falls, Idaho. 1994 to 1996.
- Traveled to clients' homes to teach cooking, cleaning, shopping, and budgeting.
- Assisted in writing, developing, and implementing program procedures.
- Taught life skills to clients; ensured the safety of the clients.
- Monitored facility maintenance and security.
- Special project: worked with young boy, age five, who would not speak. After nine months of intense therapy, patience, and special equipment, he began speaking broken words. He is still in therapy and doing very well considering the circumstances.

LAYAWAY/SERVICE DESK CLERK. K MART, Nampa, Idaho. 1991 to 1994 (Part-Time).

CASHIER/COOK. SCOT'S DRIVE-IN, Idaho Falls, Idaho. 1988 to 1991 (Part-Time).

Have lived with and cared for a sister and a brother with handicaps.

SHANNON E. RUEFLY

32 Old Schoolhouse Road • New City, New York 10956 • (845) 555-9134 • email@email.com

TESTIMONIALS

*"Ms. **Ruefly** recently completed a five-week sick leave for my position as a Resource Room/Inclusion teacher. During that time she demonstrated an outstanding ability to make connections with the students...She was a great asset to Sunrise Drive Elementary School..."*

Carolyn Daley
Special Education Teacher
Sunrise Drive Elementary School

"... Shannon has consistently demonstrated academic excellence. She has conducted herself with professional integrity and has demonstrated commitment to responsibilities and professional studies. She is a warm, caring, and energetic person. She has demonstrated initiative, intelligence, and preparedness. I, therefore, strongly recommend her to you..."

John P. Heaphy, Ph.D.
Dowling College
Teacher Education Program

"...Shannon worked with autistic populations of children in a highly structured environment of applied behavioral analysis. She taught with expertise, kindness, and consistency and thoroughly familiarized herself with classroom routines and with specific goals for each child. In addition, Shannon was a very pleasant addition to the adult staff that worked within the classroom. I would highly recommend Shannon as a teacher in any special education setting."

Janine Corona, CCC/Sp
Speech Teacher
Eastern Suffolk B.O.C.E.S.

EDUCATION

SUNY Stony Brook—Stony Brook, NY
Currently Pursuing Bachelor of Science in Elementary Education
Expected Date of Graduation • May 2002 • Dean's List

Suffolk Community College—Selden, NY
A.A. • **Liberal Arts** • Dean's List • 1996

CERTIFICATIONS

N.Y.S. Provisional Teaching Certification Elementary Education
N.Y.S. Provisional Teaching Certification Special Education

PROFILE

A dedicated elementary education professional with demonstrated experience in working with mainstream students to achieve goals while combining and implementing various teaching and organization strategies including direct/command, task limitation, and exploration methods. Able to establish and maintain solid relationships with coworkers, students, and parents. Recognized as a resourceful and reliable teacher with the ability to perform accurate student assessment and develop individualized education plans.

AREAS OF EXPERTISE

• **Special Ed Inclusion** • **Creative Lesson Planning** • **Thematic Units** • **Development of Instructional Materials and Learning Centers** • **Cooperative Learning** • **Multisensory Lessons** • **Multicultural Units** • **Integrated Activities** • **Individualized Education Plan Development** • **Parent-Teacher Conferences** • **Performance Assessments** • **Integration of Technology** • **Life Skills Training** • **NYS Learning Standards Compliance** •

PROFESSIONAL EXPERIENCE

2001   **STUDENT TEACHER**
        Short Hills Elementary—Middle Village, New York
- Develop and implement lesson plans for 2d, 3d, and 4th-grade students of varying abilities and intellectual levels with diverse backgrounds.
- Implement thematic approaches and integrated curriculum, providing opportunity for students to build upon strengths.
- Establish connections between concepts and skills.
- Integrate language arts approaches to supplement and enrich curricula standards.
- Utilize computers for both classroom lessons and one-on-one tutoring to provide independent math and writing activities.

1999 to 2000   **STUDENT TEACHER**
        Eastern Suffolk B.O.C.E.S.—Patchogue, NY
- Provide instruction for the ABA program designed to meet the needs of elementary-aged autistic children.

Maria Lozano

192-42 35th Avenue
Flushing, NY 11358
(718) 555-6804
email@aol.com

" ... exceptionally energetic and enthusiastic teacher ... projects a charisma that captures the imagination of students ... demonstrated excellent classroom management skills ..."

Robert G. Pisido
former administrator

"... business background in technology was supportive to the use of videos and computers in the class ... She volunteered for cooperative opportunities in the media center and helped teachers to accommodate computers ... I recommend her with the highest regard ..."

Tom Delaney
2nd Grade Teacher
New York City Schools

Professional Profile

Eager to bring elementary students into the twenty-first century using a unique combination of education experience coupled with ten years' business background in computer systems management.

- Hold Masters Degree in Elementary Education and Bachelors Degree in Computer Science.
- Experienced in use of the Internet and educational software.
- Dedicated to enthusiastic and dynamic teaching as a means of creating and nurturing a lifelong love of knowledge in children.

Education, Honors, & Certifications

M.S. Elementary Education
Queens College, Flushing, NY. 1995

Bachelor of Science Computer Science
Hofstra University, Hempstead, NY. 1984

Kappa Delta Pi Honor Society Member

Provisional Certifications
NY State Elementary Education. 1995
NY State Business Education. 1995

Key Qualifications

Certified in Elementary (K-6) and Business Education

Plan and instruct each subject area using wide variety of teaching aids, motivational and implementation strategies to engage students in active learning.

Incorporate learning modality principles into classroom and individual instruction. Develop and conduct intergrade activities. Utilize Heath automated math management system.

Implement technological approaches to subject material. Research educational resources on the Internet. Assist with information retrieval.

Experienced Computer Educator

Designed and conducted various faculty and student workshops for training in word processing and spreadsheet software. Instructed corporate personnel in use of word processing, desktop publishing, and drafting programs for conversion from manual typesetting and drafting to computer-assisted methods.

Maria Lozano

Computer Skills
- **Software (IBM and MAC environments):** Windows and DOS, WordPerfect, Lotus123, Microsoft Word, Pagemaker, AutoCad, Books in Print, Baker & Taylor Links, Bibbase
- Working knowledge of the **Internet**
- **System installations and debugging;** terminal/printer operations

Employment
Professional Development in Education
- **Substitute Teacher,** K thru High School, April 1995 to present
- **Graduate Adviser, Education Dept.,** October 1995 to present
  Queens College, Flushing, NY
- **Workshop Presenter,** November 1995
  First combined International Reading Association Regional Conference, Nashville, TN
- **Information Services Assistant,** May 1994 to August 1995
  Queens College, Flushing, NY
- **Student Teacher,** September to December 1994
  P.S. 32, Flushing, NY

Computer Related Training Positions
- **Workshop Presenter,** February, 1995
  East Islip High School, East Islip, NY
- **Graduate Assistant,** August 1993 to May 1994
  Queens College, Flushing, NY
- **Software Engineer,** 1989 to 1991
  Craftsman Corporation, Smithtown, NY

Corporate Computer Systems Management
- **Systems Manager,** 1987 to 1989
  Metricase Corporation, Bohemia, NY
- **Software Quality Assurance Engineer,** 1986 to 1987
  Gull, Inc., Smithtown, NY
- **Staff Administrator, Executive Department,** 1984 to 1986
  Brooklyn Union Gas Co., Brooklyn, NY
- **Student Director/Assistant, Computer Science Lab,** 1981 to 1984
  Hofstra University, Hempstead, NY

Professional Affiliations
International Reading Association
Association for Supervision and Curriculum Development

LORI PETRASK

151 W. Passaic Street • Rochelle Park, New Jersey 07662 • **(201) 555-3772**
email@email.com

SPECIAL EDUCATION TEACHER

- Experienced in successfully working with Special Education students and developing skills in students at all levels of achievement.
- Utilize creative skills to design and implement well-received lesson plans and program structure.
- Establish learning environments which meet the physical, emotional, intellectual, social and creative needs of children.
- Create yearly course work including the selection of teaching materials.
- Effectively counsel students and parents on goals, objectives and plans.
- Rapidly develop and adjust lesson plans to meet unforeseen classroom situations.

SELECTED ACCOMPLISHMENTS

- ♦ **Significantly increased enrollment and student learning by implementing innovative programs.**
- ♦ **Instrumental in State accreditation.**
- ♦ **Implemented a revised reading program to interest young children.**
- ♦ **Planned numerous extracurricular activities.**
- ♦ **Recipient of numerous letters of appreciation from parents for dedication and effort.**

PROFESSIONAL EXPERIENCE

The Windsor School - Pompton Lakes, New Jersey   1989-1998

Special Education Teacher (1997-1998)

Administered curriculum for 5th and 6th grade Special Education students (emotionally disturbed, learning disabled and neurologically impaired). Developed lesson plans and instructed all major subject areas including reading, grammar, science and social studies. Assessed student abilities and evaluated performance; conducted parent-teacher conferences to provide parents with student development reports. Counseled students and parents to resolve learning and discipline problems. Developed monthly newsletters and participated in IEP meetings for each child.

Elementary Teacher (1989-1997)

Taught 4th grade for 3 years and full day kindergarten for 4 years. Directed the preschool and junior kindergarten program for 1 year. Revised curriculum and reading program for kindergarten class. Generated progress reports and evaluated students through report cards. Authored monthly newsletters. Created lesson plans and developed learning centers. Accountable for kindergarten screening and direction/production of annual holiday pageant.

EDUCATION / CERTIFICATION

- *Master Degree in Special Education* (currently pursuing, 12 credits completed)
- *B.S. in Elementary Education* (*Concentration in Early Childhood*) • 1988
    Jersey City State College - Jersey City, New Jersey

- *New Jersey Certificate in Elementary Education (K-8)*
- *New Jersey Certificate in Special Education (pending)*

ALEXANDRA N. BOGADZIK

8762 South Washington Avenue
Carmel, Indiana 47663
(717) 555 -8776
abogadzik@msn.com

CAREER SUMMARY:

Dedicated **EDUCATOR** with 20+ years of teaching experience. Recognized for innovation in program development, instruction and administration to meet the needs of a broad range of students. Effective communicator, writer, administrator and student adviser/advocate.

CORE COMPETENCIES:

Curriculum Development & Instruction

- Assisted in the development, validation and enhancement of curricula. Introduced hands-on tools (e.g., computer technology, outside classroom activities) to improve classroom interest and retention.
- Taught a full academic curriculum (e.g., reading, writing, communications, mathematics, social science) to children ages seven to 13.
- Designed and implemented customized teaching programs to allow emotionally, physically and learning disabled students to be mainstreamed into the classroom.
- Launched a highly successful peer tutoring program designed to improve interaction between upper-level and younger students while fostering communication and mentoring skills at all levels.

Administration & Special Activities

- Appointed Vice Principal with responsibility for a diversity of functions, including faculty recruitment and scheduling, curriculum development, discipline, parent/community affairs, and special events planning.
- Prepared documentation for recertification by the National Accreditation of Schools Committee as a member of a cross-functional faculty/administration committee.
- Provided classroom training, performance evaluation and motivation as a mentor to student teachers completing college requirements for an education degree.

Community & Public Relations

- Built partnerships with local companies and developed a series of seminars to introduce junior high school students to the business world. Coordinated speaker selection and topics of discussion.
- Participated on cross-functional teams of educators and administrators to design programs to improve the quality of educational curricula, enhance parent and community relations, and increase student participation both inside and outside of the classroom.

PROFESSIONAL EXPERIENCE:

Teacher / Administrator	ST. MARY'S DAY SCHOOL, Carmel, IN	1990 to 1998
Elementary Education Teacher	INDIANA PUBLIC SCHOOL SYSTEM	1982 to 1989
Elementary Education Teacher	MICHIGAN PUBLIC SCHOOL SYSTEM	1977 to 1981

EDUCATION:

B.A., Education (Minor in History), MICHIGAN STATE UNIVERSITY, 1977

Permanent Certification in Elementary Education (K-8), Indiana
Past Certification in Elementary Education (K-8), Michigan

Graduate of 100+ hours of continuing professional education and graduate studies sponsored by the College of the Midwest, Ball State University, Purdue University and Michigan State University.

191—TELECOMMUNICATIONS ENGINEER

TECHNICAL PROFICIENCIES

Network/Operating Environments:

- Solaris, AIX, Linux, Novell Netware, VMS/CMS Mainframe, DOS, Windows 95/98/NT, Xwindows, Banyan Vines, SunNet Manager

Network Equipment:

- Cisco (1000, 2500, 4000, 7000 series Routers)
- Bay Networks (Contivity 4000 Extranet Switch, BCN and BLN series Routers, 28000, 58000, and 350T series Ethernet Switching Hubs)
- Synoptics (2813, 3000, 3030, and 5000 series hubs/concentrators)
- 3com (3100 series Terminal Servers, Netbuilder II Routers, Lanplex 2500 series, Linkswitch 3000 series)
- Cyberguard (Firewall), Sniffer, OneTouch.

Programming / Scripting Languages:

- C, C++, Assembly (370,8086,8031,8051), HTML, FORTRAN, BASIC, Visual Basic, Java, Perl, CGI, SQL, Shell Scripting

Protocols / Services:

- IPsec, PPTP, SNMP, TCP/IP, RADIUS, PAP, MSCHAP, DHCP, DNS, FTP, Telnet, RMON, x.509, DES, Triple-DES, FTTH

Applications:

- Microsoft Outlook, Word, Powerpoint, Excel, Project, Access, Bay Networks Optivity, Harris Network Management, Exceed, Lotus ccMail, Ecoscope, Netscape, Internet Explorer, Visio, Informix, Oracle

Tom Anika

123 Arlington Court, Denver, CO 80239
e-mail@e-mailaddress.com
303-555-5451

Summary

- **Voice & Data Communications Engineer** with 10+ years of experience seeking continued project leadership role, integrating emergent technologies into comprehensive communications solutions.
- In-depth knowledge of communications network operations. Proven ability to build proficiency in new technologies and collaborate with multidisciplinary project teams to ensure successful project integration.
- Strong skills in coordinating all facets of multiple complex projects, ensuring on-time, on-budget, on-target results.
- Articulate, flexible, and personable communicator, with excellent skills in client and vendor relations. Frequently selected to serve as a project consultant and task force contributor on critical corporate initiatives.

Experience

Internet Fiber, Inc., Denver, CO   1998-Present
FTTH Project Manager

- Design and build Neighborhood Networks™ (customer-owned Internet Fiber networks) using a high-speed fiber to the home (FTTH) architecture for Internet, telephony, and video.
- Perform feasibility studies, determine network requirements and specifications.
- Maintain strong partnerships with top-rated residential homebuilders. Coordinate construction schedules from rough electrical to interior finishing phases.
- Hire and manage telecommunications and network technicians and subcontractors to meet all implementation deadlines.

AT&T / Lucent Technologies, Westminster, CO   1990-1998
Telecommunications Engineer, IP-based Network Services

- Supported implementation of multiple projects, including Interspan Network, IP network services (the AT&T Worldnet backbone), frame relay, ATM, AT&T Broadband services, APS (a PC-based, Unix O/S Voice Recognition Call Processing System), and 900 MHz Spectralink phone systems.
- Determined location of hardware and schedule installations to minimize impact to customers.
- Coordinated all unit and system testing, ensuring 100% turn-up of equipment prior to cut-over.

Education

BS, Telecommunications Engineering, Cum Laude
University of Colorado at Boulder

LESLIE A. HINKLE
3600 Fillmore Street #204, San Francisco, CA 94123, 415-555-7597, lhinkle@link.net

---

PROFESSIONAL PROFILE

- 4 years in telecommunications industry
- Specialty in voice and data product management, engineering, and sales engineering support
- Developed technical sales training for Sprint sales
- Performed wide area network [WAN] designs for hundreds of Sprint customers and sales prospects

EXPERIENCE

5/99-Present **SPRINT CORPORATION** San Francisco, CA
Advanced Sales Support Manager/Field Product Manager
- Provided technical and product-related support for all West Area Sales Support divisions on leading-edge technologies. Acted as a technology consultant for approximately 200 engineering and sales management employees.
- Created and delivered strategic presentations on Converged Network solutions to premiere high-technology companies and top-tier funded E-Commerce clients.
- Developed analyses of competitors' product offerings and evaluated customer demand for new product feature offerings through market surveys. Provided recommendations to Marketing and Business Development on needed enhancements to product portfolio.
- Contributed to $1.5 million 1999 revenue for products through speaking engagements at high-profile industry conferences and executive briefings for CTOs and CIOs.
- Conducted monthly product updates and technical training sessions for Engineers and Sales Managers throughout the West area.

1996-1999 **SPRINT CORPORATION** Herndon, VA
Systems Design Engineer II, Government Systems Division
- Designed and implemented wide area networks for NASA and Energy Sciences Network (ESNET) using Asynchronous Transfer Mode (ATM) technology.
- Conducted analysis of network design to determine optimal configuration for customer's data traffic profile. Made recommendations and presented design strategy to client.
- Designated as region's Subject Matter Expert on ATM, SONET/DWDM, and Integrated On-Demand Network (ION) Architecture.
- Created product guidelines and coordinated service delivery for Sprint's first OC-12 ATM product.

July-Dec. 1996 **SPRINT CORPORATION, ASSOCIATE ENGINEERING PROGRAM** Reston, VA
Associate Engineer
- Completed 6-month rigorous training program on Wide Area Network (WAN) design and telecommunications protocols.
- Promoted to Systems Design Engineer I within 6 months of employment with company.

EDUCATION
COLLEGE OF WILLIAM AND MARY Williamsburg, VA
Bachelor of Science, May 1996

ADDITIONAL
Extensive knowledge of ISDN, Frame Relay, ATM, TCP/IP, and SONET protocols.
Practical experience with configuration of *Fore Systems* ATM switches.
Enjoy Yoga and running.

555 Lincoln Avenue
Brentwood, NY 11111

DANIEL M. WILLISON

(631) 555-5522
engineer@onetry.net

Electronics Design / Test Engineer

PROFESSIONAL EXPERIENCE

Systems Specialist, MICROWAVES, INC., Deer Park, NY   5/97 – Present

- Measure and test electrical performance of RF/IF and microwave signal processing components:
  - *frequency mixers, power splitter/combiners, high-power amplifiers, directional couplers*
  - *attenuators/switches, filters (low pass, band pass, high pass), frequency doublers, phase detectors/shifters*
  - *RF transformers, oscillators, VCOs, synthesizers, and phase lock loop*
- Test electrical performance of low band (20-100 MHZ) and midband (100-500 MHZ) RF amplifier system:
  - *VSWR, power sweep, third-order intermodulation distortion*
  - *gain flatness, harmonics, spurrious, isolation, insertion/conversion loss, % AM and FM distortion*
  - *AM, FM, and pulse modulation/demodulation, dynamic range, 1db compression point, power consumption, noise figures, vibration and temperature testing*
- Test cellular/wireless communication devices (CDMA amplifiers) utilizing Automatic Test Equipment, single tone, swept response, burst signal and digital signal (CDMA and TDMA)

Design Engineer, SCIENCE UNIVERSITY, GeoSciences Department, Great Neck, NY   1/96 – 5/97

- Assisted Senior Engineer in all phases of the MAS project involving design, testing, troubleshooting and implementation of electronics systems.
- Utilized the Canbera X-Ray Detector, Solid State Detector and Gas Proportional Detector to monitor and track a source's energy and intensity; collected data utilizing the Canbera MCA Series 135.
- Developed software programs using C programming language to perform the following tasks:
  - *calibration of Servo motors*
  - *acquire data from Canbera MCA Series 135*
  - *upload information to Excel, Quattro and Lotus applications*
- Designed an Embedded Control System to monitor water flow.
- Measured voltage, current and power utilizing the Fluke 8840A voltmeter and the Tektronic Digital TAS 465 oscilloscope; measure the intensity of beam utilizing the ionization chamber.
- Designed LVDTs, current sensors and pressure transducers; A/D, D/A, frequency to voltage; and voltage to frequency converters.
- Utilized a broad range of instruments for various testing, including Canbera High Voltage Power Supply, Canbera Manual Crate Controller, EMS 40-60 Switching Power Supply and Nim Bin.
- Assisted with the maintenance of the Seismic RF System.

Electronics Technician, DIGITAL TECHNOLOGY, Hicksville, NY   8/92 – 11/95

- Ensured audio recording equipment functionality through repair and preventive maintenance.
- Designed error detectors to distinguish audio-based glitches throughout recordings.
- Tested audio recording equipment utilizing the Tektronic FSEB 20/30 Spectrum Analyzer, TV110 Cable Scout (coaxial cable tester) and Tektronic Type 115 Pulse Generator.

— Continued —

DANIEL M. WILLISON

Page 2

PROFESSIONAL EXPERIENCE, Continued

Manufacturing Engineer, ELECTRONICS MANUFACTURING, Levittown, NY   1/90 – 2/91

- Under DoD contract, built RF devices in accordance to military specifications; as Certified Quality Assurance MIL STD 2000 Inspector, performed final inspections; trained and certified electronics technicians.

- Demonstrated devices' performance to government inspectors as criteria for selling the final product.

Electronics Technician, GENESIS LABORATORIES, Mastic Beach, NY   11/85 – 7/88

- Assisted Power Supply Group technicians with equipment repairs; cable manufacturing; and soldering, assembly, and wiring of circuit boards.

- Worked with Vacuum Group technicians on repairs and leak checks in the AGS Ring vacuum system.

HARDWARE / SOFTWARE

HP Equipment: Network Analyzer, Spectrum Analyzer,
PC Interface, Power Meter, Signal Generator, Scope;
Excel, Quattro and Lotus applications

Languages: C/C++, Visual Basic 5.0, Assembly, Fortran, and Unix

EDUCATION

STONY BROOK UNIVERSITY
Bachelor of Science, Electrical Engineering, 1994

SUFFOLK COMMUNITY COLLEGE
Associates in Applied Science, Electronics Technology, 1987

UNITED STATES ARMY ARMAMENT & ENGINEERING
Certificate of Completion, 1991

SUZANNE COUTEE-CHANG

445 East Avenue   Home (407) 555-4688
Chicago, IL 60611

PROFESSIONAL SUMMARY:

Professional UNIX Systems Administrator with seven years of experience. Experienced in analyzing, supporting and troubleshooting client/server configurations across large-scale heterogeneous networks. Also accomplished at providing a high level of customer service and training to end users. Experienced in dealing with vendors from both a hardware and a software perspective. Solid knowledge of the following hardware/software:

Hardware/Operating Systems	Software	Applications Used
Sun Sparc (5,10,20,Xterm,Ultra, 1,000,2000) **(Solaris** 1.X & 2.X)	Abaqus	FrameMaker
	Patran	Word Perfect
	C/Fortran Compilers	MS Office
HP 9000 (700,800,C100 Series)	Comsearch/SSAM	Wingz
(HP-UX 9.X & 10.X)	Mapinfo	MAE
	Informix/Oracle	Soft-Windows
Tektronix Xterminals	ER Mapper	PC-Xware
HP & Sun Printers/Plotters	FrameMaker	Action Request System (ARS)
	Paradigm Help Desk	
Sun/Dec Storage Arrays	WinDD	**Others**
DiskSuite, Auspex	Spectrum Help Desk	NFS/NIS/NIS+
	Word Perfect	TCP/IP, Automount
Backup Software	HP Jetadmin	
Legato Networker	Secureid (Security)	
Veritas Netbackup	Sun XtMgr	
Delta Microsystems Budtool	Lotus Notes	
	Tektronix Xpressware	

EMPLOYMENT

8/03 to Present

MOBIL OIL   13777 Midway Rd, Farmers Branch, TX
Position: UNIX Systems Administrator (Consultant with Decision Consultants)
Providing client/server, system hardware/software support on SUN/HP/SGI platforms to Engineers, Geophysicists and all other technical staff in the Research Development division, which consists of 10 departments. Working with each department on a project basis to implement standardization of all desktop environment, including network and operating system configurations. Coordinate user migration; provide training to help-desk support personnel on how to respond/log UNIX related calls and provide ongoing procedure documentation. Provide training to new users on general use of workstations.

5/02 to 8/03

MOTOROLA   8000 W. Sunrise Blvd, Plantation, FL
Position: UNIX Systems Administrator (Consultant with TechniSource, Inc.)
Provided client system/application support to 800+ client workstations which consisted of developers, engineers, database, and network administrators; provided backup support to server administrators; configure and maintain SUN/HP client workstations for NIS client/server environment; administer/monitor/troubleshoot help desk support calls through use of Action Request HelpDesk software (ARS). Install and configure HP network based printers/plotters. Maintain and update inventory of all HP/SUN equipment on ARS.

(continued)

SUZANNE COUTEE-CHANG   (continued)

6/01 to 5/02	**Verizon Wireless (PrimeCo)**	Six Campus Circle, Westlake, TX

Position: UNIX Systems Administrator

Provided systems support to developers, engineers, database, and network administrators; this included the RF Engineering department and the implementation of a production work environment. Also provided backup technical support to the system administrators in 11 markets on the Sun platform. Installed, configured, maintained, and upgraded Sun/Solaris servers and workstations. Evaluated, tested, installed, and upgraded software packages. Troubleshot help desk calls. Installed and configured HP network printers and plotters. Maintained an NIS+/NIS client/server environment with 15 different domains established. Maintained system backups on Legato Networker. Procured evaluation units, acquired price quotes, generated purchase orders, and tracked maintenance agreements for all UNIX hardware/software within the company and 11 national markets.

8/00 to 5/01	**Southwestern Bell Mobil Systems**	13900 Midway Road, Farmers Branch, TX

Position: UNIX Systems Administrator

Provided system support to developers, database, and network administrators. Also provided backup technical support to system administrators in other markets on both SUN/HP platforms. Installed, configured, maintained and upgraded Sun/Solaris servers and Xterminals, including SUN/HP and Tektronix. Evaluated, tested, installed, and upgraded software packages. Troubleshot help desk calls. Installed and configured HP printers on network.

1/00 to 7/00	**The Future Now**	3410 Midcourt Drive, Ste. 115, Carrollton, TX

Position: UNIX Systems Engineer

Provided presales support to Marketing department. Provided postsales support for implemented solutions at customer site. Installed and configured servers and workstations. Maintained in-house Solutions Center and assisted with internal UNIX Network support and planning. Evaluated and tested new products, and demonstrated new solutions to clients. Assisted with the development and implementation of programs. Provided on-site user-end training.

5/97 to 1/00	**SuperConducting Super Collider Laboratory**	Waxahachie, TX

Position: UNIX Systems Administrator

Provided system, software, client/server support for 600+ users on SUN/HP platforms, which included over 20 servers across 30 routed subnets. Worked closely with engineers, physicists, and technicians to determine and understand user needs, problems, and requests. Installed, configured, upgraded, and maintained SUN workstations, operating systems, tools applications, and hardware. Coordinated major events such as user migration, system relocation, and system installations. Coordinated, managed help desk requests. Set up/maintained user accounts. Configured and maintained Sun and Tektronix printers on printservers. Administered network backups for all systems. Maintained constant contact with vendors to coordinate hardware/software purchase, repairs, warranties, and upgrades.

EDUCATION

1/98 to Present	**Northwood University**	Cedar Hill, TX

Major: Business Management
(Bachelor of Arts Degree Expected Completion Date of 12/04)

PROFESSIONAL COURSES

Sun Microsystems –   Solaris Systems Administration, Network Administration, SunOS Systems Administration, Server Administration, NIS+ Administration.

Hewlett Packard -   HP-UX Systems Administration (700 & 800 Series)

Wendy Ryder

2251 Red Horse Trail   Home: 913-555-5794   Mobile: 913-555-8371   Marshall, Texas 78240
email@email.com

Education

Associate in Applied Science - Veterinary Technology
Cedar Valley College, Lancaster, Texas - 1993

Credentials

Registered Veterinary Technician
Texas State Board of Veterinary Medicine - 1993

Professional Qualifications

Accomplished paraprofessional with career focus on large animal veterinary treatment facilities.

- Highly motivated, professional and articulate. Special knack for client assistance and education.
- Enthusiastic, positive and patient-driven.
- Skilled and practiced in the following:
  - **Triage.**
  - **Laboratory procedures.**
  - **Surgical preparation and assistance.**
  - **Patient monitoring.**
  - **All areas of clinical treatment procedures—on site and on farm call.**
  - **Dental prophylaxis.**
  - **X-ray procedures.**
- Innate ability to communicate trust and reassurance to sick or injured animals.
  - Stimulate cooperation during treatment.
  - Accelerate healing process.

Professional History

Marshall Animal Hospital	Marshall, Texas	
Veterinary Assistant/Technician	1995 to Present	
Marshall County Veterinary Clinic	Marshall, Texas	
Veterinary Assistant/Technician	1993 to 1995	
Hunt County Veterinary Clinic	Greenville, Texas	
Kennel Worker/Vet Assistant	3/91 to 9/92	

Professional Associations

North American Veterinary Technician Association
International Arabian Horse Association

Personal

Avid fan, student and promoter of legendary Horse Whisperers' training methodology. Studied under renowned trainer Ray Hunt. Promote "Whisperer" training methods by scheduling and conducting clinics throughout the North Texas area.

—Related during client interview

Professional Experience

Critical Care

I remember one particular dog—a black Labrador with the sweetest eyes I'd ever seen—who was suffering from frequent grand mal seizures.

The Doc and I stayed with our patient for 3 days - 24 hours a day - searching for the right combination of meds (anticonvulsants) that would decrease the frequency, duration and severity of the seizures. (The patient was suffering severe attacks every 12 minutes at the most critical point.)

After we got the dog to a manageable level for quality of life, I'm not sure what made me happier—a thank you card from the owner, or knowing that the dog would have a happy life as long as he stayed on the meds that finally worked for him.

Initiation

I was new on the job and still pretty "green" when the Doc asked me to go out back and load up a bull for one of our clients. This animal had prevailed against other handlers and staff who had been trying to load him—without success—for most of the day.

It was just about closing time. I was tired, edgy and all the other stuff that doesn't work with bulls when I went out to the pen—a pit of freezing mud—and set to work opening an alley to push the bull through. I got stuck! Stuck in the mud up to the tops of my knee-high rubber boots! I was in a small holding pen with a 2000 lb. Beefmaster bull—and couldn't move an inch—seemed to dawn on the bull and me at the same time. It got "kinda western" for a minute...then common sense took over and I scrambled through the fence. I looked back and saw the bull charge my empty boots—still standing upright in the bog.

I got the bull loaded, but I did it from outside the pen. I'd been about as entertained by that bull as I cared to be.

Job Satisfaction

Most of a VT's job is not real pretty. If you work for a large animal vet, you persevere through freezing rain and mud, 100°+ heat, and a lot of cleaning up. But seeing an animal recover from a devastating disease or trauma makes it all worthwhile to me. I'll always remember the first time the vet told me to pull on a calf's leg—during a difficult birthing—and out he came! His momma cleaned him up and nuzzled him toward the milk factory...me and the Doc just stood in the pouring rain admiring another one of God's miracles. If it was easy, I guess everyone would do it.

383

HENRY SCHLESINGER

555 Crescent Hill
Brentwood, NY 11111
(631) 555-8888
SH@finsrvs.com

Financial Services Management

Management Information Systems…Client Services…Project Management

Senior financial services professional with a steadfast career in operations management with leading institutional and retail financial organizations. Experienced network administrator specialized in maintaining the stability of critical backbone systems that support real-time global financial activity. Effectively direct staff management functions and continuous improvement processes. Willing to travel extensively. Select qualifications encompass:

• Operations Management	• Account Management	• Regulatory Compliance
• Systems Operations	• Program Development	• Vendor Relations
• Staff Management	• Risk Management	• Disaster Recovery

Bachelor of Arts, Economics, Adelphi University, Garden City, NY
Active Member, Futures Industry Association (FIA)

PROFESSIONAL EXPERIENCE

Vice President, Futures Department, Johnson & Co., New York, NY   9/89 – present

Operations Management

➤ **Maintain dual responsibility for the management of business operations and Information Systems designed to process, track, and report daily investments of up to $38 million in Futures and Options.**

➤ **Instituted an operational infrastructure designed to manage front- and back-end operations supporting global trading of Futures, Options, government securities, OTCs, and foreign exchange instruments.**

➤ **Cross-train and supervise night operators and technicians in overnight processing of Back-office systems, billing, trading floor, and exchange fees, and mandatory generation of customer reports.**

• Build and maintain strong relationships with institutional customers, vendors, and international exchange representatives to expertly share information and consult on up-to-the-minute, market-moving financial news.

• Source for, and maintain, a vendor-network that supports mission-critical projects companywide.

• Established a front-end trading system that monitored customer portfolios for losses exceeding credit lines.

• Optimize cross-platform data systems to synchronize margin calls, cash management, wire transfers, trade corrections, give-up invoicing, trade balancing, adjustments, payouts, and floorbroker maintenance.

• Diversify overnight investments, achieving an annual increase in Return on Investment by 15%.

• Coordinate with worldwide branches concerning investments, regulatory reporting, gains maintenance, trade correction, general ledger, and cash balances to exchanges, including Japan and Switzerland.

• Strategically negotiated a 28% cost reduction in phone service contracts in 1999 that consistently decreased annual overhead expenditures by approximately $350,000.

• Track service and productivity levels to swiftly identify and resolve internal operational deficiencies.

— Continued —

HENRY SCHLESINGER

Page 2

Professional Experience, continued
Vice President, Futures Department, Johnson & Co.

Management Information Systems

➤ **Automated and simplified daily processes with an emphasis on reports and data feeds from exchanges and banks, currently utilized companywide.**

➤ **Contributed to the development of an Intranet Website for customers to view portfolios in real time, obtain end-of-day trade information, and download daily statements in PDF format.**

➤ **Spearheaded the installation and configuration of a Professional Automated Trading Systems (PATS).**

➤ **Led a six-month database upgrade project that replaced an outdated revenue tracking system and provided postinstallation support through in-service training and development of user manuals.**

➤ **Guided a GMI Back-office and Platinum General Ledger systems-upgrade project and provided ongoing systems maintenance and support for domestic and international branches.**

- Served as point of contact on a 24/7 basis to coordinate timely disaster recovery procedures directly impacting the stability of systems operations.

- Provided on-site and postinstallation support during rollouts, upgrades, networking, and optimization projects.

- Architected database programs that streamlined and enhanced sophisticated workflow efficiencies.

- Installed an in-house AS400 email delivery system, eliminating the costly need for third-party vendors.

- Produced Back-office data feeds that seamlessly interfaced with the Accounting Department's general ledger for on-demand generation of task-specific, queried reports.

- Introduced a user-friendly blotter system that sorted and emailed trades received in real time.

- Performed data storage on trade activity for Johnson and On-Commission Generation records for brokers.

- Developed custom reports and databases for staffs in Germany, Switzerland and Japan.

Treasurer, Marcus & Friedlander, New York, NY   8/85 – 9/89

➤ **Held accountability for the management of financial operations and information systems to ensure the integrity of trade entries, exchange fees, FX clearing, cash balancing, and broker commissions.**

➤ **Managed institutional accounts and margin calls for designated branches in areas of cash reconciliation, commission payouts, foreign trading reconciliation, and complaint logging and resolution.**

- Administered Back-office systems and database development projects to support daily operations in areas of computer terminal management, bank communications, wire transfers, and credit verification processes.

- Trained and supervised a staff of twenty-four operations personnel, and provided end-user support.

- Developed and beta tested newly implemented programs with the feedback from users and programmers.

MANAGEMENT INFORMATION SYSTEMS

Certified Novell Administrator; RPG III; IBM

Systems:	Windows NT/2000/98, Novell, AS/400, SQL Server
Software:	Microsoft Office, Microsoft Project, Client Access, FoxPro, Quattro Pro, Crystal Reports, Harris Cash Manager, Clearvision, WebSphere, Platinum G/L, GMI, PATS
Languages:	DB2, SQL, C++, CL, MQM
Protocols:	IPX/SPX, TCP/IP

DONALD BARRETT

555 Mackey Street • Overland Park, Kansas 55555
Home: 913-555-1313 • Cell: 913-555-5555
dbarret@careertrend.net

EXPERTISE: SALES LEADERSHIP – TERRITORY, PRODUCT AND TEAM MANAGEMENT

Generating consistent revenue streams and vaulting sales to unprecedented levels:

Year	2002	2001	2000	1999	1998	1997
% Increase Over Prior Year	60%	21%	90%	34%	28%	15%

Top-producing, highly competitive **Senior Sales Executive / Manager** with 15+ years' professional experience selling customer-focused solutions across diverse industries. A proven sales performer skilled at leading and motivating sales teams to success in highly competitive markets. Contributed to company's success in growing revenues and profits despite challenging economic and industry conditions. Perform in a fast-paced environment tasked with complex problem-solving initiatives. Experience and record of achievement with Fortune 500 firms.

- Strategic Sales / C-Level Presence
- Competitive Market Intelligence
- Major Account Retention / Development
- Operating Leadership
- Profit & Loss Management

- High-Impact Presentations
- Customer Needs Assessment
- Customer Relationship Management
- Performance Improvement
- Turnaround Management

SALES HIGHLIGHTS / PERFORMANCE

Heavily involved in multiple turnaround and highly competitive environments with track record of exceeding multi-million-dollar sales goals and spearheading innovative and profitable sales programs.

Sample clients:
Kraft Foods, General Mills, Unilever/Best Foods, Nabisco, Lipton

- **Tagged to steer an experienced group of engineers** into a cohesive and bottom-line-focused sales team, securing aggressive contracts for Major Packaging. Exceeding sales goals YTD.
- **Instrumental leader/member of sales team** that helped rescue Major Packaging, a company experiencing declining revenues and severe losses, to achieve both climbing revenues and profits.
  - Weathered challenging economic conditions, hoisting sales to record levels, punctuated by an 90% sales increase, 2000.
  - Keys to turnaround success: Revamped sales force; landed two key accounts – Lipton California / Chicago; and consummated **largest-ever agreement with General Mills, a $7M per-year deal ($15.5M in capital with a 5-year contract).**
- **Challenged with $100M annual revenue accountability** and management across 8 individuals (sales and administrative staff) as Major Packaging's Vice President of Sales.
  - Incited sales team to record performance, customizing leadership strategies across highly tenured individuals.
  - **Secured an average 30% margin** on sales.
- **Outdistanced competition by providing impressive relationship development** and problem-solving acumen:
  - **Example: Captured $3.5M in annual business** by attacking quality assurance issue at key account that involved on-site visits and problem-solving with colleagues and clients at Major Packaging's Atlanta, Georgia plant.
- **Established District as #1 Performer among 87 districts** while District Manager at ABC Leasing in St. Louis, Missouri

SALES / MANAGEMENT CAREER PROGRESSION

FOOD PACKAGING, INC., Kansas City, Missouri   2003 to Present
New and used food / retail packaging machinery and packaging equipment sales (rental, lease and refurbishment) marketing to companies in the food, pharmaceutical and novelty toy business. [www.foodpackaging.com]

General Manager – Sales

Brought on board to foster a sales mentality among 6 technically trained, but non-sales-oriented professionals. Charged with cultivating a revenue-focused inside sales team targeting an international clientele (United States, Canada and South America). Scope of day-to-day accountability is diverse and includes oversight of the entire business operation and leadership / motivation of administrative, production (shop) and sales staff. Interview, hire, coach and, as needed, terminate employees.

- **Instituted weekly sales meetings** to recognize and reinforce successful sales strategies, troubleshoot aborted sales opportunities and review actual sales vs. budget.
- **Originated and implemented use of "tough closing questions"** across sales staff.
- **Unified employee commitment** to company goals by shaping a mutually respectful environment.

MAJOR PACKAGING COMPANY, St. Louis, Missouri   1992 to 2002
Outsource provider of manufacturing and logistics capabilities to Fortune 500 food, retail, and consumer products companies. [www.majorpackaging.com]

Vice President of Sales, 1995 to 2002

Reporting directly to CEO, directed sales activities for industry segment, selling Major Packaging's products to 7 key accounts across a 50-state territory. Managed sales team (8 national sales executives) to consistently high performance levels. Recruited, hired and nurtured a well-balanced, diverse, focused team through motivation, leadership, training and establishment of relentless customer relationship management as the foundation for business success. Originated and managed/forecasted sales budget to plan, determining all pricing decisions.

- **Instrumental in catapulting Major Packaging's sales team** to record-level performance.
- **Generated year over year double-digit percentage sales increases** for the largest contract manufacturer of food and beverage products in the U.S.

Vice President of Sales – Beverage Division, 1994 • Director of Operations – Dry Division, 1993 • National Sales Executive, 1992

Initiated tenure as National Sales Executive marketing to major food/beverage companies, earning succession of promotions to Director of Operations, accountable for 4 dry food manufacturing plants, capital expenditures and budget/profitability management; and Vice President of Sales (Beverage Division); before ultimate promotion to Vice President of Sales.

ABC LEASING CORPORATION / XYZ TRUCK LEASING, St. Louis, Missouri   1987 to 1991

District Manager, (St. Louis, Missouri) • **District Manager** (Kansas City, Missouri) • **Director of Rental Operations** (Detroit, Michigan) • **Rental Development Manager** (St. Louis, Missouri) **Rental Division Manager** (St. Louis)

Aspired to turn around worst-performing district for ABC Leasing by spearheading aggressive and customer-focused sales and collections initiatives, **jacking up district to #1 of 87 districts.**

- **Charter Member, President's Award; Quota Buster Award.**
- **2 Super Awards for Best Profit vs. Plan and Best Overall Operating District.**

MAJOR TRANSPORT SYSTEMS, Des Moines, Iowa   1984 to 1986
Account Manager, Leasing Division / *Rookie of the Year*

EDUCATION

B.S. in Economics, 1984, Missouri University, Columbia, Missouri

LESTER HOLMES, JR.
(719) 555-9050
115 North Union Boulevard
Colorado Springs, Colorado 80909
lholmes@msn.com

Hospitality—Food & Beverage

Wait Staff - Host - Bartender - Trainer

EDUCATION

Undergraduate studies, General Education, Pikes Peak Community College
Graduate, Colorado Food Handling Safety Course
Graduate, Colorado Bartending School (License is current)
Graduate, Customer Service Training Program, Antonio's Restaurante
Graduate, Mitchell High School, Colorado Springs, Colorado [1993]

PROFESSIONAL EXPERIENCE

October 1995
to
Present

WAIT STAFF - TRAINER
BROADMOOR HOTEL, COLORADO SPRINGS, COLORADO
(A world renowned 5-Star and 5-Diamond Hotel and Resort with 4 gourmet restaurants)

- Assigned to all four gourmet facilities:
    (Penrose Room, Tavern, Spencer's and the Golf Club)
- Greet guests and make them feel immediately welcome
- Assist patrons with food and wine selections, including daily specials
- Prepare and serve a wide variety of menu items
- Operate and recocile a cash fund with high-volume transactions
- Responsible for training all new wait staff in procedures

June 1993
to
October 1995

[Part-time
evenings]

WAIT STAFF - HOST
PEPPER TREE RESTAURANT, COLORADO SPRINGS, COLORADO
(A small, up-scale, fine dining facility with a high-volume of repeat customers)

- Required to greet all repeat guests by their names and honorifics
- Menu presentation is 100% verbal, with kitchen creating special requests
- Extensive table-side presentation of salad and main course items
- Serve as Host on weekends, greeting guests and acting as maitre-d

June 1993
to
Present

[part-time days]

BARTENDER
PATTY JEWETT GOLF CLUB, COLORADO SPRINGS, COLORADO
(A fast-paced and high-volume public facility with a very casual atmosphere)

- Prepare a wide range of mixed drinks from well to call labels
- Significant problem resolution responsibilities
- Order, stock, control and inventory all liquor and mixes
- Troubleshoot beer-wine taps plus refrigeration and dish washing equipment

References and Amplified Background Information Available Upon Request

Dan Petry

9871 Pinecrest Place #24C
Brandon, Florida 32510
813-555-9779
emailaddress@emailaddress.com

WEB DEVELOPMENT / WEB PROGRAMMING / WEB DESIGN / WEBMASTER

Web Developer with experience in multimedia and Web design. Skilled in assessment of client needs and requirements. Capable creator of viable e-business solutions from concept to implementation. Proficiency in JavaScript and Perl scripting languages and Active Server Pages; broad knowledge of database structures. Team builder with strong customer service focus and highly effective communication skills.

Programming: HTML 4.0; ASP 2.0/3.0; VBScript; JavaScript; Perl
Operating Systems: Windows 98/NT/2000; UNIX
Applications: PhotoShop 5.5 / ImageReady 2.0; HomeSite 4.5; MS SQL 7; Dreamweaver 2.0; Microsoft Office 2000; Flash 4; CakeWalk Pro Audio 8.0; Xing AudioCatalyst

EDUCATION /
CREDENTIALS B.A. Education, State University   Graduated with honors, May 1995
            Passed Microsoft's **Network Essentials** examination   March 1999

EXPERIENCE INTERNETTRAVEL.COM
Web Developer   March 2000 – Present
Work with other programmers, database developer, graphic artists, video encoders, and content staff to create, maintain, and upgrade, travel information Web site. Integrate new products into existing Web pages. Design, develop, and code Web pages using Active Server Pages (ASP), VBScript, JavaScript, MS SQL 7, and HTML 4.0. Oversee development of intranet and Administration Web sites for company.

- **Embedded QuickTime video player into Web pages to ensure convenient and seamless viewing of video travel clips on Web site.**
- **Challenged to integrate proprietary chat and message board applications into Web site. Researched/analyzed products, acquired necessary development tools and successfully completed project, adding functionality and consumer interest to the Web site. Applications used Apache Web server on NT server.**
- **Co-supervise intern programmer; assign projects and evaluate skills and performance.**

MUNICIPAL GOVERNMENT CONSORTIUM
Web Services Administrator   April 1999 – March 2000
Maintained consortium's intranet and Internet sites, accessible by 300+ member organizations. Consulted with member groups to develop their Web sites. Created and/or modified graphics and animations for consortium Web sites. Installed software and hardware; provided technical support for users.

- Implemented online intranet auction utilizing ASP. Site has attracted interest and consultation requests from several municipalities across the country.
- Implemented online message board (Perl).
- Designed, developed, and coded legislative bill tracking system for intranet site, using ASP. System facilitated research and enabled member groups to act quickly on time-sensitive legislative issues.
- Acquired secure server certificate to acceptance of online credit card purchases.
- Compiled 400 + e-mail addresses of associates; developed database and created/distributed weekly e-mail news bulletin with links to consortium Web site. Increased Web site traffic substantially.

(Continued)

Dan Petry   Page 2

INDEPENDENT WEB DEVELOPER   February 2000 - Present
Created and maintain eCommerce site for small commercial enterprise. Assessed customer needs; collaborated with business owner to create visually attractive Web pages and to develop effective online marketing strategies. Researched site's Internet visibility potential. Currently evaluating the possibility of creating database back end for client to display inventory more quickly on Web site.

• Web site consistently ranks in top 9 views in product searches on major search engines.

MUNICIPAL LIBRARY
Computer Support/Trainer   April 1999 – October 1999
Hired to modify existing computer training curriculum for library staff. Instructed classes in Windows NT, MS Office 97 programs and Internet skills. Additionally created, modified, and taught curriculum for public computer training classes (up to ten students per class).

• Provided computer support to patrons using MS Office 97 programs and Internet Explorer 4.

ATTORNEYS-AT-LAW INC.
Legal Assistant   Spring 1994; June 1995 - July 1998
Initially a temporary placement, then hired full-time to provide administrative and clerical support for attorney. Established, organized, and maintained legal records and files. Researched, drafted, and prepared reports, forms, contracts, legal documents, Board minutes, correspondence, and IRS applications. Served as liaison to State University.

• Used MS Access to track payments to client accounts, created a variety of reports quickly and accessed information easily. Maximized productivity while minimizing mistakes.

MUNICIPAL BOARD OF EDUCATION
Math Tutor   August 1994 - June 1995
Tutored students (1st - 5th grades) in math problem-solving strategies. Maintained anecdotal records, individual folders, and periodic progress reports.

• Member of Focus Group that made recommendations for program improvement.

STATE LAW LIBRARY
Librarian Assistant   October 1987 - January 1994
Provided limited supervision of Clerks and Pages. Assisted patrons with use of IBM and Macintosh personal computers.

MUSICIAN
Guitarist/Songwriter
Co-manager: Booked performances; negotiated fees; contacted media, record stores, and radio stations; promotion and marketing; conferred with legal representative and handled other business matters.

References and samples of work available upon request

Tom Martin

8600 Aspen Ridge • Apartment 15
Ann Arbor, Michigan 48103
734.555.1492   tmartin@airmail.com

Objective

Web-head techie looking for long and short-term Web, Internet, and eCommerce projects and assignments utilizing heavy JAVA, HTML, Web browsers, and MS applications. Highly skilled in troubleshooting and problem-solving complicated situations.

Background in building and updating Web sites, researching projects, and consulting for general business, education, music, movies, games, sports, and independent retail companies.

Education

UNIVERSITY OF MICHIGAN; Ann Arbor, Michigan
COMPUTER TECHNOLOGY curriculum *(undeclared major)*

PIONEER HIGH SCHOOL; Ann Arbor, Michigan
GRADUATE, 1998
• Assisted school in hardware/software integration with all the middle-level schools in the district.
• Presented computer workshops to middle and elementary-level students.

Experience

IKANDOIT; Ann Arbor, Michigan
INDEPENDENT CONTRACTOR— Web Surfing Geek, 1995-current
Undertake challenging projects to assist companies and individuals with software and hardware concerns. Examples include:

Joe's Sport Shop — Built and maintain a Website promoting University of Michigan sport merchandise and sport memorabilia. State-of-the-art site encouraged worldwide business and quadrupled sales in the first year.

ConeZone Coneys — Developed successful marketing and promotional application tools that partnered with Sony to create a movie featurette. Fast-tracked the production and delivered final product in only five weeks.

Ann Arbor Brokerage — Assisted with online trading and brokerage Website to broaden customer base and cross-sell banking services.

TechnoLogic — Mined the Internet to locate and identify potential avenues of growth for startup business.

CosmicWare — Developed cool entertainment, sports, and game Websites (i.e., ZoneGame.com, ZoneKid.com).

BERNARD LAW
18 Allan Circle
Durham, North Carolina 27707
(919) 555-1212/email@email.com

Seeking Position as...

WELDER/FABRICATOR
Mig/Tig/Gas/Stick/and Plasma for Custom Fixtures and Finished Products

**Recognized for 100% QUALITY Work/Perfect Safety Record
Trained in Lathes, Mills, Drills, and Polishers
21 Years' Experience**

Twenty-one-plus years' experience as a professional welder/fabricator. Outstanding work ethic with attention to quality, costs, and project scheduling (deadlines).

AREAS OF STRENGTH

Strong technical and mechanical aptitude	Custom fabrication and welding
OSHA regulations and code compliance	Skills in all types of welding
Have own set of tools	Excellent trainer in high-skill work
Communication skills—verbal and written	Quality assurance
Customer service	Project coordination—expense control

EMPLOYMENT

Strong Weld, Inc., Durham, North Carolina   1995 to Present
Welder Fabricator

- Perform for all types of fixture welding, including mig/tig welding of stainless to carbon
- Work within strict tolerances; perform welding of metal .004 to $^{1}/4$ inch
- Contributing member in the fabrication of precision cloisters for HVAC applications (exceeding EPA standards)
- Fabricate various products based on customer specifications—work with major clients, including Office Depot
- Welded cooler tanks used in plastic-injection molding—developed technology to reduce welding time by 25%

O'Sullivans Fabrication, Durham, North Carolina   1991 to 1995
Welder

- Performed detailed welding for manufacturing equipment—$1 million and up
- Utilized customer's blueprints and assembled heavy machinery to withstand high-tolerance levels
- Responsible for precision welding on flat-base construction equipment
- Assembled stainless steel equipment using purge/tig, hand-free, and out-of-position welding

EMPLOYMENT (Prior to 1995)

Courier/Driver	UPS	1984 to 1995
Maintenance Supervisor	High-rise Cleaning Service	1981 to 1984

EDUCATION/TRAINING

DURHAM VOCATIONAL AND TECHNICAL COLLEGE, Durham, North Carolina
Welding and Fabrication, 1985 and 1986

EDDIE BRODY HIGH SCHOOL, Durham, North Carolina
Graduate, 1984

References and Supporting Documentation Furnished upon Request

Ensemble Group, Inc.
Orchestrating Communication Solutions
BEN WONG

WIRELESS MANAGEMENT CONSULTANT

DEPLOYMENT STRATEGIES, ORGANIZATIONAL DESIGN, CHANGE MANAGEMENT, SITE DEVELOPMENT, CONSTRUCTION MANAGEMENT, PCS/RF ENGINEERING, AND NETWORK DEPLOYMENT MANAGEMENT.

PROJECT MANAGEMENT

Multiple Engineering Department operation, staff, and resources management.

Proposal preparation and contract negotiation.

Strategy development and formation of strategic alliance(s).

Establishment of customer relationship.

Account attainment and management.

RF ENGINEERING TECHNOLOGIES

Digital: CDMA, TDMA.

Analog: AMPs – Americas, TACs – International.

Paging: FLEX (1 way), REFLEX 2.5 (2 way).

ENGINEERING

Design
Create Initial RF design(s) for bidding of wireless carrier licenses and RFP(s) using propagation, and statistical software.

Create demographic and morphology calculations for bidding of wireless carrier licenses and RFP models.

Evaluate and analyze link budgets.

Direct and create coverage, frequency, and capacity plans.

Implementation
Implement Q&A procedures to monitor effective installation of RF communication system.

Direct and implement processes for site noise and interference measurements.

Monitor Microwave Link relocation process to reduce link and designed network interference.

Present and submit technology reports to regulatory and local agencies.

(continued)

Ben Wong

Ensemble Group, Inc.
Orchestrating Communication Solutions

Optimization

- Implement drive-test procedures resulting in effective measurements in determining RF network performance.
- Train RF Engineering personnel about the effective processes and techniques.
- Create processes and procedures to manage network expansion and RF databases.
- Create procedures to monitor and record all pertinent RF OMC parameter changes.
- Implement and optimize existing and additional CBSC's to alleviate current capacity and system expansion.
- Implement Operational key indicators to persistently improve capacity and cell site dimensioning.

EQUIPMENT/TOOLS

- Safeco-MDM, OPAS; Qualcomm-DM, LPAR; Grayson-CW test equipment; Lucent-AutoPace, HP-E4900, HP-E7450 to E7480 (optimization tools), HP-E7480; MapInfo; ISG-CellDesigner; MSI-PlaNET, LCC-ANET, CelluMate, RSAT, Comarco; Safeco; AEthos-Odyssey, SUN OS UNIX.

PROFESSIONAL EXPERIENCE

PageNet Inc., Dallas, TX	Principal Consultant	6/98 – present
WaveLink Systems Inc., Dallas, TX	Principal Consultant	1/97 – 4/98
Aethos Communications, Dallas, TX	Senior Consultant	3/95 – 3/96
Mobile Systems International, Chicago, IL	Senior Engineer	3/93 – 3/95
Ameritech Cellular, Schaumburg, IL	RF Performance Engineer	5/92 – 3/93
LCC Inc., Arlington, VA	Associate RF Engineer	10/90 – 5/92

WIRELESS NETWORK CONSULTING ENGAGEMENTS

PageNet	Dallas, TX	2-way messaging
	Chicago, IL	REFLEX 25/FLEX
Sprint PCS	Salt Lake City, UT	CDMA
PrimeCo Personal Communications	Dallas MTA, TX	CDMA
PrimeCo Personal Communications	Miami MTA, FL	CDMA
Bell Atlantic Personal Communications	Arlington, VA	CDMA/GSM
Bell South Personal Communications	Atlanta, GA	CDMA/GSM
Ameritech Personal Communications	Hoffman Estates, IL	AMPS
CellNet	London UK	TACS
AirTouch Cellular	Los Angeles, CA	AMPS
Bay Area Cellular	San Francisco, CA	AMPS

EDUCATION

Bachelor of Science in Electrical Engineering, Capitol College, May 1990

13
Tips and Strategies

25 TIPS FOR USING THE INTERNET IN YOUR JOB SEARCH

1. When typing your resume out with the intent of e-mailing it, make sure it is in an ASCII format.

2. Use keywords heavily in the introduction of the resume, not at the end.

3. Keywords are almost always nouns, related to skills, such as financial analysis, marketing, accounting, and Web design.

4. When sending your resume via e-mail in an ASCII format, attach (if you can) a nicely formatted one in case it does go through and the reader would like to see your creativity and preferred layout. If you do attach it, use a common program such as Microsoft Word.

5. Don't focus on an objective in the introduction of the resume; focus on accomplishments, using keywords to describe them.

6. Don't post your resume to your own Website unless it is a very slick page. A poorly executed Web page is more damaging than none at all.

7. Before you e-mail your resume, try sending it to yourself and to a friend as a test drive.

8. Look up the Website of the company you are targeting to get recent news information about new products and look for its job posting for new information.

9. Before your interview or verbal contact, research the company's Website.

10. Use a font size between 10 and 14 points, make it all the same for an ASCII format resume, and don't create your resume for e-mailing with lines exceeding 65 characters.

11. In case your resume may be scanned, use white paper with no borders and no creative fonts.

12. Include your e-mail address on your resume and cover letter.

13. Don't e-mail from your current employer's IP network.

14. Don't circulate your work e-mail address for job search purposes.

15. In the "subject" of your e-mail (just below the "address to" part), put something more creative than "Resume Enclosed." Try "Resume showing 8 years in telecommunications industry" (if that is your chosen industry), for example.

16. For additional sources of online job searching, do a "search" on the Web for job searching, your targeted company, and your specific discipline for additional information.

17. Be careful of your spelling on the Internet. You will notice more spelling errors in e-mail exchanges than you will ever see in mailed letter exchanges.

18. Try to make sure your resume is scannable. This means it has a simple font, no borders, no creative lining, no boldface, no underlining, no italics, and limited if any columning. Though the practice of scanning is overestimated, it should still be a consideration.

19. Purchase or check out of a library an Internet directory listing the many links to job opportunities out there. There are thousands.

20. If you are using the e-mail as your cover letter, keep it brief. If the readers are reading on screen, their tolerance for reading long passages of information is reduced dramatically.

21. Always back up what you can on a disk.

22. If you post your resume to a newsgroup, first make sure that this is acceptable to avoid any problems with other participants.

23. Remember that tabs and spaces are the only formatting you can do in ASCII.

24. Make sure to check your e-mail every day. If you are communicating via the Internet, people may expect a prompt return.

25. Don't send multiple e-mails to ensure that one gets through. Try to send it with aconfirmation of receipt or keep a lookout for a notice from your ISP that the message didn't go through.

25 NETWORKING TIPS

1. Two-thirds of all jobs are secured via the networking process. Networking is a systematic approach to cultivating formal and informal contacts for the purpose of gaining information, enhancing visibility in the market, and obtaining referrals.

2. Effective networking requires self-confidence, poise, and personal conviction.

3. You must first know the companies and organizations you wish to work for. That will determine the type of network you will develop and nurture.

4. Focus on meeting the "right people." This takes planning and preparation.

5. Target close friends, family members, neighbors, social acquaintances, social and religious group members, business contacts, teachers, and community leaders.

6. Include employment professionals as an important part of your network. This includes headhunters and personnel agency executives. They have a wealth of knowledge about job and market conditions.

7. Remember, networking is a numbers game. Once you have a network of people in place, prioritize the listing so that you have separated top-priority contacts from lower-priority ones.

8. Sometimes you may have to pay for advice and information. Paying consultants or professionals or investing in Internet services is part of the job search process today as long as it's legal and ethical.

9. Know what you want from your contacts. If you don't know what you want, neither will your network of people. Specific questions will get specific answers.

10. Ask for advice, not for a job. You should not contact someone and ask if that person knows of any job openings. The answer will invariably be no, especially at higher levels. You need to ask for things like industry advice and advice on geographic areas. The job insights will follow but will be almost incidental. This positioning will build value for you and make the contact person more comfortable about helping you.

11. Watch your attitude and demeanor at all times. Everyone you come in contact with is a potential member of your network. Demonstrate enthusiasm and professionalism at all times.

12. Keep a file on each member of your network and maintain good records at all times. A well-organized network filing system or database will yield superior results.

13. Get comfortable on the telephone. Good telephone communication skills are critical.

14. Travel the "information highway." Networking is more effective if you have e-mail, fax, and computer capabilities.

15. Be well prepared for your conversation, whether in person or over the phone. You should have a script in your mind of how to answer questions, what to ask, and what you're trying to accomplish.

16. Do not fear rejection. If a contact cannot help you, move on to the next contact. Do not take rejection personally—it's part of the process.

17. Flatter the people in your network. It's been said that the only two types of people who can be flattered are men and women. Use tact, courtesy, and flattery.

18. If a person in your network cannot personally help, advise, or direct you, ask for referrals.

19. Keep in touch with the major contacts in your network on a monthly basis. Remember, out of sight, out of mind.

20. Don't abuse the process. Networking is a two-way street. Be honest and brief and offer your contacts something in return for their time, advice, and information. This can be as simple as a lunch or an offer of your professional services in return for their cooperation.

21. Show an interest in your contacts. Cavette Robert, one of the founders of the National Speakers Association, said, "People don't care how much you know until they know how much you care." Show how much you care. It will get you anywhere.

22. Send thank-you notes after each networking contact.

23. Seek out key networking contacts in professional and trade associations.

24. Carry calling cards with you at all times to hand out to anyone and everyone you come in contact with. Include your name, address, phone number, areas of expertise, and specific skill areas.

25. Socialize and get out more than ever before. Networking requires dedication and massive amounts of energy. Consistently work on expanding your network.

25 "WHAT DO I DO NOW THAT I HAVE MY RESUME?" TIPS

1. Develop a team of people who will be your board of directors, advisers, and mentors. The quality of the people you surround yourself with will determine the quality of your results.

2. Plan a marketing strategy. Determine how many hours a week you will work, how you'll divide your time, and how you'll measure your progress. Job searching is a business in itself—and a marketing strategy is your business plan.

3. Identify 25 (50 would be better) companies or organizations you would like to work for.

4. Contact the companies or do some research to identify hiring authorities.

5. Define your network (see "25 Networking Tips"). Make a list of everyone you know, including relatives, friends, acquaintances, family doctors, attorneys, CPAs, the cleaning person, and the mail carrier. Virtually everyone is a possible networking contact.

6. Prioritize your list of contacts into three categories: (1) strong, approachable contacts, (2) good contacts or those who must be approached more formally, and (3) those whom you'd like to contact but can't without an introduction by another party.

7. Set up a filing system or database to organize and manage your contacts.

8. Develop a script or letter for the purpose of contacting the key people in your network, asking for advice, information, and assistance. Then start contacting them.

9. Attempt to find a person or persons in your network who can make an introduction into one of the 25 or 50 companies you've noted in item 3.

10. Spend 65 to 70% of your time, energy, and resources networking because 65 to 70% of all jobs are secured by this method.

11. Consider contacting executive recruiters or employment agencies to assist in your job search.

12. If you are a recent college graduate, seek out assistance from the campus career center.

13. Scout the classified advertisements every Sunday. Respond to ads that interest you, and look at other ads as well. A company may be advertising for a position that does not fit your background but say in the ad that it is "expanding in the area." You have just identified a growing company.

14. Seek out advertisements and job opportunities in specific trade journals and magazines.

15. Attend as many social and professional functions as you can. The more people you meet, the better your chances are of securing a position quickly.

16. Send out resumes with customized cover letters to targeted companies or organizations. Address the cover letter to a specific person. Then follow up.

17. Target small to medium-size companies. Most of the opportunities are coming from these organizations, not from large corporations.

18. Consider contacting temporary agencies. Almost 40% of all temporary personnel are offered permanent positions. Today a greater percentage of middle and upper managers, as well as professionals, are working in temporary positions.

19. Use online services. America Online, Prodigy, and CompuServe have career services, employment databases, bulletin boards, and online discussion and support groups, as well as access to the Internet. This is the wave of the future.

20. If you are working from home, be sure the room you are working from is inspiring, organized, and private. This is your space, and it must motivate you!

21. If your plan is not working, meet with members of your support team and change the plan. You must remain flexible and adaptable to change.

22. Read and observe. Read magazines and newspapers and listen to CNBC, CNN, and so on. Notice which companies and organizations are on the move and contact them.

23. Set small, attainable weekly goals. Keep a weekly progress report on all your activities. Try to do a little more each week than you did the week before.

24. Stay active. Exercise and practice good nutrition. A job search requires energy. You must remain in superior physical and mental condition.

25. Volunteer. Help those less fortunate than you. What goes around comes around.

25 INTERVIEWING TIPS

1. Relax. The employment interview is just a meeting. Although you should not treat this meeting lightly, don't forget that the organization interviewing you is in need of your services as much as, or perhaps more than, you are of theirs.

2. The key to successful interviewing is rapport building. Most people spend their time preparing for interviews by memorizing canned responses to anticipated questions. Successful interviewers spend most of their time practicing the art of rapport building through the use of powerfully effective communicating techniques.

3. Prepare a manila folder that you will bring to the interview. Include the following in the folder:

   * Company information (annual reports, sales material, etc.)

   * Extra resumes (6 to 12) and your letters of reference

   * 15 questions you've prepared based on your research and analysis of the company

   * A blank legal pad, a pen, and anything else you consider helpful (e.g., college transcripts)

4. Dress appropriately. Determine the dress code and meet it. If their dress is business casual, you still need to be dressed business professional. Practice proper grooming and hygiene.

5. Shoes, of course, must be polished.

6. Wear limited jewelry.

7. Call the day before and confirm the appointment—that will set you apart.

8. Be certain you know exactly where you're going. Arrive in plenty of time. You should be at the receptionist's desk 10 to 12 minutes before the scheduled interview.

9. Before meeting the receptionist, check your appearance. Check your hair, clothing, and general image. Test your smile.

10. Secretaries, administrative assistants, and receptionists often have a say in the hiring process. Make a strong first impression on them.

11. Look around the office and search for artifacts that disclose the personality and culture of the company—and possibly the interviewer. This information will be helpful in initially breaking the ice, when you first begin discussions.

12. Be aware of your body language. Sit erect, with confidence. When standing and walking, move with confidence!

13. Your handshake should be firm, made with a wide-open hand, fingers stretched wide apart. Women should feel comfortable offering their hands for firm and friendly handshakes. A power handshake and a great smile will get you off to a great start.

14. Eye contact is one of the most powerful forms of communication. It demonstrates confidence, trust, and power.

15. During the interview lean forward toward the interviewer. Show enthusiasm and sincere interest.

16. Take notes during the interview. You may want to refer to them later in the interview. If you are uncomfortable with this, ask permission first.

17. Be prepared for all questions, especially uncomfortable ones. Before the interview, script out a one-page response for each question that poses a problem for you and practice repeating it until you're comfortable with it.

18. Communicate your skills, qualifications, and credentials to the hiring manager. Describe your market value and the benefits you offer. *Demonstrate how you will contribute to the bottom line.* Show how you can (1) improve sales, (2) reduce costs, (3) improve productivity, and/or (4) solve organizational problems.

19. Key in on *specific accomplishments*. Accomplishments determine hireability. They separate the winners from the runners-up.

20. Listening skills are priceless! Job offers are made to those who listen well, find hidden meanings, and answer questions in a brief but effective manner.

21. Let the interviewer bring up salary first. The purpose of an interview is to determine whether there is a match. Once that is determined, salary should be negotiated.

22. There is no substitute for planning and preparation, practice and rehearsing—*absolutely none.*

23. Practice interviewing techniques by using video technology. A minimum of five hours of video practice, preferably more, guarantees a stellar performance.

24. Close the sale. If you find that you want the position, ask for it. Ask directly, "Is there anything that would prevent you from offering me this position

now?" or "Do you have any reservations or concerns?" (if you sense that). At the very least, this should flush out any objections and give you the opportunity to turn them into positives.

25. Always send a thank-you note within 24 hours of every employment meeting.

25 SALARY NEGOTIATING TIPS

1. From the moment you make initial contact with any company or organization you wish to work with, you are in negotiation. You may not be discussing money openly, but you are making a permanent imprint on the minds of the hiring authorities.

2. Delay all discussions of salary until there is an offer on the table.

3. You are in the strongest negotiating position right after the offer is made.

4. Know your value. You must know how you can contribute to the organization. Establish this in the mind of the hiring manager.

5. Get employers enthusiastic about your candidacy and they will become more generous.

6. There is no substitute for preparation. If you are well prepared, you'll be confident, self-assured, and poised for success.

7. Before going into employment negotiations, you must know the average salary paid for similar positions with other organizations in your geographic area.

8. Before going into employment negotiations you must know, as best you can, the salary range that the company you're interviewing with will pay or what former employees were earning.

9. Before going into employment negotiations, you must know your personal needs and requirements and how they relate to items 7 and 8 above.

10. Remember, fringes and perks such as vacation time, flex time, health benefits, and pension plans have value. Consider the "total" salary package.

11. Salary negotiations must be win-win negotiations. If they're not, everybody loses in the end.

12. Be flexible; don't get hung up on trivial issues and always seek compromise when possible.

13. Listen carefully and pay close attention. Your goals most likely will be different from the goals of the employer. For instance, the firm's main focus might be "base salary." Yours might be "total earning potential." A win-win solution might be to negotiate a lower base salary but a higher commission or bonus structure.

14. Anticipate objections and prepare effective answers to them.

15. Try to understand the employer's point of view. Then plan a strategy to meet both the employer's concerns and your needs.

16. Don't be afraid to negotiate because of fear of losing the offer. Most employers expect you to negotiate as long as you negotiate in a fair and reasonable manner.

17. Always negotiate in a way that reflects your personality, character, and work ethic. Remain within your comfort zone.

18. Never lose control. Remain enthusiastic and upbeat even if the negotiations get a little hot. This may be your first test under fire.

19. Play hardball only if you're willing to walk away from or lose the deal.

20. What you lose in the negotiations most likely will never be recouped. Don't be careless in preparing for or conducting the negotiation.

21. Be sure to get the offer and final agreement in writing.

22. You should feel comfortable asking the employer for 24 to 48 hours to think about the deal if you need time to think it over.

23. Never link salary to personal needs or problems. Compensation should always be linked to your value.

24. Understand your leverage. Know if you are in a position of strength or weakness and negotiate intelligently based on your personal situation.

25. End salary negotiations on a friendly and cheerful note.

25 UNCONVENTIONAL TECHNIQUES FOR UNCOVERING AND SECURING NEW OPPORTUNITIES

1. If you see a classified ad that sounds really good for you but only lists a fax number and no company name, try to figure out the company name by trying similar numbers. For example, if the fax number is 555-4589, try 555-4500 or 555-4000 and get the company name and contact person so that you can send a more personalized letter and resume.

2. Send your resume in a Priority Mail envelope for serious prospects. It costs only $3, but will stand out and get you noticed.

3. Check the targeted company's Website; there may be postings there that others without computer access haven't seen.

4. If you see a classified ad for a good prospective company but for a different position, contact them anyway. If they are new in town (or even if they're not), they may have other, nonadvertised openings.

5. Always have a personalized card with you in case you meet a good networking or employment prospect.

6. Always have a quick personal briefing rehearsed to speak to someone who might be helpful.

7. Network in nonwork environments, such as a happy-hour bar (a great opportunity to network) or an airport.

8. Network with your college alumni office. Many college graduates list their current employers with that office, and they may be a good source of leads, even out of state.

9. Most newspapers list all the new companies that have applied for business licenses. Check that section and contact the ones that are appealing to you.

10. Call your attorney and accountant and ask if they can refer you to any companies or business contacts; perhaps they have a good business relationship that you can leverage.

11. Contact the Chamber of Commerce for information on new companies moving into the local area.

12. Don't give up if you've had just one rejection from a company you are targeting. You shouldn't feel that you have truly contacted that company until you have contacted at least three different people there.

13. Join networking clubs and associations that will expose you to new business contacts.

14. Ask stockbrokers for tips on which companies they identify as fast-growing and good companies to grow with.

15. Make a list of everyone you know and use them all as a network source.

16. Put an endorsement portfolio together and mail it out with targeted resumes.

17. Employ the hiring proposal strategy. (See *101 Best Cover Letters*.)

18. Post your resume on the Internet, selecting news groups and bulletin boards that will readily accept it and match your industry and discipline.

19. Don't forget to demonstrate passion and enthusiasm when you are meeting with people, interviewing with them, and networking through them.

20. Look in your industry's trade journals. Nearly all industries and disciplines have several, and most journals have advertising sections in the back that list potential openings with companies and recruiters. This is a great resource in today's low-unemployment environment.

21. Visit a job fair. For most professionals, there won't be managerial positions recruited for, but there will be many companies present, and you may discover a hot lead. If they are recruiting in general, you should contact them directly for a possible fit.

22. Don't overlook employment agencies. They may seem like a weak possibility, but they may uncover a hidden opportunity or serve as a source to network through.

23. Look for companies that are promoting their products by using a lot of advertising. Sales are probably going well, and they may be good hiring targets for you.

24. Call a prospective company and simply ask who its recruiting firm is. If they have one, they'll tell you, and then you can contact that firm to get in the door.

25. Contact every recruiter in town. Befriend them and use them as networking sources if possible. Always thank them, to the point of sending them a small gift for helping you out. This will pay off in dividends in the future. Recruiters are always good contacts.

Index

ABOUT THE AUTHORS

Jay A. Block, CPRW, internationally certified career coach and resume strategist, is the contributing cofounder of the Professional Association of Resume Writers (PARW). He helped develop the PARW national certification process and is a widely respected national speaker, author, and career coach.

Michael Betrus, CPRW, is the coauthor of *The Guide to Executive Recruiters* (McGraw-Hill), the most comprehensive directory of its kind.

Jay Block and Michael Betrus are coauthors of the bestsellers *101 Best Resumes*, *101 More Best Resumes*, and *101Best Cover Letters*.

The Professional Association of Resume Writers (PARW) is the official organization governing resume standards. PARW aims to elevate the skills of resume professionals. It provides the only certification process for resume writers.